MARK MORRIS'
l'allegro, il penseroso ed il moderato

PHOTOGRAPHS BY

STEPHEN BLACK

TOM BRAZIL

BILL COOPER

GADI DAGON

KEN FRIEDMAN

ROBBIE JACK

KLAUS LEFEBVRE

JANET P. LEVITT

SUSANA MILLMAN

DANIÉLE PIERRE

BILL RAFFERTY

LINDA RICH

CHRIS RYAN

BEATRIZ SCHILLER

LESLIE E. SPATT

MARTHA SWOPE

BRANT WARD

l'allegro, il pense

MARK MORRIS'
roso ed il moderato

A Celebration

EDITED BY
JEFFREY ESCOFFIER
AND MATTHEW LORE

ESSAYS BY
JOAN ACOCELLA
WENDY LESSER
ALASTAIR MACAULAY

MARLOWE & COMPANY · NEW YORK

Published by Marlowe & Company
An Imprint of Avalon Publishing Group Incorporated
841 Broadway
New York, NY 10003

Library of Congress Cataloging-in-Publication Data
Mark Morris' l'Allegro, il penseroso ed il moderato: a celebration / edited by Jeffrey Escoffier and Matthew Lore; with essays by
Joan Acocella, Wendy Lesser, and Alastair Macaulay.
        p. cm.
  ISBN 1-56924-631-9 (cloth) — ISBN 1-56924-580-0 (pbk.)
   I. Allegro, il penseroso ed il moderato (Choreographic work: Morris) I. Escoffier, Jeffrey. II. Lore, Matthew. III. Acocella, Joan. IV. Lesser,
Wendy. V. Macaulay, Alastair.
GV1790.L35 M37 2001
792.8'2—dc21
00-052098

Hardcover ISBN 1-56924-631-9
Paperback ISBN 1-56924-580-0

Designed by Pauline Neuwirth, Neuwirth & Associates, Inc.

Distributed by Publishers Group West
Printed in Italy
9   8   7   6   5   4   3   2   1

To the dancers,

who dance "as though they're singing it"

Introduction	8
JEFFREY ESCOFFIER AND MATTHEW LORE	
A Silvered World	16
JOAN ACOCELLA	

■

Part the First

Mad Crossing	26
Mad Scene	28
Three Graces	32
Sage and Holy	34
Haste Thee Nymph	38
Come and Trip It	42
Pensive Nun	44
Come, Come	46
The Diet Dances	48
Birding	52
Male Bird Solo	54
Bird Duet	56
Sweet Bird	58
The Hunt	62
Fireplace	64
Crickets	66
Hansel and Gretel	68

Each Action	70
Mountains	72
Merry Bells	76

Part the Second

Gorgeous Tragedy	82
Populous Cities	86
Hymen	88
Day's Garish Eye	90
The Stupid Men's Dance	94
The Ladies' Dance	96
The Walking Duet	100
Basilica	104
Weary Age	106
Melancholy Octet	108
Orpheus	114
Finale	120

■

Creation Myth	126
ALASTAIR MACAULAY	
An Artist for Our Time	134
WENDY LESSER	

Contents

The Making of L'Allegro   140

The Dancers of L'Allegro, il Penseroso ed il Moderato,   154
    1988–2000

Performances of L'Allegro, il Penseroso ed il Moderato,   155
    1988–2001

Acknowledgments   156

Selected Bibliography   157

About the Contributors and Editors   158

"MIRTH AND HER COMPANIONS," from William Blake's "L'Allegro"

[The Pierpont Morgan Library/Art Resource, New York]

"A FULLY REALIZED imaginative world," one early admirer called Mark Morris' dance, *L'Allegro, il Penseroso ed il Moderato*, which had its world premiere at the Théâtre Royal de la Monnaie in Brussels, Belgium, on November 23, 1988. Since then it has received adulatory and nearly unanimous accolades by critics, who have called it a work of "utopian grandeur," "a masterpiece of craft, invention, and feeling," and "among the happiest and most endearing works American dance has seen." Audiences from Paris to Brooklyn, from Berkeley to London, leap to their feet at its conclusion, applauding thunderously—

as near to ecstasy, perhaps, as it is possible for a two-hour dance set to Baroque music to bring a roomful of sedentary spectators.

L'Allegro, il Penseroso ed il Moderato is a great big thing of a dance—encompassing a range of human behavior and a depth of feeling seldom found in works of performing art in the latter part of the twentieth century. It was born in the summer of 1988, when, in a gymnasium on the campus of the State University of New York at Brockport, the 32-year-old choreographer Mark Morris began to create it. But *L'Allegro* (as it is usually referred to) is also the work of three other artists: a poet, John Milton, a composer,

Introduction

JEFFREY ESCOFFIER AND MATTHEW LORE

George Frideric Handel, and a painter, William Blake. Milton created, Handel elaborated, Blake illustrated, and then, three centuries later, Mark Morris came along and made something that was greater than the sum of its parts.

You don't need to see *L'Allegro* more than once to understand it, but it rewards repeated viewings. We have seen *L'Allegro* many times, and we believe if ever a single work of dance was created that merits a book, this dance is it. There is, simply, a lot to *L'Allegro*—a lot to love and to understand: the complexity of its gestural and movement language; the connections it makes between music, dance, art and poetry; the fertility and ingenuity of

"A YOUTHFUL POET'S DREAM," from William Blake's "L'Allegro"

[The Pierpont Morgan Library/Art Resource, New York]

its inner whirrings; and its teeming portrait of a broad swath of human experience (not to mention

"JOHN MILTON," by an unknown artist (circa 1629)
[National Portrait Gallery, London]

"GEORGE FRIDERIC HANDEL," by Thomas Hudson (1756)
[National Portrait Gallery, London]

the experiences of birds, dogs, foxes, horses, trees, shrubs, and flowers).

But opportunities to see this dance are limited. Because of the enormous expense required to put on *L'Allegro*, and because no film version has ever been made, the dance remains less accessible to us than other contemporary works of art that have achieved a comparable stature. We intend, then, with this book, to commemorate and to celebrate this dance—something glorious that we have all been given in our time.

L'ALLEGRO'S ROOTS REACH back two thousand years, to the Greek poets who first celebrated the joys of pastoral life. The revival of classical literature was near its peak in 1631 when John Milton, then a student at Christ's College, Cambridge, wrote two companion poems, "L'Allegro" and "Il Penseroso." (Milton's Italian titles were typical of his era.) L'Allegro is the cheerful man, il Penseroso the thoughtful or

contemplative man. These twin "pastoral odes," as Milton called them, articulated the divided mind of an ambitious, intellectual young man who was grappling with how he might best live his life.

When Milton was born in 1608, William Shakespeare, Ben Jonson, John Donne, and William Fletcher were active poets and playwrights. London theater audiences had not yet seen *The Winter's Tale* or *The Tempest*, though they had seen *Hamlet*, *King Lear*, and Shakespeare's other earlier plays. Milton grew up in thriving, chaotic London, a city whose population of 220,000 in 1600 would double in the next fifty years. His family's house, on Bread Street, near St. Paul's Cathedral, was surrounded by crowded tenements, windmills, theaters, brothels and mansions. Milton's father was a prosperous middle-class broker and trader—a man with a passion for music and poetry, who sought to raise his son as an educated gentleman, perhaps even a clergyman. Until Milton was eleven, he was tutored privately at home, particularly in Latin and Greek, after

"WILLIAM BLAKE IN YOUTH AND AGE," attributed to George Richmond after Frederick Tatham [Yale Center for British Art]

MARK MORRIS, 2000 [Marc Royce]

which he attended school at St. Paul's. When he was sixteen, he was sent off to Cambridge.

"L'Allegro" (152 lines long) and "Il Penseroso" (176 lines) are Milton's most accessible and popular works. "Probably no other poetry he ever wrote has pleased as many generations of English readers as have these two poems," the Milton scholar Harry Francis Fletcher wrote in 1941. Their universal appeal stems from the fact that these poems celebrate life's pleasures—not only those that Milton himself experienced, but also those celebrated in the classical pastoral tradition: the rustic charms of the country and the busy life of "populous cities"; the songs of birds and the company of women; poetry, music, and reading; masques, revels, and theater-going; dreaming and philosophical speculation; even the pleasures of church-going, with its "pealing organ" and "full-voic'd choir." L'Allegro's pleasures typically involve the company of others, or at least show him attentive to the coming and goings of

his fellow men and women. Il Penseroso's pleasures, on the other hand, are more solitary, brooding, and concerned with the individual imagination. As the critic Stephen Greenblatt has said, Milton "turns infinitely subtle shadings of active and contemplative pleasure into visible landscapes, continuously shifting scenes of hunting and harvest, country dances and urban play-going, star-gazing and religious meditation. Each of these scenes, from the rustic cottage to the philosopher's lonely tower, has a claim to truth, but the truth is at least as much inward as outward. We do not know in these poems if certain landscapes are conjuring up corresponding emotions, or certain emotions are conjuring up corresponding landscapes." Dramatic conflict isn't what propels these poems forward, but rather an urge on the poet's part to witness and depict the whole of the world and everything in it that vies for our attention, and which we must choose between.

FLASH FORWARD A hundred years, to February 27, 1740, a freezing night when the Thames River had frozen over and theaters were closed for lack of heat. Still, at least one show would go on: the premiere of George Frideric Handel's *L'Allegro, il Penseroso ed il Moderato*, conducted by the composer himself. (The audience was encouraged to attend *L'Allegro*'s premiere by the promise of a theater "secur'd against the cold.") One of the central figures of the Baroque era, Handel shaped Baroque music for the theater as thoroughly as Bach did music for the church. Born in 1685 in Germany, Handel had his first opera produced by the time he was twenty. After traveling in Italy and settling briefly in Hanover, he moved permanently to England in 1712. Over the next thirty years he composed and produced thirty-six operas in London—most of them sung in Italian and drawn from history (*Giulio Cesare*), mythology (*Acis and Galatea*), and romantic legend (*Orlando*).

"MILTON, LED BY THE MUSE CALLIOPE, PRESENTING HIS WORK TO HANDEL," frontispiece to Henry Roberts' *The New Calliope* (1743) [The British Library]

Handel had enormous success as an opera composer, but the ten years leading up to *L'Allegro* were difficult. He suffered from poor health and changing fashions in opera that made the public less disposed toward his works. The decline of his operatic ventures (he was also the producer of his own operas and concerts) so depleted his finances that his contemporary, the music historian Charles Burney, reported that Handel's affairs were "at this time so deranged, that he was under constant apprehensions of being arrested."

L'Allegro was intended to help Handel make a comeback financially; ironically, he was at the height of his powers musically. It also represented a continuation of his move away from opera toward oratorios. In the four previous years he had produced his first ventures in that form: *Saul* and *Israel in Egypt* (both 1738), as well as *Alexander's Feast* (1736) and *Ode for St. Cecelia's Day* (1739), the two latter being re-settings of poems John Dryden had written decades before for earlier composers. Handel's friends now urged him to set to music the work of John Milton, an even greater poet. Probably it was the philosopher James Harris who originally proposed setting "L'Allegro" and "Il Penseroso" to music, but it was Charles Jennens, a country squire who loved Handel's music and would later arrange Biblical texts into *Messiah*, who took on the libretto's preparation. Jennens wove Milton's twin poems into a single dramatic structure, a dialogue that alternates between the two contrasting points of view of the "characters," l'Allegro and il Penseroso. Apparently at Handel's suggestion, Jennens tacked on to the end of this dialogue a third perspective, that of il Moderato, who, in Jennens' words, was to "unite two independent Poems in one Moral Design"—suggesting that for both Handel and Jennens the voice of clear-headed and well-balanced reason was needed to unify the tensions created by l'Allegro and il Penseroso's contrasting (albeit complementary) views.

Handel worked on *L'Allegro* with amazing speed, helped by the enforced closure of his theater because of the bitter cold. "Beginning on January 19, 1740," the conductor Nicholas McGegan has related, "he finished the first part in a week, the second in another; Part Three [il Moderato] took him only two days, and he completed the draft score on February 4. The full orchestration was done by February 9, just over two weeks before the premiere. Even for Handel, this was quick work. *Messiah*, a much less elaborate score, took him much longer."

For a full orchestra, four-part chorus (soprano, alto, tenor, and bass), four vocal soloists (originally tenor, soprano, bass, and castrato, or countertenor), harpsichord, chamber organ, and carillon, Handel composed a sequence of recitatives, arias, and choruses, which, taken together, offer a variety of pictorial scenarios, musical affects, and emotional tonalities. "Since there is no dramatic action," McGegan elaborates, "Handel is forced to create each scene by sound alone. Indeed it is one of his most evocative and detailed scores; both Mirth and Melancholy are treated with equal care, and the orchestration and word painting are among his finest." Its many highlights include solos for flute and horn, the dramatic *penseroso* fugue, "These pleasures, Melancholy give, / And I with thee will choose to live," and one beautiful aria after another, including "Sweet bird, that shun'st the noise of folly," "Oft, on a plat of rising ground," "Sometimes let gorgeous tragedy," and "Hide me from day's garish eye." Among the choruses, "Haste Thee Nymph" is particularly raucous, while the piece's only duet, "As steals the morn upon the night," is widely regarded as one the very finest Handel ever composed; ironically, it is set to one of Jennens' il Moderato paeans to Reason (Jennens even managed to get in the word *intellectual*), which otherwise failed to elicit Handel's most creative musical response.

Many consider *L'Allegro* Handel's most English creation. With its simple melodies, the music reflects Handel's deep love for his adopted English countryside and puts the piece squarely in the English pastoral tradition. It was also one of a growing number of Handel's works in English that allowed locally trained English singers to perform it. An anonymous poet, writing in the *Gentleman's Magazine* shortly after its premiere, said: "Handel's harmony affects the soul. To soothe by sweetness, or by force control; And with like sounds as tune the rolling spheres. So tunes the mind that ev'ry sense has ears."

FLASH FORWARD AGAIN, another sixty years, to 1803, and to another artist, William Blake. In the midst of *his* most creative period, Blake created twelve watercolors that paid homage to the themes that Milton had explored in "L'Allegro" and "Il Penseroso." Poet, painter, engraver and seer, Blake (1757–1827), was, as the art critic Deborah Solomon has written, "one of the most poignant figures who ever strolled the streets of London. Poor and ignored in his own lifetime, he ran a print shop where he earned his living engraving other men's designs. In an age when all of London was swooning over the society portraits of Joshua Reynolds and Thomas Lawrence, Blake could be found in his rooms in Soho, a solitary mystic musing on the comings and goings of angels. Deeply religious, he saw visions and heard voices. In his great poems and engravings he recorded meetings with prophets and other transcendent beings, which led his contemporaries to speak of him as a madman."

Blake celebrated the sensual human body and passionately attacked social injustice. He denounced England's "dark Satanic mills" for the impact the new industrial economy was having on workers and their quality of life. Among his communications with angels and the dead, he reports of having spoken to Milton, who "came to ask a favor of me. He said that he had committed an error in his *Paradise Lost* which he wanted me to correct . . . he wished to expose the falsehood of his doctrine that sexual intercourse arose out of the Fall. Now that cannot be, for no good can spring from Evil." For Blake, there was innocence in sensual pleasure and sexuality, and human redemption was achieved through freedom and experience of the body.

As Blake prepared his visualizations of Milton's poems, he also wrote an extended meditation on the spiritual significance of Milton in his long epic poem, called simply *Milton*. Like Blake's other late works, particularly his epic *Jerusalem*, his twelve watercolors for "L'Allegro" and "Il Penseroso" depict the "human form divine" that so preoccupied him in the latter part of his life. A central figure or two dominates many of these watercolors; Mirth and Melancholy, of course, each star in their own illustration, while the Sunshine Holiday, the Youthful Poet's Dream, the Lark Startling the Night, and Milton himself take center stage in others. Meanwhile, around these figures (many of them clad in diaphanous robes), swirl in some cases consorts and hubs of activity, in others quieter landscapes punctuated only by a church steeple. Some illustrations are recondite and iconographically dense, especially in their margins; others, like "Milton's Vision of the Moon," are simple and elegant. But all of Blake's images give divine human form to Milton's scenes while at the same time they capture something just right about their prevailing spirit.

Finally, another leap forward—185 years, to the summer of 1988. The American-born choreographer Mark Morris has just accepted Gerard Mortier's invitation to become director of dance at the Théâtre Royal de la Monnaie, Belgium's state opera house. In a few weeks he and his dance company, the Mark Morris Dance Group, will move to Brussels to become Belgium's official dance troupe. Their first project at their new home is to be *L'Allegro, il Penseroso ed il Moderato*, which Morris has begun to sketch out at a summer workshop before he and his twenty-seven dancers fly to Brussels.

THE TRAJECTORY WE have just charted, beginning with Milton, through Handel and Blake, and now to Morris, only begins to tell the story of *L'Allegro*'s creation—it's that part of the story that answers the question all children sooner or later ask their parents: "What was your life like *before* I came along?" Our introduction also provides a frame for appreciating the dance critic Dale Harris' comment that *L'Allegro* is "a fully realized imaginative world." *L'Allegro* is exactly this in part because it represents the culmination of three hundred and fifty years of creative collaboration. But *L'Allegro* is even more so its own fully realized imaginative world because of the efforts of a single man, Mark Morris, and the dancers who are able to do the work of dancing this fully realized world into life for him—and for all of us. It is this part of the enterprise that is *L'Allegro* that this book celebrates.

Mark Morris' *L'Allegro, il Penseroso ed il Moderato* comprises thirty-two interconnected dance sequences divided into two acts, set to Handel's music, as cut and rearranged by Morris and Craig Smith, who conducted its premiere. (A more detailed description of their changes appears on page 147 in "The Making of *L'Allegro*.") *L'Allegro*'s set design is by Adrianne Lobel, its lighting is by James F. Ingalls, and its costumes are by Christine Van Loon. Each of *L'Allegro*'s thirty-two dances has a name bestowed by Morris and his dancers. Some names derive directly from the libretto ("Sage and Holy," "Crickets," "Day's Garish Eye"), others are descriptive ("Male Bird Solo," "The Hunt," "Finale"), while a few are known by their nicknames ("Mad Crossing," "Hansel and Gretel," "The Stupid Men's Dance"). This book's central section, devoted to the dance itself, begins with the first of *L'Allegro*'s dances, "Mad Crossing" and ends, thirty-one dances later, with its "Finale." We've sought to capture the spirit of each of *L'Allegro*'s sections and as many of the work's most distinctive and beautiful moments as it's possible for a book of photographs to do. (Needless to say, this is a book, not the

dance itself—for every gesture and step there is no substitute for a live performance.) To the extent we've been able even to attempt this, we're enormously indebted to the work of seventeen photographers, whose photos, taken at many *L'Allegro* performances and final dress rehearsals over the past thirteen years, grace these pages.

Appearing throughout this book are the eight William Blake watercolors from his series illustrating "L'Allegro" and "Il Penseroso" that inspired Morris.

Joan Acocella published her biography of Mark Morris in 1993, when he was thirty-eight. Here she gives the long view: *L'Allegro*'s place in history, seen from her vantage as the critic most familiar with Morris' work. In his appreciation, British theater and dance critic Alastair Macaulay, who has been writing about *L'Allegro* for more than ten years, pays close attention to how its gestural language speaks to us. *Threepenny Review* editor and publisher Wendy Lesser, who organized a symposium in 1994 on the occasion of *L'Allegro*'s West Coast premiere, offers the final personal appreciation—one that situates Morris as an artist for our time.

In "The Making of *L'Allegro*," we go directly to the source, to Mark Morris himself, five dancers on whom it was choreographed, set designer Adrianne Lobel, lighting director James F. Ingalls, and rehearsal pianist Linda Dowdell. They talk about the process of creating *L'Allegro* from the perspective of a dozen years after its premiere.

"From the moment the curtain rises on *L'Allegro*, we are almost personally involved—provoked, comforted, exhilarated, enlightened," wrote Dale Harris. "We find parallels with our daily lives, signs that our personal feelings are part of a universal order." For two hours *L'Allegro*'s twenty-four performers dance through time and space, and in so doing, have the ability to move those of us watching them to ask ourselves the deepest, most profound questions about what it means to be given life, and to consider how we choose to live that life. Ultimately, *L'Allegro* offers a profoundly redemptive view of human life, in dozens of fleeting moments and, most succinctly, in its finale, in three minutes of great joyousness, as its dancers leap toward us, offering themselves to us without reserve. What has come before has prepared us for this joyousness; it is the final piece in Morris' "universal order"—the "hidden soul of harmony," in Milton's own words.

Like the world it depicts, *L'Allegro* remains, in the end, inexhaustible.

BERKELEY, 2000 • Company, in the "Walking Duet" [Chris Ryan]

PEOPLE OFTEN SAY, of a work of art they cherish, that every time they see it, they find new things in it. Every time I go back to a favorite piece of mine, I see pretty much the same things in it. That's why I return to it, to see those things. With some works, however, what can happen, after a few viewings, is that my mind's tilt changes. I am no longer trying to understand the piece; I figure I've done that. So I relax, and other matters, more personal, seep through. In the summer of 2000, in London, I saw Mark Morris' *L'Allegro, il Penseroso ed il Moderato* for the first time in several years. It was not much different. There were cast changes, of course, and some roles were done better than before, and some not quite as well, or not as I remembered. But what crept over me, as I sat there, was the sense of *L'Allegro*'s value just to me.

I love *L'Allegro* for what a good time it is—for its pacing and excitement, like a movie. What an opening it has! After the overture the front curtain rises, but we see nothing, just darkness. And what the tenor now sings is frightening:

Hence, loathèd Melancholy,

Of Cerberus and blackest midnight born

In Stygian Cave forlorn

'Mongst horrid shapes and shrieks, and sights unholy . . .

A Silvered World

JOAN ACOCELLA

The singer is wishing away these terrors, but that's not what we hear. We hear the long vowels, the liquid consonants—"loathèd," "forlorn"—sucking us into the void we see before us. We are in the Stygian cave, in hell.

But wait. A stripe of light falls across the stage, and suddenly people are running. Still there is no promise of rescue. The people look frantic; the stage remains mostly dark. We feel we're waking up from a nightmare, pulling cobwebs off our face. At last the stage lights go on, full blare; the soprano sings, "Come, thou Goddess fair and free," and a lone nymph leaps out of the wings. But this is fully three minutes

"WAND'RING MOON," from William Blake's "Il Penseroso"

into the piece. Morris has made us wait, made us suffer.

And what he gives us is just one little nymph. That, for me, is another great beauty of *L'Allegro*: discretion, *mésure*, the way that Morris, never hurried, parcels out his beauties. The first nymph is eventually joined by two more, and the three women dance, but it is a modest number: natural, lilting, with an easy thigh. They will not need Epsom salts after the show. Not until the *next* three nymphs, in the next song—"Come, rather, Goddess, sage and holy"—do we get the hot blast of late twentieth-century dance technique, above all, the huge extensions. How excellent, how witty, that Morris gave the fireworks not to the "mirthful" nymphs, but to the "melancholy" ones. And it is even better than that, for when these women go into their fullest extension, they do so within a context of pain and necessity. The soprano is paying tribute to Melancholy: "Thee bright-hair'd Vesta long of yore, / To solitary Saturn bore." It's grand, it's holy: Vesta, a goddess, is giving birth to Melancholy. But it's also a poor woman on the floor, in labor. How many hundreds of dances have we seen, in the eighties and nineties, where women stretch their legs open, to do—what? Make an impression, knock 'em dead, assert sexuality and also disdain it. Morris' women do it for a reason, sexuality, and they do it in agony and embarrassment, covering their crotches with their hands.

That action, the opening of the thighs, comes back again, transformed, in the very next dance, "Haste Thee Nymph," where three jocund fellows sit with their legs apart and tip over and up again like Smurfs. This banishes the painful meaning that was just given to the open-thigh motif, converts it to comedy. But no sooner does that happen than the "Haste Thee Nymph" number is reprised, with women, and the motif is resexualized. It will come back again in the course of *L'Allegro*'s two hours, as people have sex, or think about it or remember it.

That is the logic of *L'Allegro*, and of almost all Morris' mature choreography, as critics have pointed out for years now. He sets up a number of motifs—often, like the open thighs, figurative motifs, actions that mean something in our lives. Then he repeats them, in new contexts: with different dancers, different accents. In the simplest pattern, canon (a device he adores), the repeats come right away. He'll set up four lines of women, say, and have the first line do a jump and then do something else as the second line picks up the jump, and then the third line. (This happens at the end of the women's section of "Haste Thee Nymph"—probably the most glorious canon Morris ever made.) Here we have the pleasure of

seeing the jump sweep down the stage, like a fire. Other motifs travel more slowly; they come, they go, they come again ten minutes later. But the results are similar. Morris is helping us understand his dance. If we miss something the first time, we get a second chance, and a third and a fourth. He lets us earn some mastery. At the same time, through these variations on a theme, he is building a world we recognize and love, the world of classical art, of Persian carpets and Beethoven's Fifth: fullness within predictability. Morris has said that he loves music more than dance. In his motif-weaving I see an emulation of music's severe economy. What do Western composers have? A set of twelve pitches. From that they build their great things. Morris is submitting, gladly, to the same law.

The result is a very firm structure, one that can withstand considerable tension. Actually, there is not a lot of tension in *L'Allegro*, or in any case not the painful division, the marriage of dread and hilarity, gravitas and effrontery, that in early works such as *O Rangasayee*, *Lovey*, and *Stabat Mater*—and in later work too, indeed in the very first piece he created after *L'Allegro*, *Dido and Aeneas*—showed us what it meant for a tough, ironical postmodern mind to pledge itself to classicism. Those were bold pieces; our jaws dropped. If our jaws drop at *L'Allegro*, it is at the sight of this thorny mind finding, for once, a moment of repose. Maybe it was enough for him that the theme of *L'Allegro*, joy versus melancholy, supplied the ambivalence. Perhaps that freed him to be less ambivalent, to portray those two states of mind, in dance after dance, with a sweet forthrightness.

L'Allegro would not be a Mark Morris piece, however, if it were wholly sweet. Here and there, he gives us the old jolt. In the dance of the Muses ("And join with thee calm Peace and Quiet"), one of the most transporting sections, the three women at a certain point open their mouths wide, in silent vocalization. There is textual support for this. The lyric says that the muses are singing. But their mouths don't seem to be singing; they look as though they're screaming. This little disturbance is not enough to cancel out the hush and ecstasy of that moment. The muses go on circling the altar; the orchestra and chorus pour on their gold. But a strangeness has been introduced, a reminder of what life is. I would call this the Greek principle: no beauty without a note of terror.

There are other oddities—hints of pain or raillery in passages that would otherwise be lyrical or sacral. The nightingale has to try four times before she gets up into the air. She fails on her first three take-offs, and we feel sorry for her. Further on, in the country scene

("Let me wander, not unseen"), the shepherd tells a tale to a gaggle of girls, and if I am not mistaken, its meaning is quite dirty. Further on, when Eurydice appears to Orpheus, she turns out to be a man—a homosexual joke. Near the end, between the ensemble's last two Penseroso numbers, a lone woman, June Omura, appears and does a little solo ("These pleasures, Melancholy, give") that predicts all the steps that will be performed in the following dance but produces them in a wholly different key—combative, fist-in-the-air, agitprop almost—and thus, like vinegar in oil, tightens and brightens a section that, with its side-by-side melancholies, could have been too evenly brooding. I cite these moments as examples of Morris' emotional seriousness, but they might also be invoked as proof of his sheer good taste. There are major artists (Poe, O'Neill) who have no taste, no sense of when things are going too far. Morris, the supposed *enfant terrible*, is not one of them. He judges things very nicely. If he did your living room, he would do a good job.

L'Allegro is the wisest work Morris ever made, possibly the wisest he will ever make. Notice how many sections feature one dancer, or maybe two or three, having some experience and then the whole company coming in to back up the point. That structure is dictated by the music—the solo voice singing about this or that and then the chorus coming in to agree—but the music was chosen by Morris, and the effect is different from in his other, comparable works. *Dido*, too, has a small main cast and a supporting chorus, but the chorus never actually tempers the opera's heat, what we sense as something personal, some inconsolability, at the heart of it. In *L'Allegro* the ensemble does have a tempering effect. The piece proposes the personal—*this* person takes walks, reads books, has moods—but soon absorbs it into the general. As its title indicates, it is a philosophical work. It shows us a mind bending itself not just around its own life, but around human life. For Milton in the seventeenth century, and Handel in the eighteenth, that was a normal stance, indeed the job of art. In the twentieth century, it is a remarkable choice, and one for which Morris needed to summon all his erudition. If the piece hadn't been so frankly historicist—if the text hadn't been by Milton, the music by Handel, if the costumes hadn't looked like Isadora Duncan's, if the spectators hadn't been able to say to themselves that Morris was a modern person talking to them about something old—it probably wouldn't have worked. But they did, and it did, and then we found out how much we still wanted to hear an artist talk about human life, how we were dying for it.

■   ■   ■

IT MAY BE of some use, for people thinking about Morris down the road, to know the circumstances under which *L'Allegro* was created. Morris was the most prominent young choreographer in New York in the 1980s, and the most controversial. This was the time of postmodernism, the dissolution of the liberal consensus. What that meant intellectually was that there was no longer a reality, something whose meaning one could fight over, but simply a multiplicity of "discourses." What it meant emotionally was the rout of earnestness by rage and irony.

Morris participated in all of this, not, I think, by choice—he was never an art-world person—but just by being a man of his time. He was raised in the sixties and seventies, in Seattle, by decent, socially responsible Presbyterian parents, and so part of him was earnest. Then he came of age in the eighties, in New York, and he was homosexual, so part of him was critical, ironical. He founded his company in 1980, and from the time it became widely known, in 1984, the critics were sharply divided over him. Some hailed him as the next great thing in modern dance, and praised him the more in that he was so clearly, so willingly, the inheritor of past great things in modern dance: musicality, idealism, body weight, body "sincerity." Others, seeing his idealism juxtaposed with irony and scabrousness—this is the ambivalence I spoke of earlier—thought he was pulling their legs. His antic personality, which came across so vividly in interviews—and there were many interviews, for he was a wonderful talker—only increased their reservations. To them, he was just a young smart-aleck who was being petted, rather revoltingly, by a group of would-be stylish reviewers. This was actually a very bitter quarrel. Still today, there are people who will cross a room to avoid greeting someone who was on the other side of the Mark Morris question in the eighties.

All that changed in 1988, when Morris accepted the invitation to become the director of dance at Belgium's royal theater, the Théâtre Royal de la Monnaie—a strange and perilous assignment. The Belgians had no modern dance tradition. What would they think of Morris' work? Furthermore, he was replacing Maurice Béjart, who had quit after a disagreement with the Monnaie's director, Gerard Mortier. Mortier was an unpopular man in Brussels. Béjart was a local hero, and now a martyr. What were the chances that the Belgians would look kindly on the person who took his place? Yet the Monnaie job offer, when it came, seemed a godsend to the Morris company. Morris at that time was bursting with ideas. He wanted to make big pieces, with lots of dancers and singers and musicians—something he had little chance of doing in the United States, with its meager arts funding. That was the lure of the Monnaie: resources. With hindsight, one can add that a side benefit of the Belgian job was that it removed Morris from the controversy that had gathered around him at home.

Whereupon he became the subject of a new, more violent controversy. The story of what happened to Morris in Brussels—indignant audiences, excoriating reviews, headlines saying "Mark Morris, Go Home!"—has been told many times. What is worth considering, though, is *L'Allegro*'s place in that history. Morris and his company knew from the beginning that they would have trouble in Belgium. What were Morris' thoughts as he went into the studio to create his first piece there, *L'Allegro*? On the one hand, he felt defiant, as is clear in the interviews that he gave at that time. ("Béjart is shit," he told Charles Siebert of *Vanity Fair*, thus kicking the Belgians' hero when he was down. The magazine printed the quote. Morris paid dearly for it.) On the other hand, he was no doubt very nervous as he set out, in a work three times as long as any of his previous pieces, and with twice the cast and many, many times the budget, to make his first impression on the Belgians. According to members of his company, his mood was simply ferocious. And out of that gloom rose this calm, confident, world-embracing piece. It is a sort of miracle, a testament to what we call the artistic imagination. In darkness, he could remember light.

Some of the Belgian reviewers enjoyed *L'Allegro*, or at least gave it the "honeymoon" benefit. But even those who praised it remarked on what seemed to them its simplicity, the fact that the dancers appeared to be not so much dancing as just moving around in a pleasant way. And once Morris presented them with further works—no longer calm or pleasant, but turbulent and strange: *Dido and Aeneas, Mythologies*—that early judgment, of his "simplicity," combined with the shock of the later shows to produce the impression that he was a foul-minded incompetent.

But as the Belgian press turned, so did the American. The American reviewers who admired Morris talked their editors into sending them to Brussels to see *L'Allegro*, and they brought back the news: this work was everything, everything, his early work had promised. Then, in 1990, the Morris troupe came back to the United States on tour and presented *L'Allegro* in New York. At that moment—October 6, 1990, when *L'Allegro* had its U.S. premiere at the Brooklyn Academy of Music—the American press war over Mark Morris ended. I have never seen an ovation such as the one that night. The audience was up long before the curtain was down. In a single sweep, the conductor, Nicholas McGegan, made his final stroke, the dancers raised their faces to heaven, and the spectators jumped to their feet, clapping and halloing, to say "Mark Morris, come home."

Of course the success of the company's U.S. tours meant little to the Belgians, and there is no reason it should have. They still had to live with Morris—he had a three-year contract—and they didn't like him any better because the Americans did. I hope, in telling this story, not to seem wholly biased. To my knowledge, the theatergoers of Brussels were having a sincere aesthetic response; they were not being paid to dislike Mark Morris. On the other hand, it would be confusing, for anyone trying to make sense of these events, not to record what many American reviewers felt (and some Europeans too—then as now, Morris has had many fans in the British press) about the treatment Morris received from his Belgian audiences. I remember a show at the Monnaie in November of 1989: *New Love Song Waltzes, Love Song Waltzes*, and *Wonderland*. When the dancers took their curtain call, there was some clapping, some booing. Then Morris walked on stage, and the booing doubled, quadrupled, rang from the rafters. Americans are unaccustomed to booing. (And we had to be told that some of it was done by claques.) Still, what was this? The audience seemed ready to lynch him. And he, seemingly oblivious, walked to the center of the stage and bowed and smiled and bowed again, as if their booing were clapping.

This too was reported in the American press, with predictable effects on local pride. He became a hero. But curtain calls were the least of it. His real triumph was not on the stage on Saturday night, but in the studio from Tuesday to Friday. Many people, in his situation, would have given up and gone home. He did not. Amid catcalls from the audience, insults from the press, he went on doing his work, better work than ever before: not just *L'Allegro*, but *Dido, Love Song Waltzes, Wonderland, Behemoth, Going Away Party, The Hard Nut*. Nothing stopped him. In 1991, as he was preparing to come home, the MacArthur Foundation in Chicago granted him one of its prized five-year fellowships. I think this award was given as much for his moral courage as for his artistic achievement.

That was almost a decade ago. Morris' status is different now. He is considered one of America's foremost artists. He is probably the most popular choreographer in the country, and *L'Allegro*, which has been shown throughout the United States (and also in France, England, Scotland, Israel, Australia, New Zealand, and Hong Kong, as well as Belgium), is probably his most popular piece. Meanwhile, the events surrounding its creation, and its place in the history of Morris' reputation, are largely forgotten. That is just as well, for much of the tale has to do with extra-artistic matters: politics, group loyalties, nationalism, even. It's a war story, and the war is over. Who remembers, now, the lawsuits that attended the American publication of *Ulysses*, or the bitter reviews that greeted Keats' early poetry? They are gone; the works remain.

So does *L'Allegro*. History, I feel, will judge my generation better because this work was made in our time, but the piece does not feel bound to its time. On the contrary. Though its roots can be identified—this artist, with this sort of musical education, this kind of dance training, in this place and period— its great sweep and philosophic ambition extend its boundaries. And then there are moments—I think particularly of the passage where the nightingale watches the moon, or actually two moons, crossing the sky as the soprano mounts the ladder of her song, up and up—when all boundaries seem to dissolve. We too climb the sky, and gaze down on a silvered world, and time and place are gone.

l'allegro, il pense

MARK MORRIS'

roso ed il moderato

"I FIRST SAW *L'Allegro* by accident. It was 1990 and I was in my first year at Juilliard. I remember the day.

A friend of mine at Juilliard asked me, "Do you want to see the Mark Morris Dance Group with the

White Oak Dance Project?" They were alternating shows—*L'Allegro* and a mixed program.

I really wanted to see Baryshnikov dance and that's the show I thought I was going to see. I got to

BAM after a huge day of work and rehearsing. I was still wearing my sweats. We ran, I remember

I hadn't eaten anything. We got there to find out that it's not Baryshnikov; it's a two-and-a-half-hour

dance piece, and really, my heart sank. I thought, "Oh my God, I don't know if I'm up for this."

I have to say—it changed my life to see this dance. I left the theater trembling. And not because

I was starving. I thought it was one of the most beautiful works of art I'd ever seen."

[JOHN HEGINBOTHAM, DANCER]

Part the First

OVERTURE
George Frideric Handel
Concerto Grosso in G major, Op. 6, No. I
(*A tempo giusto—Allegro*)

MAD CROSSING

MAD SCENE

THREE GRACES

SAGE AND HOLY

HASTE THEE NYMPH

COME AND TRIP IT

PENSIVE NUN

COME, COME

THE DIET DANCES

BIRDING

MALE BIRD SOLO

BIRD DUET

SWEET BIRD

THE HUNT

FIREPLACE

CRICKETS

HANSEL AND GRETEL

EACH ACTION

MOUNTAINS

MERRY BELLS

[The Pierpont Morgan Library/Art Resource, New York]

"NIGHT STARTLED BY THE LARK," from William Blake's "L'Allegro"

MAD CROSSING

ACCOMPAGNATO FOR TENOR

Hence, loathèd Melancholy,

Of Cerberus, and blackest midnight born

In Stygian Cave forlorn

'Mongst horrid shapes, and shrieks,

and sights unholy,

Find out some uncouth cell,

Where brooding Darkness spreads his

jealous wings,

And the night-Raven sings;

There under Ebon shades, and

low-brow'd rocks,

As ragged as thy Locks,

In dark Cimmerian desert, ever dwell.

BERKELEY, 2000 • [L–R]: Lauren Grant, Michelle Yard, Rachel Murray
[PARTIALLY OBSCURED], Joseph Poulson [Ken Friedman]

l'allegro

BERKELEY, 2000 • [L–R]: Ruth Davidson, Joe Bowie [Ken Friedman]

"THE OPENING OF THE PIECE IS TREMENDOUS.

In black darkness—nothing onstage, nothing anywhere—a tenor voice rises up out of the pit, 'Hence, loathèd melancholy, / Of Cerberus and blackest midnight born,' it sings, and it goes on singing of the black world of Melancholy—the Stygian cave, the night raven, the ebony shades—for ten long lines. The effect is spooky, sepulchral, as if we too were in the Stygian cave, or some dark ditch in Dante's Hell, with someone addressing us from the inside of a tomb. . . . Then a dim, murky sort of swamp light goes up behind a black scrim, and dancers begin racing across the stage. Life! But inchoate at first: little groups form and vanish, trailing away like fog or cobwebs. This is day struggling to be born from night, and consciousness from dream. Creation from chaos."

[Joan Acocella in *Ballet Review*]

MAD SCENE

il penseroso

ACCOMPAGNATO FOR SOPRANO

Hence, vain deluding Joys,

Dwell in some idle brain,

And fancies fond with gaudy shapes possess,

As thick and numberless

As the gay motes that people the Sun Beams,

Or likest hovering dreams

The fickle Pensioners of Morpheus' train.

BERKELEY, 2000 • [L–R]: Joe Bowie, Lauren Grant, Shawn Gannon [Ken Friedman]

BERKELEY, 2000 • [L–R]: Gregory Nuber, Matthew Rose, Shawn Gannon, Lauren Grant, Kim Reis, Joe Bowie [Ken Friedman]

THE STAGE REMAINS ONLY FAINTLY

ILLUMINATED: As yet we are in the land of

Morpheus, son of sleep, god of dreams. The world of

L'Allegro begins to unfold. From its first moment the dancers

are dancing to the music, illuminating the text—showing us

the dance's essential propelling energy. We begin to see

gestures and images that will recur throughout the dance.

BERKELEY, 2000 • [FACING US, L–R]: Marjorie Folkman, Peter Kyle, Ruth Davidson, Shawn Gannon; [BACKS TO US, L–R]: Charlton Boyd, Rachel Murray, David Leventhal [Ken Friedman]

BERKELEY, 2000 • [STANDING, L–R]: Marjorie Folkman, Peter Kyle, Shawn Gannon [HELD ALOFT], Ruth Davidson; [ON THE FLOOR, L–R]: Charlton Boyd, Rachel Murray, David Leventhal [Ken Friedman]

BERKELEY, 2000 • [L–R]: Shawn Gannon, Kim Reis, Gregory Nuber, Matthew Rose, Lauren Grant [Ken Friedman]

THREE GRACES

AIR FOR SOPRANO

Come, thou Goddess fair and free,

In heav'n yclept Euphrosyne;

And by men heart-easing Mirth,

Whom lovely Venus, at a birth,

With two sister-Graces more,

To ivy-crownèd Bacchus bore.

l'allegro

NEW YORK CITY, 1995 • [L–R]: Tina Fehlandt, Mireille Radwan-Dana, Megan Williams
[Beatriz Schiller]

BERKELEY, 2000 • [L–R]: June Omura, Mireille Radwan-Dana, Julie Worden
[Ken Friedman]

"THEN—BANG! . . . [O]ut onto the stage flies the goddess Mirth, Tina Fehlandt, her skirts dancing on the air behind her. Morris has never lacked for boldness, but the sheer simplicity of this image really takes your breath away. Here at the very opening is the patron saint of the piece, and her dancing tells you right away who she is and hence what the piece will be. She is history, and the history of art. As she leaps and prances, and as she is joined by her two sisters—together, they are the three Graces—you see before you the maenads of Attic sculpture and the three Graces of Botticelli's *Primavera* and Isadora Duncan, would-be maenad, who so much loved that Botticelli."

[Joan Acocella in *Ballet Review*]

BERKELEY, 2000 • [L–R]: June Omura, Julie Worden, Mireille Radwan-Dana [Ken Friedman]

SAGE
AND
HOLY

AIR FOR SOPRANO

Come rather, Goddess, sage and holy;

Hail divinest Melancholy,

Whose saintly visage is too bright

to hit the sense of human sight;

Thee bright-hair'd Vesta long of yore,

To solitary Saturn bore.

LONDON, 2000 • [L–R]: Michelle Yard, Joe Bowie [Bill Coop

il penseroso

BERKELEY, 2000 • [L–R]: Matthew Rose, Ruth Davidson, Marjorie Folkman, Michelle Yard, Joe Bowie [Ken Friedman]

BERKELEY, 2000 • [L–R]: Matthew Rose, Ruth Davidson, Marjorie Folkman, Joe Bowie, Michelle Yard [Ken Friedman]

BERKELEY, 2000 • [L–R]: Ruth Davidson, Marjorie Folkman, Michelle Yard, Matthew Rose [HELD ALOFT], Joe Bowie [Ken Friedman]

"**IN THE FIRST** Allegro dance, you see three Graces do a hand-on-head gesture to illustrate the word *ivy-crownèd*. . . .[T]he way that their hands rise, during that bounce, forms a visual counterpart to a motif introduced in the succeeding Penseroso dance, where the dancers' hands shield their eyes ('Hail divinest Melancholy, / Whose saintly visage is too bright / to hit the sense of human sight'); when the dancers then lift their hands into the air, we have an image of sight, which will recur, with variations, throughout the work. And so Morris shows resemblance between Allegro and Penseroso motifs. In that same Penseroso dance, verbally addressed to Melancholy, he has three women lie on the floor, legs apart, as if in labor ('Thee bright-hair'd Vesta long of yore, / To solitary Saturn bore'), one downstretched arm between their thighs. The image is full of stress; Morris answers it with a visually similar but a temperamentally opposed image in the next Allegro dance, when he has dancers sit on the floor, legs apart, hands on their sides, laughing ('And Laughter, holding both his sides')."

[Alastair Macaulay in *The Dancing Times*]

Haste
Thee
Nymph

BERKELEY, 1994 • [L–R]: Derrick Brown, Kraig Patterson, John Heginbotham [Brant Ward/*San Francisco Chronicle*]

AIR FOR TENOR

Haste thee, nymph, and bring with thee

Jest and youthful Jollity,

Quips and cranks, and wanton wiles,

Nods, and becks, and wreathed smiles,

Such as hang on Hebe's cheek,

And love to live in dimple sleek;

Sport, that wrinkled Care derides,

And Laughter, holding both his sides.

CHORUS

Haste thee, nymph, and bring with thee

Jest and youthful Jollity;

Sport, that wrinkled Care derides,

And Laughter, holding both his sides.

l'allegro

HASTE THEE, NYMPH! And make way for all her consorts—
for this is their dance. Three male soloists prance onto the stage bringing with
them "jest" and "jollity," their dancing pyrotechnics full of the "quips and
cranks" and "nods and becks" of Milton's text. As the tenor embellishes the
word *La . . ha . . ha . . ha . . ha . . aughter* the dancers run through a routine of
gestures that suggest the physicality of laughing, while on the words "holding
both his sides" they roll on the floor doing just that, holding both their sides
(a gesture inspired by Blake's depiction of Mirth). All twelve women dance the
chorus—like the men, they arrive in groups: the first six on the vocal line, the
rest on the instrumental echo. We see reprises of all the quips, cranks, nods
and becks, shaking with *La . . ha . . ha . . ha . . ha. . aughter* and rolling on the floor.
It's a dazzling, jubilant four minutes of dancing.

BERKELEY, 2000 • [L–R]: Derrick Brown, David Leventhal,
John Heginbotham [Susana Millman]

HONG KONG, 1997 • [L–R]: Tina Fehlandt, Derrick Brown, Kraig Patterson, John Heginbotham [Stephen Black]

NEW YORK CITY, 1995 • [L–R]: Rachel Murray, Juliet Burrows, Katharina Bader, Deniz Oktay [PARTIALLY OBSCURED], Julie Worden, Ruth Davidson, Megan Williams, Victoria Lundell, Tina Fehlandt, Marianne Moore [Janet P. Levitt]

LONDON, 1997 • [L–R]: Ruben Graciani, Matthew Rose, Dan Joyce, Charlton Boyd, Donald Mouton, Joe Bowie, Guillermo Resto, Shawn Gannon [Bill Rafferty]

COME AND TRIP IT

l'allegro

AIR FOR SOPRANO

Come, and trip it as you go,

On the light fantastic toe.

CHORUS

Come, and trip it as you go,

On the light fantastic toe.

LONDON, 1997 • [L–R]: Tina Fehlandt,
Mireille Radwan-Dana [Leslie E. Spatt]

"ALL HIS MOTIFS—some mainly lower-body, others upper-body—have a certain 'mime' emphasis in their timing: the delivery shows you that something is being depicted even when you can't tell what it is. But *L'Allegro* is never just a collage of mime gestures. What makes these motifs work is the way they're strung together into phrases. For example, in the Allegro air and chorus 'Come, and trip it as you go, / On the light fantastic toe,' there are movement motifs for 'Come,' 'trip,' 'go,' and 'light fantastic toe.' The motifs come round again and again, just as those words do in Handel's setting."

[Alastair Macaulay from "Creation Myth"]

PENSIVE NUN

ACCOMPAGNATO FOR SOPRANO

Come, pensive Nun, devout and pure,

Sober, steadfast, and demure;

All in a robe of darkest grain,

Flowing with majestic train.

il penseroso

A BRIEF AND SOLEMN

interlude: A lone dancer glides across

the stage, turning slowly, pausing only

to measure heaven and the earth. As he

pirouettes off the stage, another dancer

follows him, imitating his gestures.

LONDON, 1997 • Guillermo Resto [Leslie E. Spatt]

45

COME, COME

ARIOSO FOR SOPRANO

Come, but keep thy wonted state,

With even step, and musing gait;

And looks commercing with the skies,

Thy rapt soul sitting in thine eyes.

LONDON, 1997 • [L–R]: William Wagner, Mireille Radwan-Dana [Robbie Jack]

"TWO FIGURES . . . are separated from one another by several lines of dancers crossing the stage laterally. The two look at one another, reach out for one another, and in the only direct connection between their story and il Penseroso's, they bob up and down on the soles of their feet, as if in excitement, when the singer speaks of 'thy rapt soul sitting in thine eyes.' Otherwise, they walk back and forth, gazing at one another and the company walks between them ('with even step and musing gait') until the song is finished and they part, exiting in opposite directions. This beautiful little story—I think of it as the 'Some Enchanted Evening' number—Morris has spun out of two simple ideas in [Milton's] text, walking and yearning."

[Joan Acocella in *Ballet Review*]

il penseroso

BERKELEY, 2000 • [L–R]: Michelle Yard, Rachel Murray, Matthew Rose, Joe Bowie, Maile Okamura, David Leventhal, Seth Davis, Mireille Radwan-Dana, Kim Reis, Julie Worden, Charlton Boyd [Ken Friedman]

THE DIET DANCES

ACCOMPAGNATO FOR SOPRANO

There held in holy passion still,

Forget thy self to marble, till

With a sad leaden downward cast

Thou fix them on the earth as fast.

ARIOSO FOR SOPRANO

And join with thee calm Peace and Quiet,

Spare Fast, that oft with gods doth diet,

And hears the Muses in a ring

Round about Jove's altar sing.

CHORUS

Join with thee calm Peace and Quiet,

Spare Fast, that oft with gods doth diet.

"IN THE DANCE OF THE MUSES ('And join with thee calm Peace and Quiet'), one of the most transporting sections, the three women at a certain point open their mouths wide, in silent vocalization. There is textual support for this. The lyric says that the muses are singing. But their mouths don't seem to be singing; they look as though they're screaming. This little disturbance is not enough to cancel out the hush and ecstasy of that moment. The muses go on circling the altar; the orchestra and chorus pour on their gold. But a strangeness has been introduced, a reminder of what life is. I would call this the Greek principle: no beauty without a note of terror."

[Joan Acocella from "A Silvered World"]

LONDON, 2000 • [L–R]: Ruth Davidson, June Omura, Julie Worden [Bill Cooper]

BERKELEY, 2000 • [BACKS TO US, L–R]: Charlton Boyd, Jonathan Pessolano, Matthew Rose, Derrick Brown, David Leventhal; [FACING US, L–R]: Joe Bowie, Seth Davis, Gregory Nuber, John Heginbotham [PARTIALLY OBSCURED], Joseph Poulson, Peter Kyle [Ken Friedman]

BERKELEY, 2000 • [BACKS TO US, L–R]: Jonathan Pessolano, Matthew Rose, Derrick Brown, David Leventhal, Shawn Gannon; [FACING US, L–R]: Joe Bowie [PARTIALLY OBSCURED], Seth Davis, Gregory Nuber [PARTIALLY OBSCURED], John Heginbotham, Joseph Poulson, Peter Kyle [Ken Friedman]

BIRDING

BERKELEY, 2000 • [L–R]: Michelle Yard, Derrick Brown, Mireille Radwan-Dana [PARTIALLY OBSCURED], Rachel Murray, Matthew Rose, Ruth Davidson, Christina Amendolia, Peter Kyle, Gregory Nuber [Ken Friedman]

l'allegro

RECITATIVE FOR TENOR

Hence, loathèd Melancholy,

In dark Cimmerian desert ever dwell

But haste thee, Mirth, and bring with thee

The mountain nymph, sweet Liberty.

RECITATIVE FOR SOPRANO

And if I give thee honor due,

Mirth, admit me of thy crew.

BERKELEY, 2000 • [L–R]: Michelle Yard, Mireille Radwan-Dana, Derrick Brown, Rachel Murray, Matthew Rose, Ruth Davidson, Peter Kyle, Christina Amendolia, Maile Okamura [PARTIALLY OBSCURED] [Ken Friedman]

"IT'S A HUGE SECTION of beautiful music

that really brings home the natural world. The whole suite

is nothing but birds— birds, and the moon."

[June Omura, dancer]

MALE
BIRD
SOLO

AIR FOR SOPRANO

Mirth, admit me of thy crew

To live with her, and live with thee

in unreprovèd pleasures free;

To hear the lark begin his flight,

And singing startle the dull night;

Then to come in spite of sorrow,

And at my window bid good morrow.

Mirth, admit me of thy crew.

BERKELEY, 1994 • Kraig Patterson [Brant Ward/San Francisco Chronicle]

BERKELEY, 2000 • David Leventhal [Ken Friedman]

"THE LARK . . . COMES IN AND HOPS AROUND
the whole big stage all by himself, jerking his little head this
way and that and picking up one little foot and then the
other. . . . What a composition this is—all that space and
this one small creature. This must be what the sky feels like
to a bird: so big and yet not at all frightening. Then,
suddenly, it all changes. As [the lark] crosses the stage again,
in flies the rest of the company behind him, their arms
extended, winglike, and they swoop this way and that in
those pulsing triangular formations that flocks of birds fly
in. The pleasure here is not just to have the portrait of
birdhood expanded on (one bird hopping versus a whole
flock flying) but a purely formal joy—to have emptiness
suddenly filled—and also a deep, half-mad kinesthetic
thrill: to have something going pick-pick, sharp and little,
give way to something huge and sweeping, like a tidal wave."

[Joan Acocella in *Ballet Review*]

BERKELEY, 2000 • David Leventhal [Ken Friedman]

LONDON, 2000 • David Leventhal [Susana Millman]

l'allegro

BIRD DUET

ACCOMPAGNATO FOR SOPRANO

First, and chief, on golden wing,

The cherub Contemplation bring;

And the mute Silence hist along,

'Less Philomel will deign a song,

In her sweetest, saddest plight,

Smoothing the rugged brow of Night.

"AN ESPECIALLY TELLING VIGNETTE, during a long orchestral passage, is when one Allegro lark actually meets one Penseroso nightingale center-stage. The two 'birds,' in profile to us, just stand there and gaze into each other's eyes, as if contemplating an opposite number. Nowhere else in the work do we see Allegro and Penseroso emblems so plainly sharing the stage; and the meeting seems for a long while to freeze them. Next, as the music softly builds, they behave like the birds they are—listening, with wonderfully birdlike inflections of head and eyes—but both in completely the same way."

[Alastair Macaulay from "Creation Myth"]

BERKELEY, 2000 • David Leventhal, June Omura
[Ken Friedman]

SWEET BIRD

BERKELEY, 2000 • [FOREGROUND]: Julie Worden, Peter Kyle
[Ken Friedman]

AIR FOR SOPRANO

Sweet bird, that shun'st the noise of folly,

Most musical, most melancholy!

Thee, chantress, oft the woods among,

I woo to hear thy even-song.

Or, missing thee, I walk unseen,

To behold the wand'ring moon

Riding near her highest noon.

il penseroso

BERKELEY, 2000 • [FOREGROUND]: Julie Worden, Peter Kyle; [BACKGROUND]: Lauren Grant and Marjorie Folkman lifted by [OBSCURED]: Gregory Nuber, Joseph Poulson, Charlton Boyd, Seth Davis; and June Omura [Ken Friedman]

"HANDEL'S 'SWEET BIRD, that shun'st the

noise of folly' transmutes nature into music, a

virtuosic colloquy for soprano and flute in

which bird song is referred to rather than

imitated naturalistically. Mr. Morris' setting of

the aria is more directly mimetic. As the dancers

leap into one another's arms, flutter their hands,

preen themselves, dart about the stage with

avian movements, nature reappears."

[Dale Harris in *The Wall Street Journal*]

BERKELEY, 2000 • Julie Worden [Ken Friedman]

LONDON, 1997 • [BIRDS L–R]: Julie Worden, Marjorie Folkman, Derrick Brown, Katharina Bader, Rachel Murray; [LIFTERS, L–R]: Ruben Graciani [PARTIALLY OBSCURED], Guillermo Resto [PARTIALLY OBSCURED], Joe Bowie, John Heginbotham, Dan Joyce [PARTIALLY OBSCURED] [Leslie E. Spatt]

l'allegro
THE HUNT

RECITATIVE FOR BASS

If I give thee honor due,

Mirth, admit me of thy crew!

AIR FOR BASS

Mirth, admit me of thy crew!

To listen how the hounds and horn

Cheerly rouse the slumb'ring morn,

From the side of some hoar hill,

Through the high wood echoing shrill.

BROOKLYN, 1990 • June Omura and Clarice Marshall [CENTER] and company [Tom Brazil]

"IN THE MOST obvious tour de force of the piece, Morris builds from Milton's four-line 'hounds and horn' suggestion a swiftly traveling narrative hunt scene in which the dancers depict—with whimsy, hilarity, and tremendous poignancy— every last obligatory element: trees and hedgerows, proud steeds conveying smug aristocrats, eager, slobbering dogs with their sly handler, and a pair of innocent, terrified little vixens who escape with their lives yet convey the idea that for every living creature, animal or human, respite from peril is only temporary."

[Tobi Tobias in *New York* magazine]

NEW YORK CITY, 1995 • Company [Tom Brazil]

FIREPLACE

Oft, on a plat of rising ground,

I hear the far-off Curfew sound,

Over some wide-water'd shore,

Swinging slow, with sullen roar;

Or if the air will not permit,

Some still removèd place will fit,

Where glowing embers through the room

Teach light to counterfeit a gloom.

BERKELEY, 2000 • [L–R]: Marjorie Folkman, Matthew Rose, Rachel Murray, Peter Kyle and company [Ken Friedman]

LONDON, 1997 • June Omura and company [Bill Rafferty]

"**WORDS LIKE** *birth, smoothing,* and *stream* are enacted for us [throughout the piece] with the same gleeful inventiveness as the hunting scene in which the dancers become 'the high wood' with a pack in full cry running through it, or the astonishing moment in "Oft, on a plat of rising ground," in which Handel's thrilling simulation of the distant curfew is realized by the group bunching into a bell shape with one of its members lifted to and fro as a clapper."

[Jonathan Keates in *The Times Literary Supplement*]

CRICKETS

NEW YORK CITY, 1995 • [L–R]: Joe Bowie, Tina Fehlandt, Katharina Bader [Beatriz Schiller]

AIR FOR TENOR

Far from all resort of Mirth,

Save the cricket on the hearth,

Or the bellman's drowsy charm,

To bless the doors from nightly harm.

il penseroso

BERKELEY, 2000 • [L–R]: Joe Bowie, Kim Reis, Seth Davis, Lauren Grant, Julie Worden [Ken Friedman]

"CRICKETS IS SO STRANGE, an odd little thing. This little good-luck cricket is chirping, interspersed with these couples changing partners and thinking that they're so special prancing through the landscape. And also, there are the people coming in from the side. It's a little tiny bit of the dance but it's one of the hardest parts. It's hard because you have very little room and you're supposed to be spinning and crossing with somebody and getting back into the wings without smacking your head. There's a real vaudeville gesture, palm out, very presentational, like the one in 'Gorgeous Tragedy.' The other sort of vaudevillian thing is the bellman. I love the bellman lurching and hurtling across the stage. When Mark read 'the bellman's drowsy charm,' he imagined the town crier late at night getting drunker and drunker."

[June Omura, dancer]

BERKELEY, 2000 • [L–R]: Julie Worden, Joe Bowie, Lauren Grant [Ken Friedman]

BERKELEY, 2000 • [L–R]: June Omura, Joe Bowie, Charlton Boyd, Kim Reis, Seth Davis [Ken Friedman]

RECITATIVE FOR TENOR

If I give thee honor due,

Mirth, admit me of thy crew!

AIR FOR TENOR

Let me wander, not unseen

By hedgerow elms, on hillocks green:

There the ploughman, near at hand,

Whistles over the furrow'd land,

And the milkmaid singeth blithe,

And the mower whets his scythe,

And every shepherd tells his tale

Under the hawthorn in the dale.

a tale to a gaggle of girls, and if I am not

mistaken, its meaning is quite dirty."

[Joan Acocella from "A Silvered World"]

l'allegro

LONDON, 1997 • Kraig Patterson and [L–R]: Rachel Murray, Ruth Davidson
[PARTIALLY OBSCURED], June Omura, Julie Worden, Victoria Lundell, Tina Fehlandt
[Leslie E. Spatt]

AIR FOR TENOR

Each action will derive new grace

From order, measure, time, and place;

Till Life the goodly structure rise

In due proportion to the skies.

EACH ACTION

il moderato

BRUSSELS, 1988 • Company [Klaus Lefebvre]

[Joan Acocella from "A Silvered World"]

l'allegro

LONDON, 1997 • Kraig Patterson and [L–R]: Rachel Murray, Ruth Davidson
[PARTIALLY OBSCURED], June Omura, Julie Worden, Victoria Lundell, Tina Fehlandt
[Leslie E. Spatt]

AIR FOR TENOR

Each action will derive new grace

From order, measure, time, and place;

Till Life the goodly structure rise

In due proportion to the skies.

EACH ACTION

il moderato

BRUSSELS, 1988 • Company [Klaus Lefebvre]

"THROUGHOUT THE IMAGES and anecdotes and rites that make up Morris' movement language in *L'Allegro*, certain motifs recur. . . . [The] upper arm-movement becomes 'fire' itself. In the Moderato air that Morris places in Part One, 'fire' becomes one of four motifs that depict the four elements: earth, air, fire, water. In 'earth,' the dancers crouch with hands on the ground, and a ripple passes through their spines and arms, briefly lifting their hands off the ground. 'Air' is an adorable 'blowing' mime, in which the dancers (standing and leaning forwards) become the personifications of winds, as on old maps: They blow with puffed cheeks and fanning hands, and the action of puffing passes right through them, so that they hop briefly off the floor. The image for 'water' again passes right through the dancers, as they lean from one side to the other, but its emphasis is on rippling hands, as if tracing the surface of the sea, in a sweeping left-to-right gesture. Here, as on several other occasions, there's no cue in the words for these motifs."

[Alastair Macaulay from "Creation Myth"]

MOUNTAINS

l'allegro

ACCOMPAGNATO FOR BASS

Mountains, on whose barren breast

The lab'ring clouds do often rest;

Meadows trim with daisies pied,

Shallow brooks, and rivers wide

Tow'rs and battlements it sees,

Bosom'd high in tufted trees.

BERKELEY, 2000 • Mireille Radwan-Dana [Ken Friedman]

"**FROM PRETTY EARLY** on I knew that I

wanted everything to double or reflect or to be in some

way symmetrically two. That includes something that seems

like a long solo, like 'Mountains.' The duet there shows up

only at the very end, when another dancer goes across. In

my head that implies that it's going on in parallel,

somewhere out of range."

[Mark Morris in "The Making of *L'Allegro*"]

MERRY BELLS

l'allegro

LONDON, 1997 • [CENTRAL QUARTET, L–R]: Victoria Lundell,
Guillermo Resto, Marjorie Folkman, Shawn Gannon;
[LEFT GROUP, L–R]: John Heginbotham, Katharina Bader,
David Leventhal; [RIGHT GROUP, L–R]: Tina Fehlandt, Matthew Rose
[Leslie E. Spatt]

AIR FOR TENOR

Or let the merry bells ring round,

And the jocund rebeck sound

To many a youth, and many a maid,

Dancing in the checquer'd shade.

CHORUS

And young and old come forth to play

On a sunshine holiday,

till the livelong daylight fail,

Thus past the day, to bed they creep,

By whisp'ring winds soon lull'd asleep.

BRUSSELS, 1989 • [L–R]: Joachim Schlömer, Tina Fehlandt, Charlton Boyd, Megan Williams [Daniéle Pierre]

BERKELEY, 2000 • Company [Ken Friedman]

"**WHAT TO MY MIND** is the most breathtaking compositional effect occurs at the end of Part One. The dancers join hands to form six circles, and run in those circles, when suddenly, before you can see what happened, they are four circles, and as you are trying to understand how they did it, they are now two circles, and then one, and still running, running, never missing a beat. And the fact that every time the break occurs it falls, from what I can tell, on a different count within the musical phrase makes it seem more thrilling, unstoppable, like a bomb exploding. Then peace. The dancers stand still in their big circle, holding hands: what was separate is now together, a human community. They lie down and, still in the circle, roll over one another (lovemaking). Then six pairs stay put on the floor: they are sleeping. Six others leave, as if their bedrooms were upstairs."

[Joan Acocella in *Ballet Review*]

"FOR ME DOING *L'Allegro* IS LIKE GOING ON A JOURNEY—from the moment

the overture starts playing with everybody backstage, the curtain down, and you're all excited and

jumping with extra energy, to two hours later—Boom! [on the count of] seven . . . two . . . three, and

you hit that final pose, the lights black out. After some performances, we're all screaming on stage

because it's our third show in forty-eight hours, and we're like, 'Aaahhh! We did it!' You've wanted to be

a dancer since you were a kid, and here you are, you're making a living at it, you're dancing—that's the

fulfillment of you as a human being. Mark has created this piece that's just beyond what you could

ever hope to do, and yet here you are doing it. I wish every dancer could have a chance to be in it, and

I wish that everyone in the world could see it because it would really change people. *L'Allegro* is a gift

everyone should enjoy."

[GREGORY NUBER, DANCER]

Part the Second

GORGEOUS TRAGEDY

POPULOUS CITIES

HYMEN

DAY'S GARISH EYE

THE STUPID MEN'S DANCE

THE LADIES' DANCE

THE WALKING DUET

BASILICA

WEARY AGE

MELANCHOLY OCTET

ORPHEUS

FINALE

[The Pierpont Morgan Library/Art Resource, New York]

"MILTON'S MYSTERIOUS DREAM," from William Blake's "Il Penseroso"

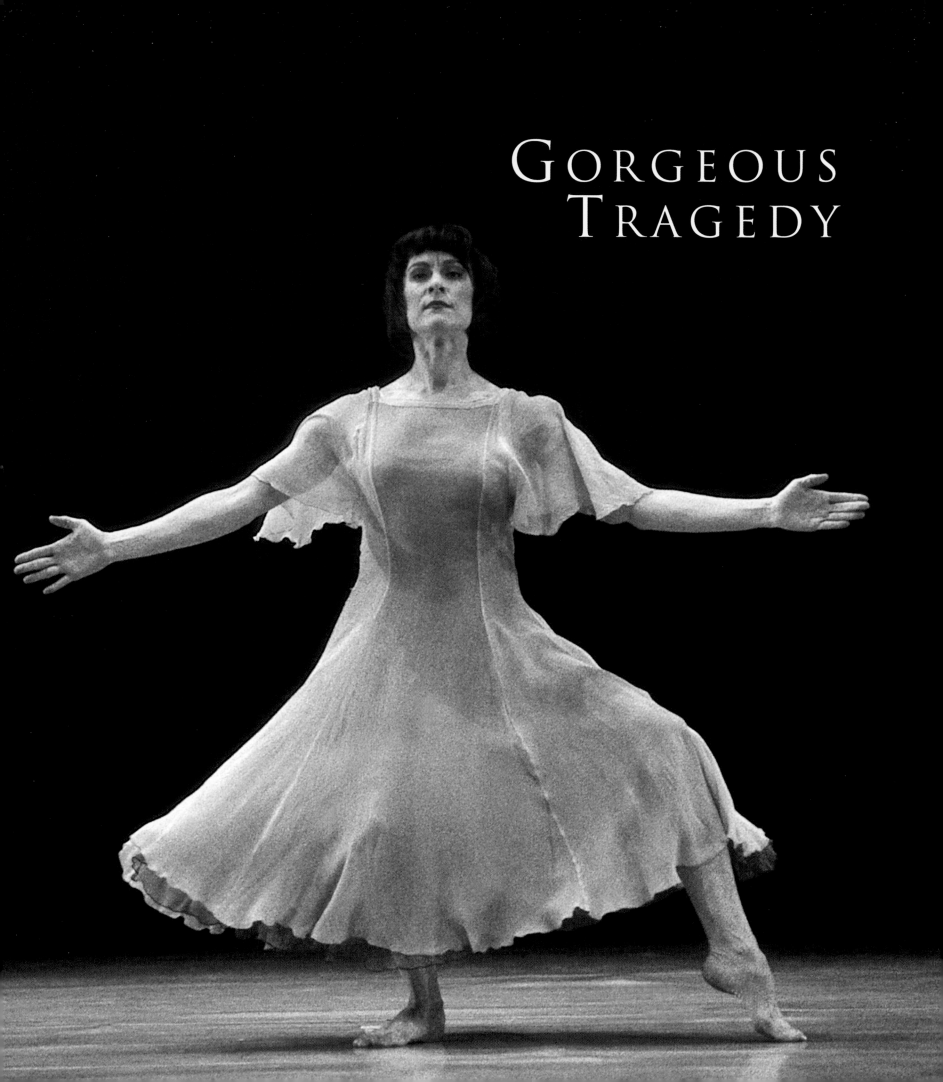

GORGEOUS
TRAGEDY

ACCOMPAGNATO FOR SOPRANO

Hence, vain deluding Joys,

The brood of Folly without father bred

How little you bested,

Or fill the fixed mind with all your toys!

Oh! let my lamp, at midnight hour,

Be seen in some high lonely tow'r,

Where I may ofte out-watch the Bear

With thrice-great Hermes, or unsphere

The spirit of Plato to unfold

What worlds, or what vast regions hold

Th'immortal mind that hath forsook

Her mansion in this fleshly nook.

AIR FOR SOPRANO

Sometimes let gorgeous Tragedy

In scepter'd pall come sweeping by,

Presenting Thebes, or Pelops' line,

Or the tale of Troy divine;

Or what, though rare, of later age

Ennobled hath the buskin'd stage.

RECITATIVE FOR SOPRANO

Thus, Night oft see me in thy pale career,

Till unwelcome Morn appear.

LONDON, 2000 • Ruth Davidson [Susana Millman]

BRUSSELS, 1989 • [L–R]: Dan Joyce, Ruth Davidson, Penny Hutchinson [Daniéle Pierre]

BERKELEY, 2000 • Ruth Davidson [Ken Friedman]

TEL AVIV, 1996 • Ruth Davidson [Gadi Dagon]

"IL PENSEROSO, from the pit, sings of the joys of the mind—how when everyone else is asleep, he will sit alone in a dark tower, reading Neoplatonic treatises—and [Ruth] Davidson, all alone on the . . . stage, does a dance where her arms seem to be the book that is opening. Meanwhile, however, her legs perform turns so exacting that she must surely be not any *thing* in this scene but rather the image of Penseroso's mental act as he scales the heights of thought: so beautiful and so difficult at the same time."

[Joan Acocella in *Ballet Review*]

SOLO FOR BASS

Populous cities please me then,

And the busy hum of men.

CHORUS

Populous cities please us then,

And the busy hum of men,

Where throngs of knights and barons Bold,

In weeds of peace high triumphs hold;

With store of ladies, whose bright eyes

Rain influence, and judge the prize

Of wit, or arms, while both contend

To win her grace, whom all commend.

BERKELEY, 2000 • Company [Ken Friedman]

l'allegro

POPULOUS CITIES

BERKELEY, 2000 • John Heginbotham and company [Ken Friedman]

"THE 'POPULOUS CITIES please us

then' vignette is a cityscape as hectic as Wall Street on a

Monday morning."

[Christine Temin in the *Boston Globe*]

HYMEN

BERKELEY, 2000 • [FOREGROUND, L–R]: Mireille Radwan-Dana, Charlton Boyd;
[BACKGROUND, L–R]: Julie Worden, Michelle Yard, Derrick Brown
[PARTIALLY OBSCURED] [Ken Friedman]

AIR FOR TENOR

There let Hymen oft appear

In saffron robe, with taper clear,

And pomp, and feast, and revelry,

With mask, and antique pageantry;

Such sights as youthful poets dream

On summer eves by haunted stream.

l'allegro

"GYMNASTIC LOVERS" is the alternate name the dancers have given this section, and appropriately so: How rarely are we reminded of the sheer physical vigor lovemaking requires. But even as the various lovers tumble over each other performing routines worthy of an Olympics competition, they also gaze longingly and caress tenderly. A poet dreams and gives birth to a fantasy of love and marriage as the "horse and carriage" we see elsewhere in the dance passes through, on the way to its next rendezvous.

TEL AVIV, 1996 • Mireille Radwan-Dana, Guillermo Resto [Gadi Dagon]

DAY'S
GARISH
EYE

ACCOMPAGNATO FOR SOPRANO

Me, when the sun begins to fling

His flaring beams, me goddess bring

To arched walks of twilight groves,

And shadows brown that Sylvan loves;

There in close covert by some brook,

Where no profaner eye may look.

TEL AVIV, 1996 • [L–R]: Vernon Scott, Ruth Davidson, June Omura, William Wagner [Gadi Dagon]

AIR FOR SOPRANO

Hide me from day's garish eye,

While the bee with honey'd thigh,

Which at her flow'ry work doth sing,

And the waters murmuring,

With such consorts as they keep

Entice the dewy-feather'd sleep;

And let some strange mysterious dream

Wave at his wings in airy stream

Of lively portraiture display'd,

Softly on my eyelids laid.

Then as I wake, sweet music breathe,

Above, about, or underneath,

Send by some spirit to mortals good,

Or th'unseen genius of the wood.

TEL AVIV, 1996 • [FRONT TO BACK]: June Omura, Ruth Davidson [OBSCURED], William Wagner, Vernon Scott, Ruben Graciani [Gadi Dagon]

BERKELEY, 2000 • [L-R]: Shawn Gannon, John Heginbotham, Jonathan Pessolano
[Ken Friedman]

"IN [DAY'S GARISH EYE] we can make out a bee or stream. But Morris also suggests less tangible ideas like music or painting or even the poet's state of mind, like when the poet enters the grove of trees, we can really sense his thoughts turning inward. That's really what's so extraordinary about Morris' choreography. He gives logical shape to music, ideas, and emotions while at the same time he's making a very sophisticated dance."

[Judith Mackrell in *The Hidden Soul of Harmony*,
South Bank Show, London Weekend Television]

TEL AVIV, 1996 •
[L-R]: William Wagner, Ruth Davidson, Ruben Graciani;
[FLOOR]: June Omura [Gadi Dagon]

LONDON, 2000 • [FRONT TO BACK]: June Omura, Ruth Davidson, John Heginbotham [OBSCURED] [Susana Millman]

BRUSSELS, 1989 • [L–R]: Olivia Maridjan-Koop, Jean-Guillaume Weis, Penny Hutchinson, Mark Nimkoff, Joachim Schlömer [Daniéle Pierre]

LONDON, 2000 • [L–R]: Shawn Gannon, John Heginbotham, Jonathan Pessolano [Robbie Jack]

LONDON, 2000 • [L–R]: Shawn Gannon, John Heginbotham, Jonathan Pessolano [OBSCURED] lifting June Omura, and Ruth Davidson [Susana Millman]

THE STUPID MEN'S DANCE

BROOKLYN, 1990 • [L–R]: Joe Bowie, Guillermo Resto, Keith Sabado, Mark Nimkoff, Erin Matthiessen, Hans-Georg Lenhart [Tom Brazil]

l'allegro

BERKELEY, 2000 • [L–R]: Matthew Rose, Joseph Poulson, Derrick Brown, Jonathan Pessolano, Shawn Gannon, David Leventhal, Joe Bowie, Seth Davis, Peter Kyle, Charlton Boyd, Joseph Gillam, Gregory Nuber [Ken Friedman]

AIR FOR TENOR

I'll to the well-trod stage anon,

If Jonson's learned sock be on;

Or sweetest Shakespeare, Fancy's child,

Warble his native wood-notes wild.

"**ALL TWELVE MEN** stand in a ring. First they embrace, then they sock one another in the face . . . then they do a nice, jolly, tripping circle dance. Then they start punching one another again; then they dance again, and so on. So that's what boys are made of." "Sometimes [Morris] will pun on [the text], as when l'Allegro, speaking of going to the theater, mentions Ben Jonson's 'learned sock'—that is, Jonson's learned comedy, 'sock' being the *soccus*, or low-heeled shoe, worn by actors in Attic comedy—and Morris has his dancers sock one another. (They also stick their feet out, as if to show us their socks, but I think the pun was intended.)"

[Joan Acocella in *Ballet Review*]

THE LADIES' DANCE

And ever against eating cares,

Lap me in soft Lydian airs;

Sooth me in immortal verse,

Such as the meeting soul may pierce

In notes, with many a winding bout

Of linkèd sweetness long drawn out;

With wanton heed, and giddy cunning,

The melting voice through mazes running

Untwisting all the chains that tie

The hidden soul of harmony.

l'allegro

"THE MEN'S PUNCHOUT is followed by a quintessentially wafting number for the women. This is another circle dance—we are meant to see the two as a pair—but instead of revolving forcefully, it flows and winds like a moving wreath: twelve enchanted princesses, perhaps, or twelve priestesses, descendants of Doris Humphrey, dancing around an invisible altar."

[Joan Acocella in *Ballet Review*]

BERKELEY, 2000 • [L–R]: Kim Reis, Michelle Yard, Lauren Grant, June Omura, Rachel Murray, Julie Worden, Ruth Davidson, Maile Okamura, Mireille Radwan-Dana, Karen Reedy, Christina Amendolia, Marjorie Folkman [Ken Friedman]

LONDON, 2000 • [L–R]: Michelle Yard, Kim Reis, June Omura, Rachel Murray, Lauren Grant, Julie Worden, Ruth Davidson, Maile Okamura, Karen Reedy, Christina Amendolia, Marjorie Folkman [Susana Millman]

LONDON, 2000 • [LEFT SIDE OF ARCH, FRONT TO BACK]: Kim Reis, Michelle Yard, Maile Okamura; [CENTER]: Ruth Davidson, Julie Worden; [RIGHT SIDE OF ARCH, FRONT TO BACK]: Karen Reedy, Marjorie Folkman, Christina Amendolia [Susana Millman]

"THE SUBJECT HERE IS SONG—specifically, how singing, while it may lead us through a thousand complications, still reveals itself in the end as something *rational*, with its basis in harmony. Milton tells this story by poetic means, Handel by musical means. Morris hears all that, but out of it he makes his own dance story. Discarding the subject of song and going just for the point about reason and fancy, he arranges twelve women in a braided wreath and has them dance in and out among one another. The wreath winds and turns, twists and untwists—this is the 'wanton heed,' the 'giddy cunning'—but always with the simple, rational circle (the 'hidden soul of harmony') at its center. As the song nears its end, the drama intensifies. The women break into groups of three, and in each trio, one woman dips down while the two others join their hands over her head, imprisoning her. Then, on the final cadence, she bursts up through the barrier: the hidden soul of harmony, rising, sweet-faced, out of apparent confusion. So Milton's image is there, but it has become a dance image, a matter of hiding and revealing through dancing. The same is true in most of *L'Allegro*. Goddess, nymph, bird, dream: the thing is indicated, but then it begins to change. It sprouts new meanings, flows back into the dance."

[Joan Acocella in *Mark Morris*]

BRUSSELS, 1988 • [REAR GROUP, L–R]: Penny Hutchinson, Clarice Marshall [PARTIALLY OBSCURED], Susan Hadley;
[FRONT GROUP, L–R]: Olivia Maridjan-Koop, Ruth Davidson [PARTIALLY OBSCURED], Tina Fehlandt [Klaus Lefebvre]

THE WALKING DUET

BERKELEY, 2000 • [L–R]: Joe Bowie, Maile Okamura, Charlton Boyd [Ken Friedman]

DUET FOR SOPRANO AND TENOR

As steals the morn upon the night,

And melts the shades away:

So truth does Fancy's charm dissolve,

And rising Reason puts to flight

The fumes that did the mind involve,

Restoring intellectual day.

il moderato

BRUSSELS, 1989 • Company [Daniéle Pierre]

"**WHAT IS WONDERFUL** here is to see how
Morris can find beauty not just in those two sexy extremes
[Allegro and Penseroso] but in Moderato as well. To the
steady, churning beat that Handel uses for Reason's march
against Fancy, Morris creates a Thracian line dance, in which
the twenty-four dancers form two lines and march toward,
away from, and into one another in patterns that seem to
multiply endlessly. Each time the two lines meet, center stage,
a new surprise is born. Thus Reason, though steady, is no
school-marm."

[Joan Acocella in *Ballet Review*]

BRUSSELS, 1989 • [L–R]: Megan Williams, Hans-Georg Lenhart, Mireille Radwan-Dana, Joachim Schlömer, Keith Sabado, Alyce Bochette [Daniéle Pierre]

"[THE WALKING DUET], based on the folkdance axiom of linked bodies executing a steady tread in simple geometric patterns, elevates one of Morris's formative influences to a means of transmitting feeling so primal words could not possibly interpret it. . . . The effect is so graphically satisfying and so touching that you could die happy at the moment the chain of bodies—replete with human dignity, deeply and rightly enigmatic—passes across your field of vision."

[Tobi Tobias in *New York* magazine]

BASILICA

RECITATIVE FOR SOPRANO

But let my due feet never fail

To walk the studious cloisters' pale,

And love the high-embowed roof,

With antique pillars' massy proof,

And story'd windows richly dight,

Casting a dim religious light.

CHORUS

There let the pealing organ blow

to the full voic'd choir below,

In service high and anthem clear!

SOLO FOR SOPRANO

And let their sweetness, through mine ear,

Dissolve me into ecstasies,

And bring all Heav'n before mine eyes!

il penseroso

"BASILICA" launches us into *L'Allegro*'s final Penseroso sequence. With quiet dignity, the dancers walk onto a stage made to resemble a sanctuary. Beneath a radiating light, they pause to listen to the "pealing organ" and the "full voic'd choir." They depart walking backwards, like cars in reverse.

BERKELEY, 2000 • Company [Ken Friedman]

WEARY AGE

il penseroso

AIR FOR SOPRANO

May at last my weary age

Find out the peaceful hermitage,

The hairy gown and mossy cell,

Where I may sit and rightly spell

Of ev'ry star that Heav'n doth shew,

And ev'ry herb that sips the dew;

Till old experience do attain

To something like prophetic strain.

"THE LAST PENSEROSO passage of Part Two has five musical sections. The central one is the air 'May at last my weary age'; in the dance quartet that Morris sets to it motif after motif that we've seen before comes back to roost. Back come 'earth,' 'air,' 'fire,' and 'water'—now in a simple canon, like recycled memories. Other motifs, in this Penseroso context, acquire often a quite different meaning. In Part One, you saw dancers sitting, holding their knees, and rolling over from side to side, as 'Laughter, holding both his sides'—a thoroughly Allegro image. But here it lacks its former pulse: once helpless laughter, now recollected in tranquility."

[Alastair Macaulay from "Creation Myth"]

BRUSSELS, 1989 • [L–R]: Keith Sabado, Dan Joyce, Clarice Marshall, Penny Hutchinson [Daniéle Pierre]

BERKELEY, 2000 • [L–R]: Mireille Radwan-Dana, Shawn Gannon, Ruth Davidson, Charlton Boyd [Ken Friedman]

MELANCHOLY OCTET

il penseroso

SOLO FOR SOPRANO

These pleasures, Melancholy, give,

And I with thee will choose to live.

CHORUS

These pleasures, Melancholy, give,

And we with thee will choose to live.

BROOKLYN, 1990 • [L–R]: Jon Mensinger, Tina Fehlandt,
Alyce Bochette, Erin Matthiessen, June Omura,
Rachel Murray, Ruth Davidson, Kraig Patterson,
Joachim Schlömer [Martha Swope/TimePix]

"MELANCHOLY OCTET," set to *L'Allegro's* only fugue, accumulates enormous power as it moves to its climax. Each of the fugue's four vocal parts is shadowed by a pair of dancers: soprano, by a woman leading a woman; alto, by a woman leading a man; tenor, by a man leading a woman; and bass, by a man leading a man. Each pair of dancers cycles through the same sequence of gestures as their vocal part sings Milton's couplet, and when their vocal part is at rest, each couple stands in an embrace. (One dancer, June Omura, begins the section by previewing the sequence, then stands at the back of the stage, her back to us, her right arm held aloft, her hand made into a fist.) As Mark Morris has explained, "The dance is done as a steady crescendo. It starts out gentle, and gets more emphatic. It gets bigger. Walking turns into running, and it gets wilder as it goes along. The dancers start out very gently embracing, and by the end they're smashed together. At the very end everybody embraces at the same time because there's a full bar of rest. It's the only time that all voices are rested at the same time. That's the reason that it looks like a fabulous passionate climax."

TEL AVIV, 1996 • [L–R]: Tina Fehlandt [PARTIALLY OBSCURED], Guillermo Resto, June Omura, Kraig Patterson, Joe Bowie, Rachel Murray, Ruth Davidson [Gadi Dagon]

TEL AVIV, 1996 • [L–R]: June Omura, Kraig Patterson, Joe Bowie, Rachel Murray, Ruth Davidson [Gadi Dagon]

TEL AVIV, 1996 • [L–R]: Victoria Lundell [PARTIALLY OBSCURED], June Omura, Kraig Patterson, Joe Bowie [Gadi Dagon]

TEL AVIV, 1996 • [L–R]: Victoria Lundell [PARTIALLY OBSCURED], June Omura, Kraig Patterson, Joe Bowie, Rachel Murray, Ruth Davidson [Gadi Dagon]

LONDON, 1997 • [L–R]: Rachel Murray,
Ruth Davidson [Bill Rafferty]

LONDON, 2000 • [L–R]: Julie Worden, John Heginbotham [Bill Cooper]

LONDON, 2000 • [L–R]: David Leventhal, Julie Worden, John Heginbotham [Bill Cooper]

LONDON, 2000 • [FOREGROUND]: John Heginbotham, Julie Warden; [BACKGROUND, L-R]: Ruth Davidson, Rachel Murray, June Omura [Bill Cooper]

ORPHEUS

Orpheus' self may heave his head

From golden slumbers on a bed

Of heap'd Elysian flow'rs, and hear

Such strains as would have won the ear

Of Pluto, to have quite set free

His half-regain'd Eurydice.

LONDON, 2000 • Shawn Gannon and women of the company [Susana Millman]

BERKELEY, 2000 • Shawn Gannon and women of the company [Ken Friedman]

LONDON, 2000 • Shawn Gannon and [L–R]: Rachel Murray, Karen Reedy, Lauren Grant, Maile Okamura, Julie Worden, Kim Reis, Anne Sellery, June Omura, Marjorie Folkman [Susana Millman]

BRUSSELS, 1989 • Keith Sabado and women of the company [Daniéle Pierre]

"[T]HE FINAL ALLEGRO SECTION begins with the tale of Orpheus. Here the imagery of sight and death are extraordinarily linked—more so than Milton's words alone would sanction. By looking at his beloved, dead Eurydice, Orpheus kills his lover a second time over. Milton's words merely refer to Orpheus the heroic musician, who half-regains Eurydice from the Elysian fields with his music; but Morris rattles through the whole tragic myth as if it were a comic, cautionary tale. Orpheus sleeps, dreams, wakes, plays music, enchants his listeners, is no sooner allowed to take his (male) Eurydice than he looks at him, loses him forever, recoils in horror, goes distracted, is chased by the maenads (who, seconds before, had been his musical groupies), and is torn apart by them. Morris quickly 'wipes' this image, just as he 'wipes' the Penseroso pair of male lovers at the end of the previous number."

[Alastair Macaulay from "Creation Myth"]

LONDON, 2000 • Shawn Gannon and women of the company [Susana Millman]

BERKELEY, 2000 • Shawn Gannon and women of the company [Ken Friedman]

AIR FOR TENOR

These delights if thou canst give,

Mirth, with thee I mean to live.

CHORUS

These delights if thou canst give,

Mirth, with thee we mean to live.

l'allegro

LONDON, 1997 • Julie Worden [Bill Rafferty]

FINALE

BERKELEY, 2000 • [L–R]: Gregory Nuber, Anne Sellery, Michelle Yard, Karen Reedy, Joseph Gillam, Lauren Grant [Ken Friedman]

"THE END OF *L'Allegro* is even more thrilling than the beginning. The stage is opened to its full depth, fully lit, and as the singers' voices go up in their final hymn to Mirth, the dancers, in ones and twos and threes, come leaping out of the back wings, join hands with others flying in from the other side, and race downstage toward us in a transport of joy. As one group exits, the next one enters, wave upon wave breaking. Then they all disappear, and after a moment's pause, like a delayed heartbeat, they reenter, forming three concentric circles. And as the drums pound and the trumpets raise their fanfare, the circles begin running: the outer one clockwise, the middle one counter-clockwise, and the inner circle—three women, just like the Muses—clockwise, as before, around Jove's altar. . . . In its fusion of geometry and dynamism, it is the embodiment of Milton's and Handel's and Morris' meaning: the coming together of the two poles of the mind—reason and energy, contemplation and enjoyment, Apollo and Dionysus, seeing and being, Penseroso and Allegro."

[Joan Acocella in *Ballet Review*]

BERKELEY, 2000 • [L–R]: Gregory Nuber, Michelle Yard, Joe Bowie, David Leventhal, Ruth Davidson, Rachel Murray, Karen Reedy, Lauren Grant [Ken Friedman]

LONDON, 2000 • [L–R]: Julie Worden, Bradon McDonald [Bill Cooper]

"DEPARTING FROM BOTH MILTON (who ended with Melancholy) **AND HANDEL** (who, in typical eighteenth-century mode, ended with Moderation), Morris begins *and* ends the piece with Happiness. That is, he turns Milton's and Handel's linear structure into a circle—just as he does in the final moments of the dance itself, which ends as a large, fast, joyous circle dance culminating in a single moment of upward-reaching stillness. The many dancers have become a single motion, and unity has been imposed on division, but not by arriving at a logical and irrefutable compromise. Morris has simply chosen— arbitrarily, personally, and whimsically—to end on a note of happiness. Nothing in either the world or this work of art leads you to conclude that happiness is a necessary or permanent outcome; and yet the moment feels right, and final, and true."

[Wendy Lesser from "An Artist for Our Time"]

LONDON, 2000 • Company [Susana Millman]

IN THE BEGINNING, primeval darkness. An Allegro tenor sings "Hence, loathed Melancholy. . . ." The darkness remains. You seem to be staring into the void. Then the music shifts into Penseroso mood. Suddenly you glimpse atoms (dancers) running dimly through the dark, running, running, until— bang! stop! wheel!—two of them collide, join, circle. A molecule! These "atom" dancers were running pell-mell in criss-crossing diagonals. To watch them missing each other had the perilous excitement of observing an experiment in nuclear fission. But what happened? No Big Bang. Instead—as if the proscenium arch were now a

microscope—the magnified beginnings of organic life. One cluster forms and dissolves; then a larger one; then one larger yet. A young world has begun.

At the end, in the Finale, glowing enlightenment. You see dancers running through the light, running, running, like blithe and illumined immortals, until—one circle! a second! a third!—they become three concentric rings, revolving clockwise, counterclockwise, clockwise: harmony and complexity fused. In the eighteenth century, the Reverend Sydney Smith proposed that one idea of heaven is "eating *pates de foie gras* to the sound of trumpets." In their *L'Allegro, il Penseroso ed il Moderato*, Handel and Morris seem to agree about the sound

Creation Myth

ALASTAIR MACAULAY

of trumpets. Bright fanfares sound, in great runs and trills. The dancers wheel around each other, ring within ring within ring, in their ultimate mortal/immortal paradise. Bright light glows above.

Chaos into order; darkness into light; instinct into knowledge. *L'Allegro, il Penseroso ed il Moderato* seems to start like an either/or choice: this way of living or that, Melancholy or Mirth. But it becomes—of course—a celebration of both/and. Watching and listening, you recognize Allegro and Penseroso principles in yourself, and do not find yourself tragically torn between the two poles. Instead, you feel the richness of each system growing harmoniously within yourself.

"MELANCHOLY AND HER COMPANIONS," from William Blake's "Il Penseroso"

[The Pierpont Morgan Library/Art Resource, New York]

The Milton/Handel/Morris *L'Allegro, il Penseroso ed il Moderato* is that rare thing, a work of art that has made many thousands of people feel proud to belong to the same era as it. In the vast creation-myth history of the world that it traces, and in its families of expressive motifs, I think of it in the same breath as Wagner's "Ring" Cycle. In its musically structured, philosophical analysis of separate impulses in human thought, I set it beside the Hindemith-Balanchine ballet *The Four Temperaments*. It is "full of *things*"—the quality that Pasternak loved in the poetry of Pushkin—and the kaleidoscope that these "things" add up to in Morris' staging reminds me of the greatest of the nineteenth-century ballets, the Tchaikovsky-Petipa *Sleeping Beauty*, with its crowds of people suddenly laid to sleep, its hunt scene, its chain-dance farandole danced by peasants, lords and ladies, its Romantic vision, and its fires suddenly flickering in the grate. And in its changes of scale—cosmic/human, comic/transcendent—it recalls Shakespeare's *A Midsummer Night's Dream*.

ON ONE LEVEL, *L'Allegro, il Penseroso ed il Moderato* is a guide to natural movement. This was Morris' debut presentation as resident choreographer of the Théâtre Royal de la Monnaie in Brussels, and it seemed then—1988—as refreshing an American landing in Europe as that of Isadora Duncan at the beginning of the same century—Isadora, the great American dance pioneer of the early twentieth century, who drew inspiration from her ideas of ancient Greek art, from European music of the eighteenth and nineteenth centuries, from her own body, and from her liberal ideals of womanhood and society. Back to basics! Stand. Walk. Run. Lie down. Gesture. Twirl. Hop. Skip. Jump. *L'Allegro*'s language is very largely Isadora's. The feet are bare, as are the shoulders and arms; the costumes are Grecian. Here and there in Morris' choreography, virtuosity briefly blooms. The lone woman who opens Part Two (Ruth Davidson at all performances to date) performs a gorgeously full revolution-and-a-half several times: a turn that looks wholly original because, throughout it, she holds an unusual three-dimensional sculptural position. You see how she turns on the ball of her foot and the full length of her toes; you feel the texture of the foot and its friction while you watch. Mainly, however, you feel that this is movement

you could do yourself; and, even if in fact you couldn't, that feeling is right. The world of *L'Allegro* is something you belong to.

The movement abounds in literal imagery. Most of the images pour easily forth from Milton's twin poems: Laughter, holding both his sides; the lark bidding good morrow at the window; the nightingale and the wand'ring moon; the hounds and horn; the cricket on the hearth; the milkmaid singing blithe; the city's store of ladies; the bee with honey'd thigh; th'unseen genius of the wood. . . . Some of these allegories are so sustained that you cannot help but recognize them. Others pass as transient incidents. Group tableaux suddenly coalesce into stage-filling pictorial images with their own inner narrative life, such as a pair of huge fireplaces with flames flickering in either grate, with one dancer warming her hands at either fireplace before suddenly departing and closing the door behind her. (Penseroso: "Where glowing embers through the room / Teach light to counterfeit a gloom.") Some of these scenes have far more interior detail than can be taken in at any one viewing; I had seen the work more than a dozen times before I ever noticed the milkmaid's actual gesture of milking.

Some of the first personages you see in it look mythological—nymphs, goddesses, graces, or muses. The two women in the Allegro air "Come, and trip it as you go / On the light fantastic toe" even remind me of Picasso giantesses: not just in their weight

"WARMING HER HANDS" • LONDON, 2000 • Marjorie Folkman and company, in "Fireplace" [Bill Cooper]

and solidity but in the block-like way they stretch out into the space around them. In due course, most of Morris' characters start to look more like ordinary human beings, though their world, as in Homer, is one they share with deities. And, as these humans form into groups, you see the birth of society. There are male or female soloists, male or female couples; then images of birth; and then (only then!) images of marriage. Soon there are also male/male couples and female/female.

There's a Noah's Ark feeling to the first half of *L'Allegro*: we keep seeing two of each kind. Two giantesses; two pensive nuns; two larks; two nightingales. . . . There may have been various structural reasons for all this duplication in Morris' mind, but one reason in the back of our minds is connected to the dualism of Allegro and Penseroso. Even when you're watching a thoroughly Allegro or Penseroso number, it never remains singular for long. You see the "wand'ring moon," but it consists of two women facing in opposite directions, each lifted by a pair of men, all revolving together, so that the image is of a circling orb with, yes, two sides, like the moon's bright and dark faces.

An especially telling vignette, during a long orchestral passage, is when one Allegro lark actually meets one Penseroso nightingale center-stage. The two "birds," in profile to us, just

"TWO OF EACH KIND" • **BERKELEY, 2000** • [L–R]: June Omura, Julie Worden, in "Sweet Bird" [Ken Friedman]

stand there and gaze into each other's eyes, as if contemplating an opposite number. Nowhere else in the work do we see Allegro and Penseroso emblems so plainly sharing the stage; and the meeting seems for a long while to freeze them. Next, as the music softly builds, they behave like the birds they are—listening, with wonderfully birdlike inflections of head and eyes—but both in completely the same way.

The work grows in complexity. The Allegro tenor air "Haste thee, nymph" (near the beginning) is a dance for three men; then, as Handel takes up the tune with a mixed chorus, Morris turns it into a dance for twelve women. This is one kind of multiplication (Morris goes on to use this method—the few and the many—in several different ways); and perhaps it prepares you for multiplication of another kind, where you see onstage not just this world but also—through this gauze or that—another: some Platonic realm, idealized by this one. The structural justification for this comes from various distancing or expanding methods in Handel's musical arrangements. But what Morris shows is that, for him, structure is metaphysics.

The structures of *L'Allegro* have many kinds of complexity. The "lark" air is mainly a solo dance for one male lark; but its orchestral passages are for an entire flock of larks male and female. Somehow this has the effect of suggesting the Platonic idea in reverse. You've seen the lark ideal; now you're watching a host of wannabe larks. More sophisticated yet are the structures Morris uses for the Penseroso "nightingale" soprano air ("Sweet bird") that follows. First, he turns its several recurring orchestral passages into a series of exercises in—of all unlikely things!—dance deconstruction. He shows you a whole group of men and women crossing the stage. What they're doing—together, or one after another as they pass across—is practicing lifts. (One of the couples, you may notice, is male-male. No special attention is drawn to this fact.) What you see is how the men really collect themselves before the lift, bend down to catch the woman (or man), push her (or him) up into the air for a moment, then deposit her (or him) once more. The next time these dancers return, you notice that some of the men are lifting— what?—nothing! thin air! And so, for once, you observe analytically the bare mechanics of lifting, without any illusion of weightlessness.

"THE BARE MECHANICS OF LIFTING" • EDINBURGH, 1994 • [L–R]: Joe Bowie, Deniz Oktay, Charlton Boyd, Rachel Murray, Dan Joyce, William Wagner [OBSCURED], Victoria Lundell, John Heginbotham, in "Sweet Bird" [Robbie Jack]

Next time, Morris shows you *all* the men lifting thin air, again and again. Finally, he shows you just one male-female couple, doing the lift alone. Morris forces the point so hard that you can't help but think about it while you're watching.

And these thoughts about the mechanics and the meanings of lifting and of being lifted come to you during the intervals of the solo dance for the female nightingale: a dance in which the "sweet bird" herself strains and flutters this way and that—yet almost always stays on the ground. We see and feel her wings, but we don't really feel that she's flying. However, in the middle section of this A/B/A da capo aria, this nightingale wistfully observes "the wand'ring moon," through a gauze at the back, as it crosses the stage—held high without any apparent effort while it revolves. And our nightingale runs longingly towards this moon, and now is lifted high (by a male partner, who materializes here only for this purpose) and is held aloft in a sustained lift. Hers is the definitive form of the lift that the others had been practicing. Those dancers wanted to share the nightingale's winged condition—and the nightingale longs to share the moon's suspended condition. After all those wannabe nightingales, our nightingale seemed like the one true

nightingale—but now we see that she regards herself as a wannabe moon! Next, the other nightingale appears behind the gauze; and the two nightingales keep up a you/me duet, in which "our" nightingale often follows the lead of her fellow; then is inspired by her; and finally resembles her perfectly.

Throughout the images and anecdotes and rites that make up Morris' movement language in *L'Allegro*, certain motifs recur. The flames that flicker in the grate and at which two girls warm their hands: their upward arm-movement becomes "fire" itself. In the Moderato air that Morris places in Part One ("Each action will derive new grace"), "fire" becomes one of four motifs that depict the four elements: earth, air, fire, water. In "earth," the dancers crouch with hands on the ground, and a ripple passes through their spines and arms, briefly lifting their hands off the ground. "Air" is an adorable "blowing" mime, in which the dancers (standing and leaning forwards) become the personifications of winds, as on old maps: They blow with puffed cheeks and fanning hands, and the action of puffing passes right through them, so that they hop briefly off the floor. The image for "water" again passes right through the dancers, as they lean from one side to the other, but its emphasis is on rippling hands, as if tracing the surface of the sea, in a sweeping left-to-right gesture. Here, as on several other occasions, there's no cue in the words for these motifs. Those dance clusters that I have previously described as "molecules" and "the beginnings of organic life" (in the first danced passage of all, the Penseroso recitative "Hence, vain deluding Joys") are, in fact, almost entirely made up of gestures, movements, patterns that will recur as motifs throughout the work (one of them is "water").

This way of working with motifs is highly Wagnerian. (This is ironic; Morris generally expresses aversion for Wagner's music.) Wagner took pride in the fact that all the orchestration of *Götterdämmerung* was made up of leitmotifs; and the same is very nearly true of the movement in *L'Allegro*. But it's important to say at the outset that Morris, like Wagner, is often highly ambiguous about these motifs and their meaning(s)—so that they act as a subtext: an undercurrent suggesting something we hadn't suspected in the words and music alone.

All his motifs—some mainly lower-body, others upper-body—have a certain "mime" emphasis in their timing: the delivery shows you that something is being depicted even when you can't tell what it is. But *L'Allegro* is never just a collage of mime gestures. What makes these motifs work is the way they're strung together into phrases. For example, in the Allegro air and chorus "Come, and trip it as you go, / On the light fantastic toe," there are movement motifs for "Come," "trip," "go," and "light fantastic toe." The motifs come round again and again, just as those words do in Handel's setting. The method begins to look schematic—Fit The Motif to The Word—but, if you analyze it, you find that Morris *doesn't* actually slap on the motif each and every time the appropriate word crops up; and his timing varies, too. What you also notice is how smoothly the motifs all run smoothly into each other, in ways that complement the contours of Handel's phrases. Yet the motifs here are all different types of movement. The "Go" motif is principally upper-body (a pointing gesture, though maintained with a full-bodied arabesque shape), whereas "light fantastic toe" is principally lower-body (a side-skipping step). As for "trip it," only Morris would show the dancers actually tripping! As their feet trip up and down, as if over an obstacle, their torsos lurch right over; and yet Morris gives this a rhythmic continuity that makes it feel dance-y, not like a mime illustration. And it's this rhythmic and lyrical current that brings together all the distinct motifs into a coherent phrase. Of all Morris' musical gifts, this dynamic sense is among the most extraordinary: somehow, the mime emphasis he and his dancers bring, to gestures and even to steps, never blocks the larger dance rhythmic continuity of a melodic phrase. The communicative impulse and the lyrical impulse work brilliantly—naturally—together.

In this number, the motif for "Come" has a particular marcato emphasis. Squatting, their legs planted well apart in deep *demi-plié*, the dancers hold a forward oval shape with their arms, and for each utterance of the word "Come," they inflect this shape with a beckoning impulse. It's a small impulse, but it passes through the entire body, starting both in the forearms and pelvis. Now, although the word "Come" has already occurred during three earlier musical items of this oratorio, it's only here that Morris has chosen to illustrate it. And, having done so in this Allegro item, he

"THE 'GO' MOTIF" • WASHINGTON, D.C., 1999 • [L–R]: Mireille Radwan-Dana, Tina Fehlandt, in "Come and Trip It" [Tom Brazil]

promptly re-employs it in the Penseroso arioso that follows: "Come, but keep thy wonted state." Sure, in each case, he's responding to a rhythmic repetition ("Come, come") in Handel's word-setting. But, by showing the same motif in successive musical items, he shows you how Allegro and Penseroso—here, as at each stage of the work—share the same language. That's why, though the words seem to urge us towards an either/or choice between the two philosophical systems, you never feel compelled to make that choice. The music suggests and the dance shows that no choice is necessary or even possible.

The last Penseroso passage of Part Two has five musical sections. The central one is the air "May at last my weary age"; in the dance quartet that Morris sets to it motif after motif that we've seen before comes back to roost. Back come "earth," "air," "fire," and "water"—now in a simple canon, like recycled memories. Other motifs, in this Penseroso context, acquire a quite different meaning. In Part One, you saw dancers sitting, holding their knees, and rolling over from side to side, as "Laughter, holding both his sides"—a thoroughly Allegro image. But here it lacks its former pulse: once helpless laughter, now recollected in tranquility.

Sometimes, precisely when Morris is at his most dogged in connecting motifs to words, what hits you is how odd his choice of movement is: eloquent, but not explanatory. A motif will accompany a word again and again, and yet you can't help seeing that it's by no means a neat illustration of that word's primary sense. Just look at the dance's last two Penseroso sections: a solo and then a four-part choral fugue with the words "These pleasures, Melancholy, give, / And I (we) with thee will choose to live." Morris sets the solo for female soloist (June Omura, at all performances to date); the fugue for four couples. Each couple answers a choral part. (It's interesting that only now, near the end of the work, does Morris employ what used to be his standard compositional formula: one male/male couple, one male-female, one female-male, one female-female.) There are motifs for "These pleasures," "Melancholy," "give," "we," "choose," and "live": so far, so neat. But some of these motifs are legato, some staccato; some aim up, some down. And all of them are very strangely floated on a surprisingly hesitant dance current.

The mime emphasis here is unusually strong—especially in the four-part fugue—both in the force of certain upper-body gestures and in the staccato timing with which some of them are held. Can we work out what they "mean"? Well, one of these motifs, to "Melancholy," makes sense in context of the rest of the work: this has an arm folded across the chest (hand on the opposite shoulder), and we've seen it several times (mainly in Penseroso contexts) since the opening recitative. We've seen "give," too—a half-crouch, with the palms of the hands clasped together in a pointing gesture. But this crouch, in Part One, occurred in a different light, illustrating "the cricket on the hearth." Here (the dancers' heads now are facing down, and the whole tone is darker), it looks like an image of prayer. What's it doing here? And why does Morris provide a dark, figure-of-eight stirring gesture for each utterance of "These pleasures"? Why the odd hold-out-one-wounded-arm gesture for "choose"?

The fugal structure of the choreography seems schematic— "I'm a real structure queen," Morris said in London, back in 1985, with good reason—but these individual movements are intensely expressionist. Yet their individual meaning hardly matters; what becomes disturbing, as you go on watching this fugue, is the collective meaning they add up to. Why the heroic gesture of defiance (like Liberty on the barricades) for "live"? Why the gestures—both

also set to various parts of the line "And we with thee will choose to live"—of (a) raising and waving both arms to the skies (b) a tragic embrace? What do all these images add up to mean?

One seasoned follower of Mark Morris' work finds that this solo and fugue put him in mind of the Spanish Civil War. To him, the stirring gesture is an image of cooking meals on the ground outdoors, as if by campfire; the heroic gesture (with clenched fist) is a Communist party salute; the wounded arm (with one hand splayed) suggests a Catholic Spanish examination of stigmata; the tragic embrace is not a lovers' clinch but the desperate collapse of one harrowed warrior onto the breast of another stronger one. The meaning of these images accumulates as the four-part fugue builds up: comrades in war, the Communist ideal in adversity, prayer, wounds, despair, defiance. . . . It's worth noting, too, that while the fugue occurs, the female soloist stands at the back. She's like a presiding muse, but she holds one fist aloft throughout, which suggests she is less Penseroso than Communist. The more I watch this last Penseroso dance, the more I like this Spanish Civil War theory. But Morris isn't using Milton and Handel as a platform for some fantasy about the Spanish war between Communists and Fascists. Rather, the specific imagery, in this verbal and musical context, seems, by meditating on Spanish Civil War ideas, to transcend them. And so what mainly impresses us as we watch are the dance's larger qualities of tribulation, heroism, pain, and endurance—so timed and reprocessed here that we seem to be not experiencing them direct but to be meditating upon them, feeling them like the traces of the historic past. Morris is not explaining the music; he's providing one highly ironic and dramatic illustration of it.

THERE ARE TWO main families of motif throughout the work, I believe. One of them is to do with the floor. I've mentioned Laughter, holding both his sides, sitting on the floor and rolling over. This (initially Allegro) motif is a visual counterpart to the (initially Penseroso) image of childbirth. Here, too, the legs are bent and apart; but the rest of the body is in much greater strain. The dancer's back and head lean back in travail; and one straight arm bisects the groin.

The ultimate use of the floor is when dancers extend their full length upon the ground. First of all, you see this as an image of sleep—most emphatically at the end of Part One ("Thus past the day, to bed they creep, / By whisp'ring winds soon lull'd asleep"), when sleep comes to a whole group of dancers. But sometimes it's the big sleep. All of *L'Allegro* suggests, I think, that "Our little life is rounded with a sleep"—especially in that last Penseroso air, "May at last my weary age," for four dancers.

The other family of motif consists in the use of both arms held forwards with equal stress. In the very first danced recitative, we see the hands closed before the face, then opening out, then falling downwards. When this recurs in the opening dance of Part Two, it seems to illustrate the word "Tragedy"—as if the dancer had been holding the book of Tragedy before her face. This is a Penseroso image; its Allegro counterpart has the hands like a crown, illustrating "ivy-crownèd": the back of the wrists are held to the head, the hands point upwards, like the sides of a crown, and the arms then "bounce" this crown shape on and off the head, in time to the music. This, in turn, finds a counterpart in an image in the next Penseroso dance: the image of "sight," in which the dancers bring the backs of their hands over their eyes, shielding them, then (more pointedly) lifting the hands, opening the eyes, and opening the arms to suggest the view.

It is especially il Penseroso who is shown as a see-er, a spectator. (L'Allegro is a doer.) Il Penseroso looks into this or that other world. In "Come, but keep thy wonted state," two Penseroso dancers see each other (and mime "sight" very fully at each other), through a gauze and as if "across a crowded room." (Morris, who sets this episode amid four horizontal lines of dancers passing across the stage, nicknames it "Some Enchanted Evening.") One plain suggestion is that they have fallen in heart-stopping love with each other at first sight; another is that they have found Romantic love just because there is an unbridgeable gap between them.

There is a Penseroso walk, by the way—the "musing gait"—in which one hand is held forward and parallel to the floor, with the dancer looking at it or perhaps past it to the ground. This brings out, exquisitely, the "pensive" quality of il Penseroso: the life of contemplation. But all the Penseroso dances are to do with sight—

or, rather, to do with looking. The Penseroso nightingale looks at the moon. In the astonishing stream of dream imagery in the Penseroso recitative and air "Me, when the sun begins to fling. . . . Hide me from day's garish eye," you see the dreamer and her dream, the visionary and her vision, the artist and her muse.

As Part Two approaches its close, it presents—though little emphasis is paid on this, and though it is easy not to notice—two quite specific images of death onstage. At the end of the final Penseroso fugue ("These pleasures, Melancholy, give"), the female soloist—who has been standing motionless, back to the audience, with that heroic Communist fist brandished throughout—turns, gravely walks downstage, and, like Fate, softly with a small gesture lays one male–male couple suddenly into their final sleep. (It lasts only a moment. But I am invariably reminded at this moment of the Greek army of male lovers whom archaeologists found together centuries later.)

Next, the final Allegro section begins with the tale of Orpheus. Here the imagery of sight and death are extraordinarily linked—more so than Milton's words alone would sanction. By looking at his beloved, dead Eurydice, Orpheus kills his lover a second time over. Milton's words merely refer to Orpheus the heroic musician, who half-regains Eurydice from the Elysian fields with his music; but Morris rattles through the whole tragic myth as if it were a comic, cautionary tale. Orpheus sleeps, dreams, wakes, plays music, enchants his listeners, is no sooner allowed to take his (male) Eurydice than he looks at him, loses him forever, recoils in horror, goes distracted, is chased by the maenads (who, seconds before, had been his musical groupies), and is torn apart by them. Morris quickly "wipes" this image, just as he "wipes" the Penseroso pair of male lovers at the end of the previous number; and the work ends with the great rush of Allegro enlightenment I have mentioned. But the meaning of these deaths is clear. "Seeing" can bring wisdom; or ruin. Meanwhile human life has its terminus, whether at the end of idealistic practical endeavor or amid the intense and emotional pursuit of art. Live now, live intensely, live fully. Life holds much; there is much to live for; this life is all the life you have.

*I*BEGAN FOLLOWING THE Mark Morris Dance Group in 1990, when I arranged a trip to New York specifically to see them perform at the Brooklyn Academy of Music. I had heard a lot about the company from friends, so I expected to like what I saw. But I did not expect to be completely smitten—to spend the rest of my New York visit urging everyone I knew to get out to BAM, telling them that I had finally seen a great artwork, a masterpiece, made in my lifetime.

The piece I saw that first time—the evening-length *L'Allegro, il Penseroso ed il Moderato*—remains, for me, an exemplary high point. Choreographed to a Handel piece which itself was composed as the set-ting for poems by Milton, *L'Allegro* displays many of Mark Morris' virtues and virtuosities. It is at once rooted in history and strikingly contemporary. The line back to the seventeenth-century words and the eighteenth-century music feels strong and unbroken, and yet the dancers are performing steps and com-binations that seem thoroughly modern. Mimetic gestures of book-reading, bird-singing, game-hunt-ing—gestures which evoke the pastoral scenes on medieval tapestries—combine with the vigorous rhythms and patterns of Eastern European circle dances. Archaic courtliness intertwines with humor-ous inventiveness, as a female soloist's graceful ada-gio emerges from a full-group rendering of arm-

An Artist for Our Time

WENDY LESSER

shaking, leg-swinging mirth. Men and women share and exchange roles, with one ensemble dance having the women lift the men, followed by the men lifting the women. (It is part of Morris's acute intelligence as a choreographer—a social as well as aesthetic intelligence—that he thought to have the lifts performed in this order. Had the men lifted the women first, the women's lifts would have seemed a mere joke on traditional techniques. Coming first, they have a tenderness, a maternal protectiveness that is all their own; only secondarily do they become part of the joke about relative sex roles that is indeed being made. The pairing, in this order, evokes a moving revelation rather than a guffaw.)

"SUNSHINE HOLIDAY," from William Blake's "L'Allegro"

Mark Morris himself does not dance in *L'Allegro*, so the first time I ever saw him was when he came out at the end to take his curtain call. Morris's curtain calls are an art form in themselves—I have come to be quite a connoisseur of them, in the years since—but I didn't realize that then. All I knew was that I couldn't take my eyes off this tall, slightly bulky, curly-maned, weirdly beautiful, absolutely commanding figure. (The next day, watching him perform in a mixed program with Mikhail Baryshnikov, I had the same experience, to my even greater surprise: I had never before seen anybody who could draw my eye away from Baryshnikov.) Standing to applaud at the end of *L'Allegro*, surrounded by the rest of the clapping, screaming BAM audience, I felt the charge of the choreographer's presence as if it were a blast of electricity. "He's like a rock star!" I said to my friend Mindy, a dance critic who had brought me to the performance.

Later, as we were climbing into our taxi in front of the auditorium, I saw Morris emerge from the building with a small group of people—heading out for a late dinner, perhaps. When they passed near us, I stuck my head out the taxi window and yelled at him, "You're great! It was great!" He turned toward me and beamed an angelic "Thanks!" Hiding within the taxi, torn between

her embarrassment at my outburst and her pleasure at my enthusiasm, Mindy wryly pointed out to me that the name of the cab company, which was emblazoned on the side of the car facing Morris, was CHEERS.

I knew nothing of Mark Morris' history at the time, but I subsequently learned that this particular production was something of a watershed in his career. Before *L'Allegro* he was widely viewed as the bad boy of modern dance. "Boy" can be taken almost literally here: he was twenty-four when he founded his own company, and all of thirty-two when he choreographed *L'Allegro* in 1998. The choreographer of John Adams's opera *Nixon in China* and the director of dance for the Théâtre Royal de la Monnaie in Brussels, Morris was famous for spitting in the face of bourgeois audiences, for taking previously inoffensive art forms and lending them an earthy, streetwise capacity to offend. This reputation does some violence to the truth, for all of Mark Morris' work is in some way respectful (to its musical sources, at the very least) and none of it has the irritating "Gotcha!" quality that one finds in the work of artists who have one eye cocked on audience reaction. Nor was *L'Allegro* Morris' first

BROOKLYN, 1990 •
[L–R]: Joachim Schlömer and Katharina Bader, Keith Sabado and Tina Fehlandt [BACKGROUND], Jon Mensinger and Olivia Maridjan-Koop, Erin Matthiessen and Rachel Murray [BACKGROUND], Mark Nimkoff and Holly Williams, in "Merry Bells" [Tom Brazil]

satisfyingly beautiful piece—though it remains, I think, his most satisfyingly beautiful piece to date.

I am using the term "satisfyingly beautiful" in a very specific sense, a sense that's been suggested to me by the choreography of Mark Morris. From what I have seen of his dances (and I've seen less than a third of his hundred or so pieces—some, alas, only on videotape), I conclude that Morris is after two very distinct effects. One of these has to do with asking a question, testing out a theory, opening up an area of inquiry; the other has to do with providing a worked-out, completed (if only temporarily final) answer. In the first category I would put such dances as *Ten Suggestions* (which he originally choreographed in 1981, to piano music by Tcherepnin) and *Three Preludes* (made, to Gershwin's music, in 1992). Each of these pieces carries its tentativeness in its title; each, as it happens, is a solo in which Morris has alternated with Baryshnikov. In such works he seems to be trying out certain ideas about dance and about life. What difference does it make to have the same gestures performed by two very different bodies? How can casualness combine with precision? How can props be used? (*Ten Suggestions* features a hula hoop.)

How do hands dance, as well as, or in contrast to, feet? How is stillness a kind of dancing? How can we keep a dance in our mind once the dancer has disappeared? Where do dances come from, and where do they go? You can watch these two pieces over and over again, with Morris or Baryshnikov, on stage or on tape, and still feel that, however much you discover each time, their essence has escaped you. Their only graspable point is that they cannot be grasped. They experiment with and comment on the ephemerality of dance.

And then there are the other Mark Morris dances, the ones that seem to hand you a full goblet and allow you to carry it, ever so carefully, away. These pieces from which you can drink your fill include *Dido and Aeneas*, his evening-long work to Purcell's opera, in which Morris himself plays both Dido and the Sorceress. But the dance needn't be long to be complete; *Gloria*, an early work to Vivaldi, has this quality.

There does seem to be a connection, though, between Morris' use of vocal music and the kind of satisfaction I'm referring to. His questioning, what-if, how-does pieces are all set to purely instrumental music—or, in the case of the 1990 *Behemoth*, to no music at all.

BROOKLYN, 1990 •
[L–R]: Holly Williams and Mark Nimkoff,
Rachel Murray and Erin Matthiessen,
Alyce Bochette and Kraig Patterson, in
"Merry Bells" [Martha Swope/TimePix]

In the vocal pieces, the words are not just there to provide plot (a device which we sometimes confuse with satisfaction or completion), for a Mark Morris dance can include elements of plot and still be both wordless and open-ended—as is *Wonderland*, for instance, the 1989 dance-noir set to Schoenberg. No, the importance of vocal music appears to be that through it, in combination with dance, Morris can engage the whole body. The satisfying beauty of a piece like *L'Allegro* comes from the sense that everything which can possibly be used *has* been used—that the world, at least for a brief moment at the end of the dance, has no inexhausted possibilities.

With his particular form of choreographic genius, Mark Morris has managed to incorporate some of this changeability, this lifelikeness, even into a completely satisfying work like *L'Allegro, il Penseroso ed il Moderato*. Departing from both Milton (who ended with Melancholy) and Handel (who, in typical eighteenth-century mode, ended with Moderation), Morris begins *and* ends the piece with Happiness. That is, he turns Milton's and Handel's linear structure into a circle—just as he does in the final moments of the dance itself, which ends as a large, fast, joyous circle dance culminating in a single moment of upward-reaching stillness. The many dancers have become a single motion, and unity has been imposed on division, but not by arriving at a logical and irrefutable compromise. Morris has simply chosen—arbitrarily, personally, and whimsically—to end on a note of happiness. Nothing in either the world or this work of art leads you to conclude that happiness is a necessary or permanent outcome; and yet the moment feels right, and final, and true.

Part of what makes it feel final and true is that, like any moment in dance, the ending of *L'Allegro* is only temporary and contingent. This is one of the things dance and its ephemerality can teach us; this is one of the things Morris has taught himself through his experiments, his "suggestions" and "preludes." When one gets to the end of the music, one must choose an end to the dance, but that end is not a permanent stoppage, not a closure for all time. It is an end only to that particular piece, and in another work, under other circumstances, the choreographer might just as arbitrarily and personally choose the opposite course.

When you attach yourself to a cherished artist, as I have attached myself to Mark Morris, you cede to that artist a certain portion of your own intellectual development. You are not just the learned critic, commenting on the work; you are also the novice, being molded by that work. In such cases you sometimes have to trust the artist more than you trust yourself. He (or she—but for me such artists are almost always "he") may be working a few steps ahead of you, and you may not be ready to absorb what he has made. Sometimes the new piece itself will teach you things you need to know to respond to it, but that process can take years, and your first impulse may be to resist the new direction because it is not exactly what your beloved artist has done before.

I think it is useful for critics, especially extremely opinionated critics, to have a few touchstone artists of this sort. If I don't like something in a Mark Morris dance, I will ask myself whether I am wrong to feel that way. I will see the dance over and over, if I can, and I will keep asking myself this question. Sometimes I come out on my side; less often I come out on his. But either way, the process of thinking about what he has done and why he has done it alters me as a critic.

An artist with a strong personality, like a critic with a strong personality, is always at risk of seeing things too much his own way. He needs to rely on his own judgments, but he must also temper those judgments by recognizing the needs and capacities of the people around him. If he is a choreographer, he will necessarily shape the dancers who work with him; and if he is a good choreographer, he will also be shaped *by* them. One of the things I appreciated the very first time I saw the Mark Morris company was the individuality of the dancers' styles. Varying as they do in shape, age, sex, weight, height, race, nationality, and background, they could hardly convey a chorus-line rigidity of style. But their variety goes beyond superficial appearance. What Morris' choreography does is to allow his dancers to express their own distinct personalities even as they are dancing his steps.

And yet, there is a kind of unity to their effort. This is not just the unity of their impressive musicality (though here they triumph over any other company of dancers I have ever seen: *no one* misses the beat), but a stronger and deeper sense of coherence. When I saw *L'Allegro* I had not yet seen Mark Morris dance, but I knew what he must be like as a dancer. I saw bits and pieces of Mark Morris in all his dancers' styles, individual and singular though they were—so that the next day, when I saw Morris himself perform, he was utterly recognizable, almost familiar. And something in his choreography was also recognizable to me, as if I had seen it before in dreams, or had been waiting a lifetime, expectantly, to see it.

I am roughly the same age as Mark Morris—to be exact, I am four years older—and, like Morris, I was obsessed by Balkan folk dancing in my teens. (I took longer to outgrow it than Morris did: I was still performing with a Balkan dance group during college. But then he had other kinds of dance to move on to.) When I hear people talk about the influence of Balkan dance on Morris's work, I want to say, "Yes, but . . . " Yes, it was a search for roots and community in the sixties and early seventies. Yes, it was a way of bringing together song and dance, audience and participant, couple and group, tradition and novelty. But it was darker, more divisive, more interesting things as well. It was getting out of the house when you were a teenager, escaping from your own family into some other, less personal simulacrum of a family. It was excitement, late nights, and parties after the parties. It was the lure of sex and the safety of displacement. It was getting to dance without being asked, evading the teenage hell of sock hops and cheerleaders, exerting a more adult kind of attraction on people older than yourself. It was a realm of dance in which skill still mattered, in which you couldn't just get up and wiggle (as any fool could do during sixties happenings and rock concerts) but I had to master the steps, acquire a style, become a *dancer*. It was precision in a world of sloppiness, and "heightened awareness" of a predictable, self-induced, non-drug-related variety. It was a place in which everyone was accepted, but in which discriminations (of grace, skill, knowledge) nonetheless mattered. It was a kind of community that was ideal for someone who was essentially, secretly solitary.

Morris' adulatory critics, Morris' dancers, and even, in some interviews, Morris himself repeatedly emphasize the role of "community" in his artworks and his artistic life. It is true that Mark Morris favors the ensemble dance and even the trio over the duet in his choreography. It is true that some of his dancers have been with him for twenty years, and that many of them go out drinking and partying with him after rehearsals, night after night. There is, indeed, a sense of the group in his life and in his art. But there is also, just as strongly, a sense of the solitary, individual artist leaving his own personal signature on the world. To view Mark Morris as a product of the sixties, complete with commune-like dance group, is utterly to misread what he is doing. At the core of Morris' work is allegiance to something other than the group—something I can only characterize with the inadequate words "artistic truth."

Such a sensibility is both omnivorous and highly discriminating. When he uses Indian ragas or Texas country music as the settings for his dances, Morris is not just being cute or fashionable: he is selecting the piece of music that, of all the music in the world, best suits his needs at the moment. People praise (or, less frequently, condemn) Mark Morris for fluttering between high and low art, for crossing boundaries between Western and Eastern music and dance, for being "multicultural" and "populist." But none of these distinctions has any meaning for Morris. He takes whatever he needs, wherever it comes from. He may be broad-minded, but he is also a snob. He wants only the best: the best dancers, the best music, the best performance of that music, the best literary texts, the best visual inspirations, the best lighting and set design. He deeply believes in the concept of "the good," "the best"—he would not be able to work without it—and this very belief distinguishes him from the vast majority of iconoclastic artists who are wrongly grouped with him.

The gift Mark Morris gives us cannot be a permanent one. No choreographer's can. Without Morris to supervise every rehearsal, train every dancer, adjust every gesture, his dances soon fade away, be travestied, cease to be themselves. The sense of completion they give us is an illusion. The sense of fulfillment, however, is not. Dance disappears, but the feeling it creates is left in the mind of the audience. We are its beneficiaries and its repositories. Years ago, witnessing for the first time this marvelous company and its marvelous work, I was grateful to be alive at the moment in history when Mark Morris was making his dances. And that feeling is with me still.

The process of making L'Allegro, il Penseroso ed il Moderato *as a dance work began more than a year before Morris actually started sketching dances for various sections of Handel's music. Morris first heard a recording of Handel's* L'Allegro, il Penseroso ed il Moderato *in 1985, while living in Seattle, and he knew immediately that he wanted to choreograph it. The following comments are based on our conversations with Mark Morris; five of the dancers on whom it was originally choreographed and who performed at its premiere: Ruth Davidson, Tina Fehlandt, Dan Joyce, Rachel Murray, and June Omura; and Linda Dowdell, the Mark Morris Dance Group's rehearsal pianist in Brussels, and later the company's music director.*

—JEFFREY ESCOFFIER AND MATTHEW LORE

MARK MORRIS: A good friend of mine played me the music. I'd never heard it before, which shocked me because I was already a giant Handel devotee. I listened to it all the time. I thought, "Oh my God, this is so great and beautiful."

I didn't make it up until 1988. But there was sort of a semi-plan to do it with Boston Ballet. That's why I was so ready when I got to Brussels because I had started actually thinking of doing it as a production. I'd started thinking how the stage picture might work. We were thinking—I don't remember who or why—but we were thinking of having the band on the second story of the stage, above the dancers, which happened occasionally in some baroque spectacles.

When asked [by Gerard Mortier, then the director of the Monnaie] if I had a big project in mind I immediately thought of *L'Allegro* because I had been working on it in my head and finally something could happen. I also checked out the Milton in its original form. And because of the prints that were in an edition of the Milton, Blake came into the picture too. There's one hundred years or so between all these people. What was interesting was how all those things could work together.

I worked on it at Brockport [where Morris conducted a workshop on the campus of the State University of New York (SUNY) there] the summer before we moved to Brussels. I was working already with Adrianne Lobel on the sets. We were looking at sketches of a million little panels and I was looking at row after row of possible color combinations in watercolor. We were in this horrible hot, hot, hot summer at Brockport. I worked on what

The Making of L'Allegro

urned into the contra dances in "Merry Bells" and the walking dance of "Come, Come" that I made up there in its entirety and dance figure studies that I used later on in the dance in "Merry Bells" and some other stuff. There's some material that I didn't use then but have used since. So that's what I was working on for a long time. I remember those two movements very specifically because I worked on them a lot.

TINA FEHLANDT: Mark started before we went to Brussels during the summer of 1988. We were teaching a workshop at SUNY Brockport. There was a heat wave. We were staying in these apartment dorms on campus, and we were freaking out because we were moving to Belgium. Mark started working and he did "Come, Come." That was one of the first things he made up, in the gym. And he made up "Come and Trip It" there and parts of the "Diet Dances." And I remember being in the gym, doing "Come, Come" and trying to learn the tune, because that's a walking dance, and just going insane. I felt like already then he had a clear picture of what he wanted it to look like.

I think the first pieces he did were reference pieces. "Come and Trip It" is choreographed absolutely to the lyric. "Haste Thee Nymph" he did early in Brockport. I think of those two pieces as being quintessential *L'Allegro* pieces. To me, you find whatever you're going to see in the rest of the dance in them. That's where Mark makes his statement: "This is how I work." Here are women and men, men and women. There are mirror images, there are patterns, the use of folk dance, the gestural

"MILTON AND THE SPIRIT OF PLATO," from William Blake's "Il Penseroso"

[The Pierpont Morgan Library/Art Resource, New York]

stuff. In those two sections he lays his cards on the table, he says, "This is what my dance is going to be." He culled from those sections a lot going forward. I think that's why he made them up first.

LINDA DOWDELL: Mark started working on *L'Allegro* at Brockport the summer before we went to Brussels and I was there for that. That's when the singing and dancing really started. The section he worked on there was "Merry Bells," the part where they sing "Dancing in the checquer'd shade." It was all these little square dances. Also he worked on parts of "Come, Come," "Haste Thee Nymph," "Come and Trip It." Mark was already very familiar with this music. I think his ability to read music has influenced him a lot. Plenty of us—music readers or not—listen to music, but we don't necessarily know what meter it is. Mark likes to choreograph to music he's very familiar with. It's interesting how reading a score and also knowing the text so well are such motivators for him.

With *L'Allegro* we really did a lot with just piano and us singing. The rehearsal process was truly in the ballet tradition. There you usually have a pianist playing piano reductions of the works that will be played live during performance and that keeps the live thing going and that's definitely Mark's model for it, too. We certainly did a lot of singing in rehearsal. Mark would refer to my Blossom Dearie vocal style, which in my case meant more breath than tone and not much range—unlike him, whose singing style ranged from George Jones to Dietrich Fischer-Dieskau.

■

In L'Allegro, Morris' choreography draws on an eclectic range of dance vocabularies, including ballet, modern, and a wide variety of folk dances. It displays a broad emotional palette that allows for irreverent humor, slapstick, spirituality, and intellectual seriousness; and, as many have remarked (both friends and foes), it demonstrates a rich gestural imagination unafraid of being literal. Nevertheless, L'Allegro's choreography reflects both an architectural impulse and the creation of a coherent dance language.

■

MARK MORRIS: In Charles Rosen's genius book, *The Classical Style,* he talks about Haydn establishing the language for a piece and then having to finish it by finding the way back to the home key or by dropping in the keystone that will resolve the whole piece in its language. I thought about that a lot because that's the way I work.

That to me is really a keystone itself in the idea of classical style.

Originally, I wanted the palette to change through the course of the evening. The idea was that one person at a time would change costumes from the dark version to the pale version so that you wouldn't notice until by the very end of the change everyone would have changed. It would have happened gradually. It's a fabulous idea that didn't work. So, we made it act by act: Melancholy costumes in the "Act the First," and Mirth costumes in the second.

In this case, I thought because of the way I was using men and women in this piece, and because of the English tradition, I wanted little green wooden batons for the men to use and pink silk handkerchiefs for the women—both are props in Morris dancing, and also they then can be flowers or structures or whatever. I thought it was a great idea. But I never even tried it. I always get rid of those things. That led me to why there are no set pieces, and why in some of the movements I use the dancers like Baroque scenery. I could have, of course, with my budget, had actual shrubbery—but that's not as interesting for me as a choreographer.

I don't have it in my head when I make up a dance, but from pretty early on, I knew that I wanted everything to double or reflect or to be in some way symmetrically two. That includes something that seems like a long solo—like "Mountains." The duet of that shows up only at the very end, when another dancer goes across. In my head that implies that it's going on in parallel, somewhere out of range. Sometimes, I go exactly word by word with what's going on, sometimes just the sense of it, sometimes just what's happening musically and not so much the text. But, actually I would say all of it reflects, in my opinion, very directly what's happening textually.

I decided, for example, that the Moderato sections would be for every single person, for twenty-four people. We wanted the stage in those sections to be pretty open and white. Just sort of nothing instead of everything. Those two movements are the most open and have a different kind of symmetry. For two recitatives, "Pensive Nun," and the one before the "Diet Dances," I knew I wanted two sets of dancers very alone in a corridor because they're both small and they match each other and they're fabulous. So I knew those matched. I decided early that the aria for "Haste Thee Nymph" would be men and the chorus would be women and then the opposite in [the next section] "Come and Trip It." I also knew that eventually I was going to have a men's dance and a women's dance. I had contiguous pieces from different parts of it and then once those were kind of resolved and that decided the personnel, I would do some connective recit stuff and transitional things. That's important to me because of the way that Handel dealt with the text mostly.

L'Allegro was mostly just bigger than other pieces that I'd done. But my approach wasn't that different. I'd already decided a lot about it, not steps necessarily. But whenever I make up something, then I have that material that I can either use or not, somewhere else within the piece. So certain moves have multiple purposes like, for example, that rolling on the floor thing which is from "Laughter, holding both his sides." I thought that would be kind of fabulous looking. So we do that and later it comes back in "Weary Age" in a totally sad and lonely context. Or like the move that in "Weary Age" is like a star-gazing thing is also in "Gorgeous Tragedy" with less of a direct literal word-meaning. Sometimes I'll take something that I've made up, something that is similar enough to something else that I either make it a little different, or I make it the exact same thing so it gives an illusion of thematic continuity as well as being the thematic continuity. It's both. It's real and fake continuity.

RACHEL MURRAY: One of the things I remember most about the making of *L'Allegro*, given the largeness of the piece, was that Mark knew exactly what he was doing. It was as though he had the whole thing already planned out before we started. Not that he didn't get blocked a couple of times, but it rolled out of him. So, it was quite organized as a working process, especially considering the huge number of people he was working with, and under a huge amount of stress, being far away from home and displaced.

It was really such a remarkable thing to me that he was so in control of his material from the get-go and that he knew exactly what he wanted and was making. It was my introduction, as a dancer, to the working process with Mark. He'd basically teach a theme phrase and then he'd immediately start manipulating it—

manipulating it and knowing quite quickly what he was doing, so it was constantly unfolding before our eyes. That's where the rhythm thing was always very clear, right away. Sometimes he would be making it up right on the spot. He doesn't plan the movement. That's the extraordinary thing. The whole thing is in his head but he hasn't been at home making up the steps. You're coming in the morning and he's just taught a class. So it's not like he was even sitting there. I would have been sitting there going through it making sure I had everything. No! He's been up doing something up all night, then doing something totally different. He comes in looking at the score and then he decides, okay. You know, he might have thought, "Okay, I have this jump," this one idea for a jump, or this one little step. He'd have a few key bookmarks on that section. But then he'd be like hmmm. Yump dump dump, he gives you some movement. So you're just feeling that you're just going in and imitating. But it's all very specific right away. When it happens. When exactly *that* [gesture] happens. And then the music plays and then you see, Oh, well it was really hard, and at first it was confusing, but with the music it's getting easier. And then, okay, suddenly Linda's playing and she starts singing, and then she and Mark are singing and you're like "Haste thee, nymph, ha!" And this is all maybe fifteen or twenty minutes, half an hour into it. It would be revealed very quickly. It was *very* satisfying. And the great thing was, it wasn't handed to you too quickly, either. It was revealed in a very exciting way. It would be one layer after another. Then it would be: "Oh you now solo with the men and then the women." And suddenly that would kind of happen at the end. There it was. I don't know exactly how long it took to make up "Haste Thee Nymph" but I'd wager a bet that it didn't take more than a few hours. Ultimately to sketch it out. Three hours, maybe?

I do know that we all had to be there all the time, in the room. I remember that was a big deal because some of the older company members were over that a little bit. "Can't you just know what you're going to do, because if I'm not going to be in this section, I'll go down to the other end of the hall and stretch my calves." I, of course, couldn't dream of being anywhere else but the room. It wouldn't have *occurred* to me to leave the room. He'd say, "Okay, you four over there come here," and he'd make something up and then the next thing you knew you were sitting there for two hours trying to look alert and stay alive while he was working on a smaller section. Then in the middle of it, he'd tell everybody, "OK, everybody needs to know everything" and you'd jump up and start doing things. Now, of course, I understand exactly how the older dancers felt. So, we were all in the room all the time, and we were called to duty either as a group or in couples as was necessary, which was often true because he was developing material all the time, obviously with the repeating themes.

RUTH DAVIDSON: *L'Allegro* was the first piece Mark created in Brussels. A lot of people weren't sure where it was going. He was working with imagery, making scenes with dancers, and that wasn't something we did. I remember that some of the original company members felt a bit insecure: "Oh God, this is what we moved to Brussels for?" It was a little tense. People felt uncomfortable about it or sort of slighted. "I've studied all these years to do this!" It's like: "Hey Mom, I'm a tree!" To me, it's fun. It's theater. The truth is, everyone is an important part of the scene. In Part One, I'm either running in a flock of birds, crawling on my hands and knees as a shrubbery or a sheep, rolling on the floor being water, or lifting someone. It's physically taxing. I need to pace myself in Part One for all the dancing I do in Part Two, where I'm highlighted more.

When Mark started to show me the steps in "Gorgeous Tragedy," I realized that it was harder than it looked, as is all of Mark's work. It takes a lot dramatically and technically to sustain that dance. The parts of this section where I'm alone everything is on one leg or turning. In the beginning it was really difficult. So I started reading the libretto and talking with him about it—what it was about. The piece was about the theater. As an aid for myself, I thought to conjure some great theatrical female character—like Lady Macbeth, or person, like Dame Judi Dench. But technically, I have to practice the steps all the time. I feel like I have to put myself wholeheartedly into dancing *L'Allegro*. Hanya Holm, whom I worked with, used to say, you have to find a thread throughout the whole dance. You have to be in it, and you have to go with it. You

can't break that thread, it's a concentration thing. The amazing thing about being in Mark's work is that he sets the pattern. It's not like I have to do it. I really just go in and ride it.

■

Gesture, dance and language are inseparable in L'Allegro*. Handel's music provides the dynamic context for their performance. While complex patterns of footwork are essential to maintaining the dance's rhythmic momentum, the gestures tie the language of the libretto into the dance action.* L'Allegro's *gestural language is permeated by a vast and subtle network of metaphorical transformations: Two clasped hands in a gesture of supplication are transformed into the wings of crickets rubbing together to make the sounds of chirping. Later in the dance, that gesture is transposed back again into two hands in melancholy prayer. The dancers' gestural doubling of the libretto, in effect, makes the dancers into singers—their bodies literally dancing the words.*

■

MARK MORRIS: William Blake did a series of drawings. From a portrait of Melancholy and her companions, I directly stole several moves, for example, and Blake's image of the moon, which also happens several times in the dance. It happens in "Me, when the sun begins to fling / his flaring beams . . . " [the introduction to "Day's Garish Eye" in Part Two]. Then, there are other things, just positions like sitting curled up on the floor from a detail in one of the Blakes, of a little old guy [used in "Haste Thee Nymph"]. There's also a part in "Day's Garish Eye" where one person's asleep and the other one is being frightened by this nightmare figure: There's a wing picture, it's almost like a peacock tail where there are different figures hidden in this wing and it's sort of like a horrible opium dream.

I also had a little bit of experience with American Sign Language (ASL) so I decided the gesture for "come" [in "Come and Trip It"] which is very close to what you do in ASL—if it's emphatic, it's two hands. So I decided that was going to be the sign for "come" because it is anyway, so you don't even have to make it up. And I thought because of the way that happens every time, because "come" is said every five seconds.

NEW YORK CITY, 1987 • Mark Morris [Chantal Regnault]

TINA FEHLANDT: Mark had used ASL before, in *Strict Songs* (1987) with music by Lou Harrison—in that he illustrates the text not just with a hand language, but theatrically. Mark has done what I call word painting from the beginning. In the text of *L'Allegro*, there is a lot to illustrate even though there isn't really a story. The moods are the story.

RUTH DAVIDSON: Gesture is very important to Mark. He works so much with hand gestures—hands and finger things. He also uses sign language symbols. Gesture is his language. He often says, "God is in the details."

DAN JOYCE: If you can sing something, it's more true than if you're counting. Mark often said, "Pretend like you're singing it." You're expressing with your body what the singer is singing.

JUNE OMURA: There are gestures for all five senses. The "Diet Dances" have an eating gesture, appropriately, since Milton is talking about eating ("with gods doth diet"). This wonderful gesture where you wipe something into your mouth and your mouth is supposed to stay open—it comes back later, in the "Ladies' Dance" ("And ever against eating cares"). I started thinking about the senses because of all the sight gestures. In "Sage and Holy" and "Hymen" and in "Day's Garish Eye" there's sort of a blindness or a sight gesture. When Mark was choreographing this . . . I happened to know this because my sister studied early Flemish painting, and she had taught me about all the saints who were in all these paintings. St. Lucy is the saint you always see pictured with a plate that looks like she has two fried eggs on it. But they're actually her eyeballs. She was martyred by having her eyes plucked out. So Mark did this gesture, and he said: 'It's like you're holding your eyeballs on two stalks. Who's that saint? Who's that saint?' and I said, "St. Lucy." But there's another sight gesture too, which either means seeing or blindness, depending on where it happens. In "Mountains" Mireille does it on the words, "It sees," but she covers her eyes, so it's ironic there, and in "Sage and Holy," it's a shielding from something too bright. There's this kind of faraway sight that happens most notably in

"Gorgeous Tragedy," but also in "Weary Age," where your hand is scanning the horizon.

I was thinking about the senses because of that, and I had the taste one, and touch was obvious because it's throughout *L'Allegro*. Hearing, there's a lot of this holding your hand to your ear like for the "far-off Curfew sound" in "Fireplace." But then I thought, there's no smell gesture. And then just that week in rehearsal Mark reminded us that this gesture [fanning the dress behind our backs] in the knights and ladies section of "Populous Cities" is not just being sexy and flirtatious with your skirt. Actually you're fanning pheromones out to your suitor. And I thought that's *it*. There *is* a smell gesture. Mark didn't necessarily put that in so he could complete the five senses, but it just comes naturally to him, to have that gusto for life that would naturally include all the senses.

■

Unlike most other modern dance choreographers, Morris draws on folk dance in his choreography. L'Allegro includes many steps suggested by Eastern European folk dance. Growing up in Seattle, Morris studied flamenco, ballet, and folk dancing, and as a teenager, he spent three years dancing with the Koleda Folk Ensemble, a group that specialized in performing Balkan folk dances. The most common form of Balkan folk dances are group dances, in which the dancers are linked in a circle or a line. Many of the open circles, which usually have one dancer as a leader and another as an "end man," transform themselves into straight or serpentine lines. In addition, many Balkan dance rhythms are irregular. The limping walk that the dancers perform in "Walking Duet" in Part Two is characteristic of certain folk dances in Thrace, a region that overlaps contemporary Greece and Bulgaria.

■

MARK MORRIS: Personally, I have gotten a whole lot of information from different ethnic dance forms that has changed my work. I think that they are much, much more interesting in general than concert dancing. When I'm choreographing something, very often the first thing I'll know about it beside the music is the basic geometry of it. I do line dances and circle dances because I love them. They're also pretty early in dance history. When you're allowed to watch a dance of another culture you watch something happen between people as a community. In classical ballet, the dance positions are designed to be seen from the front only. I don't do that. I use a circle that's closed and we're allowed to watch it just like you'd be allowed to watch a dance from another culture. I want people to look like people when they're dancing.

Because of the text, the section called "Merry Bells" reminded me of a Morris dance or a reel. The rhythms in "Haste Thee Nymph" reminded me of a pretty direct quotation of a fabulous Croatian dance which is just jumping up and down. The dance is jumping up and down, holding hands. That's how the dance goes. And that's spliced in with this heel-clicking dance which is from the Vlach country of Yugoslavia and Romania. Not exactly, but that seemed to belong there because of "Haste Thee Nymph." And then "Come and Trip It" is completely made up. For the "Walking Duet," I decided that because it's a Moderato section. The rhythm that Handel made up there sounded like something I knew only at quarter speed, and so I thought: "How better than to have this kind of Thracian harvest dance going on during that?" The folk dance stuff is there for the same reason that the early modern dance stuff is there or the ballet stuff or anything else. It's just part of my thinking and my background. And I think it's a lot more interesting than what people think of as abstract dance.

■

Morris eliminated most of Handel and Jennens' il Moderato (Part Three of their version), though he kept two of its most musically interesting sections—"Each Action" in Part One and the "Walking Duet" in Part Two. Morris' change would have made his dance end on the piece's final Penseroso section known as "Melancholy Octet"—a fugue of profound gravitas. Morris wanted the ending of the piece to resolve the dramatic and musical tension of the entire work. He moved what were Handel's last two Allegro sections—"Orpheus" and "These delights if thou canst give" (the "Finale") to the end.

■

MARK MORRIS: The finale? What is there left to do? That's why the stage is fully open for the only time. Everything is gone. It's never

been open before. There's always been a little shred of something masking. "These delights if thou canst give / Mirth, with thee I mean to live"—every single repetition of those lines passes down in a different rhythm. Musically, the rhythm of "These delights . . ." is *never* the same. It's interrupted. That piece is very hard. One of the great things about Baroque and classical music is that the resolution, the final cadence of something is very often the downbeat of the next thing. So, it's actually fifteen bars long or seventeen bars long and the Western ear hears it as perfectly square but it never is. That's one of the thrills of Baroque music to me. So, in this case, if the dancer changes parts in this she or he may have to learn a whole different track because there's different numbers and syncopations within it that's exactly with the text.

The vocal line [in the Finale] is pairs of people, and there's one solo trumpet line which is a single person, and then it becomes quartets, and then if there's a trumpet line it's a duet. So when it's not sung, it's smaller, when it's sung it's bigger. Then this happens, the chorus is from the sides—same thing. This canon that happens from the sides—there's no canon in the music, of course. That chorus ends with a leap. It's a little one and then a bigger one and then it crosses. It starts like that and it just keeps waving bigger until it goes . . . until everybody is on the other side. It's an attempt to get across and then it happens, so hooray for everyone!

Then the waves happen one way, then the S-es, and then there's nothing left to do, except a circle. There's nothing left in the geometry of the piece. And of course the steps have all been done before. The running, the circle which is the finale of act one, is the outside circle. The inside circle is the men skipping which happens in the "Stupid Men's Dance." That's all men. And then, the core of it is the three women, the three graces, doing the spin that comes from the "Diet Dances." You can't see it unless you're upstairs. The women that are doing that exact spin, the men are doing this skipping thing, and then there's the running on the outside. So that's a summation in a certain sense of all the material that the sexes have done before. So it's women in the middle, then a ring of men, and then men and women alternating. I don't know half of this until I start talking about this.

The Set Design and Lighting

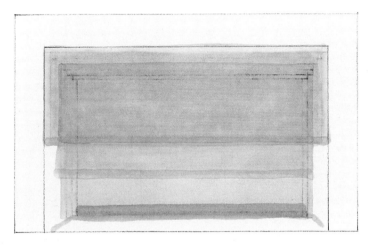

"Hence, loathèd Melancholy,
Of Cerberus, and blackest midnight born"

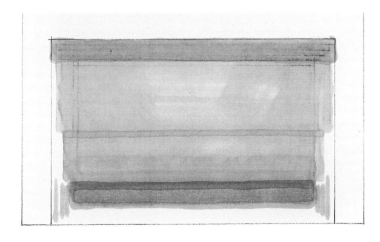

"Hence, vain deluding Joys,
Dwell in some idle brain"

*I*N THE SPRING *of 1988 Morris invited Adrianne Lobel to design the sets for* L'Allegro. *They had previously worked on Peter Sellars' production of John* Adams' opera, Nixon in China, *for which Morris had choreographed the dances. Lobel had worked with Sellars on a number of earlier productions, including his production of Igor Stravinsky's opera,* The Rake's Progress. *She also has extensive experience on Broadway working with George C. Wolfe on the Leonard Bernstein–Jerome Robbins' musical,* On the Town, *on Stephen Sondheim's musical* Passion, *as well as Francesca Zambello's productions of* Lady in the Dark *(at the Royal National Theatre in London) and* Street Scene *(Houston Grand Opera). After* L'Allegro, *Lobel designed the sets for Morris'* The Hard Nut, *his radical* *rreworking of* The Nutcracker, *and most recently Morris' own production of Rameau's opera,* Platée.

The set that Lobel designed for L'Allegro *makes a significant contribution to the piece's success. It creates an enormously varied and complex series of spaces within which the dancing takes place. Edwin Denby, the great dance writer, stressed that a set design "has to stand up under steady scrutiny almost as an easel painting does. At first sight it tells a story, it has local color or period interest or shock value. But then it starts to change the way a picture in a museum does as you look at it attentively for five or ten minutes. The shapes and colors, lines and textures in the set and costumes will act as they would in a picture, they will seem to push and pull, rise and fall, advance and retreat with or against*

"Hail, divinest Melancholy,
Whose saintly visage is too bright
to hit the sense of human sight"

"Haste thee, nymph, and bring with thee
Jest and youthful Jollity"

"Come, and trip it as you go,
On the light fantastic toe"

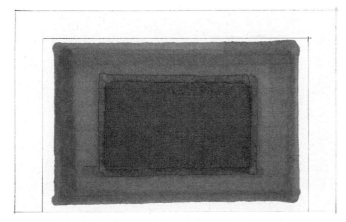

"Sometimes let gorgeous Tragedy"

"Populous cities please me then,
And the busy hum of men."

their represented weight. . . . A good ballet decor, like a good painting, does different and opposite things decisively; like a painting, it presents a bold equilibrium of pictorial forces. And when the bold equilibrium in the decor corresponds in vitality to that of the dancing and that of the score, then the ballet as a production is alive and satisfactory."

Very early on, Morris had told Lobel that he wanted "the stage to be broken into different sizes and areas." "I didn't know anything about color or opacity or framing. I only knew that I wanted small areas to do stuff," Morris recalled. In response, Lobel created an unusual stage space by an elaborate series of scrims. Thus L'Allegro's set is not a series of painted backdrops, as in many traditional ballets, but rather is a thorough modeling of three-dimensional space that performs several important functions: It frames the dancing by establishing a left-right continuum across the front of the stage and also by implicitly imposing a grid on the floor; it is also a little like a compass because it orients both the dancer and the spectator to the other, and it creates a three-dimensional space that suggests both depth and plasticity. Below is an excerpt from an essay by Lobel on designing the set for L'Allegro.

Adrianne Lobel on the Set Design

I N LISTENING TO the music, I heard that for every verse of
poetry there were distinct changes in tone. Handel had already
accomplished his musical "illustration" of the verses. My job, it
seemed, was to illustrate with scenery.

I started to sketch. At first I made some really literal pictorial
choices. If sheep and clouds were mentioned, I drew sheep and
clouds. But soon I realized that this was not my job at all. We heard
the words—we didn't need to repeat the images that were written. I
needed to create a fluidly shifting and expressive environment in
which the dancers could move from thought to thought. I got rid of
all specifics and began to work with abstract planes of color. In
arranging and rearranging these color planes, I could create both literal landscapes—of green fields and blue sky—of sunset and dawn,
of monasteries and cities—that were also non-literal landscapes—
of joy, of sorrow, of peace, of excitement. I looked at Mark
Rothko and Josef Albers and studied the emotional impact of
color: of color against a color and the changing of composition of
more of one color and less of another.

I explained my moving Rothko color-tone-poem idea to Mark.
He seemed intrigued but said he needed to see it. I sent him a
story-board of each verse. He didn't object to what I was doing and
I felt pretty strongly that I had found the approach, so I continued
on to the model phase.

It became clear that the color planes would be drops bordered
by white portals that receded upstage in perspective like the borders
in an Albers print. In this way you could see the edges of the pure
color of one drop against the portal behind it as well as the different color that would be created by the drop against another drop,
both behind or in front of it. In the model I figured out the spac-
ing of the portals and the amount I wanted them to perspect.
Mostly, I spent hours in my kitchen over steaming pots of boiling
dye, dying organza different colors. (Organza is a semi-sheer and
semi-stiff material that is commonly used for emulating theatrical
scrim in models.)

There is a technical problem with scrim that I needed to consider also. If you put one scrim drop too close to another it causes
an unpleasant op art–like moiré pattern that moves and wiggles and

*The following is the letter that Lobel wrote to
Morris after she had started working on the set design.*

■

May 2, 1988

Dear Mark,

Here are some sketches.

*The [music] is completely beautiful and I love working on it—the
problems I am struggling with are as follows:*

*Though the moods are abstract the verse is really very literal—how
much does one illustrate? How much scene shifting is allowed? There is
plenty of music for set changes but will they be too distracting?*

*Some of the scene shifts could be done with one color seeping into anoth-
er or getting lighter or darker while others could be actual moving scenery.*

*I looked at Rothko—whose paintings are mood landscapes but to me
also literal landscapes of earth, sun and water. I've tried to do the same.
There is dawn, rows of trees, green fields next to rivers—a moon that
becomes a window—all in simple color planes that can be be re-positioned
in hopefully an unlimited number of ways. Sometimes we can be completely
literal—sometimes expressionistic.*

*What is hard to tell from the sketches is the materials that things might
be—I'm not sure yet but I'm thinking of a combination of scrim, painted
plastic and dyed translucent muslin.*

*Until I start the model the spaces will not be clear. Some scenes will be
deep, some shallow—I need you to tell me any thoughts on which should be
which.*

*These sketches are just a beginning but I'd like to know your initial
impression. Do you like it or does it look too much like wrapping paper? Is
it too serious? (I have inflatable cows waiting in the wings.)*

*My plan is to have more finished sketches to present in Brussels—there
isn't time now to do a presentable model before I go to Amsterdam though I
am going to start a rough model right away.*

*I know you must be nuts in Seattle but if you have a chance—let me
know if you hate these or not so that I can continue.*

*Love,
Adrianne*

"There let Hymen oft appear"

"Haste thee, nymph"

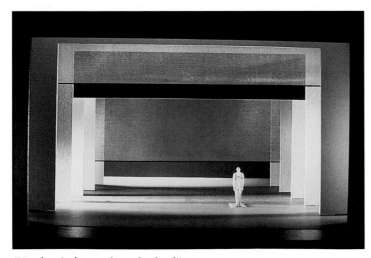

"Orpheus' self may heave his head"

that is distracting. This could be used for effect somewhere, but for my purposes, where I wanted clean flat planes of color, it would not do. In alternating the scrim drops with dyed muslin drops, I believed that I could control this problem.

Dyed muslin is not transparent like scrim but it is translucent. It can be lit to glow like stained glass. When scrim is lit on the front, it will go opaque, when it is lit from behind it will go transparent and disappear, and by balancing the light there are many levels of translucency in between. The combination of these two materials allowed for endless painterly possibilities.

I made dozens of colored scrim drops out of organza and translucent drops made of different colors of Pantone paper. In this way, I could see how one color would affect another and work out how many drops and of what color I needed to create the landscapes I wanted. I could also work out their positioning and start to play with the order of their movement loosely following the storyboard. I remember one wonderful meeting at Jacob's Pillow, where the dance group always does a summer residency. Mark had started making dances for *L'Allegro* so there was something to see! I brought up the model and Mark and Jim Ingalls and I went through the show with shifting drops. We were very clear of the look of some of the verses and vague on some of the others. Most important was to know when the drops came down to the deck because they would divide the stage up into corridors and limit the space.

I delivered the designs to the Théâtre de la Monnaie and went away. The drops and scrims were industrially dyed in Germany to match my color swatches exactly. The white portals were built and painted at the [Monnaie] opera's shop. Aside from the geometric modernity of the set, it could have been a nineteenth-century ballet setting with its portals and drops. That was easy, the hard part was coming.

The hard part was tech. Some of the theater's fly lines were manual, which means someone had to fly in a drop on cue. About two-thirds of the fly lines were computerized, which meant that one person could push a button and on cue three drops could move at three different speeds and fly to three different trims. This system made the creation of *L'Allegro* possible. The set resembled a giant musical instrument—like an organ that was capable of accomplishing great complicated chords.

The first run-through was a mess. I was sure I would be asked to cut half of the scenery. Fortunately, Gerard Mortier, the very supportive director of the theater, could see the potential and asked what I needed. I said, "Time." For the next three days Mark kindly took the dancers off to a rehearsal room leaving me, the lighting designer Jim Ingalls, the stage manager, and their rehearsal pianist, Linda Dowdell, to continue to tech the show. With the enthusiastic crew, we ran the shifts over and over again, adjusting light cues, changing trims, changing timings, and generally playing the set until

the shifts started to flow with inevitability. If the drops moved at what seemed like a musically appropriate speed, and landed on a perfect note, they were invisible. They merged seamlessly with the music. We would work all day and the dancers would come onstage in the evening. We would run through the dance and I would take new adjustment notes for the next day's call. They were three of the most intense and thrilling days of my life.

James F. Ingalls on the Lighting Design

Shortly after Morris had asked Adrianne Lobel to design the sets, he invited James F. Ingalls to design the lighting for L'Allegro. *Ingalls has designed many works for the Mark Morris Dance Group, including* Dido and Aeneas, The Hard Nut, Love Song Waltzes, New Love Song Waltzes, *and* Wonderland. *Recently, Ingalls designed the lighting for Morris' production of Rameau's opera,* Platée.

L'Allegro IS UNIQUE in its use of stage space. The usual dance space is a big open box and that makes the lighting approach for a traditional dance piece a lot easier. Adrianne's white perspective portals chop the space down sideways and the drops and scrims cut the space above. Backlighting—a useful angle because it reveals the dancer's form and "separates" him or her from the background—was difficult because there was too much in the way. I decided to use sidelight extensively and emphasize the various planes of the space, layers really, which opened up and closed down for the different sections. But the design isn't only about how each dance section

looks. The sequence of light cues had to make sense with the movement of the dance, the music and the changing space. The lighting and the set, in essence, are dancers, too.

Lighting design, especially in dance, often needs to be made very quickly—the stage time is so short. It's like action painting. You have to work in the moment and respond quickly to what you see using whatever elements you've assembled. I didn't write the light cues ahead of time—I waited to see the dancers on stage. In the studio we planned the set and lighting for the "Walking Duet" to be one single volume of white. But in the theater I made a subtle pull down of the lighting in the "B" section to emphasize a central hot spot—the center is the focus in that section. The light pulls down and then rebuilds all within the same look, a modulation within the main idea, or theme, of that section.

Stage design (the set, lighting, and costumes) is not an appliqué, like makeup. It is integral to the piece at hand, like the strands that make up a woven fabric. Mark uses the text as closely as he uses the music, and so we have to, too. The references in the text to light and darkness were helpful "clues" for Adrianne and me. The opening line is "Hence, loathèd melancholy, / Of Cerberus and blackest midnight born." *L'Allegro* starts from dawn or an even murkier beginning—creation, from nothing. So we started in the dark. The whole thing fell together from there. Rehearsals were incredible—to be in rehearsal with Mark and the company is a joyous experience.

The Dancers of L'Allegro, il Penseroso ed il Moderato, *1988–2000*

The following is a list of all of the dancers who have appeared in performances of *L'Allegro* and the years in which they performed. Dancers are members of the Mark Morris Dance Group, unless their names are followed by a dagger (†), which denotes supplementary dancers. An asterisk (*) denotes members of the premiere cast.

Christina Amendolia, † 2000

Katharina Bader, † 1989, 1990, 1991, 1994, 1995, 1996, 1997

Alyce Bochette, * 1988, 1989, 1990, 1991, 1994

Joe Bowie, 1989, 1990, 1991, 1994, 1995, 1996, 1997, 1998, 1999, 2000

Charlton Boyd, 1989, 1994, 1995, 1996, 1997, 1998, 1999, 2000

Raphael Brand, †* 1988

Derrick Brown, † 1994, 1995, 1996, 1997, 1998, 1999, 2000

Juliet Burrows, † 1994, 1995, 1996, 1997, 1998, 1999

Ruth Davidson, * 1988, 1989, 1990, 1991, 1994, 1995, 1996, 1997, 1998, 1999, 2000

Seth Davis, 1999, 2000

Tina Fehlandt, * 1988, 1989, 1990, 1991, 1994, 1995, 1996, 1997, 1998, 1999

Marjorie Folkman, 1997, 1998, 1999, 2000

Michael Gallo, †* 1988

Shawn Gannon, 1994, 1995, 1996, 1997, 1998, 1999, 2000

Joseph Gillam, † 2000

Ruben Graciani, † 1994, 1995, 1996, 1997, 1998, 1999

Lauren Grant, 1998, 1999, 2000

Susan Hadley, * 1988

John Heginbotham, 1994, 1995, 1996, 1997, 1998, 1999, 2000

Penny Hutchinson, * 1988, 1989, 1990, 1991

Dan Joyce, * 1988, 1989, 1990, 1991, 1994, 1995, 1996, 1997, 1998

Peter Kyle, † 1999, 2000

David Landis, * 1988

Hans-Georg Lenhart, 1989, 1990, 1991

David Leventhal, 1997, 1998, 1999, 2000

Paul Lorenger, †* 1988

Victoria Lundell, 1994, 1995, 1996, 1997

Olivia Maridjan-Koop, * 1988, 1989, 1990, 1991

Clarice Marshall, * 1988, 1989, 1990, 1991, 1994

Silvia Martins, † 1989

Erin Matthiessen, * 1988, 1989, 1990, 1991

Bradon McDonald, 2000

Jon Mensinger, * 1988, 1989, 1990, 1991

Marianne Moore, 1994, 1995, 1996, 1997

Donald Mouton, * 1988, 1994, 1995, 1996, 1997, 1998

Rachel Murray, * 1988, 1989, 1990, 1991, 1994, 1995, 1996, 1997, 1998, 1999, 2000

Mark Nimkoff, † 1989, 1990, 1991, 1994

Gregory Nuber, 1999, 2000

Maile Okamura, † 1998, 1999, 2000

Deniz Oktay, † 1994, 1995, 1996

June Omura, * 1988, 1989, 1990, 1991, 1994, 1995, 1996, 1997, 1998, 1999, 2000

Kraig Patterson, * 1988, 1989, 1990, 1991, 1994, 1995, 1996, 1997, 1998, 1999

Jonathan Pessolano, † 2000

Joseph Poulson, † 2000

Mireille Radwan-Dana, * 1988, 1989, 1990, 1991, 1994, 1995, 1996, 1997, 1998, 1999, 2000

Gene Reddick, † 1990, 1991

Karen Reedy, † 2000

Mara Reiner, † 2000

Kim Reis, 1999, 2000

Guillermo Resto, 1989, 1990, 1991, 1994, 1995, 1996, 1997, 1998

Matthew Rose, 1997, 1998, 1999, 2000

Keith Sabado, * 1988, 1989, 1990, 1991

Joachim Schlömer, * 1988, 1989, 1990, 1991

Vernon Scott, † 1994, 1995, 1996

Anne Sellery, † 1998, 1999, 2000

Torbjörn Stenberg, † 1989

Jordana Toback, † 1991, 1994, 1995, 1996, 1997, 1998

William Wagner, * 1988, 1990, 1991, 1994, 1995, 1996, 1997, 1998, 1999

Jean-Guillaume Weis, 1989, 1990, 1991

Teri Weksler, * 1988

Megan Williams, * 1988, 1989, 1990, 1991, 1994, 1995, 1996

Holly Williams, 1989, 1990, 1991

Julie Worden, 1994, 1995, 1996, 1997, 1998, 1999, 2000

Michelle Yard, 1997, 1998, 1999, 2000

In Memoriam

Michael Gallo

Jon Mensinger

Performances of L'Allegro, il Penseroso ed il Moderato, *1988–2001*

BRUSSELS, BELGIUM • Théâtre Royal de la Monnaie • November 22–December 20, 1988
  World Premiere: November 23, 1988

BRUSSELS, BELGIUM • Théâtre Royal de la Monnaie • November 26–December 7, 1989

BROOKLYN, NEW YORK • Brooklyn Academy of Music Opera House • October 6–13, 1990
  United States Premiere: October 6, 1990

PARIS, FRANCE • Théâtre des Champs-Élysées • May 21–25 1991

ADELAIDE, AUSTRALIA • Festival Theatre • March 10–13, 1994

BOSTON, MASSACHUSETTS • The Wang Center for the Performing Arts • June 2–4, 1994

EDINBURGH, SCOTLAND • Festival Theatre • August 20–22, 1994

BERKELEY, CALIFORNIA • Zellerbach Hall • September 30–October 2, 1994

SEATTLE, WASHINGTON • Meany Hall • October 26–30, 1994

MINNEAPOLIS, MINNESOTA • Northrup Auditorium • November 18–20, 1994

NEW YORK, NEW YORK • New York State Theater at Lincoln Center • July 12–15, 1995

TEL AVIV, ISRAEL • Tel Aviv Performing Arts Center • January 31–February 4, 1996

HONG KONG • Grand Theatre • February 22–25, 1997

COSTA MESA, CALIFORNIA • Orange County Performing Arts Center • April 3–6, 1997

LONDON, ENGLAND • London Coliseum • June 5–10, 1997

WELLINGTON, NEW ZEALAND • St. James Theatre • March 18–22, 1998

WASHINGTON, D.C. • John F. Kennedy Center for the Performing Arts • May 6–8, 1999

HOUSTON, TEXAS • Jones Hall • January 27–29, 2000

BERKELEY, CALIFORNIA • Zellerbach Hall • March 1–5, 2000

LONDON, ENGLAND • London Coliseum • June 30–July 7, 2000

BROOKLYN, NEW YORK • Brooklyn Academy of Music Howard Gilman Opera House • March 22–25, 2001

THE CREATION OF this book would not have been possible without the cooperation of dozens of generous and extraordinarily talented people. We are indebted, first and foremost, to Mark Morris, and to Barry Alterman and Nancy Umanoff. From the start they shared our belief in this book, and they supported its preparation at every turn. We are particularly grateful to Nancy, who, quite simply, is a saint, and whom we thank for never once making us feel as though we were imposing, no matter how much we asked of her. We would also like to thank the rest of the staff at the Mark Morris Dance Group (MMDG), for their ready and unflagging help: Lisa Belvin, Lesley Berson, Eva Nichols, Michael Osso, Lee Streby, and Lynn Wichern.

For their assistance at a special photo shoot in Berkeley on March 3, 2000, we would like to thank MMDG technical director Johan Henckens, lighting director Rick Martin, wardrobe supervisor Pamela Anson, and all the dancers: Joe Bowie, Charlton Boyd, Ruth Davidson, Marjorie Folkman, Shawn Gannon, Lauren Grant, John Heginbotham, David Leventhal, Rachel Murray, June Omura, Mireille Radwan-Dana, Matthew Rose, Julie Worden, Michelle Yard, Christina Amendolia, Derrick Brown, Seth Davis, Joseph Gillam, Peter Kyle, Gregory Nuber, Maile Okamura, Jonathan Pessolano, Joseph Poulson, Karen Reedy, Kim Reis, and Anne Sellery. We would also like to thank Robert Cole and Hollis Ashby at Cal Performances, and photographer Ken Friedman. Photographs by Ken Friedman appearing on the title page and the following pages—32, 33, 36 (3), 46–47, 48, 52, 53, 55 (2), 59, 60 (3), 65, 67 (bottom), 78, 79 (2), 84, 85 (3), 86, 87, 88, 92, 95, 97, 100, 104–105, 107, 115, 116, 119, 122 (2)—are used courtesy of Cal Performances, University of California, Berkeley, Robert Cole, Director, from the production presented on March 1–5, 2000, at Zellerbach Hall.

For their recollections and insights, we would like to thank Charlton Boyd, Ruth Davidson, Tina Fehlandt, Marjorie Folkman, John Heginbotham, Dan Joyce, David Leventhal, Rachel Murray, Gregory Nuber, June Omura, and Matthew Rose. A special thanks to Marjorie Folkman for compiling the complete list of dancers. We are particularly grateful to set designer Adrianne Lobel, for her recollections and for allowing us to reprint excerpts from her essay on *L'Allegro* and original drawings and slides of set designs; former MMDG music director Linda Dowdell; and lighting designer James F. Ingalls.

We are extremely grateful to the seventeen photographers whose work appears here: Stephen Black, Tom Brazil, Bill Cooper, Gadi Dagon, Ken Friedman, Robbie Jack, Klaus Lefebvre, Janet P. Levitt, Susana Millman, Daniéle Pierre, Bill Rafferty, Linda Rich, Chris Ryan, Beatriz Schiller, Leslie E. Spatt, Martha Swope, and Brant Ward. Thanks also to Marc Royce, Chantal Regnault, Gary Fong at the *San Francisco Chronicle* and Tom Gilbert at TimePix.

We want to thank Joan Acocella, Wendy Lesser, and Alastair Macaulay for their contributions and incalculable support of this project. At the Avalon Publishing Group we would like to thank Neil Ortenberg, Susan Reich, Dan O'Connor, Ghadah Alrawi, Sue McCloskey, Catheline Jean-François, and Jamar Wilson. At Publishers Group West, thanks to Charlie Winton, Trigg McLeod, Mark Ouimet, Kim Wylie, Kevin Votel, Brittin Clark, Bill Getz and all the other reps. Thanks also to John and Susan Hale at Robert Hale Limited, Candace Groskreutz at CG Rights Agency, Shawneric Hachey for his invaluable assistance on the permissions front, and William Zinsser for his judicious editing. At Neuwirth & Associates we are grateful to John Nora, Beth Metrick, and, most considerably, Pauline Neuwirth, for her enthusiasm, steady grace under pressure, and titanic competence—and for crafting a beautiful book.

We would also like to thank Chris Bull, Ani Chamichian, Amber Hollibaugh, Bob Hughes, Claire Jagemann, Hans Johnson, Patricia and Gerald Lore, Andrew Lynch, Karen and Gill Newton, Michael Rothberg, Michael Sexton, Alice Simmons, Andrew Spieldenner, Leith ter Meulen, Iris Wendel, and Yasemin Yildiz.

Finally, we would like to recognize the late Dale Harris. Although he was not the first critic to praise *L'Allegro*, his review of its U.S. premiere, which appeared in *The Wall Street Journal* on October 19, 1990, first alerted us to the dance, and thereby set this book in motion more than ten years ago.

Selected Bibliography

Acocella, Joan. *Mark Morris*. New York: Farrar, Straus & Giroux, 1993.

———. "L'Allegro, il Penseroso ed il Moderato." *Ballet Review*, Summer 1989.

Ackroyd, Peter. *Blake: A Biography*. New York: Alfred A. Knopf, 1996.

Burrows, Donald. *Handel*. New York: Schirmer Books, 1994.

Denby, Edwin. "About Ballet Decoration." *Dance Writings*. New York: Alfred A. Knopf, 1986.

Downey, Roger. "Secular Dialogues." Monnaie Dance Group/Mark Morris souvenir program. Brussels: Théâtre Royal de la Monnaie, 1988.

Gardiner, John Eliot. Liner Notes to Handel's *L'Allegro, il Penseroso ed il Moderato*. Soli, Monterverdi Choir and English Baroque Soloists, conducted by John Eliot Gardiner. Erato, 1992.

"George Frideric Handel." Monnaie Dance Group/Mark Morris souvenir program. Brussels: Théâtre Royal de la Monnaie, 1988.

Greenblatt, Stephen, Nicholas McGegan, Joan Acocella, and Alastair Macaulay. "A Mark Morris Symposium." *The Threepenny Review*, Spring 1995.

Harris, Dale. "A Morris Masterwork." *The Wall Street Journal*. October 19, 1990.

Keates, Jonathan. *Handel: The Man and His Music*. New York: St. Martin's Press, 1985.

———. "The Soul's Embrace." *Times Literary Supplement*, June 13, 1997.

Keefe, Maura, and Marc Woodworth, "An Interview with Mark Morris." *Salmagundi*, Fall 1994.

Leishman, J.B. *Milton's Minor Poems*. London: Hutchinson, 1969.

Macaulay, Alastair. "L'Allegro, il Penseroso, ed il Moderato." *The Dancing Times*, August 1994.

———. "The Last Great American Choreographer." *Dance Theatre Journal*, Summer 1995.

Morris, Mark. "The Hidden Soul of Harmony," in Selma Jeanne Cohen and Katy Matheson, eds., *Dance as a Theatre Art*, second edition. Princeton, N.J.: Princeton Book Company, 1992.

Solomon, Deborah. "The Gallery: William Blake, Artist." *The Wall Street Journal*, April 23, 1997.

Tobias, Tobi. "Paradise Regained." *New York* magazine, October 29, 1990.

Wattis, Nigel, director. *The Hidden Soul of Harmony*. South Bank Show, London Weekend Television, 1990.

Whittington, Stephen. Program Notes, Cal Peformances presentation of *L'Allegro, il Penseroso ed il Moderato*, September 30–October 2, 1994.

Wilson, A. N. *The Life of John Milton*. Oxford: Oxford University Press, 1983.

JOAN ACOCELLA is the dance critic of *The New Yorker*. She is the author of the book *Mark Morris* and the editor of *The Diary of Vaslav Nijinsky*. Her most recent book was *Willa Cather and the Politics of Criticism*. She is a fellow of the New York Institute for the Humanities and a former Guggenheim fellow.

STEPHEN BLACK is a Hong Kong–based photographer.

TOM BRAZIL has photographed the Mark Morris Dance Group since 1983, in Becket, Berkeley, Boston, Brooklyn, Brussels, Cedar Rapids, Columbus, Fire Island, Manhattan, Princeton, and Washington, D.C. His book of photographs, *Dances by Mark Morris,* was published in 1992.

BILL COOPER is a London-based photographer who specializes in the opera arts.

GADI DAGON is a photographer in Tel Aviv, Israel.

JEFFREY ESCOFFIER writes on dance, sexuality and gay social theory. He is the author of a book of essays on gay cultural politics and a biography of John Maynard Keynes. He lives in Brooklyn.

KEN FRIEDMAN is a Bay Area photographer who specializes in dance, theater, opera, and popular entertainment.

ROBBIE JACK has been photographing the performing arts for almost twenty years. He first photographed the Mark Morris Dance Group when they visited Edinburgh in 1992, and he has photographed many of the world's leading dance companies, including the Kirov Ballet, the Bolshoi Ballet, the Royal Ballet, and the Rambert Dance Company. He lives in London.

KLAUS LEFEBVRE has taken photographs of theatrical productions since 1980. His photographs have been published in many German and international newspapers, magazines, books and programs. He lives in Ennepetal, Germany.

WENDY LESSER is the founder and editor of *The Threepenny Review*. In 1997, she received the Morton Dauwen Zabel Award from the American Academy of Arts and Letters. She is the author of five books, of which the most recent is *The Amateur*, a collection of her essays.

JANET P. LEVITT has been a dance photographer for over twenty years and has worked with all the world's major ballet and modern dance companies. She is a contributing photographer for *Dance Magazine* and *The Dancing Times* of London, where her work appears every month in the "New York Newsletter."

MATTHEW LORE is editorial director of Marlowe & Company and the creator, with his brother Mark, of *Rubberneckers*. He lives in Brooklyn.

ALASTAIR MACAULAY, who lives and works in London, is the theater critic of the *Financial Times*. His published books include the biography *Margot Fonteyn* and a book of interviews with the choreographer Matthew Bourne. He is currently preparing a book on the choreographer Merce Cunningham.

SUSANA MILLMAN has come to a career in photography somewhat late in life, after experience as a psychologist, traveler, and importer. She has a great love for shooting live entertainment of all sorts, from the Grateful Dead to theater and modern dance, as well as travel and interior photography. She lives in San Francisco with her husband, author and publicist Dennis McNally, and has one daughter, social entrepreneur Season Ray.

DANIÉLE PIERRE specializes in set photography, theater, opera, dance, and feature film. She lives in Brussels, where she photographed the Mark Morris Dance Group when it was the resident dance company of the Théâtre Royal de la Monnaie.

BILL RAFFERTY has worked for forty years at the English National Opera, where he is the company photographer. He lives in London.

LINDA RICH has specialized in dance and theater photography since 1980. Her work has been exhibited at the Sadler's Wells Theatre, the Royal Festival Hall, and the Royal Photographic Society members' gallery. She lives in London.

CHRIS RYAN is a photographer based in the San Francisco Bay Area.

BEATRIZ SCHILLER, a photographer living in New York City, shoots opera, dance, and theater. Her work has been published in *Art in America*, *Graphis*, *Opera News*, *Dance Magazine*, *New York* magazine, *The New York Times*, *Time*, and *Newsweek*.

LESLIE E. SPATT, although born in New York City, has been a London resident for more than thirty years. She has worked with the Royal Ballet, Sadler's Wells/Birmingham Royal Ballet, Stuttgart Ballet, Dutch National Ballet, Kirov Ballet, and Bolshoi Ballet. She lives in London.

MARTHA SWOPE has been one of the leading photographers of dance for almost fifty years. She was the official photographer of the New York City Ballet, the American Ballet Theatre, the Martha Graham Dance Company, and the Dance Theatre of Harlem. She lives in New York.

BRANT WARD has been a staff photographer at the *San Francisco Chronicle* since 1984. He has covered stories all over the world, including earthquakes in Mexico, famine in Somalia, and political upheaval in Haiti. He lives in Petaluma, California.

OVERLEAF: LONDON, 2000 •
Marjorie Folkman and Lauren Grant lifted by
[L–R]: Charlton Boyd, Matthew Rose [OBSCURED],
Seth Davis, Joseph Poulson, in "Sweet Bird" [Bill Cooper]

NORTH
OF
BOSTON

ELISABETH ELO

headline

Excerpt from 'Memento' from *Face Behind the Face: Poems* by Yevgeny Yevtushenko,
translated by Arthur Boyars and Simon Franklin (Marion Boyars, London, 1979). Used
by permission of Marion Boyars Publishers.

1

Cataloguing in Publication Data is available from the British Library

ISBN 978 1 4722 0633 6

Printed and bound in Great Britain by Clays Ltd, St Ives plc

Headline's policy is to use papers that are natural, renewable and recyclable products and
made from wood grown in sustainable forests. The logging and manufacturing processes
are expected to conform to the environmental regulations of the country of origin.

HEADLINE PUBLISHING GROUP
An Hachette UK Company
338 Euston Road
London NW1 3BH

www.headline.co.uk
www.hachette.co.uk

In memory of my father,
William Jacob Panttaja

Acknowledgments

Many thanks to Holly Robinson, Terri Giuliano Long, and Virginia Smith, who critiqued early drafts of the manuscript. To Esmond Harmsworth, who saw something good in it. And to Pamela Dorman, who made it much better. My gratitude forever flows to Ben and Ellen, who are my pride, joy, and inspiration, and to Robert, without whose love and support none of this would have happened.

North of Boston

Chapter 1

He was a loser," Thomasina says, head lolling. "But he was a good loser." A fifth of Stolichnaya has put her in a nasty, forgiving mood. I'm tempted to take a few shots myself to medicate my grief and survivor's guilt. But someone has to stay sober for Noah.

Thomasina paws something she sees in the air—maybe nothing, a spark of hallucination, or a particle of dust—and her tone goes flat. "I never loved him. I just wanted sperm." She pushes the bottle halfway across the kitchen table and lays her head down on folded arms. Her shoulders heave a few times. Sorrow? Nausea? In her state it could be either, or even a hiccup of indifference. But when she picks up her face, it's tear-stained. "But I must have loved him some, 'cause right now I feel *wicked* bad."

Noah pokes his head around the corner. He doesn't have the heavy, square look of Ned or what was formerly the haunting, big-eyed beauty of Thomasina. He's small, thin, pale. Dark eye rings give him a monkish quality. He doesn't talk much, doesn't have friends. Maybe that's why we get along.

"Noah, baby. Let mama get you something to eat." Thomasina lurches to her feet and staggers to the refrigerator. When she opens the door, Noah and I look inside. Lime Gatorade, half a tomato, mold-speckled hamburger buns. "You want a tomato sandwich, baby?"

"No, thank you," Noah says. He's always been polite. He wanders back to the living room to continue whatever intricate activity he was engaged in. I've seen him build entire futuristic cities out of tongue depressors, popsicle sticks, and toothpicks.

Thomasina sways in a widening arc, her eyes start to roll back in her head, and her eyelids flutter and close. She slides down the refrigerator and collapses. I get one of her arms around my neck and haul her up, drag her across the scuffed linoleum to the dank bedroom at the back of the apartment. Clothes and shoes litter the floor. I recognize the lizard-skin cowboy boots she wears out at night. I let her fall across the king-size bed and push her legs onto the mattress.

The fall brings her back to consciousness. She mumbles, "You have to tell him how it happened, Pirio. He trusts you. He *loves* you. And you know better than anyone what to say—you were *there*." She turns her face toward the closed window shade and says mournfully, "Remember, long time ago, when we were just little girls no one cared about? So we cared about each other. It was sweet, but we were so sad. Weren't we, Pirio?"

"We were OK," I say firmly, trying to steer her away from the rabbit hole of old pain.

"Can you believe it, Pirio? I can't. Ned dead. Hey, it rhymes! Now Noah has no father. My baby's half an orphan. Poor little kid."

I don't say anything. I can't believe it either. I'd do anything to make it different. I keep asking myself what I could have done, but I keep coming up empty. No one could have saved him. Except the cowards on the ship.

"Want to know who I dreamed about the other night?" Thomasina asks musingly. Sometimes I'm jealous of the way booze gives her mind permission to wander up every alley and side street it sees. "Biggest asshole *ever*. You know who it is. You and me, we're like peas and carrots, peas in a pod. Whatever. Insert your vegetable." She puts two fingers over her lips in self-censorship. "Oops. Didn't mean it that way." Her hand flops away from her mouth, and her eyelids begin another rapid-fire fluttering. "Guess, Pirio. You'll get it on the first try, I bet. Biggest asshole *ever* was . . . It was . . ." Her voice becomes a whisper. "It was . . ." Her eyes close.

"It was Dickhead Bates," I say softly.

I push some pillows under her head and shoulders to prop her up so she won't choke if she vomits, and pull a blanket over her. I take a minute to collect myself, then go into the living room.

Noah looks up from his project. "How's my mom?"

"Sleeping."

He nods. With his limited life experience, he has no idea how worried to be. He knows his mom's been trying hard not to drink so much. Sometimes he comes to my apartment in the evenings so she can go to meetings; then for days she doesn't go out at all. He's used to her taking naps at odd times.

I get a whiff of indoles and uric acid. Translation: shit and piss. There's a small plastic cage on a table in the corner. I slide back the cover, reach inside, curl my hand around a quivering little body huddled in a pile of sawdust, and place the hamster in Noah's cupped hands. He starts cooing to it, rubs his cheek against the rodent's fur. *Hi, Jerry. Are you OK, Jerry?* It takes me a little while to clean the cage. When Noah places Jerry back inside, he makes his body round and hunkers down into the fresh sawdust, which smells confusingly of sweetened pine and searing ammonia. I try to imagine how the cheap chemical additives affect his tiny olfactory glands and decide he probably preferred the smell of his own waste. I hate the whole idea of keeping animals in pens. If he weren't Noah's pet, I'd let him go.

"Come on, Noah. I'll buy you a hamburger," I say.

3

Thomasina and I went to boarding school together. I'd been at the Gaston School since seventh grade; it was one of the only schools my father, Milosa, could find that warehoused kids that young. It was located in Boothbay, Maine, but to me it felt like Tomsk, Siberia, which is where I'd been told the Russian government lost track of my maternal grandparents around 1944. My mother died when I was ten, Noah's age. Never an angel, I became increasingly defiant, noncommunicative. I pretty much just stopped answering adults' nosy questions and heeding their hysterical warnings. Several of Milosa's girlfriends tried hard to figure out what was wrong with me but came up clueless. Then he remarried, and my stepmother, Maureen, wasted no time pronouncing me a true, definitive problem child. She had stacks of books to prove herself right and got a doctor at Children's Hospital to agree. A boarding school with lots of "structure" just made sense. In fact, Headmaster Richard (Dickhead) Bates was not even close to being the biggest asshole at the Gaston School. There were others more sadistic than he.

Thomasina arrived at Gaston in ninth grade, the detritus of a bitter divorce that left neither parent wanting permanent custody. She was eating-disorder thin, deeply tanned from a vacation with her mother in the Azores, bedecked in silver hoop earrings and bracelets that rose halfway up her left arm. And because she still wore braces, top and bottom, on her big square teeth, she gave the impression of being a starving small brown animal trapped in a metal cage. Her eyes looked wet, as if a tear were poised to spill, only it never did. She was too deeply, everlastingly skeptical to cry about anything.

We sized each other up, saw ourselves for what we were, and accepted what we believed to be our dismal fates. We skipped class; drank Boone's Farm, Budweiser, and Lancers Vin Rosé; climbed over the high stone wall surrounding the school's eighteen acres and jumped down onto the tarry shoulder of Route 27; hitchhiked into town. Wherever we went, we gloried in pissing off as many people as we could. After two years of being alienated in isolation, it felt good to have someone to get in trouble with.

Neither of us was interested in college, so after graduation I came home to Boston, and Thomasina joined me. We rented apartments a few blocks from each other in Brookline, a mostly ritzy, part-run-down urbanish neighborhood, and settled into independent lives. I joined the family business, a perfume company named after my mother, Inessa Mark. Thomasina's parents—one in France, one on the West Coast—have scads of money and bottomless guilt, which essentially means she's never had to work.

For the first few years, Thomasina and I caroused aimlessly. The nicer bars soon bored us; all those guys in Brooks Brothers suits took themselves too seriously. We gravitated toward the seedier taverns, especially down at the waterfront. Dockworkers and fishermen would literally follow us around. We enjoyed the power we had, flattering ourselves that we were breaking hearts wherever we went.

Then Thomasina met Ned, and the two of them fell away from the bar scene to snuggle into their supposed love nest. I boozed and dated a little longer, until I got tired of hearing lame pick-up lines from belching idiots, and eventually put down the bottle to go to UMass Boston, where I studied Russian language and literature. I guess it was some kind of roots thing—my attempt to understand the Russian character, to be connected to my Russian past. It didn't work; I wasn't really sure what I was looking for, and it wasn't much of a surprise when I didn't find it. But I did encounter suffering more brutal and prolonged than anything my poor-little-rich-girl story could offer, and that bit of historical perspective nudged me to start growing up.

It came as no surprise when Thomasina and Ned's relationship disintegrated. He was working-class Irish-Italian from South Boston. She's a brilliant, privileged, slothful iconoclast. At first they seemed to transcend all that. They smiled at each other like angels lit from the inside with megawatt bulbs. That phase lasted, by my amazed reckoning, almost three months. Then, probably figuring he'd gone far enough in the conversation department, he started in with the blank stares and inopportune groin scratches, and she began to display the full power of her underused intellect with put-downs so brilliantly satiric he didn't even understand them. Alcohol brought them to the brink of violence—dinners ruined, plates smashed, neighbors yelling out the windows to shut up. She just couldn't forgive him for being dull. By the time Noah came along, they'd already split.

They never married, and Ned's parents and sister refuse to accept that Noah is related to them at all. They prefer to think that Thomasina bewitched Ned into providing for another guy's brat. I confess that I've wondered about Noah's paternity myself, and I know Ned occasionally felt baffled at having spawned a genius kid who didn't look like him or act like anyone he knew. But Ned was always a good father, at least as good as anyone could be under the circumstances. He insisted on paying child support, although no court required it and Thomasina didn't need it. He got tickets to the Bruins, Red Sox, Patriots. Winter, summer, fall—Ned and Noah always had their outing. He visited Noah every other weekend—lunch and a trip to the park or library, depending on the weather. If Thomasina asked, he would even pick up Noah after school. Sometimes Thomasina let Ned stay overnight, and when he did, he seemed glad for it. I imagine him trying to curb his Southie manners, trying not to be stupid. People will do just about anything to get one tender caress.

But even with Ned doing his part, Thomasina was overwhelmed by single motherhood. The parents who hadn't had time for their only daughter were even less interested in a grandchild, and she didn't exactly fit in at PTA. But none of that really explains why what used to be a fairly standard type of admittedly ugly but relatively contained debauchery has morphed over the last year into a fierce, pathetic addiction.

She knows she's in trouble. She's tried it all. Not just AA, but also

Rational Recovery, Tarot cards, the Enneagram, therapy, spas, meditation, confession, reading to the blind, and drinking only wine. Nothing's worked. She gets a few days of sobriety here, enjoys a clearheaded week or two there, but eventually her shaking hand rewraps itself around the neck of a bottle. Looking at Thomasina today, you'd never guess what she used to be like—that at sixteen she learned flawless French in a few months, knew every character in Shakespeare, and could recite most of the Gettysburg Address backward, collapsing in gales of laughter when she was done. But you'd probably have no trouble guessing that the bulges in her handbag are little pops of airplane gin.

You stand by helplessly; you start getting truly scared. You sense something desperate inside, something far darker than what you thought was there. I'd like nothing better than to turn away from the spectacle of Thomasina's relentless, incremental self-destruction. But then I remember Noah, and pick up the phone. Hear myself saying, *How are you? How's Noah? What's up?*

I'm Noah's godmother. Seriously. It's a Catholic thing. When he was two months old, I stood with Thomasina and Ned at the side altar of a big church, holding him in my arms. The baptismal font was cool white marble; a priest hovered at my shoulder, his pastoral vestments smelling of rich, rotting medieval leather flattened by a dry cleaner's press. He asked me a question: *Do you renounce Satan and all his ways?* I blinked, taken aback. *Satan?* But Ned and Thomasina were watching and Noah was in my arms, so I thought about it seriously and replied, "If I ever met him, I'd know what to do."

This answer must have been good enough, because the priest gestured for me to hold Noah over the font. He tipped the cup he'd been holding, and water flowed across Noah's forehead into the marble bowl. Noah screwed up his wrinkled face but only cried a little. Even as a baby he kept his emotions in check, as if he knew there wasn't going to be a lot of space for his feelings in this world. To my surprise, my eyes were wet with all the godmother blessings I wanted to bestow, but all I had to give him was a kiss. I saw Thomasina and Ned squeeze hands, and we looked at one another with a bit of shy nakedness, knowing we had stumbled across a perfect moment in our lives. A moment as fleeting as any other, already gone.

Now, at Taffy's, a restaurant on the corner, Noah squares off in front of a hamburger and fries. He gets his fingers around the bun, lifts it to his mouth, and takes an enormous bite. He chews like a lion, gulps it down. He admitted he was hungry when I asked. It's possible he's actually starving.

It's been three days since his father drowned. I have no idea how much he knows about the accident. The story was on the news in a slightly-more-than-sound-bite form. A picture of Ned's regular-guy mug hovered in a small box next to the news announcer's perfect cover-girl face, then expanded to fill the entire screen. When his face was in the box, he looked like a nice guy you knew in high school who forgot to comb his hair. When it bloomed to fill the screen, you could see the brown discolorations on the side of his face from years of being outside. His tea-green eyes looked bloodshot, wary, possibly dishonest. Or maybe he only looked that way because, on the news, everyone tends to look like a criminal. In any case, it would have felt drastically wrong to Noah to see his deceased father on a television screen.

"You want to know how it happened, Noah?"

"OK." He's learned to be accommodating.

"It was a crash, like the kind on highways, only this one was on the ocean."

"I *know* that already." He dips a French fry in a little paper bucket of ketchup to show how uninteresting this is.

Of course. He knows everything about crashes; he's seen a million on TV. Sparks fly, buildings dissolve, cars burst into flame. *Ho-hum.*

I take the paper place mat from under the plate my BLT is on and turn it over. With a pen borrowed from the waitress, I sketch the coastline from Cape Cod to Maine. I put in the islands in Boston Harbor and roughly shade in Georges Bank. "Your dad and I were here," I say, pointing to a spot that correlates to about twenty-five miles northeast of Boston. "The fog came in thick. Your dad was in the wheelhouse. I was in the stern baiting lobster traps. It was really quiet. I couldn't even see the bow. The next thing I knew, something huge crashed into us. Huge, Noah. A freighter. It hit starboard, broadside. That means right in the middle of the boat. I bailed, and when I broke the surface and looked back, your dad's boat was in splinters and the freighter was passing by."

"My dad swam away, like you did."

"The Coast Guard looked for him for about five hours that day, until the sun went down, and then from daybreak to sunset the next day. They had two patrol boats, two helicopters, and a C-130 search plane. Almost twenty hours of searching, Noah. Some fishermen were out there, too—your dad's friends. A lot of people were involved. They searched an eight-mile radius from where I was found."

"Cool," he says. His eyes are vacant, as if he doesn't know what I'm saying is real.

"They didn't find him, Noah."

"He got away like you did. He swam underwater."

"He'd have to come up for air sometime."

"Not if he went to Atlantis."

"Atlantis is a made-up place."

"No, it isn't." He looks at me reproachfully.

I've babysat him since he was an infant. I'm his good fairy godmother, the one who plays games and willingly accompanies him on flights of fancy, who doesn't ever tell him to be sensible or brush his teeth. This is a new me he is seeing.

I wait.

Noah dips another fry in the ketchup. He draws it several times across the thin paper at the bottom of his hamburger basket, leaving reddish streaks. Maybe he's writing a hieroglyph, trying to communicate. If he is, I'm probably the only person left in the world who would try to decipher it.

"A monster killed my dad," he says, attempting.

"He drowned, Noah," I say gently. "He's gone."

Fury knits his brows together, makes his tiny nostrils flare. "Why did that boat crash into him? Why didn't they look where they were going?" He's been told that a hundred times. *Be careful. Don't run. Watch what you're doing.* But he's already figured out that adults don't play by those rules.

"It was an accident, Noah. Collisions at sea happen more often than you'd think." I could kick myself for making it sound mundane.

"Why didn't the people stop to look for him?"

"Good question," I say, buying time.

I feel helpless to the point of despair. I don't want Noah to see my rage. If the captain had stopped the freighter immediately, as soon as he realized what had happened, he could have saved us both easily. But he didn't. He just kept going. He probably wanted to spare himself an official inquiry and whatever damage his reputation would suffer.

I can't say that to Noah. So I give the typical response. "The Coast Guard is looking into it. They're going to find the people on the boat and ask them that."

He looks at me with the weary, perplexed eyes of a disappointed man. He knows I'm holding back.

"It's possible that the people on the ship didn't even know they hit us," I say. "That freighter could have been five hundred feet, and I don't even know how many hundreds of tons. Double steel hull. Bridge about three stories up. And in fog like that, what's the point of looking out anyway? They rely on radar in that weather. But the ocean is big and they're not expecting anything, so if they see something small like your dad's lobster boat, they might think it's just sea clutter, like floating oil drums or garbage."

Noah's lip is trembling. He's trying not to cry. His tears are so rare that the prospect of just one falling makes my whole body hurt.

But he gets himself together, gazes out the window. Across the street there's a lamp store, a Walgreens, and an Indian grocery. Down the street there's a park with a playground where he often went with his dad and where I've taken him, too. As a small child, he liked the swings but not the slide. On the swings he could keep an eye peeled for unusual occurrences; the slide was too disorienting.

I wonder what he's thinking. Maybe that the world is deeply unfair and dangerous, only he wouldn't have the words for that. Maybe he isn't thinking at all, just soaking it up. Cars, boats, fog. Drunken mothers, distant fathers. Crash. I wish now I hadn't said his dad's boat could have been mistaken for garbage.

I draw a vessel that looks like the *Molly Jones*. "There's something important I want you to know. Your dad probably could have jumped overboard and swum away, like I did. But if he'd done that, we both would have died because nobody would have known we were out there. So your dad stayed in the wheelhouse and called the Coast Guard."

Noah is staring at me, and I'm having a hard time looking back.

"Your dad saved my life."

Noah frowns. He picks up his hamburger slowly. "Did he want to marry you?"

"No. We were just friends."

"Why?"

"Why were we friends?"

"Why didn't he want to marry you?"

"He just didn't. Marriage is a special thing. We were happy being friends."

"How come my mom and dad didn't get married? Were they just friends?"

This one's tricky. I tell him they used to be more than friends, and then they became friends.

He puts what's left of his hamburger down, takes the bun off, peels a pickle out of its mustard-ketchup goo, and places it carefully on the wrapper. Without looking at me, he says, "If you and my dad got married, you'd be my stepmom."

That's how I know how bad he's hurting; he's never said anything like this to me before. I take my time before I answer. "I'm not cut out for parenthood, Noah. But if I had to be someone's stepmom, I'd want to be yours."

He looks into my eyes with as much trust as he can give to anyone, and I think three words I haven't used since my mother died. *I love you.* I would say them to him, but I'm afraid I haven't got what it takes to make good on the promise they imply.

Noah takes something out of the pocket of his jacket. It's a yellowish-white disk riddled with tiny veins and holes. Two inches in diameter, an inch thick, the edges smooth as glass.

"That's nice," I say. "Where'd you get it?"

"My dad. He gave me other stuff, too."

"Where'd he get it?"

"Off a whale."

"Is that what he told you?" It looks vaguely like it could have come from an animal, but I've never seen a bone like that. My guess is it's some kind of rock. It's obviously been cut and appears to have been polished.

Noah leans forward and whispers, "My dad fought a whale once. He got in a little boat and followed it and killed it with a harpoon. The whale didn't die right away. It pulled my dad all over the world, but he hung on with all his might. The whale was bleeding the whole time and finally it bled to death, and my dad pulled it back to the ship. He stayed up all night cutting it into pieces, and he took some of its bones. See?" He waves the ivory disk. "A whalebone." He gives it to me.

When Noah was a baby, he had enormous dark blue eyes. His lips would pucker in tiny exhaled kisses, as though he couldn't help sending the love that filled him into the world. We used to play a game together: We would sit face to face, he in a high chair, me in a kitchen chair. We would pass something—a rubber duck or ninja figure or some other little toy—back and forth for a long time while we smiled into each other's eyes. This reminds me of those times. Only when I try to return the disk, he pushes it right back to me.

Maybe the kind of hero I described—the kind who radios for help—isn't good enough. He needs one who wielded harpoons.

I turn the treasure slowly in my hand, inspecting it, respecting it. "Nice, Noah. Really nice."

He grabs it and stuffs it in his jacket pocket, closes and buttons the flap, and looks around the restaurant at the people eating. Suddenly he's a restless kid again, perked up by a hamburger, secure in his right to believe stories that comfort him and to ignore facts he can't understand. There's still some time until he has to do homework, and he says, "Hey, Pirio, after this can we go to your place and play dominoes?"

Chapter 2

It's Saturday morning, one week after the accident, and I'm sitting in a hushed television studio in Brighton. There's a live studio audience on the other side of the glaring stage lights—more than two hundred fans of the famed Jared Jehobeth, who occupies the club chair directly across from me. He appears completely relaxed. He shuffles his tie, apparently lost in thought, summoning his showtime personality from wherever he keeps it stored. A tiny table is on my left. I note that a glass of water has been thoughtfully provided, in case I choke.

This is one of the last places I ever thought I'd be. I hate television in general and morning shows in particular. So when the executive producer called me after reading the *Globe*'s account of the incident and asked me to appear as a guest, I immediately declined.

Then I thought about it. No one had come forward to take responsibility for the collision. The more time that went by, the more likely it was that the freighter that sank the *Molly Jones* would get away. What if publicizing the story got a crew member to confess or to drop an anonymous tip? So I called the producer back.

Right now I'm doubting the wisdom of that choice. I sweep my hair off my neck and twist it loosely over my shoulder, which causes an assistant producer to materialize at my elbow, spritz, comb, and put my hair back just the way it was. Under the hot lights, the pancake makeup they slathered on me is already starting to slide off my face. I'm glad I refused the rest of the cosmetic camouflage they tried to persuade me to wear. A young producer in a T-shirt and jeans stands below the stage, holding up fingers, counting down the seconds until the red on-air light will flash.

Now the producer points his index finger silently, emphatically, at the two of us on the stage, and the on-air light blooms red in my peripheral vision. A rush of fear dizzies me. It's as if a scaffolding has been pulled away. I look down to discover that I am, in fact, wearing clothes—a red silk shirt, a short gray skirt over black tights and high black boots. Meanwhile, Jared Jehobeth has lit up like a neon bulb. He exudes such confidence and charm that even his nondescript brown suit looks dapper somehow. He welcomes his studio audience and television viewers to *Jared Jehobeth in the Morning*. The vaguely suggestive implications of the title do not make him blink. Instead, his eyes shine like innocent blue balloons, and his mop of brown hair and the pink powder blush they put on him make him look as trustworthy as a Franciscan friar. But he has a reputation for hard-hitting interviews—he has exposed the perpetrators of defective products to public scorn, made abusers and deadbeat dads break down and beg forgiveness from their families.

He explains that today he has a very special guest, a young lady of exceptional courage, who is here to tell an amazing tale that can barely be believed. This sounds so good that I forget for a moment he's talking about me.

"Turn off *Survivor*, folks; this is the real thing. After a collision at sea sank the fishing boat she was on, leaving the captain presumed drowned, this incredible young woman spent nearly four hours stranded in the North Atlantic in water temperatures of forty-two degrees before she was rescued. As far as we know, no one has ever done such a thing before, my friends. The longest the average person can expect to survive in such temperatures is one to two hours, max. She's an inspiring survivor, a medical marvel, and one very lucky young woman!" He turns to me, eyes glowing with generous admiration. "I thank you for coming, Pirio Kasparov. Now tell us what happened out there."

My throat closes up. I feel like bolting off the stage. I look at him in silent, apologetic horror.

He slides a microexpression of intense irritation my way.

I tell the truth, knowing it sounds like a hedge. "I don't remember much, I'm afraid."

Jared Jehobeth rears back in dramatic disbelief. "You swam clear of a sinking boat and spent hours paddling in icy water—still conscious when they found you, I was told. You must remember something!"

OK. *There's no way out but through.* I gather courage, concentrate, go back in time. Immediately, as if it had been waiting a few feet offstage for its cue, a vast wall of streaked gray water appears above me, hovers, arches, and begins to fall. I hold my breath instinctively. There's a horrible roar in my ears, and I feel such utter terror that I would willingly give my life to be released from it.

I must be blanching visibly, because Jared Jehobeth intervenes. "Go back to the moments just before the accident. What were you doing?"

"It felt like . . . well, first . . . I was standing in the stern. My friend, Ned Rizzo—"

"The man who died. A father of one, am I right?"

"Yes." I trust Noah's not watching. He doesn't watch much TV, and *Jared Jehobeth* is not his kind of show, but I told Thomasina to keep him away from the television this morning anyway.

"I was baiting lobster traps. It was very foggy. From where I was standing, I could just make out Ned in the wheelhouse. He was wearing a yellow oilskin. Those things are so bright, you know?" I'm veering off into irrelevant details, anything to keep from plunging ahead.

Jared Jehobeth holds my gaze in a sort of visual headlock. His eyes are compassionate, imperious. When this interview is over, I'll never see him again. But for now he is like a best friend, of sorts.

"I stopped baiting when I saw blood oozing from the base of my right thumb. The hinges on the lobster traps are really sharp. I dropped an empty bucket over the stern rail, pulled up seawater, and dipped my hand inside to numb it and make the bleeding stop." I hear myself speaking and am impressed. I sound so competent!

"You must have known that being immersed in water that temperature for even a short period of time was potentially fatal." He is a genius, this man.

"I wasn't thinking about that."

"But you knew."

"Yes."

Jared Jehobeth shoots a triumphant grin at the audience. He's going to make me a hero; that's what this is all about. I feel silly for not having seen it coming. And slightly awed. To think a person can be reinvented so easily and so falsely. All I did was jump out of a doomed boat to save myself. Then my body, all by itself, went into some kind of medically mysterious, rarely documented hibernation that somehow managed to preserve a minimum temperature in my critical organs until the Coast Guard arrived and hauled me out of the drink. I was a limp sack of bluish, water-saturated flesh when they found me. Nothing there I can take credit for, nothing I *want* credit for.

"I was feeling seasick, actually. I'm not an experienced fisherman. I didn't like being cold and wet."

The audience titters affectionately. I'm just like them.

"Ned told me I'd get used to the motion eventually, but it was the smell I couldn't stand. All those diesel fumes mixed with the bait, which is basically just putrefied herring guts."

The audience groans sympathetically.

"Anyway, I was pretty miserable, and the fog made it worse. I kept peering into it, trying to find the horizon line, but I could barely see the bow. Right before the, uh, collision, everything was quiet—too quiet. I noticed a huge black wall a few feet off the bow, sort of lurking there in the haze. At first it didn't seem to be moving. Then I realized it was sliding quickly along the starboard side. The next thing I knew the steel hull of a huge ship—so high I couldn't see the top—was crushing the gunwale about ten feet from where I stood.

"The deck started cracking under my feet. There was a horrible loud noise. The next thing I knew I was diving over the side. I don't remember being afraid. I was just thinking how unfair it was, that I was already miserable and now I would be soaked."

"What else were you thinking?" Jared Jehobeth asks breathlessly.

I close my eyes and concentrate. "I was thinking . . . *Don't die, Ned.*"

"Ah." He sits back, well pleased. "And then what happened?"

"You feel shocked when you hit water that cold. Every bit of you, shocked. Then you don't feel anything. I swam underwater for a while, surprised that my arms and legs could move."

"What was it like under there?"

I almost smile. He wants a travel report, as though I'm just back from a foreign place. The world of Little Nemo, possibly. Or Planet of the Giant Squid.

But my story is rushing along, no time for questions. "I didn't gasp. My airways just closed up. My arms and legs were going like crazy—it was all instinctive. I used to swim in high school, and I still swim a couple of times a week at the Y. That probably helped me—I don't know. I saw a glow and figured it was the surface, so I went that way. Then I was in the air, gagging, trying to keep my head above water. Finally, I looked back."

"What did you see?"

I ever so slightly shake my head. This part I won't say. It hurts too much. Yet, in my mind's eye, the scene is perfectly clear: the front half of the *Molly Jones* rolling away from the huge slicing ship like a severed head falling from a guillotine, listing, pausing, then sliding under the waves, faster than I would have thought possible, while the freighter glides soundlessly out of one fog cliff into another, a huge floating fortress of steel.

Ignoring Jared Jehobeth's drama-seeking eyes, I go on with the story. "A board bumped into me as I floated there. I grabbed it, slid one end between my legs, and lay along its length. Eventually the wake of the ship surged over me in huge swells. I'd be submerged, then come up again. That's when I was the most scared, I think."

"Were you in pain?"

"No. Hypothermia doesn't hurt. You get groggy and just sort of . . . go to sleep."

Jared Jehobeth lifts his tie, pats it down, and smiles. "Well, we certainly are glad you're with us today, Miss Kasparov. Now tell me how it felt when you realized that you were being rescued, that after everything you'd been through, you were going to be safe."

"I wish I could answer that question, but I don't recall the actual rescue. They tell me I was conscious, but all I remember is waking up naked in a sleeping bag, curled in the strong arms of a very warm, very living man."

"Ah, wonderful!" Jared Jehobeth says, brightening up and winking at the audience. "The exchange of bodily warmth is an accepted treatment for hypothermia. Were you surprised?"

"I thought I'd died and gone to heaven."

The audience erupts in applause, and I swear Jared Jehobeth gives a nanosecond wink at me, too, recognition from one performer to another. I grin in spite of myself, not quite believing it. I'm acing this thing. It feels sickening and delirious.

"You were in fact on a Coast Guard helicopter, being transported to safety," he explains. "That is truly an amazing tale. Thank you so much for sharing it. Ladies and gentlemen, I give you Pirio Kasparov, a true survivor!"

The audience resumes enthusiastic clapping. I can't see beyond the blazing lights, but I can feel their amassed approval flowing toward me. It's surprisingly nice.

Jared Jehobeth swirls in his chair to face the cameras. "Stay with us, folks. We'll be back on the other side of this short station break."

The on-air light goes off. Jared Jehobeth deflates. He takes out a handkerchief, mops his brow. The assistant producer appears at my elbow and ushers me off the stage, back to the drab greenroom where the next guest, a diet guru, is being led in. She thanks me, hands me my coat.

"Is that it?" I say.

She smiles coolly. "Yes, you can go now."

Minutes later, I'm in the parking lot, a light rain misting in my face. I feel a bit helium brained, a bit unreal. Cars on the Mass Pike scream on one side of me; monster industrial buildings loom on the other. I head back toward the city in my twelve-year-old Saab, wondering if anyone will call in with a tip.

Chapter 3

The high, medieval-looking façade of Gate of Heaven Church in South Boston has fallen into a damp shadow. If you did not fear God before you saw this church, you would after. Or at least whoever commissioned such a looming, unmerciful structure. Mourners file through the heavy nail-studded doors, collapsing their umbrellas, unbelting their trench coats. It is the same church where Noah was baptized; as I enter I recognize the marble font to one side of the distant altar. I slide into a back pew and watch Ned's friends file in.

You can tell the fishermen by their red, weathered faces. One of them limps—perhaps from having a leg struck by a flying hook or crushed against a gunwale. Most have probably been to funerals without caskets before. They look uncomfortable being indoors, breathing dry air, walking a pace behind their stout, practical wives.

Ned's parents, his sister and brother-in-law, and their unruly twins are already seated in a front pew. So are Thomasina and Noah, but on the other side of the aisle. Ned's mother, Phyllis, is probably aghast at that, probably wishes she'd cordoned off the area to keep Thomasina out of the limelight. But Thomasina apparently arrived early enough to claim the exalted spot before anyone else did, placing

Noah beside her like a mascot. *See? This is his child, despite what you think.* She's wearing a voluminous black hooded cape that brings to mind either the grim reaper himself or an excessively pious nun. I'm guessing that underneath its folds she's got on a tight, near-transparent, possibly spangled T-shirt and even tighter three-hundred-dollar designer jeans, and I'm willing to bet that her eyes are rimmed with eyeliner and gobs of mascara, which, when she cries, will ghoulishly run. At this stage of her addiction, she is incapable of proper decorum, not that she was ever any good at it.

The priest keeps everyone waiting, then appears from a side door like an ecclesiastical rock star in a lush purple robe, and is ushered to the altar by a flock of boys in fluttering white tunics. He turns his back to us, raises his arms to the huge crucifix above the tabernacle, lowers them in prayer, and proceeds to a lectern at the left side of the altar, where he begins to speak. He has a boyish face and a clear, calm voice; I try to listen but feel as if cotton is plugging my ears. I'm deaf to religion, and can only fidget. The service drags on and on. You'd think the lack of a body would make things go a little faster.

Finally the priest leaves the altar, makes his magisterial way down the center aisle, robe flapping. Thomasina and Noah are quick to fall in behind him. Ned's parents and sister and her family are forced to follow in her wake. Thomasina surprises me with her solemn carriage and dignity; in a pinch she is able to fall back on impeccable upper-class breeding. It's Phyllis who's red and heaving, dabbing her eyes. We mourners let them pass, give them plenty of room. The family of the deceased occupies an inner circle of grief that everyone wants to honor, and avoid.

People begin to file out of the pews. I stay behind, strangely reluctant to leave. I needed something from this service. Some kind of solace, I guess. My eyes fill with an image of Ned, glassy-eyed and bloated, floating a few feet off the scoured-by-trawlers ocean floor, his hair waving around his skull like sea grass in the current, one of the lobsters he wanted to catch trundling across his orange quilted vest.

My gaze wanders blindly across the painted statues of saints, the flickering red votive candles, the wood-carved stations of the cross. All of it designed to reconcile humanity to suffering and death. I heartily wish that the weird myths of religion worked for me, but they don't. Still, right now I can't seem to tear myself away. What if I'm missing something hidden in plain sight? What if I'm wrong?

I manage to collect myself and join the last stragglers flowing into the marble foyer. There's a commotion at the front door. I can't see through the people, but I hear raised voices, then, heart sinking, Thomasina's shriek.

"What are you doing? Take your hands off me!"

I push my way forward, and the first thing I see when I break through the crowd is Phyllis, stiff and bloated with rage, barring the exit against Thomasina and Noah. She's wearing a small round hat, dark coat, and dark pumps; her hair is tightly curled and sprayed. She looks like a woman who has worked hard, sacrificed much, asked for little, and played by the rules. A woman, therefore, who considers bitterness her right. One hand clutches a small black purse close to her chest; the other has apparently just shoved Thomasina.

"How dare you walk in front of us! How dare you come here at all! You ruined my son—he was never the same after he went with you. And now you barge in here and take the first pew as though you were his wife. Why did you come? You don't belong here! You have no right to walk in front of us!"

I wince. I see Noah stiffen. Thomasina reaches for his hand. Dozens of people are watching, and no one makes a sound.

At this point Ned's father, standing slightly behind his wife, snaps out of his dazed disbelief and steps forward, takes Phyllis by the elbow, and steers her to the door. She stumbles out, her face painfully red, calling over her shoulder, "Look at you! You come into a church dressed that way—like a slut! I don't care if I burn in hell for saying—"

The massive door closes on her voice, and the crowd stands stock-still for a moment. Then people begin to move again, to dip their fingers into the holy water and make the sign of the cross with bowed heads and mumbled prayers. It's as if they've decided that whatever just happened maybe didn't. Or, if it did, it can't be helped now. Nevertheless, in their exodus, they leave a good five feet of empty space around Thomasina and Noah, who stand just where they were, like two human statues on a square of marble lawn.

"Thomasina—" I touch her arm.

"It's fine, Pirio. I can handle this," she says in a firm voice.

Her eyes are fixed on the door. Beyond it, there'll be a gauntlet of stone stairs she must walk down. Followed by a crowded sidewalk and a corner at which small groups of people will be talking. Stares, whispers, smirks. Then the car ride home with a bereaved, repudiated ten-year-old. But, yes, she'll handle it. Walk through the crowd without showing any emotion. Make up something vague and almost believable to tell Noah about what just happened. *It's not your fault. It's mine. Your grandparents don't like me very much. Silly, isn't it?* Nobody could meet this challenge better than Thomasina. She'll even make it look easy. But tonight when she's alone she'll reach for the Stolichnaya again, instead of her usual wine. Polish off a fifth with a vengeance and pass out on the couch, where Noah will find her in the morning and briefly have to wonder if she's still alive.

She inhales deeply, firmly grasps Noah's hand; he glances at me in fearful confusion, and I nod encouragement. So they go, backs erect, eyes straight ahead. A man holds the door for them, but looks away when they pass. Perhaps in cowardice, or simple pain, I linger in the foyer until it's empty. When I finally go outside, there's no sign of Thomasina and Noah or Phyllis and her family.

It's just dusk. The air has a muted violet tone. A fat white pigeon waddles toward me, tottering from side to side as if on legs of differing heights. In this light, its feathers appear luminescent. On an impulse I squat down, and the pigeon approaches my outstretched palm. It pecks at my fingers for a bit, and walks unhurriedly away.

This is the second strange thing that's happened to me recently. Last night I heard bagpipes in the middle of the night. I opened the window and leaned out. It was a peaceful song I'd never heard. I listened for a long time, and when I went back to bed, the music was still playing. I felt like the bagpipes were singing me back to sleep.

My pigeon flies to the top of the building across the street and disappears over its roof. A man is standing on the sidewalk just below that point. He's looking at me in troubled concentration. He's in his thirties, medium height, with a wide face, heavy black glasses, and curly brown hair that almost reaches his shoulders. He's got one hand in his pocket. There's a sense of decorum, of strength being reined in, words held back by pursed lips.

He crosses the street, ascends the steps briskly, sticks out his hand. "Larry Wozniak, old friend of Ned's."

I shake his hand—it's warm and dry. I realize I'm shaking his left hand with my left hand.

"Terrible, isn't it? He was so young." He seems to know he's mouthing platitudes.

I agree vaguely and proceed down the steps. It's been a long funeral, and I'm not in the mood for small talk.

"You were on the boat, right?" he hastily adds, following me. "I recognized you from the newspaper photo. I, uh . . . I wanted to know if . . . Were you and Ned, uh . . . ? How well did you know him?" He's flushed and floundering.

"If you're asking whether we were lovers, the answer is no. Friends, yes. But only to a point."

"Really?" He says this as though my answer were a lot more interesting than it was, and adjusts his steps to match mine. "What do you mean 'to a point'?"

"I mean that I'm friends with his ex-girlfriend and godmother to his kid. I went out on his lobster boat because he needed the help. It was a new boat, he was just getting started and hadn't found a regular stern man yet. It was a Saturday, and I had nothing else to do, so I agreed. I like to try new things."

"Oh, I didn't realize you're not an actual fisherman."

"No, just a pretend one. A fishing dilettante, you might say. Although once a person's been involved in a fatal tragedy at sea, I don't think that distinction should really matter."

"No, probably not." He appears chastened in a way that lets you know it's only momentary. "I guess Ned explained what to do."

"He taught me how to bait lobster traps before we left the harbor. Said he'd show me how to haul the pots on the way back. We were supposed to be home before dark."

"Did he ever say anything about why he wanted to switch to lobstering all of a sudden?"

"He worked on corporate factory trawlers and long-liners for twenty years. Maybe he got tired of spending weeks at sea hauling groundfish for a soulless corporation and wanted his own boat, his own little business. Makes sense to me."

"But he never said exactly why?"

"He wasn't into self-disclosure. He talked about the Red Sox, Bruins, and Patriots in depth. And the weather. As in, *Nice day, huh?* Or, *Looks like rain to me.*"

Larry has been weaving his way around lampposts and mailboxes, trying to stay abreast of me on the narrow sidewalk. He's wearing a ratty old trench coat over a dark gray pin-striped suit jacket, black T-shirt, and jeans. I think he could at least have found some nicer pants for the occasion. Sometimes it feels as if the whole world is giving up, going over to shabbiness. I guess I've got a bit of Phyllis in me.

"Why do you want to know all this?" I ask, my irritation mounting.

"Just curious, I guess. We fell out of touch. I didn't know what he was up to." Then, as if he just thought of it, he asks, "Can I walk you to your car?"

"We're here." I manually unlock the door of my Saab.

He shuffles his feet awkwardly. "One more thing: Did you, uh, did you see who hit you?"

"You mean the boat that ran us over?" I can't believe he's asking me this question right now.

His eyes slide sideways. "Yeah, did you happen to catch the name on the stern transom or any numbers on the side?"

"No, I didn't see the name. It was just a boat to me. A great big fucking boat."

Chapter 4

The second half of the ritual—the after-funeral party—takes place at Ned's favorite watering hole, Murphy's Pub. All of his friends are there, none of his immediate family. There's a buffet table with cold cuts, lasagna, garden salad, cakes. There's a DJ who's been told to play sixties, seventies, and eighties music—the songs Ned lived his life to. It's like a wedding reception, only without the happy kissing couple and the girls in horrid dresses. But everyone talks, laughs, cries, and drinks the same way, as if their lives depended on it, and it's a safe bet that many of them expect to make a long night of it, so that the rowdy hell that is in them can break loose if it wants to.

I see Noah and Thomasina sitting at the bar and make my way across the crowded room. Noah has been served a ham sandwich, chips, pickle, and Coke. The bluish shadows under his eyes and the fact that he's loosened his tie make him look like a tired banker. He seems relieved to be out of God's jurisdiction, but uncertain how to behave among grown-ups who are acting like unruly kids. Thomasina steals a maraschino cherry from the bartender's store and offers it to him. He refuses—he's a stickler for the rules—so she pops it into her mouth and lays the stem on her cocktail napkin. The glass in front of her is full of a clear liquid, tiny bubbles, and a lemon wedge. "Sparkling water," she informs me immediately, but her eyes slide sideways, because she knows it won't last.

Noah's looking at the baseball game on the TV above the bar. One of the guys watching the game passes Noah a bowl of peanuts and starts talking to him, man to man, about who's going to win. Noah moves to the stool closer to him so he can eat the peanuts and see the TV better, and I take his place. The man sitting on the other side of Thomasina has dark hair, smooth olive skin, and a youthful, feminine face. He's leaning toward her, paying close attention to the dramatic brunette in the skin-tight jeans. Between the music and the television, there's a lot of noise.

"Was she a bitch, or what?" Thomasina says. "I didn't say half of what came to mind. But when she ever put her hands on me . . . I could have killed her."

The dark-haired man says, "Killed who?"

"Phyllis Rizzo."

He finds this amusing, but doesn't speak.

"Honestly, Pirio. Can you believe she said that stuff in front of Noah?"

"In front of everyone," the man obligingly amends.

"Oh, well. Every funeral needs a scene," I say, hoping to move the conversation along.

A large man sidles up, his eyes locked on mine. It takes a few seconds for me to recognize John Oster, and then the bottom of my stomach falls away. *Whoosh.* Like an elevator plummeting twenty floors in two seconds. You can't help having this reaction when you suddenly run into someone you used to have intense sex with, no matter how long ago it was.

He's changed a lot in a decade. The flaming hair that used to fly around his head is thinner now and neatly buzzed, exposing the white skin of his skull. His hairline's crept back, too. John Oster's red hair used to be a reckless celebration, so I can't help seeing these changes as a loss. More sadly, all the once-sharp bodily angles are rounded, as if it had been decided by the gatekeepers of middle age that they'd be better off padded for their own protection by a layer of fleshy bubble wrap.

But he's still John Oster. The gunmetal flash in his eyes; the brash, square-to-the-world stance that seems to be taunting fate—these things are his alone. No one ever called him John: it was always Crazy John, Johnny O, or Oyster Man. He told more stories than Jesus, most of them about daredevil challenges and nick-of-time survival. About things that shouldn't have happened and did. About losers who got what they deserved. He was bitter, shocking, loyal, and often insincere. He had enemies, but many more friends who respected him for doing and saying the things they wished they could. Occasionally, I was granted glimpses of his soul. Angels and demons were doing battle in there. Most of the time the score was close; occasionally, however, the demons streaked ahead. You could see him getting out of control—the sudden spells of dark brooding; the petty, nasty cruelties; the vicious lack of self-respect. Women thought him sexy, but most of them stayed away.

He and Ned had grown up together in Southie and were never far apart. When Thomasina and Ned started going out, it seemed reasonable for Johnny and me to do the same. I was drinking a lot back then, even more than Thomasina, and didn't think too much about what I was doing, just bobbed along like a cork in whatever current was flowing, as long as it was fast. My relationship with John Oster had a kind of discordant poetry to it at first, lasted longer than I thought it would, predictably foundered when it hit our very significant differences, and got ugly at the end. I had heard news of him occasionally over the years, mostly from Ned. The two of them worked side by side on trawlers and purse seiners for a company called Ocean Catch up until Ned quit.

Johnny drapes a lazy arm around Thomasina's shoulders in a half-assed condolence hug, while keeping his eyes on me. "Howdy, stranger."

"I heard you got married," I say. "Congratulations."

"That's right. Four boys now. Keep us busy."

"Four? You don't waste time."

"Kevin, Sean, Riley, and Patrick. Not a dull moment at my house." But his eyes are saying something else. Like, there are a lot of dull moments.

"Will I have the pleasure?"

"They're home with the wife." A pause. "I heard you *didn't* get married."

"I like my freedom."

His eyes gleam. "Yeah. You always did."

That's the kind of statement that needs a wide berth, especially coming from an ex.

"You ever think about me?" he says bluntly.

"I try not to."

"I don't think about you either."

Thomasina, who's been following the conversation with strange delight, emits a kind of strangled bark.

"How about a dance anyway, for Ned and the good old days?" Johnny says.

It sounds about right to me. What else do you do at an Irish funeral but dance with a guy you used to fuck to honor the departed? We move onto the tiny parquet floor in the middle of the room. Only one other couple is there, swaying slowly to the sound of "Beast of Burden." I'm glad, actually. My body feels as if it's been locked inside a tomb, and I need to bring it back to life. Johnny lumbers for a while, then finds a groove. His eyes are half closed, and his skin is luridly tinted in the glow of the colored bulbs strung along the wall. It feels weirdly OK to be swaying across from him. Because I know he cared about Ned. Because he's grieving, too.

By this time others have joined us on the floor. I dance for a long time without stopping—with Johnny, with another guy, with Noah in his adorable tie. I whirl and let the music flow through me until it washes away all the tension I've been carrying. Thank-yous flow from my sore heart to the Band, Led Zeppelin, and the Rolling Stones.

The guy who introduced himself outside the church, Larry Something-or-other, is sitting at a table with a noisy group of Ned's fishing buddies. Most of them are in blue dress shirts with loosened blue striped ties. Blue-on-blue seems to be the color combo of choice for men who would rather be wearing something else. Larry isn't talking much. Maybe he doesn't approve of wild Irish funeral parties. Every so often he turns his head and watches me. Doesn't stare, just watches. Like I'm someone he's not personally interested in but needs to keep an eye on. A kid sister, maybe. It seems pretty obvious that we're going to speak to each other again before the evening is done.

Thomasina and Noah have moved to a large round table in the corner, away from the music. The dark-haired guy who had been sitting next to Thomasina at the bar is there, too, hunched over, leaning close to Noah, hands gesticulating in front of Noah's impassive face. I get a not-right feeling from it, pull up a chair, join their tête-à-tête.

"You gotta upgrade," the guy is saying. "These smartphones are so much better. You got a girlfriend yet, heh? You can text her all day with this thing." He points to a cell phone between them on the table—a flat black thing with a shiny display.

"I don't have a girlfriend. I'm in fifth grade," Noah says.

"Don't have a girlfriend? What's with that, bro? Gotta be some hot girls where you are. Anyway, you get a girlfriend, you'll impress the hell out of her with this thing. You go bowling or something, whatever you kids do, you keep it in your pocket, and when the time is right, you pull it out like it's nothing much. Her eyes will pop, I'm telling you." He turns the phone on, starts tapping through the touch screens. "Look: You got a computer, a phone, a camera, and Internet all in the same place. And your iPod—you just load it in. Books, too. Boom, just like that. You're reading William fucking Shakespeare while you're waiting for your Big Mac. Or your oil change. Whatever you want. One click, and it's all happening."

Noah looks at the guy thoughtfully, trying to figure him out. Reverts to manners when he has no luck. "Thank you very much, but I don't want an upgrade right now."

"It's free if you give me your old phone."

"I told you, I don't have it. My mom said I couldn't take it 'cause she didn't want me playing video games."

"You didn't leave it in the car, did you?"

Noah shakes his head.

"Well, it's a shame you can't get your hands on it, because you just missed the deal of a lifetime." The guy sweeps the new phone off the table and stows it in his pocket. "I would have traded fair and square. And, hey, when you find the old one, I still will. OK, little man? That a deal?"

"Hey, Noah," I say, eyeing the guy. "Who's your friend?"

"Max," Noah says heavily, as if the one syllable is one too many.

Max stretches out his hand, and we shake over Noah's head, but it's perfunctory. The fingers barely clutch mine.

"Pirio," I tell him, though he didn't ask.

"Say what?"

"Pirio." I enunciate slowly.

Max nods like he gets it, but looks bothered by the nominal challenge, and turns his attention back to Thomasina, who's chatting with others at the table.

Noah is drawing the stages of evolution in a notebook he brought with him. So far he's done one-cell organisms, amoebas, and some strange-looking fish.

"That one needs a mustache," I say, pointing.

"Whiskers, maybe," he says, humoring me.

"Wait. Do fish have whiskers?" I'm actually not sure.

"Pirio—" This could mean either yes or no.

"I think I saw whiskers on a fish in the aquarium. A blue, bulbous, bug-eyed guy with droopy jowls. Looked just like my uncle Fred."

"You don't have an Uncle Fred."

"How do you know? I could have six Uncle Freds back in Russia. All kick-dancing on the steppes, yelling *Oie!*"

"*Oie?*" he repeats, squinting.

"Russian for 'Hey, pretty lady, will you marry me?' "

Noah smiles.

It's work to get a smile from him, but worth the effort, because his face softens and turns beautiful.

"You want to go home now?" I ask.

He looks at me gratefully. "Yeah."

Two hours later Murphy's Pub is emptying out. Only three big round tables are still occupied by reveling mourners. The DJ is playing sad-sack tunes; the same couple has been shuffling on the dance floor for an hour, collapsed into each other, either drunk or half asleep; and two disheveled women are in the corner crying loudly like it's a job they've been hired to do. Only crumbs are left on the buffet table— cake plates with nothing on them but plastic knives coated with sticky clumps of icing, salad bowls with limp, oil-smeared lettuce clinging to the rims. A half hour ago the bartender put about twenty shots of Irish whiskey on the bar for whoever wanted one—his spiritual offering to his old pal Ned. A bunch of people gathered round, raised the glasses, took a big religious swallow, and felt the holy burn.

Thomasina, Max, Johnny, some other people, and I are sitting together at a big table. Noah's been dropped at home with a babysitter, and Thomasina's slipped off her high-heeled boots and long since switched to vodka on the rocks. The guy sitting next to me leaves. Larry approaches the table, asks if he can sit down. I say sure and ask what took him so long. He says he was waiting for a seat to open up next to me. An answer worthy of respect.

We give conversation another shot. Somehow we get onto skiing, which he likes, roll over onto fishing, which he doesn't like (too boring), and spiral around some other topics of no importance. If he gets too personal, I say something flippant. If I get too personal, he changes the subject. We spend some time suspended in this weird ballet.

Thomasina bobs her head in our direction. The glimmer in her eye lets me know she's sized up Larry and found him to be acceptable dating material—whether for herself or me it's hard to say.

"What's your name?" she calls out, as if he's at the other end of an airplane hangar. The vodka's anesthetized the part of her brain that judges distances.

"Larry," he calls back good-naturedly, joining her in the fun of distant greetings.

"Larry? Larry? You're kidding me! *Larry* rhymes with *marry*!" She's delighted, lets a sly glance sweep across us both. Her drunkenness is so obvious and endearing in its way that she can get away with saying infantile things like this. She points to Max, who's got a rapt face turned toward her trust-fund body, which curves like a nubile dollar sign. "And what do you think of *this* guy, Pirio? He's way cute, isn't he? Max, Max, Max!" she crows.

If you stopped her in this moment and checked to see what's in her brain, you'd probably find a photo of a brilliant white, double-whammy wedding atop the caption *Pirio and Thomasina Find Decent Guys and Settle Down to Happy Lives at Last.*

Max takes her show of enthusiasm as an opportunity to kiss her dramatically on the cheek. She throws her arms around him like he's Daddy home from work. "I can't believe how much I already like you," she says.

I take a closer look. Max is as quick and trim as a featherweight boxer, with restless eyes, and a dimple that flashes on and off. There's a sense of excited distractibility about him. He's constantly in motion: an eyebrow peaks, his hands speak, his knee bounces. He whispers something in her ear that makes her laugh. I immediately try to gauge how he would treat a child—specifically, an emotionally complex ten-year-old with a genius-level IQ. The thought is too depressing to continue.

Thomasina swats Max playfully for whatever indecency he proposed, then leans across my lap to have a pseudo-intimate talk with our newfound fourth. "Have you ever been in love, Larry?"

"Once or twice," he admits.

"That's all? Crazy boy! I've been in love a *hundred* times." She sweeps her arms out as if to embrace the world, then leans forward again cozily. "But never for real. Real, true love. But maybe this guy's the one, huh?" She jabs a cocked thumb at Max, who is looking on with glee. "Stranger things have happened. You meet a guy at your not-husband's funeral. . . . So? Maybe not kosher, you say. But I say, what's wrong with that? You gotta meet him *somewhere*, right? *The funeral-baked meats did coldly furnish forth the marriage table.* That's Shakespeare, in case you're wondering. I used to know a lot of Shakespeare. And not just *Out, damned spot!* and *My kingdom for a horse.* Hey, you want to know what this guy's totally complete name is?"

Larry produces a look of interest.

"Maxwell Little-Pierce. That's his real, true name. Mr. Maximum, I call him. Max-i-*yum*. Descended from the *Mayflower*." She rears back and raises her index finger to make her next point professorial. "And *that* was a hell of a boat!" Such a sterling idea requires a long belt of vodka.

Larry, to his credit, doesn't comment, letting Thomasina veer off to other subjects. Johnny has been watching all this silently, occasionally tipping a beer bottle to his mouth. His chair is pulled back a little and cocked at an odd angle to the table in a way that seems both aloof and mildly threatening.

A heavy sadness settles over me as Thomasina continues to rant.

Max nuzzles her, she shoves him away, tries to pull him back by balling the front of his sweater in her hand.

"Whoa! Hold on there, lady. You'll stretch it!" he says in mock outrage, and leans in for a kiss.

That turns out to be as much as I can take. I say my good-byes, and Larry pushes back his chair and stands up, apparently ready to leave as well.

In a cold sober voice that travels straight across the table, Johnny says, "Hold on there, Larry. It's Larry, right? You never told us how you knew Ned."

The question seems to startle Larry. He delays a beat too long, says they went to school together. "A long time ago," he adds, with a self-mocking laugh, resting the fingers of one hand lightly on the back of his chair.

"Really? Where?" Oyster Man's not going to let him off the hook.

Larry looks around the bar as if trying to get his geographic bearings. "Uh . . . South Boston High."

The table goes silent.

"*What?*" I stare at Larry in disgust.

"Oh, honey," Thomasina slurs. "My not-husband went to BC High on a basketball scholarship. Even the ducklings on the Common know that."

The look Johnny is giving Larry right now could make the duck pond freeze.

Larry doesn't deny or try to explain. He follows me to the door.

The coats are a jumbled mess, hanging on hooks and fallen to the floor in the tiny coatroom. I find mine and, while I'm putting it on, Larry says, "I was wondering . . . before you go . . ."

Well, hell-on-a-stick, I think, *the shameless bastard's going to ask me out.*

There's no excuse for what I start thinking now, but there are mitigating factors: I'm lonely, I'm sad, I fear death by drowning, and I've got survivor's guilt. That's probably why I start thinking about love, and how it's escaped me, and how I never believed in it anyway. Friendship, maybe. Eroticism, definitely. Finding those two things in the same person would be more than enough for me. But romantic love, *true* love, the kind of thing Thomasina's gushing about? No, not really. Nothing more than *égoïsm à deux*. The simple fact that it's easier while drunk ought to raise some alarms. Not that I haven't experienced something like it once or twice, been swept away, lost my sense, felt the thatched hut of my heart grow into a palace overnight. But the palace was ransacked every time, the grand halls laid to waste. My latest debacle, with a guy who turned out to be married, is still making me feel like shit. So with cold eyes I look at Liar Larry standing there with his question about to be asked, roll a big fat *No* onto the tip of my tongue, and get ready to deliver it.

But instead of asking me out, he asks what kind of food I like. His is the slow approach.

I tell him I like all kinds. Food is a gift from the gods, and I don't play favorites.

He tells me he cooks Indian. Makes a good chicken korma.

I congratulate him while I button my coat. He better ask fast because I'm about to slip out the door.

"Would you—?"

"No! Because you lied. You didn't go to school with Ned."

"Elementary school, not high school."

"No, no, no. You didn't say elementary school. You said South Boston *High*. And you don't have a Boston accent. If you're going to impersonate a townie, you could at least learn to say *cahhhh*."

He holds his eyes steady. Doesn't reply.

"Are you some kind of ambulance chaser? Personal injury lawyer? Or just a fucked-up party crasher?"

"Look, I was wondering, if you ever want to talk about what happened out there—"

"Out where?"

"On the ocean. If you recall any details—"

"Jesus, you *are* an ambulance chaser, aren't you? What, are you going to give me your card now? What kind of scumbag are you? You come to a *funeral* and do this?"

"I guess I deserve that." He blinks slowly. Embarrassed, but taking the heat. "Here's my number in case you want to talk later. In case there's anything, anything at all, you want to say."

His left hand gives me a slip of paper. I notice now that his right hand doesn't move much. It's not like raw meat dangling off the end of his arm; it's more like a small package he's holding close to his side. It's a testament to his subtlety that I didn't notice the paralysis before.

I don't feel sorry for him. Pity is an insult. And I'm royally pissed. I shove the slip of paper in my pocket and go out the door.

A cool, wet night. The neon shamrock above the pub reflects in a sidewalk puddle. At the deserted intersection, a traffic signal blinks to red. I cross the street, walk and breathe, walk and breathe. These days if I'm not hearing strains of bagpipe music or befriending pigeons, I'm angry—at big things, little things, everything. Surviving should make a person grateful to be alive, and I am. But I'm angry also, like some part of myself I really needed was stolen out there on the Atlantic, and now I'm some kind of cripple, too.

At the end of the block, I look over my shoulder. He's standing on the sidewalk, his collar up, his eyeglass lenses glinting. He turns slightly, pretending that he wasn't watching me walk away.

Chapter 5

Home from work the next evening, I reach absentmindedly for the ringing telephone on the kitchen counter, but when I glance at caller ID, my hand freezes in midair. He's a little late with the condolences, the congratulations for being alive. But then I'm surprised he'd call at all, given the things that were said the last time we saw each other. As he pointed out (always quick with this), he'd never promised *blah, blah, blah*. . . . All he owed me was honesty. I countered with "Analyze this koan: The cheating husband speaks of honesty."

I don't pick up the phone, and he starts leaving a message: "Pirio? Pirio? Are you there? I saw the news—sorry I didn't call earlier. Just wanted to check in, make sure you're all right. Don't be mad forever, OK? Don't act like what we had was nothing. It was precious, special. You know it was. I care about you, think about you all the time. At least let me know you're all right—"

His voice feels like dusk in August, when the warm day meets the cool night and they kiss. From the portal of my ear, it spreads into every part of me, ripples along every inch of skin. The mind, they say, is plastic—always dismantling and remaking itself. I am waiting for

40

the day when it dismantles my memory of the thrill and contentment, the illusory *completion*, I felt for a short time with him.

I hit the delete button before he can finish, and for a while I just stand there looking at the mute answering machine on the counter. It lies there flat and black, ugly as roadkill. The familiar ache in my chest begins. I must not call him back.

Desperate for distraction, I turn to the pile of mail that I brought up with me from my mailbox in the foyer, and immediately start thumbing through a home-and-garden catalog. Wistfully, I imagine a life in the country, where I could have a shed, a wheelbarrow, and digging tools such as a bulb planter. It is a short step until I see myself presiding over fields of blooming tulips—flower farming must be a very uplifting career. But soon the glossy pages bore me, and I dump the catalog unceremoniously into the recycle bin. Then stop short.

I'm looking at a white letter-size envelope with an embossed seal in the corner, return address in four lines of dark blue traditional font: Navy Experimental Diving Unit, U.S. Naval Sea Systems Command, U.S. Naval Support Activity, Panama City, FL. My first reaction is paranoia: I did something wrong. My second thought is that they want something from me.

Dear Ms. Kasparov,

Please accept our condolences regarding the tragic loss of Mr. Edward Rizzo, captain of the fishing vessel *Molly Jones* coming out of South Boston, MA.

It has come to our attention that in the course of this disaster you survived ocean temperatures of 42–48 degrees Fahrenheit for a period of four hours.

The Navy Experimental Diving Unit (NEDU) is the most credible and respected research, development, and test and evaluation center for diving, as well as the focal point of leadership for biomedical and bioengineering solutions for undersea military operations.

We are interested in knowing more about the circumstances of your survival and your body's ability to withstand extreme conditions. Our research into this area suggests that there may be distinct biochemical pathways and neurologic functions that contribute to an enhanced physiological response. We are currently in the process of trying to identify these functions to aid in the selection and training of military personnel.

We would appreciate it if you would submit to a complete physical exam, stress test, and DNA screening in our Panama City headquarters. Results will be kept strictly confidential and used for scientific purposes only.

Please contact our office at your earliest convenience to make arrangements. Travel and accommodation will be paid for by the U.S. Navy. We will also be able to offer a small honorarium for your participation in military research.

Thank you for your service to our country.

Yours sincerely,
Commander Audrey Stockwell

I have to read the letter several times. Is this for real? Did I just go from being a lucky local girl on a morning talk show to a potential secret weapon for the USA?

I google Panama City and see photographs of a sparkling bay and sandy beaches, two-story buildings with charming façades, cars devoid of rust, palm trees like sculptures of palm trees, ready to be molded in plastic miniatures and placed on cold northern windowsills as proof of the tropics. Average September temperature: 83 degrees.

I've never been a big fan of the military. Nothing against it, just never wanted to participate in the whole warfare thing. But I'm pretty sure there isn't going to be a comfortable way out of this—duty to my country and so on—and I need to do something to stop myself from picking up the phone when he calls again. At least in Florida there'll be sunshine to keep me warm.

Two enormous gray eyes stare at me. The irises are circled by a darker rim, and black liner has been heavily penciled along the upper and lower lids. Together the eyeliner and the irises' dark rim make almost concentric circles around the pupils. The effect is hypnotic. If you look into these eyes long enough, you begin to feel as if you could fall in.

The hair is white blond and cropped all around to about an inch from the skull. On the crown a few cowlicks are standing shock-straight. This is obviously not a conventional woman. She is sitting on a park bench in falling snow, wearing a long bulky coat. The background of the photo is flat and fuzzy, overexposed. You can just make out two rows of dark evergreens stretching into the distance, a white corridor between them, pristine and cold. Tiny snowflakes have settled on the shoulders of the woman's coat and glisten in her hair. The top half of the coat is partway open, showing that she is naked underneath. Her breasts are small, very white, and gently round, the nipples hidden by the coat's lapels.

Scrawled across the bottom of the photograph in a loose, handwritten script like a celebrity's autograph is the caption: *L'Amour du Nord. From Inessa Mark.* This was the ad and the fragrance that brought my mother's fledgling perfume company national attention and, eventually, international success.

The photograph is huge; it occupies an entire wall in the entranceway of Milosa's Beacon Hill town house. I believe that at first he kept it displayed to intimidate his bimbos. He thought that as soon as they saw her famous, haunted beauty, they would realize that no matter how hard they tried, they would never rise to the level of his first and probably only love. I don't think any of them cared. They seemed happy enough to be one-night or weekend guests of Milosa Kasparov, whom they called Mike.

Maureen was different—more intelligent, more ambitious. As the young director of marketing, she was the logical choice to take over the company's day-to-day operations when my mother died. She became Inessa Mark, Inc.'s steady hand as Milosa indulged in several years of depressed debauchery that ended with his marriage to her. She saved the company; she saved him. She clearly deserves more credit than I'm willing to give.

Now she approaches, holding out a long-stemmed glass of white wine. Perfectly chilled, it cools the palm of my hand. Maureen's face is a dainty inverted triangle; her hands are small as a girl's. She stands next to me companionably, her head tilted in casual appraisal of her predecessor. "She certainly was lovely, wasn't she?"

Maureen stretches her words out so long you have no choice but to hang on them. The languid cadence feels slightly southern, even though she was raised in an ordinary suburb of Boston, the kind of place that flattens people with its plotted comforts and unease.

"But those bulky coats were not the most attractive style, don't you agree?" She arches an eyebrow at me as though we're sisters who care about such things.

Style is something that Maureen has spent her adult life trying to set. Style in scent, in furnishings, in dress. At the moment she's wearing a satiny dark green sheath over bare legs, and ballet flats, no doubt donned for dinner. Usually, she goes barefoot in the house, but always in a dress. She must have a hundred dresses in her closet, most of them slightly costumey, like Barbie's. She tends to package herself like a birthday present, with bows and belts and matching thises and thats.

"I like bulky coats," I say.

My mother's will left her majority share of Inessa Mark, Inc., entirely to her husband, with a few conditions—first, that if I wanted it, her share would come to me on my twenty-first birthday, and, second, that again if I wanted it, full ownership of the company would revert to me upon his death. Of course I wanted it. To me, Inessa Mark, Inc., is my mother, my connection to my mother, and my destiny. It's a sacred trust that's given my life purpose and direction, and saved me from the typical flounderings of my twenty-something peers. After working part-time at the company doing lower-level jobs while I was studying at UMass, I was glad to move to a full-time management position when I got my degree. Milosa set about teaching me the business end of things, and as my skill and confidence increased, he gradually pulled back. It was never the company he loved anyway; it was my mother. These days he comes into the Boylston Street office no more than a few times a week, while Maureen keeps everything running smoothly, just as she's always done. It often strikes me as odd and amazing that three such different individuals, with such complicated webs of tension running among them, nevertheless manage to work together reasonably well.

Jeffrey, our cook and housekeeper, announces that dinner is ready, and Maureen and I move into the dining room. The table is spread with an impressive amount of china, silver, and crystal. There's a small crowd of Wedgwood plates and Waterford glasses at each setting, two lavishly twisting candelabras, a centerpiece of gorgeous white lilies in a cut-glass vase. The walls of the room are painted pea-ish green, an authentically colonial color, and a threadbare oriental rug stretches across the floor. Royal Doulton figurines people the shelves of the Queen Anne sideboard, while gold silk drapes with tasseled swags adorn the two windows that open onto the historic cobblestone street where darkness has fallen. Every time I enter this bastion of stilted tradition, I want to scream. Although he would strenuously deny it, and often acts (pouring on the brio) as if the exact opposite were true,

Milosa is deeply ashamed of his impoverished Russian origins. So he out-Cabots the Cabots, out-Brahmins the Brahmins. Beacon Hill never saw a more loyal bastard son than he.

Maureen and I take our places at the table—Maureen at one end, me in the middle. Milosa's place remains unoccupied. He always comes to dinner last: keeping people waiting is his way of establishing dominance. Jeffrey announces the menu: swordfish with sun-dried tomato and black olive paste, garlic risotto, green beans amandine, and rustica from a nearby bakery.

"Jeffrey, the curtains," Maureen says, wagging her index finger slightly.

He pulls them closed and hurries out of the dining room, the bright tea towel that he uses to wipe his hands flapping from the back pocket of his jeans. In a few seconds he's back, carrying two small plates. Jumbo shrimp on beds of crushed ice next to silver bowls of cocktail sauce and horseradish.

Maureen waves the plates away. "Let's hold off on the appetizers until Mr. Kasparov is seated."

Jeffrey gives me a look that says *Oh, please.*

Milosa's footsteps are audible on the stairs. When he enters the dining room, Jeffrey plunks Maureen's shrimp plate in front of her. Milosa takes his seat, and the three of us shake out our linen napkins and place them in our laps.

"What happened to you is extraordinary," my father tells me. He speaks with a Russian accent, and he always gets right to the point. I haven't seen him since the accident. It was Maureen, as usual, who arranged this dinner.

He picks up a pink shrimp with his fingers, inspects it, puts it whole into his mouth. He believes the hard tail end of the shrimp that most people leave on the plate is good for one's digestion. His jaws crunch the shell slowly, with a rotating motion like a goat's.

"And of course we're sorry about your friend," Maureen adds. One of her most cherished delusions is that she and Milosa share a common set of emotions.

"How did you manage to survive?" Milosa asks.

I have to smile. This is always his question: *How?* He'd never think to ask God why there is human suffering. He'd want to know how the universe was made. And he'd pay close attention to the answer because in the back of his mind he'd be wondering if he could do it himself. His pale eyes right now are murderously inquisitive, awaiting my response.

"I have no idea."

Maureen laughs as though I've said something charming. "You must be a good swimmer."

"Decent, I guess. I do a mile three times a week at the Y. But you know that."

"Of course. Silly of me to forget."

Milosa looks directly into my eyes. "Like a cat, you escaped death. You must have done something."

"I lay across a piece of wreckage and floated for hours."

"No. If you were passive, you would have died. Maybe it was just a thought or a decision. But you did *something* to survive."

Spritzing lemon on my shrimp, I say that I got very cold and very wet, and the Coast Guard picked me up.

He glances at me in sharp disgust. *"Vy ne byli gotovy umeret,'"* he insists. *You weren't ready to die.*

I realize that Milosa has a hidden, irrational belief that he wants my experience to confirm: Not that I, Pirio, wasn't ready to die. But that one doesn't have to die until one is ready. That sufficiently stubborn individuals can call the shots. Individuals like himself.

He brings another curled shrimp to his mouth, and I notice that his eyes are unusually dull and glassy. At seventy, Milosa could easily be mistaken for a much younger man. He stays fit with squash and swimming (he taught me when I was a child), and takes a regimen of dietary supplements that costs more per day than most families pay for food in a week. Every three months he goes to one of the most elite doctors in Boston for a full battery of expensive tests that all show him to be in perfect health. Milosa is terribly afraid of dying. He can't abide the prospect of defeat.

"Oh, let's not talk about those things," Maureen says with a little shudder.

She announces that her new product line for teenage girls is coming along nicely. (Whenever we Kasparovs encounter emotional challenges, we start talking about work.) She intends to call it Sweet Surprise. It will be fruity—top note of grapefruit, bottom note of mango. Fresh and sassy, happy and brash. Target market: preteens and teens, thus inexpensive and gaily packaged in watermelon pinks and greens. First market entry: an eau de toilette, followed in quick succession by several flankers—a gel, talcum, and body wash, with possible spin-offs into facial soap and the kind of tubed lip gloss teenage girls are never without. All of it sold in drugstore chains with free scratch-and-sniff cards and a stand-alone display. Soon to be decided: the final formula, on which will depend the manufacturing schedule and launch date. Maureen's fondest wish now is for a famous celebrity face.

I agree to come to the meeting to finalize the formula when she's ready.

"Remember, we're talking preteens and teens," she reminds me.

"In other words, fruity."

"Exactly." She seems relieved that I'm on board and shoots an anxious glance to Milosa, who hasn't said a word.

Jeffrey has cleared the entrée dishes and served his famous low-fat lemon custard by the time Maureen and I finish discussing the new line.

Maureen looks at her husband for several pensive seconds. His shoulders are slumped down like a pigeon's, while his spoon clatters clumsily against the small china dessert bowl. The words on the tip of her tongue don't fall, and her face lengthens in apparent disappointment. She wants his support, his admiration, but knows she won't get it because she never has. He married her, but he doesn't love her, and has always kept his heart to himself. Shadows flit across her face, probably flashed memories of previous hurts. Her jaw clenches; she bites her lip. I've seen her get to this point before—struggling to adjust to the yawning emotional gulf that stretches between her and the man she's still trying to love.

Maureen hasn't touched the mildly caloric custard, and now she seems to find it repulsive. She throws her napkin on the table and lobs a sharp question at me while glaring at Milosa. "Do you suppose that if we found your mother's private fragrance, Pirio, your father would take an interest in *that*?"

Milosa picks up his head, looks at her blandly for a second or two, and proceeds to finish his dessert. Maureen storms out of the dining room.

Another family dinner at the Kasparovs'.

Soon after, Milosa leaves the dining room as well, and I'm left sipping the coffee that Jeffrey serves me, glad to have a few moments by myself. I've spent a fair amount of time trying to piece together my parents' story from random details I learned growing up, and from my own insistent questioning of people who knew them well. There has always been a great deal of secrecy around them, possibly rooted in shame. What I've learned so far goes like this: Milosa was born in a godforsaken village whose name he pretends to have forgotten, into a family he barely mentions. As soon as he could, he went off to Moscow, hungry for the spoils of capitalism. He says he started a modeling agency; it's more likely that he was a pimp. I've tried to get him to admit it, but he masterfully evades the question. In any case, one of his clients was a famous American designer, and soon he was supplying Slavic and Baltic beauties to the New York fashion world.

My mother was one of them, a six-foot, nineteen-year-old Estonian whose parents had been deported to Siberia during the Soviet occupation. She was raised in Tallinn by a brick-laying uncle who treated her badly in ways I can only guess. Like Milosa, she fled as soon as she was able.

They were ardent lovers from the beginning and remained so for two turbulent decades. Betting everything on her modeling career, they moved to the United States. They chose Boston, thinking they would have more peace here than in New York, but he grew bitterly jealous of her long absences, of her stratospheric rise, of so many desiring eyes upon her. The more he tried to control her, the more independent and mercurial she became, almost taunting him with her success. He wanted a traditional marriage; naturally, she refused. It wasn't until he understood her passion for creating scents, showed her the way to make her hobby a viable and then profitable business, that she in her late twenties agreed to a legal bond, achieving with my arrival a facsimile of a stable life.

If my mother was the heart and soul of Inessa Mark, Inc., he was the brains. He made her company happen, emphasis on *made*. His realm was in the shadows, where no one cared to look. He kept no records other than the minimum the government required, and these I suspect were mostly fictional. No one really knew what he was up to—it's likely that he had more than one business going on. We only saw the spectacular results.

Although my parents all but devoured each other in the realm of love, there is no doubt that their business partnership was as brilliant as they come.

The fact is that Milosa *would* take an interest if the formula for my mother's private fragrance was ever found. So would I. After creating L'Amour du Nord and some other perfumes for her line, Isa made a scent she never named. It was produced one bottle at a time at the factory in Grasse, according to a formula she didn't allow to be kept on file. It was her private fragrance, worn only by her. Professionals who knew it said it was exquisite, a scent that could rival the best of what was out there. A sure moneymaker, said some. I knew it only as the smell of my mother. I couldn't have separated the two. The fragrance belonged to her the way light belongs to a sparkling pool. The woman and the scent of the woman—both together made me feel happy, loved, and safe.

If only a few drops of the perfume had survived, we could have subjected it to a gas chromatograph and learned the formula. But when Isa died, the women Milosa hired to clean out her room took the last remaining bottle. When accused, they flatly and volubly denied it. It still rankles me that something so precious could have been lost that way. Now whenever someone at Inessa Mark mentions Isa's Scent, a moment of silence usually follows in honor of what might have been. It seems to me sometimes that what disappeared was not just a single perfume, but the possibility of her company someday becoming a true luxury house.

The ringing telephone wakes me. I grope for it.

"Who hit you?" Milosa asks without preamble. Normal words such as *Excuse me for calling at two a.m., but I have something really important to say* are not in his repertoire.

"What?"

"Who hit you? What ship?"

"Oh, that. I don't know." I rise to one elbow, turn on the light.

Grumbling sounds emerge from the receiver. Milosa gives a shallow cough. Rachmaninoff's Piano Concerto no. 2 is playing in the background. I'd recognize those brooding, passionate chords anywhere. He's obviously ensconced in his book-lined office on the third floor of the town house. I have no idea what he does up there, other than drink brandy, smoke cigars, listen to classical music, and play chess with his computer.

"How can you not know? There must have been an investigation," he says.

I tell him that the Coast Guard is looking into it.

"What do you mean, *looking into it*? This was a violent crime."

"Please, Milosa. It's the middle of the night."

"You believe those people? The Coast Guard?"

"Of course. Their job is figuring out stuff like this. It's what they do."

He whoops at my stupidity. Distrust of public officials is ingrained in the Russian psyche. "You're too trusting. Always, too trusting. You Americans are soft."

"No, we Americans just happen to live in a functioning society, where people are basically sane and rational." I get some satisfaction out of making him feel boorish, since he so often makes me feel naive.

"Ha! You know nothing of the world."

I swing my legs out from under the covers, rise to a seated position. "A little late for this kind of thing, don't you think?"

"You said it was a big boat, a freighter. How can it take so long to find a boat that size?"

"Size has nothing to do with it. There are procedures they have to follow that may be time-consuming, but in the end I'm sure they'll they get it done." Now I'm beginning to doubt it myself. It's been nine days, and no word from the Coast Guard. But I'm not about to let Milosa disturb my sleep with his dark, theatrical views.

"What are you going to do?" He plows right into this question as if the premise—that I'm supposed to do something—were already clearly established.

"What can I do?"

"You ask me what you can do?" One of his most irritating habits is the way he repeats the stupid question you just asked in a voice that makes it sound ten times stupider.

"What I'm saying, Milosa, is this: it's not my job."

A pause. He's letting me hear the fading notes of my passivity. "Remember *The Maltese Falcon*?"

Oh, another thing Milosa does in his third-floor study: he watches detective movies. Not thrillers, with their busty, panting women and trashy special effects. Detective movies, where the protagonist has to think.

"It's two a.m. What are you getting at?" I say.

"Sam Spade said, 'When a man's partner is killed, he's supposed to do something about it.'"

I groan. "Please, Milosa. Go to bed. Put down the brandy and go to bed." I hang up and turn out the light. Flop on the pillow, twist and turn, come to rest with a sigh, eyes wide open. The headlights of a passing car flicker across the ceiling. I wait for the next sweep of headlights. There it is. I start counting the number of cars that pass by on the street below. When I get to ten, I swear and fling back the covers. I shuffle to the kitchen, open the refrigerator door, stand barefoot in the spill of yellow light. *Sam Spade,* I think as I reach for the orange juice. *Jesus fucking Christ.*

Chapter 6

At nine in the morning, I call the Coast Guard from my office at Inessa Mark. I'm put through to Captain Anthony Cavalieri, chief of staff of the U.S. Coast Guard First District. He apologizes for not having gotten in touch with me before this. The initial accident report, dated September 7, has been reviewed. There are some complications, some concerns. He'd like me to come down to the station to make a more detailed statement. He bumps me back to his secretary, who tells me that he has an opening in his schedule at three o'clock.

My stomach knots. *Complications, concerns.* Every day since the collision I've been expecting the Coast Guard to call with news that they'd found the freighter and that official sanctions were being enforced. Instead, I discover that mysterious problems have cropped up, and no one even bothered to let me know. I'm glad that I dressed for work carefully this morning: a black wool below-the-knee dress over black tights and ankle boots in soft hunter-green suede. An indigo Jil Sander single-breasted coat with a demure round collar, Mikimoto pearl earrings, hair in a smooth bun at the nape of my neck. Clothes (except the boots) that might remind me to behave myself.

I skip out of work in the afternoon, and on my way downtown I try

to remember what I said the day of the accident, when I was interviewed for an hour by a shy officer with strawberry-blond curls and
endearingly chubby hands. He asked question after question, sometimes circling back to ask the same question again in a slightly different form, which made me wonder later if he'd been trained in interview
techniques. It seemed that he was jotting down volumes of information, more information than I was actually providing, studying me
occasionally with pink-rimmed, brotherly eyes.

I have no idea what I told him. I felt loopy, as if I'd drunk a few
glasses of champagne. I knew they hadn't found Ned, but what that
meant hadn't sunk in. Instead, the foggily pleasant thought that he
was bound to turn up soon intermittently crossed my mind. When I
saw him, we'd laugh in relief. What a day we had! The miraculous-
ness of my own rescue wasn't apparent to me either at that point. I
liked that the guys were making a big fuss over me, but why they
kept telling me I was amazing was anyone's guess. I'd been given a
spare Coast Guard uniform that felt like love. A warm blanket was
draped across my shoulders. Everything was sweet and nifty in my
book, even the watery hot chocolate my interviewer served me in a
paper cup.

By the time he flexed his dimpled knuckles and assured me that a
thorough investigation would commence immediately, I was ready to
be handed a stuffed animal and tucked into bed. I had no brain cells
left to pay attention to the procedure he explained—something
involving ships' logs, physical evidence, and an official-sounding
agency. All I heard was that I was to go home and not worry. That
sounded pretty good.

My old Saab courses down Stuart Street, through Chinatown, to
the waterfront, up Atlantic Avenue to the North End. It's a chilly gray
day in Boston. They usually are. I park in a garage, cross tides of tour-
ists strolling along the wharves. The Coast Guard building is a plain
brick square with some glass-and-steel triangular structures popping

out of the top. Minus those modernist architectural oddities, it's as clean and upright as a buzz cut on a skull of tar.

I looked up Cavalieri on the Internet this morning, so when he introduces himself it's like meeting someone I already know. The posted picture was kind, and about ten years out of date. In person, his eyes are closer set, his cleft chin less cleft, and his neck not so beefy. His office is as depressingly functional as everything else in the building.

"I'm sorry about Mr. Rizzo," Cavalieri says as he ushers me to a seat. He walks behind his desk. He is trying not to check me out but can't help it, and he's not sophisticated enough to be furtive. He must like what he sees because when he sits down he's smiling way too much for someone who just delivered condolences.

"Four hours in forty-two-degree water. I've never heard anything like it. Not exactly a lot of fat on your bones either," he says, taking another opportunity to survey my body.

"I bruised a rib," I say, which is true. It still hurts.

His smile widens, as if my bruised rib only makes me more spectacular.

My rib, hearing its name, starts to ache.

"Twenty-seven hundred vessels pass through this harbor a year," Cavalieri explains. "That's roughly seven or eight ships a day. On September 7, three were in the area of the incident at the right time of day, but they were all within established shipping lanes, anywhere from three to six nautical miles from where you were picked up. We photographed the ships' hulls at the waterline a few days after the event and found no forensic evidence, no paint chips, scrapes, or dents. Written statements from the captain, chief officer, second officer, and chief engineer of each vessel were obtained and put on file. They all deny being involved in an accident. The ships' logs show nothing unusual and correspond as expected to the positions recorded by the Vessel Monitoring Systems. Satellite views are useless because of the fog."

He pauses. "The search turned up your boat's EPIRB—it had drifted a few miles by the time we found it."

"EPIRB?"

"A small device that's designed to emit a radio signal on being submerged in water. Unfortunately, the signals aren't always monitored as closely as they should be." He looks dutifully apologetic. "There wasn't much at the location of your recovery. Just some wooden wreckage, an uninflated life raft, and an oil slick. The raft probably didn't inflate because part of the sea-painter was wrapped around it."

"Sea-painter?"

"That's the line that attaches the life raft to the boat. A mistake due to inexperience is my guess. The *Molly Jones* was a brand-new boat, and I suspect Mr. Rizzo was unfamiliar with all the equipment on board." He shrugs. "The life raft wouldn't have done any good anyway if you were struck with little or no warning."

He sits back, loops his fingers together behind his head, elbows pointed out. He's done his job, and now it's as if he's waiting for the start of a movie he's been dying to see. He asks me to tell him what I remember.

I say I saw a big boat, but I don't know what kind. Thought it was a freighter, but it could have been a tanker or container ship. When I was in the water, looking back, I didn't see much more. The fog obliterated all but the portion of the ship that was crossing directly over the *Molly Jones*. I never saw what was on the deck, never even saw the deck, much less any identifying marks. I'm actually not sure of the general shape of the thing. The one thing I think I know is the color: gray.

"You *think* you know?" he repeats.

I nod.

"Gray," he repeats gingerly, as if he's trying out an unusual hors d'oeuvre.

Admittedly, that isn't much to go on.

Having read Cavalieri's Internet bio this morning, I know he's had vast seafaring experience. He's been an engineer aboard an ice-breaker, a commercial vessel inspector, instructor at the Coast Guard Training Center, a federal on-scene coordinator, a federal maritime security coordinator, and a search and rescue mission coordinator. My eyes glazed over as his titles and awards accumulated. For me the takeaway was this: Cavalieri's used to dealing with bad stuff and delivering bad news.

"Ms. Kasparov, I'm sorry to tell you this, but we're coming up short on this thing. Other than your eyewitness testimony, I don't even have proof that a collision occurred."

"What do you mean, *other than my eyewitness testimony*? Isn't that enough?"

"Of course. What I'm saying is, I have no hard evidence of a collision. I can't corroborate your story."

"My *story*?" This is worse than I thought it would be. "What sank the *Molly Jones* wasn't a story, Captain."

Cavalieri stands, paces behind his desk. He's not liking this any more than I am.

"At least one of those ships' logs must have been falsified," I insist heatedly. "Don't tell me it hasn't happened before."

"No, no." He waves away my question. "It happens. One degree off course is enough for a large vessel to slip outside the shipping lanes. Once they realize what happened, they adjust their course, but in the meantime they can't turn, can't maneuver, can't even slow down very well. The crews are notoriously inattentive, and they don't want to be blamed. There've been plenty of cases of maritime hit and run, especially with the foreign carriers, we suspect, and there are relatively simple ways to cover it up. I just wish I had more information to put in my report to the NTSB."

"Am I supposed to know what those letters mean?"

He hears the edge in my voice, eyes me warily in case I'm about to become hysterical. "National Transportation Safety Board. The governmental agency that deals with accidents at sea."

"You mean you don't do it?"

"The Coast Guard submits an initial report, but the NTSB carries out the investigation and files a final comprehensive report. Their version is the official story."

At the mention of the federal government, my worst fear turns into certainty. I'm now convinced that the ship that crushed the *Molly Jones* and took Ned's life will never be identified. This is when I realize I've been holding my breath for the last ten days, waiting for justice. Also truth, solace—whatever you want to call it. Wanting it not for my sake, but for Noah's. That day at Taffy's, when I tried to explain to him why his father died, and heard how flimsy and ridiculous the reasons sounded, I realized how important some kind of real explanation would be. Because if a child's parent has to be killed in a freak accident, that child deserves to see an aftermath of concern and accountability. He deserves, at minimum, an apology from the people who screwed up.

I ask Cavalieri how long the NTSB investigation will take.

"It depends on what they find. It could be anywhere from a couple of weeks to a couple of months, even a year if things get complicated. They're careful, and slow. Which reminds me—you can help by filling this out."

He takes a clipboard with some papers attached to it off the side of his desk and hands it to me. The top sheet is Form 157K3 Collision Report. It's several pages, small type, answers to be written in the spaces provided. For my convenience, a pen has been attached to the clipboard by a chain.

"I've already given you all the information I have."

"We need the forms for the file," he says, mildly apologetic. His voice turns smooth as he prepares to dismiss me. "I want to assure you that everything that can possibly be done is being done. I'll let you know the minute I get any new information."

"What about Mr. Rizzo's remains?"

"We're not equipped to find bodies in water that deep. The Navy could do it with special divers or an undersea robot, but they won't look unless it's part of a larger research project."

I stand so we're eyeball to eyeball. "What are the names of the three ships near the site of the collision on September 7?"

His chin pulls back a notch. He wasn't expecting this, but he's quick on his feet. "Let us take care of it, Ms. Kasparov."

"I want to know."

"I know this must be hard for you. . . ."

"I want to *know*."

He sizes me up again. He must be pretty sure at this point that I'm not going to be slipping off to a motel room with him after work, because he lets his voice dip to a cold governmental temperature. "I'm afraid I'm not at liberty to divulge that information."

"Why not? It's got to be public information. How could it not be?"

"The situation is sensitive," he replies, blinking slowly.

Ah, I see. He doesn't want me harassing captains, making accusations, clambering aboard restricted vessels, creating an international scene. I almost smile. He must think I'm just a woman in a black designer dress who'd rather be on Newbury Street shopping. "It's OK, Captain. I don't need your help. I'll find the ships myself."

A flinty light comes into Cavalieri's eyes. "As you wish."

He comes around the desk quickly and opens the door to his office. I see his secretary look away. He motions me to a bench in her area where presumably I am to fill out the form.

I leave his office, sit on the bench, and fume. If it were up to me, I'd leave the form on the bench and walk out. But for Noah's sake I pick up the pen.

The first section asks for a large amount of useless information about the crew members aboard the affected vessel. I don't even look at the rest. I crumple the paper in my hand, trusting Noah would understand. My hands are shaking, and I realize that I am roiling with stored trauma—enraged, powerless, and still terrified.

Cavalieri's secretary regards me with sympathy. "Go home. Leave the form. No one reads them anyway."

I sigh. Why are the reasonable people never the ones in charge? I place the clipboard on her desk, the wad of paper on top of it.

"He had a son, a very special kid. Maybe a genius, I don't know. His mom's an alcoholic. Now his dad's dead. What happens to a kid like that?"

"They survive somehow. Children are resilient."

I think about it carefully. "No, they're not. They're easily damaged and don't always recover."

She nods slightly, averts her eyes. Hardly anyone can think about that.

I walk out of her office toward the main entrance. I feel like kicking the fake potted plant in the empty vestibule, but I don't. That's the kind of acting out behavior I got in trouble for at the Gaston School. Detention, weekend house restriction, and so on. A teacher once told me that Fuck You was just a familiar place I ran to when I felt threatened, like a bed that a frightened little girl hides beneath. I said I understood that. Everyone wants safe harbor; hardly anyone gets it. But there's a big difference between the floor under a bed and Fuck You, I remember telling her. They're really not at all alike. The floor under a bed is dim and dusty. Fuck You is a hot, sharp place.

The sun is setting without much fanfare behind low clouds. I drive south, then east to the seaport district. Past the post office warehouse, a retail fish market, a trucking company, and a boat repair. To my left Boston Harbor is slick with oil. There are four or five large vessels in some kind of sluggish motion on its surface. Not one of them is silver or gray. Now I recall that the ship that hit the *Molly Jones* looked black at first, but it could have been dark blue. The silver could have been fog. Memories of the collision emerge in sketchy pieces and dissolve a minute later. The more I think about it, the less certain of anything I am.

Chapter 7

At six in the morning I'm at the YMCA for the first time since the accident. I stand on the edge of the pool and gaze apprehensively into the turquoise water. Knowing it's only five feet deep doesn't quell my fear. The other lanes are filled with before-work swimmers. I recognize most of them. We regulars don't talk to each other much, but we know who we are. A man in a Speedo comes out of the locker room, looks around, and takes a seat on the bench. He'll be first in line for the next lane that opens up. If I just keep standing here, he'll be rightfully impatient. I've either got to dive now or surrender the lane, and if I do that, the fear will chalk up a victory, and it will be twice as hard for me to come back.

So I dive. The first few laps are like reliving a nightmare (actually, I *am* reliving a nightmare), but then, slowly, it gets easier. My stroke comes back; my body starts to feel supple and strong. Rhythmic breathing soothes me, and the water gradually begins to feel like my natural element, like a perfect whole-body caress. Tears of gratitude seep out of my eyes. I'm OK. My old self is still here—the good, open, graceful me. For an hour I swim up and down my lane with increasing zeal. I love to swim. If I couldn't do this one thing, I don't know who I'd be.

I feel so good that when I get home I call in sick to work. Since I took the afternoon off yesterday, it seems only reasonable that I'd be sick today. In any case, since I'm the heir apparent, no one's going to question it. I get comfortable in sweat pants, make a big pot of coffee and a three-egg omelet, and flip on my computer. The hell with Cavalieri and his coy secrets. It can't be *that* hard to find three freighters.

I surf the net, entering terms as they occur to me: Boston Harbor, shipping lanes, collisions at sea, etc. I note cargo capacities and how to fill out a bill of lading. I discover the correct procedure for unloading a container vessel, the exact role of the customs officer, how a million tons of steel the size of a city block is supposed to navigate a complicated system of locks. I find out that 242 container ships, 32 auto vessels, 481 bulk cargo vessels, and 113 cruise vessels docked in Boston Harbor in 2012. At one point color pictures of rusted booty from the wreckage of an eighteenth-century Spanish galleon bob before my eyes. At another I come face to face with a coelacanth.

In other words, I find nothing to lead me to the ship that sank the *Molly Jones*, and become mentally numb in the process. I keep clicking, though. I figure I'm just looking in the wrong places, but I wouldn't know the right place if it froze on my computer screen. I read randomly, learn randomly, exit randomly. Go everywhere and nowhere. For several hours I do compulsive, soul-deadening battle with the Information Age.

I lose.

All right. Enough. I detach from my computer, clean the kitchen, put some laundry in. I gaze out my front window without really seeing the blue sky and tree-lined street. I need a human being, an insider. That's when I remember Johnny. At the funeral, he gave me his number and told me not to be shy if I needed anything. I'm not sure what he meant by that, but right now I feel like using the one contact in the fishing world I have. I call and leave a voice message on his cell. He calls back half an hour later, tells me to come to his house in Dorchester at four o'clock.

Back in the bad old days, whenever there was a full moon, Johnny and I would sit out on the jetty in Scituate where his parents had a summer house. We'd be bathed in yellow moonlight, swigging from a bottle of Jack Daniel's, and making up half-true things to tell each other. The tide would roll in, black waves crawling ever higher up the rocks, until frothy seawater crowded in on us. Finally we'd decide to head back to the beach, not knowing if a portion or all of the jetty was already submerged. We'd pick our way across slippery boulders as the waves smashed into them, shooting up jets of cold spray. We didn't talk much so as not to give away our fear. We could have been stranded, or any large wave could have knocked one of us off, but that was why we did it. The adrenaline rush of cozying up to danger. The closer we got to shore, the cockier we'd get and the faster we'd go. By the time we splashed into the shallow water, we'd be running, falling, dragging each other by the arms out of the low churning surf. Soaked to the bone, salt in our nostrils, we'd fall on the upper reaches of the beach, where the soft, sheltering dunes began, and pass the bottle until it was done.

We'd peel off our wet clothes and make love. We used to copulate with abandon, Johnny and me. Then fall back exhausted, two sand-encrusted amphibians under a distant moon. Some people are risk averse; others need risk to feel alive. Attraction to the edge was a mystery Johnny and I didn't have to explain to each other. So, yes, there was a certain bond. Destructive maybe, especially with the booze thrown in. But a bond is a bond. And when you're young and haven't yet learned to live in your own solitude, even a destructive bond can seem better than none.

He lives in a split-level ranch behind the district courthouse on a street where the trees, being recently planted, are only about eight feet high and the thickness of your wrist. I park next to a dented mailbox adorned with flower decals. As I approach the front door, I hear a brotherly dispute in progress. The jeers of the powerful, the heart-rending wail of the vanquished. Through an open window I can even hear Oyster Man talking at his sons with patient reasonableness, like a suburban Kofi Annan intent on bringing about détente and having just about the same amount of luck. It is said that world peace starts at home. If that's the case, we're all in serious trouble. I'm almost expecting a chair to come crashing through the window. One of the little darlings opens the door before I push the bell—he must have seen me coming. He snaps his nearly hairless eyelids at me and bellows "MAAAA!" down the hallway like an outraged goat.

Johnny's wife shuffles to the door. She is a tired, root-showing blonde in a stained cotton shirt that reveals that she is braless. I am surprised to feel that irrational jolt you get when you meet an ex-lover's lover. Like they shouldn't exist. But there she is—a woman whose lips have kissed John Oster's and whose womb has borne him four sons. Perhaps she senses something about me, because she doesn't seem to like me much.

Johnny appears behind her in a hallway crammed with gym bags, skateboards, and baseball bats. He ushers me to a door at the back of the house, his sons peering and scattering like rascally terriers, and we are released from the after-school, predinner pandemonium into a quiet garage with one half dedicated to what appears to be his reigning passion: birdhouses. An unfinished birdhouse is sitting on a work-table, and the rafters are hung with finished birdhouses big and small. One that looks like a Congregational church, one modeled on the Taj Mahal. Houses for single birds, houses for extended avian families. Lovingly crafted in different woods—pine, cherry, teak—some of them painted fancifully, some not.

Birdhouses? I never would have guessed. It's strangely moving to see how Johnny's fantastical, obsessive streak is being so harmlessly channeled now that he's a responsible citizen and family man.

"What's on your mind?" Perched on a high stool in front of his workbench, he looks me over, but doesn't allow his gaze to linger.

"I talked to Captain Cavalieri at the Coast Guard."

"Fucking asshole."

"Right. He said there were three freighters in the area of the *Molly Jones* on September 7, but there's no evidence to link them to the collision. He wouldn't give me their names."

Johnny smiles at me with a residue of affection and judgment. "So you want to find them yourself."

"Of course. Cavalieri's given up. He bumped the case to the National Travel Safety Board. It sounds like a lot of bureaucracy. He says it could take a year."

"Don't know what to tell you other than you gotta be patient. Not so easy for you, as I recall."

"Nor you."

"That's where you're wrong." He gestures toward his crammed shelves. "These birdhouses. They're teaching me patience. I've learned to bide my time."

I sit on a bench, lean back against a painted cement wall. There are curled wood shavings everywhere, giving off a sweet, saucy smell. "People must have talked about the collision. Fishermen, whoever. You must have heard something."

"All anyone talked about was you. Woman throws herself from sinking boat, swims around in Atlantic Ocean for longer than humanly possible. That news made the rounds of the barrooms, for sure. Another sea story like *The Perfect Storm* to entertain America. We're waiting for the book and movie to come out."

"Ned was the real hero." I have a compulsion to keep repeating this to whoever will listen. I can't get over the fact that Ned, who saved my life, is being turned into a footnote, while I, who did nothing, am becoming the stuff of legend.

Johnny's thick blunt fingers have begun assembling a tiny birdhouse chimney for a tiny birdhouse roof. He keeps his face turned slightly away from me, to pay attention to what he's doing but also, I suspect, to give us space. "Damn fingers don't always behave. It's frustrating. Part of my own body, but I swear they got a mind of their own."

"Come on. Be straight with me, Johnny. If anyone in this town knows something, it's you."

He gives a flattered chuckle, tries without success to get the chimney to stand up. "I'm way ahead of you, darlin'. Ned was my buddy, remember? You think I'd let him die that way without looking into it? I did my own investigation. Talked to anyone who might know something, and a dozen more guys just in case. Even went over to discuss the situation with that asshole Cavalieri, and let him treat me like shit, as I knew he would. The Coast Guard hates fishermen, in case you didn't know. What do you think I came up with after all that? Huh?" He turns to me. His face is a sheet of white paper on which nothing is written. "Damn thing was a hit-and-run. That's all. Just a bad, sad freak accident, with the perp disappearing as fast as he can. We can search all we want, but we ain't gonna find him. Sorry. That's the maritime world for you, sweetheart. Lots of thin air to vanish into. That's why every fuckup in the world is drawn to it."

There's pressure on my chest, like someone's standing on it.

He shoots me a crooked smile. "I know you don't want to hear that. But hit-and-run is the answer we both gotta live with right now. My advice is, let the feds waste all the time on it they want." He turns back to his workbench, picks up a tiny whittling knife. "And by the way, you're not going to be doing yourself any favors if you start asking around."

"So they're out there, whoever did it—"

"Well, sure. They gotta be out there somewhere, right?"

"How does somebody get away with a thing like that?"

"Easy. If they've got paint chips on their hull, they repaint right away. The VMS signal only gives a position once an hour, so as long as they're roughly where they're supposed to be when the signal goes off, they're safe. And the VMS malfunctions a lot, conveniently. I hate to clue you in, but it happens. No one wants to get in trouble. Bad publicity for the company, insurance claims. The captain out of a job. He'll cover it up if it's at all possible and think of it as a good day's work."

"What about the crew?"

"Same thing. Why should they give a shit? It only blackballs them if they say anything. Most of them will be glad to take a bribe if it's offered, and the rest don't friggin' care. Don't forget. The majority of these ships are foreign. You know the laws we have here?"

"In America?"

"No, I mean *on land.*"

"Uh-huh."

"Well, those laws don't apply on the ocean. It's a whole different world out there. Like the Wild West before there were sheriffs." He pauses, looks over at me with concern. "You all right?"

"I guess." I'm thinking of Noah. His trusting eyes, the whalebone in his pocket. How can I tell him the bad guys got away?

"What about that guy you were talking to? The one at the pub," Johnny says. He flicks his meaty thumb across the edge of the whittling knife to test its sharpness.

"Oh, him. I don't know him. He just appeared."

"Remember his name?"

"Larry, I think. Last name begins with a W."

"What did he want?"

"He asked some questions about the collision. Wanted to know if I could identify the ship and why Ned quit Ocean Catch."

"You tell him anything?"

"I said Ned got sick of corporate trawlers and wanted his own little business. That's what he told me."

"He tell you anything else?"

"I don't know. Like what?"

"Like why he got sick of Ocean Catch."

"No. I figured he just wanted a change."

"Yeah. That was it." Johnny starts shaving wood off a stick with the knife. "What about Thomasina? Did Ned talk to her much about his work?"

"I don't think so. Nothing she ever told me about anyway."

Johnny nods slowly, bent over his creation. A slice of the knife, and a splinter comes away, revealing tender white pulp.

I peer at a birdhouse on a shelf above his work area. A little arched entrance opens to an airy living room. There's a second floor, too— tiny slanted ceilings. Maybe an in-law suite. I do a double take, look closer. Someone painted a braided rug on the floor. Delicate, painstaking work that must have been done with the world's smallest brush. I start to get a creepy feeling. The mind that made these is not completely sane.

"You must spend a lot of time on these. When do you do them?" I ask.

"I get up at four. Don't sleep very well."

"Oh, yeah? Funny, I was up at four this morning, too. With me, it's stress. How about you?" I'm not sure I want to get this personal, but I'm curious. There's some kind of weird disconnect between the Johnny I knew and the one I'm talking to. For starters, the Johnny I knew wouldn't be so cozy with the term *hit-and-run*.

"Probably that. Don't know." He puffs out his chest, rolls his shoulders to work out the kinks. He squeezes glue from a tiny tube onto a Q-tip, examines the drop in the light. "Can't use too much. Smears, and then you have to chip it off."

There's yelling coming from the house. Stomping, a slammed door. "You know, I could fucking kill those little bastards sometimes. You're not supposed to feel that way about your kids. But sometimes I just want to bolt. How'd I get here anyway? Married, four kids. Nothing but bills everywhere I go. Sometimes I feel all fucked-up." He places the Q-tip carefully on a piece of newspaper, screws the top on the tube of glue. "I didn't like that guy at the pub. Him pretending to be a friend of Ned's. If he calls you, let me know."

"Why, what are you going to do?"

"Nothing, darlin'. Nothing at all."

Now I get the look, the eyes along my body that rise slowly to my face. "You look great, by the way. Always have." His voice gets softer, deeper. "My wife's so busy with the kids these days. I have a lot of freedom, lot of time to myself. I could take you out on my boat sometime."

"I'm not big on boats anymore."

He blinks slowly, not sure where to go with that. Am I declining the offer, or do I simply need a different vehicle of seduction? "Maybe a beer, then. Don't say no right away; think about it first. You seem lonely, Pirio. Always a loner, complicated. I never figured you out. But I know you must be hurting, and I always want to be there for you, lamb."

The endearment is disgusting for three reasons. First, because it's an endearment. Second, because his wife's inside the house, feeding hungry mouths and wiping sticky fingers. Third, because long ago Johnny used to call me *goat* and I used to call him *monkey*. The terms were not without their wisdom. A *lamb* I never was.

"I'll pass on that kind offer, ape."

He nods as if he expected nothing more.

I walk through the open garage door onto the smooth black-tar driveway. I pass a shiny red Lexus, get in my old car and pull away from the curb, thinking that, if nothing else, I'm off the hook with Milosa: Johnny did the Sam Spade thing, so I don't have to. It's a relief, sort of.

On the highway I'm stuck in rush-hour traffic. I play my favorite jazz pianist, Akiko Grace, and try to relax. But for once the beautiful music doesn't take my mind off my problems. As Sister Corita's painted gas tanks come into view, I flash on a vivid image of a guy in a crappy bar, throwing back his boilermaker and laughing like an idiot. So pleased with himself and his sterling career. Thinking he got away with leaving a little fishing boat in splinters and the human beings inside it to bob on the waves in terror until they sank. My hands grip the wheel so tightly that my knuckles whiten. It probably didn't occur to him that anyone would survive.

Chapter 8

Nothing's out of place; nothing's been moved. The last rays of sun slant through the vertical blinds the way they usually do on a September evening—long, honey-gold beams latticing the rug and coffee table. And yet. Something's off. A subtle scent hangs in the air. Just the merest whiff. A woody smell, but sour. An olfactory note foreign to my apartment.

Every home has its smell—a unique aromatic blend of male and female occupants, carpets, dirty and clean clothes, and the kinds of food the family tends to eat over and over again. Even the grass and trees outside the windows lend their influence. Children know this better than anyone. A child could pick out her own home by nothing but smell if she had to. This sensitivity is blunted in time. She stops trusting her nose, eventually stops using it. Eyes and ears take over, while smell, our most primitive sense, is relegated to the animals. That is, unless your mother was a perfumer who taught you that everything has a special smell as well as a look, sound, and feel—and that of all the senses, smell is the least likely to deceive.

That's why I'm sure someone's been in my apartment. If they'd stayed a bit longer or been there more recently, I might hazard a few guesses at their cologne's components. Right now all my nose can pick up is a few of the last, large, persistent molecules of a deep base note. I'm thinking oud wood or oak moss, which are common fragrance ingredients and don't even give me the wearer's likely gender. I close my eyes, try again. It's oud wood. Yes, I'm sure of it. Dark, soft, spicy, medicinal. The smell of South Asian religious rituals. To make oud wood oil, resin is drained from trees that have been infected with a parasitic mold—the distilled odor is legendary for its strength and longevity. You either love oud wood or hate it; and there's no confusing it with anything else.

Computer on the desk. Laptop in the closet. Everything just where I left it. What else is there to take? I go into the bedroom. My jewelry box is untouched. If it wasn't a burglary, what was it?

I'm suddenly panicked at the question of how an intruder got in. I'm on the third floor. There's a front door, a back door, and a fire escape. The back door has a chain, which is still intact. The fire escape is old and rusty and could not have been used without half the building knowing about it. Then I remember that I fiddled with the front door when I came home—thought I'd unlocked it, but it seemed to stick, so I locked and unlocked it a couple of times before I felt the bolt slide. The door must have been unlocked when I put my key in the first time. The intruder picked the lock to get in but didn't have the key to lock it when he or she left.

I go next door and ask my neighbor if she saw anyone. She's suspicious of everyone—has been known to report a car idling too long in the street. She says no. Then her eyes narrow, and her door inches a few more degrees toward closed. She's even suspicious of me.

I call the super, tell him someone was in my apartment. The baseball game's going in the background, so loud we have to shout. He tells me to call the cops. So I do. They'll send a car.

While I'm waiting, I retrace my steps, check all my valuables one more time. Nothing's missing. Maybe I'm wrong about the oud wood, but I swear I can still smell its traces in the air.

I wonder if someone was watching the apartment this afternoon and saw me leave. Maybe whoever it was is still out there. I sidle to the window. On Tappan Street cars are parallel parked along the curb. A couple strolling. A kid on a skateboard. Teenage girls with long hair and bulky scarves. Am I going to live this way now, watching everything like a hawk? I go to the back of my apartment, where the bathroom window overlooks the parking lot. Peer through the blind. Cars, the usual cars. That's all.

The cops fill the apartment with their big chests and beer guts, their snapped-shut leather holsters. Handcuffs, flashlights, nightsticks clanging in their belts. Loud, husky voices. *Hey, don't worry. It happens.* Like they've known me for years. They walk around being big and strong. Touch nothing, jot some fictitious notes. It's just another call for them.

"Didn't take anything, huh?" one of them says.

"No."

"Sure there was someone here?"

"There was a scent," I say. "Oud wood."

"What?"

"I know fragrance. I can tell."

"What wood?"

"Oud wood."

"Uh-huh." An exchange of glances. The memo pad's stuffed in a pocket. They're sure I'm a crackpot now. They tell me to change the locks, then leave the door wide open when they go.

I used to steal into my parents' room on Sunday mornings and watch my mother sleep. Milosa rose religiously at five to disappear into his life, so Isa would be alone on the king-size bed until she rose at noon or one. All week she would have been busy, coming and going, mostly going, a whirlwind of early mornings and late nights. Sunday morning was one of the few times she stayed in one place. She slept clumsily, almost aggressively, helter-skelter in the sheets.

Work and sleep, work and sleep. That was her cycle. No middle gear, no liminal time. All that changed every year in late June, on the eve of the summer solstice. It was Jaaniõhtu, a national holiday in her native Estonia, and my mother always chose that day to begin her monthlong summer vacation. In Estonia, the shops and businesses close, and people gather outside to sing, dance, and drink around bonfires that blaze all night. My mother's lonelier Americanized version of the holiday was to take me by plane to St. John's, Newfoundland, and from there by ferry and rented car up the coast of Labrador to a secluded house on the beach, close to the Hudson Strait. The house had been designed by its owner, an architect from Montreal who vacationed in it with his family every August and rented it to my mother in July. It was so far north that we wore jackets and sweaters, daytime lasted until nine or ten o'clock, and the night sky occasionally swirled with the eerie parabolas of the northern lights.

We'd buy groceries and gas at a little Inuit settlement called Hopedale. The next part of the journey—from Hopedale to the house—sticks in my mind as the longest, possibly because it consisted of bouncing crazily on narrow, deeply rutted roads that couldn't possibly have accommodated another car, had we ever met one, and were probably impassable when it snowed. When we finally rounded the last curve and the architect's creation rose in the dusty windshield, it looked to my tired eyes as splendid and unlikely as a storybook house.

The interior of the house smelled like what lay outside the windows—pine and birch forests, smooth gray rocks, the dark blue Labrador Sea. We spent much of our time on the cedar deck, reading or talking or playing go fish, my mother usually in a wide-brimmed hat, smoking occasionally, smiling easily and often, sometimes stretching out and murmuring dreamily like a person floating on a cloud.

Within a week of our arrival, the rough-hewn kitchen table would be heaped with treasures of the natural world—berries, lichen, mosses, grasses, flowers stuck in jars of water or left to dry, clumps of dirt still hanging off their roots. Most days we'd roam outside without counting the hours, carrying wicker baskets that in my memory are always filled to the top. I remember how she would pick something, hold it, look at it, rub it between her fingers, put it to her nose. I'd follow, doing the same, not knowing anything in particular, simply putting into my basket whatever was pretty or strange, whatever gave off a scent that brought pleasure, comfort, excitement, or shock.

A local man acted as our guide, brought us to places we could never have found by ourselves, through marshes and on woody trails. He had a son a few years older than I was, with long black hair that shimmered in the sunlight when he ran. We played in an intense, wordless way. One day he laughed at me over his shoulder, so I climbed a dipping birch branch, scrambled higher, and enjoyed his anxiety when he couldn't find me. When he got close enough, I pelted him with broken-off twigs, and shimmied down the smooth trunk. And we set off again.

There were flowers everywhere. Blue flag irises dotted the fields, emitting their sweetly seductive odor. The pitcher plant, which captured insects in its thick, waxy petals, smelled old and sour.

The flower that would eventually change our lives was called Labrador tea. It grew in bogs and swampy forests and bloomed obligingly in our month of July—clusters of tiny white flowers with dark elliptical leaves fuzzy brown on the underside. When a whole field was in bloom, the plant's strong aroma hung over the area like a fog. Some people thought it had a narcotic effect, that you could fall asleep in a field and wake up with a headache. Others believed that it inspired creativity and love. Labrador tea is a slow-growing species, so we picked only a few flowers and leaves from each plant and put them in cloth bags. At home we hung them to dry, an act they seemed unwilling to perform, stubbornly emitting their brash, soporific, bright lemony fragrance, remaining moist long after other flowers had become brittle and easy to crush.

The most exotic of our treasures was ambergris, which is an oily, resinous substance that a whale either vomits or excretes into the ocean. It achieves a rich, dirty marine smell after years of floating under the sun. We found it by scouring the shores, where it occasionally washes up in black chunks that can be as small as a pebble, as big as your fist, or as huge as a piece of driftwood. I remember my mother's delight whenever we came across a piece. Though it was a rare find, there is probably no better place in the world for collecting ambergris than the area around Hopedale, whose Inuit name, Agvituk, means "place of the whales."

Add to all this the essences my mother brought from home—jasmine, tuberose, frankincense, bergamot, sweet orange, and others I couldn't begin to name—all lining the kitchen counter in small glass vials with cork tops. *Voilà:* a perfumery. But we never called it that. The kitchen was simply my mother's happy laboratory, where she worked with intense focus and a deep calm emotion that she didn't exhibit during the other months of the year. Looking back, I realize it was joy.

At some point during these summers of my childhood, L'Amour du Nord was born. A fragrance is difficult to describe. In colors, it would be deep blues and whites, with traces of magenta and neon green. In experience, it would be setting off across snow in a warm fur coat in a musty twilight, toward the bronze light of a distant cabin. In chemicals, it is B-selinene, trans-p-mentha-1(7), 8-dien-2-ol, and other substances whose spellings are as complicated as the molecular structures they represent. In dressing, it's a woman's lace slip and her red leather glove. In love, it's *Mmmm* until it ceases to be.

Isa said L'Amour du Nord was the smell of a place. Whenever I'm lonely or upset, I put a drop of this perfume on the inside of my wrist and let it take me home.

Chapter 9

The receptionist's desk floats on gleaming white linoleum. The storied Florida sunshine pours through spotless floor-to-ceiling windows that have no doubt spelled ruin for countless birds. A woman in a pencil-thin skirt and fitted jacket greets me. Her shoulders are squared by epaulets; her pretty blond hair is folded into a smooth bun below the rim of her Navy cap. Her smile when I introduce myself reveals pearly, child-size teeth, with just a flashing hint of sharpness in the canines.

I'm disconcerted by the awful, cool hush of the place, which convinces me, paradoxically, that there's a great deal going on, but that it's all beneath the surface, behind the walls, on the other side of the closed doors we are now passing, our footfalls clicking noisily like two metronomes out of sync. By the time we enter Commander Stockwell's office, my fight-or-flight response has duly considered the likely outcomes of *fight* and determinedly cast its lot with *flight*. But it's too late to run; the comely receptionist recedes, leaving me in a spacious office, feeling trapped. If I'm Commander Stockwell's idea of a bionic woman, she ought to be more worried than she looks.

She gives a forthright smile, rising from her flag-flanked desk.

Light brunette hair, sensibly cut, sturdy on her feet, midfifties. Short dry fingers that exert just the right amount of strong-but-warm pressure when they wrap around my hand. In civilian clothes, she could be your childhood friend's mother, the one who had more fun with the Girl Scout troop than any of the girls did. Right now she's doing a fine hostess routine, lobbing inquiries about my trip, my accommodations, my postdisaster health. With pleasure she relates a few of her city's main attractions. I must visit Ripley's Believe It or Not Museum. The white sand beaches are unsurpassed, and the ocean has been described as *emerald*. There is no word but *gracious* to describe her demeanor, but still I can't relax. There are guarded gates at every egress of this compound (upon entering I was subjected to a thorough search), and the whole time she's talking, what I'm hearing is: *Welcome to my war palace, where you will be well cared for, and carefully observed.*

We sit down across from each other, smiling like girl chums, and she starts as all good persuaders do, by telling stories:

March 24, 1999. Marine Corps Physical Fitness Academy, Maryland. Seven elite marines, all trained as water survival instructors, capsize while paddling a war canoe across the Potomac River. They have seat cushions but no life jackets. The water temperature is 37°F. Within minutes, all seven have drowned, approximately 90 yards from shore.

October 28, 2005. Sebasticook Lake, Maine. Two adults and a twelve-year-old girl, all wearing life jackets, capsize while paddling in 60°F water, in clear view of other boaters. In the time it takes rescuers to reach them, they have drowned as a result of hypothermia.

February 3, 2008. Congaree River, South Carolina. A volunteer firefighter described as experienced comes out of his kayak on a small wave, struggles to get back in, but disappears under the water less than thirty seconds after capsizing. His submerged craft is recovered with grappling hooks four days after the accident. His body is never found.

Commander Stockwell spins her computer monitor to face me and runs a YouTube video in which a young woman, clad in a one-piece Speedo, bathing cap, and goggles, dives off a skiff into ice-clogged ocean water. In the background loom the blue glaciers of what appears to be Antarctica. A pale wafer of sun hangs low on the horizon as the swimmer surfaces and begins to stroke.

"Lynne Cox," Stockwell explains. "Forty-five years old when this video was taken in 2002. You see her as she's about to become the first person to swim a mile in ice water. Most people would be dead in five minutes. She stayed in for twenty-five. Before that she'd swum the Strait of Magellan, Cook Strait in New Zealand, the Cape of Good Hope, and the Bering Sea. If you ask her why she does it, she can't say.

"And then there's this man," she says, sliding a photograph across her desk. The beautiful arc of a near-naked male body, caught midair as it dives off an ice ledge into the sea. "Lewis Gordon Pugh. In 2007, he swam .62 miles across the North Pole in twenty-nine degrees Fahrenheit water. In 2010, he swam across Lake Pumori on Mount Everest in thirty-five degrees Fahrenheit water." She pauses. "Do you know why you're here, Ms. Kasparov?"

I nod. I've got the main idea.

"The Navy spends a great deal of its resources carefully selecting and training personnel for special underwater operations. We need to know why some people, regardless of their training level, succumb to hypothermia rapidly in cold water while others are able to adapt and perform their duties successfully." She pushes away the photograph of Lewis Gordon Pugh with a trace of disdain, as if she's glad to be done with her theatrical opening gambit. "We know a great deal already, of course. The risk of hypothermia increases dramatically when low temperatures are combined with moisture. That's because water transfers heat from the body seventy times more efficiently than air. In very cold water, heat is sucked out of the human body with dangerous speed. Core temperature only has to fall to ninety-five, just a few degrees below normal, for hypothermia to set in.

"For most people there's also a gasp reflex, completely involuntary, followed by unavoidable massive hyperventilation. Even Pugh cannot avoid it. He reports that gulps of icy water rush down his throat when he is first submerged, but he is able through long practice to get his head above water and slowly even out his breathing. Most people find the shock of immersion so disorienting that this kind of control simply isn't possible. Obviously, if you gasp while your head is submerged, you may not come up again at all." She sighs a little, but pushes through to the logical end. "Because of the gasp reflex, the lungs can fill up very quickly. Then water flows into the stomach, setting off another involuntary reflex, vomiting, which opens the airways again. Need I say more?"

I shake my head numbly, trying to avoid imagining the kind of death she's describing. It occurs to me that if I'd known these details before the collision, I would probably have been driven to panic and not survived. When I was in the water, I didn't know I was supposed to drown. Ignorance is bliss.

"For a long time we relied on training to prepare our soldiers for sudden cold-water immersion. We have an ocean simulation facility and an experimental test pool in which we worked under the theory of habituation. We believed that coaching our divers to withstand progressively colder temperatures would help them change their physical and mental reactions, and to some extent this proved to be true. But overall, habituation has proved to be a failure. The body's main responses to cold—constricting blood vessels near the skin, shunting blood to the body's core, and shivering—simply did not improve significantly. And there appears to be no consistent way for most divers to control their gasp reflex, even with months of practice."

"But what about the cold-water swimmers?" I ask.

"Interesting, isn't it? Cox and Pugh have remarkable physiologies, extremely high pain thresholds, and exemplary mental toughness. But none of that adequately explains what they're able to do. The fact is that successful cold-water swimmers raise more questions than they answer: Why can some people develop Cox's and Pugh's abilities while others can't? How do you train for it? What draws athletes like Cox and Pugh to the unusual activity in which their bodies are designed to excel? How can a person *know* if he or she has capacities that remain hidden until experience itself calls them into action? How many other people have these abilities, and how can they be identified?

"You see, Ms. Kasparov, we're really just beginning to understand the physiological and psychological components of survival in extreme conditions. In the future we'll be able to give new recruits a battery of physical and mental tests that will allow us to place them immediately into the positions to which they are most suited and most likely to succeed—optimizing results while minimizing casualties. But we're still far from that goal."

I have a slightly sick feeling in my stomach. Maybe it's the offhand use of the word *casualties*. In another minute I'll find out exactly what she wants from me. I'd like to get this over with so I can go to the beach.

She offers me an uneven demi-smile in which I see a bit of the sycophant bursting through. "No one's ever done what you did, Ms. Kasparov. Not Pugh, not Cox. Forty-eight degrees, four hours. Unheard of until now."

"And you want me to—"

"Undergo testing. Medical, psychological, genetic. Allow us to observe your responses in a simulated extreme environment."

"How long will all this take?"

"A few days. No waiting around, I promise. You'll be our top priority."

The vagueness of her answer bothers me, but I can't think of a reason to object. I'm taking today and tomorrow, a Friday, off work and had planned to spend the weekend enjoying the beach anyway. Stockwell gives me a time and place to report the next morning, assures me that Eileen, the receptionist, will personally see to any needs I have.

By the time I make it to the beach, it's late afternoon and a bit chilly. I sit down on my hotel towel, watch the birds wheel overhead and the sand crabs trundle around. After a while I go into town for a cheeseburger, stroll under some palm trees, go to bed early in a mauve room so climate controlled I feel as if I've been vacuum-packed. I get that awful chain-hotel feeling, like I could be anywhere—Paris, Hong Kong, Detroit, or Schenectady. Or nowhere. My dreams seem to wander, unsure where they belong.

Over the next two days I'm given every medical test known to man. I run on a treadmill hooked up to machines; I blow into a tube as hard as I can. My blood is analyzed; my brain is mapped. I spend an entire evening in the cardiopulmonary laboratory, where I'm subjected to respiratory function tests and aerobic performance measurements before, during, and after what the Navy calls thermal exposure and what I call freezing to death. I take an IQ test, fill out a biographical survey, give information about every member of my family—a short task, given that neither Milosa nor Isa was given to family reminiscences. I tell the story of the collision over and over again. I surrender my DNA.

Everyone I meet is perfectly polite, which I dislike. It's hard to tell one individual from another when they all act the same. Ron, Bob, Bill, Jane—interchangeable as far as I can tell. And the weather: one perfect day following another. It gets boring after a while. I feel as if I left the best part of myself in Boston and need to go back and find it again amid the bad drivers and dirty streets.

Finally I'm told it's time to take the plunge. Sunday is a day of rest, so my cold-water swim is scheduled for Monday morning at nine, which means I have to call work and get another day off. The swim will take place at the Experimental Test Pool, a fifty-thousand-gallon freshwater indoor tank measuring fifteen by thirty by fifteen feet.

Eileen takes me to see it. There's a medical and engineering deck, a communications suite, full video capability, and pressure and gas monitoring. About six people will be present, she says, including a doctor and a sports scientist. She gives me a one-piece bathing suit, bathing cap, and goggles. No flip-flops, which disappoints me. I tell her I would have liked them in green to match the cap. She smiles prettily because I'm such a good sport.

She explains that I'll have something to float on in the pool, just as I did in the ocean, though I've been told over and over that activity is essential to maintaining body heat. A transmitter strapped to my chest and linked to a laptop will show my heart rate and breathing rate, and they'll use a thermal imaging camera to measure heat loss. The swim will last until it's dangerous for me to continue, however long that takes. Maybe a minute, maybe an hour, or four. But I'm trying not to think that far ahead. She tells me in all seriousness to avoid testing the water with my toe before I dive, and I almost laugh out loud maniacally. Now I can think of nothing but the initial pain and shock. The pool sustains temperatures ranging from 34 to 105 degrees Fahrenheit. Based on the results of the testing so far, the Navy will set the thermostat for me at a numbing 40 degrees.

Patriotism is the only motivation I can find for agreeing to undergo this bizarre experience, and that doesn't go very far. I suppose, on a deeper level, I'm also cursed with the human need to know who and what I am.

I spend a few hours at the beach Sunday morning, have lunch, and return to the hotel room. I fall asleep and wake with a start from a nightmare about drowning. It seems almost more terrible than reality because it's part of my own mind. My lungs feel seared from seawater; there are phantom traces of salt on my lips. My heart doesn't know it was only a dream: it's beating in a frenzy, bent on survival. The hotel clock's digital display says 3:36 p.m. I slept less than an hour.

I get up and, even though the room is filled with sunlight, turn on all the electric lights—the one next to the closet, the ugly fluorescent bulb in the bathroom, the shaded lamp on the desk. I scatter ghosts as I go, brush away the nightmare cobwebs. I tidy things. I can't even imagine what this tank experience is going to do to me, and having things in order just makes sense. I check my phone. There's a text from Johnny: *Thinking about you, darlin. How about that beer?* I send it to the trash.

My e-mail is stuff and garbage. I answer a few, delete them all, and begin pacing the narrow room. I am colossally restless, and the inanity of television will only make it worse. I decide to practice my own version of sports psychology: I visualize the warm shower I'll take after I leave the pool. What is there to worry about, really? They won't let me die. I've got a ticket for a 6:35 p.m. flight to Boston tomorrow night—one stop in Atlanta—arriving at Logan at 12:27 a.m. Come Tuesday morning, I'll be sitting at my desk, and when people ask what I did on my mini-vacation, I'll have another watery story that can't be beat.

My cell phone rings. Caller ID says Thomasina, but it's Noah's whispered voice I hear: "Pirio?"

"I'm here, Noah. Is something wrong?"

"No." A pause as big as Texas.

"What's wrong?"

"Nothing."

"Why are you calling?"

"I don't know." A tone of mild reproach: the question was too hard, or too direct.

"OK, Noah. Is your mom there? Can I talk to her?"

"She's not here." He's playing with something plastic, maybe Legos or a Ninja man.

"Where is she?"

"In jail."

"What?"

ELISABETH ELO

There's silence on the other end, but I can hear him choking back a sob.

"Did she call you?"

"Uh-huh." Weak as a kitten.

"How long has she been gone?"

"Ummm . . . maybe? Just a day."

"You've been alone all day?"

"Night, too."

"Noah, are you OK?" Stupid question.

"I think there's something wrong with Jerry."

"Jerry? Who's Jerry?"

"You know, Pirio. My hamster."

"Oh, right. Jerry. What's wrong with him?"

"I think he died." There's a catch in his voice, another swallowing of emotion. I can see his face not crying; I can see it not being scared. The thought of what his face looks like right now is enough to make me mad with grief.

"Is there someone you can visit with until I get there, Noah?"

"No. I don't want to go anywhere."

"How about your grandmother?"

"She'll make me leave my mom."

"How about the people next door?"

"They're mean. They'll just yell at me."

"How about Daniel? Can you go to his house?"

Pause. His voice drops to a whisper. "Pirio, I don't want anyone to know."

"Uh-huh. I see. I can probably change my flight and get there at about one a.m. Are you OK with that?"

"Can you come any faster?"

"I can't, Noah. I'm in Florida. But I can call you on my cell a lot, and you can call me, too."

88

"OK. I'll do my homework now," Noah says, sounding reassured and too mature.

As soon as we hang up, I dial Thomasina's cell, get bumped to voice mail. I send her a text, then an e-mail from my computer. Thomasina's never done anything this bad before. Now she's crossed a terrible line. I call the Brookline Police, but they won't give me any information. Out of anger, I'm tempted to bring in DSS. But what will they do? Start a frightening and humiliating investigation, maybe remove Noah from his home. It would be a catastrophe for Noah, another sudden, devastating loss. Not to mention a brutal betrayal of Thomasina, one she doesn't yet deserve.

I change my ticket in plenty of time to make this evening's 6:35 flight, pack quickly, and call for a cab. In transit, I'll leave a voice mail for Eileen. The Navy will have to wait.

Chapter 10

It's past one when I get to Thomasina's apartment and let myself in with the key she gave me a long time ago. Noah's sleeping, though not in his bed. He's hunched in a chair like an old man, his head hanging on his neck precariously, looking as if it might roll off his shoulder onto the floor. He's wearing jeans, sneakers that have been neatly tied with double knots, and his fake Army jacket. A gym bag is on the floor next to the chair. I don't have to look inside to know it contains whatever he considers his most important possessions, and maybe, if he remembered, his toothbrush and clean underwear.

Always a light sleeper, Noah raises his head, squints in the light I turned on when I came in. He says hi. I say hi. No big emotion, because that's how we are, he and I. Just two creatures surviving from one fucked-up thing to the next.

The phone machine is blinking. Number of messages: 7. I ask if he checked them.

His shrug is equally a yes and no.

Granted, it was a dumb question. If he had listened to the messages, the red light would not be blinking. Maybe he heard them when they were being recorded, obeying his mother's law not to pick up the phone unless it was someone he knew, or maybe he was asleep.

I push the button and listen in distaste as boyfriend Max asks his fairest where and when. He mentions that it's Saturday morning, which gives us a fact. Then he says he can't wait to cover her with kisses and lick the insides of her thighs. The words are out before I can press the skip button. Neither Noah nor I have any comment. The next messages are the kind of random nonsense with which we citizens are routinely anesthetized: a school announcement, a solicitation. Then a voice that sounds like cracking pond ice accuses Thomasina of stealing Ned's computer out of his house. It takes me several seconds to identify Phyllis, Ned's mother, spewing her usual vitriol. It's unlikely that Thomasina, who has everything, stole Ned's computer, so I figure this is just Phyllis's way of carrying on the vendetta that seems to give her life meaning.

Now Thomasina's voice comes through. "Noah? Sweetie? Noah, baby, pick up the phone." Pause. "Noah, come on. Please pick up." Pause. "OK, so you're not picking up. Maybe you're still at the science club meeting or Daniel's mother took you guys to the skate park after. I tried you on your cell but didn't get through. Did you forget to turn it on? I'm sorry I didn't tell you this morning I'd be out when you got back. I don't know how much longer I'll be; I'm tied up here with something I have to do. Just make yourself a sandwich for dinner. There ought to be peanut butter, and there's still ice cream in the freezer. And when you get this message, *call*. My phone is on. I may not be able to pick up if I'm really busy, so just leave a message to let me know you're OK. I love you, sweetie. Don't worry, I'll be home soon."

Noah and I look at each other without blinking. We both know there's another shoe to drop.

In the next message Thomasina is clearly drunk. There's background laughter of the kind adults make when they're not being at all funny. Male and female voices swirl together. Over the noise, she says something about trying to call Pirio, says she can't reach me. Tells Noah he should just go to bed, and when he wakes up in the morning, she'll be right there in the kitchen toasting bagels. *Like a good mother,* she adds. I can feel Noah flinch. Then she giggles like someone is tickling her, shrieks like a teenage girl meeting her friends at the mall, and yells *Be good, baby,* into the phone.

I don't look at Noah. I don't want to see what's on his face, don't want him to see me seeing it. There were no messages from Thomasina on my cell. Maybe she called my apartment, not knowing I was away.

I try to imagine what kept Noah from picking up the phone. Maybe he couldn't fathom what to say. *Don't worry, Mom. I'll make dinner and clean up. I won't watch too much TV, and I won't be scared or lonely. You go on. Have a great time.* That's a higher order of lying than Noah at his tender age can manage. Of course, he might have been honest. Picked up the phone and cried real tears into it. Tears that would have been lost in the delirious carnival atmosphere of adults having fake fun. Longing, worry, anger, fear. Chasing his mother with the very emotions she was running from.

The last message is from her, too. In this one, she sounds tense, clear, and logical, like a flight attendant explaining emergency landing procedures. She says she has been arrested and is being kept overnight. She doesn't want to waste her one phone call trying to reach me again, and asks if Noah will keep trying my number until he gets through. Her voice is so controlled that I imagine whoever was listening on the other end had no idea she was talking to a ten-year-old.

Noah's face is a sickly, frozen ash. No doubt he is imagining the steel-and-concrete prisons he has seen on TV, the ones that swallow people like flies and treat them like garbage.

"It's not a real jail," I tell him. "Just the police station down the street. I'll give them some money, and they'll let her come home."

He nods, dazed by the complexity of the grown-ups' world, then shifts his eyes toward the hamster cage in the corner of the room.

We approach it together, slowly, as if it's a bomb that might go off. Although Jerry is only a rodent with a short life expectancy, although it's not out of the ordinary for a rodent to die suddenly from unknown causes, although adults have been known to use the deaths of these kinds of pets as relatively benign lessons for children in the great issue of mortality, I'm scared. What if he's not really dead yet, only suffering? Or he's been dead for a long time and is as stiff as cardboard? Death is death—shocking, in whatever size it comes in.

Instinctively, Noah and I hold hands. I open the cage. No Jerry. With my free hand, I grope around and find the little body under a pile of wood shavings. It's cold and hard. The fur, if this is possible, feels synthetic.

"You were right," I tell Noah.

He nods curtly, playing the little man. But his hand is squeezing mine.

In the kitchen we wrap the remains of Jerry in a dish towel and look for a box, but can't find one. We end up using a plastic container with a snap-on lid.

We go to my apartment, bringing the plastic container with us, and I get Noah something to eat. We don't discuss his mother or his lost pet. Instead, we have a conversation about a man who wants to put a wind turbine in his backyard. City council won't let him. I call it civic inertia, unforgivable ignorance, and tragic mass hysteria. I know I'm overreacting. Noah wonders how big the turbine would be. Neither of our hearts is in the conversation. It's three in the morning. We're just marking time.

His eyelids are so heavy that when they fall his head follows. He jerks awake, tries to continue the conversation, but forgets what it's about. No, he doesn't want to go to the station with me to pick up his mother. Can he stay here and watch TV? Once on the couch he's asleep in seconds. Mouth part open, long lashes feathering his cheeks. I don't like to leave him, but I don't want to wake him up. And he doesn't need to see his mother getting out of jail. I tuck a blanket around him, leave my cell number with a note. *Back soon.*

The police station is only a few blocks away, but I drive anyway along the deserted streets, and park at a metered space out front. My heels click across the spotless linoleum floor. No line at the counter, no one waiting. A short uniformed woman with a square jaw looks me over, trying to figure me out. I explain my business, write the bail check. It's all done with a minimum of words.

I was afraid that Thomasina would act belligerently when she emerged from behind locked doors, but she is subdued and self-possessed. Our eyes meet briefly. She has twisted her hair into a bun and buttoned her black sateen jacket as if she's on her way to a job interview. Her voluminous leather purse is returned to her by the policewoman. She checks to make sure everything's there, and we walk out of the cold building into the night's last hour of darkness. In the car she doesn't say anything, just sits white-lipped behind big, bla-tantly unnecessary sunglasses. We get all the way to my parking space before she starts to explain.

"I'm not going to say anything about what I did. I know it was wrong. But I honestly didn't think I'd be gone so long. Or that I'd get caught. Not like this anyway." She takes off her sunglasses and looks at me appealingly.

Here I am, judge and jury, two jobs I never wanted. "Uh-huh. What happened?"

"Well, first I just went to Max's house and then to a party, you know, with Max and some other people, and it got kind of wild"—this means that the sex and hard drugs spread out of the bedrooms and bathrooms into the living room—"so I left to go home. It was only ten o'clock. But then I got this idea. . . . It was a bad idea, I must have been drunk. . . . Anyway, I got this idea that I could find some photos of Ned. For Noah. We don't have any."

She looks to see if I'm following the logic.

"See, a few days ago I called Phyllis asking for some, but she hung up on me. So I called Ned's sister, and she did the same. It made me so mad. I mean, what's a few photos? That's not too much to ask, is it? We don't have even one. I thought we did, but I must have thrown them away when I was pissed. Anyway, I wanted to make, like, a little album or scrapbook or something so Noah could have it to remember the good times, and what his father looked like. He *needs* that, don't you think? It's *important*. But those two . . . what's their problem? Why can't they think about Noah for a change? Who cares who his friggin' biological father is? Ned loved him, and Noah loved him back. So I thought, *I'm gonna get some fucking pictures if it kills me. Ned probably had a bunch of pictures. They don't own his shit.*"

She describes how she went to Ned's house in East Milton, climbing in through a broken basement window. I raise my eyebrows.

"OK, so I broke it myself," she amends.

The place was picked up, the bed was stripped, and there was no perishable food in the refrigerator, so she knew Phyllis and Ned's sister had already been there. Ned's desk hadn't been touched, though. Stacks of paper and mail on the top, and, sure enough, a photo of Ned and Noah in a nice frame. Leaning close together, holding hot dogs, the green monster of Fenway Park in the background, Noah with a mustard mustache and big grin. Thomasina slipped it into her handbag and went looking for more. The center drawer was crammed; she started moving stuff around, found a few more pictures. One really sweet one of Ned holding Noah as an infant. It almost made her cry. There was even a picture of herself in a bikini and big straw hat, laughing and whipping a slimy rope of seaweed at the photographer. Feisty Thomasina. Too feisty, maybe, looking back. She pulled out a manila envelope marked *Boat Stuff* and opened it on a whim.

"A whim? Really?" I say.

She sighs. "I thought there might be an insurance policy or something. There wasn't."

What she found instead were the documents required to register a boat in Massachusetts: title, bill of sale, proof of payment of state sales tax, pencil tracing of the twelve-character serial number from the upper right corner of the transom, and completed application. Everything was there but a check for the fees. Legally, Ned had twenty days after the date of purchase to file the papers. He was just past the deadline when he and the boat went down.

"You think he didn't have the money?"

"No. I think he just put off going to the registry. He procrastinated a lot."

Suddenly there was heavy pounding on the front door. She looked up to see blue lights pulsing through the picture window. There were two cruisers—one in the driveway behind her car, one on the street. She didn't bother running. Where would she go, and why should she? She just slipped the photos and envelope into her purse, let the cops in, and tried to explain rationally who she was and what she was doing. She wasn't a criminal. No, just a former girlfriend, mother-of-his-child, and so on. But they didn't like her story, the time of night, the broken basement window, or the fact that the neighbors had called in a burglary in progress. They cuffed her, packed her into a cruiser. One of them felt her up. For a while she was panicked because she thought she probably had a gram or two of coke in her purse that they would find. But when the cops at the station dumped out her purse right in front of her, there wasn't anything illegal on the table.

"Thank God." She sighs. "This whole thing would have been a lot worse if I'd had something on me." All this time she has been staring out the window; now she looks at me with big mournful eyes, trying to gain my sympathy for her ordeal.

Back at the Gaston School, Thomasina and I used to find our ways into locked rooms just for the fun of it. Either through a window, or with a stolen key, or by taping the locks. We liked to steal exams and personal items from teachers' desks. We didn't care about the stuff at all; most of the time we just threw it away, even the exams, which were as boring before they were given as they were during the actual test. But taking things made us feel powerful.

So I'm not really surprised at Thomasina's breaking-and-entering behavior. There's even a perverse sweetness to it, because she did it for Noah's sake. It does bother me, though, that she is trying to cull a bit of virtue out of the situation for not having had drugs on her. As if dodging that bullet was more significant than the fact that she left Noah alone. It is part of the general craziness of Thomasina these days that nothing she does is properly described. She blows smoke as unthinkingly as she exhales.

"But wait," she says suddenly. "You've got to see this." From the folds of the purse comes the manila envelope, curled at the edges from being stuffed inside. She opens it and hands me the title and bill of sale.

"What?"

"Look," she says impatiently, pointing to the lines on the title marked *seller* and *buyer*. "Ned bought the *Molly Jones* from Ocean Catch." She flips to the bill of sale. "For one dollar." She stares at me. "Do you get it?"

"Not sure." My head is molasses that doesn't want to be stirred. "Maybe. Yeah, I guess so."

"Even used, this kind of boat is probably worth over a hundred thousand dollars."

"It was a gift."

"Exactly. Now look at the date. It was purchased *after he quit*. Why would they do that?"

"Severance?" I say, grasping at straws.

"Please. Ocean Catch? They're the greediest bastards around. The only reason people around here work for them is that they're the only big fish company left. And guys are always quitting. Nobody cares if you quit."

"But Ned had been there for twenty years, so maybe they figured they owed him some kind of reward for his loyalty."

"A gold watch, maybe. But a lobster boat? I don't think so."

The invoice describes the *Molly Jones* as a steel-plate offshore Gamage lobster boat with a length of 45 feet, a weight of 26 tons, and a 660-gallon fuel capacity.

"He told me he was disgusted with the way Ocean Catch was fishing," Thomasina says. "He didn't say why, but I figured they must be exceeding quotas or trawling illegally. You know, breaking some of the sustainable fisheries things. But I was surprised, because he never cared about that stuff before. *Let the environmentalists worry about the environment,* he used to say."

"If Ned was criticizing the company, why would they turn around and buy him a boat?"

"Right. That's what I'm saying! And he quit so suddenly. Never breathed a word that he was even thinking of leaving, then all of a sudden he's gone. Out of there. And he's lobstering practically the next day in the *Molly Jones.*"

We're still sitting in my car in the parking lot. The brick back of my apartment building rises in front of the dirty windshield. The sun is claiming a tiny portion of the eastern sky now. I see in the rearview that one of my neighbors is a real early bird. She gets in her car and drives away.

I flatten the documents on my lap, go over them again. There's a handwritten note at the bottom of the invoice, just a sentence in a small, dainty cursive, the kind of genteel penmanship they used to teach in parochial schools years ago. *May the wind be always at your back. Take care, Mrs. Smith.*

Thomasina and I are silent, thinking things over. Ned. The boat. Quitting. Ocean Catch. A metaphoric brick wall to match the real one we're staring at.

"By the way, did you steal Ned's computer?" I say.

"Steal his computer? Of course not."

"Phyllis thinks you did."

"Did she tell you that?"

"She left a nasty message on your machine."

"Jesus, what a bitch."

"No argument."

"His sister probably took it for her kids." Thomasina stirs, turns her head to gaze out the passenger side window. The extra distance helps her admit something difficult, personal. "I'm worried, Pirio. About me and Noah."

"You ought to be. You're in deep shit, and you're hurting him."

She gives a short, ironic laugh. "What kind of friend says something like that?"

"An honest one."

She sighs. "I know I've got to do something. I have to take control of my life."

"It's more specific than that. You have to stop drinking and doing drugs."

She turns to me abruptly, allowing herself a flash of anger. "I'm *trying*, Pirio."

"Really? How hard were you trying last night?"

"It's not as easy as you think," she says wearily.

"Noah was terrified. I traveled all night to get here. What if I wasn't around?"

"I promise it won't happen again."

I shake my head in disgust. "I wish you hadn't said that."

As I start to get out of the car, she puts her hand on my arm. "Wait. Would you mind driving me out to East Milton? I need to pick up my car."

"Take a cab," I say curtly. It's early, and I haven't slept. And I'm getting that familiar creeping resentment about cleaning up after her mistakes. I have my own life, my own worries, a job I've got to get to, a freezing tank to swim in at some point. And Noah's got to get to school.

At five that afternoon, at Noah's request, the three of us trudge up a hill behind one of the parks with which our city abounds. Thomasina is carrying a Christmas gift bag she dug out from her closet. The plastic container with the remains of Jerry is inside. The path up the hill is twisted and rutted from runoff. Noah scampers; Thomasina and I step carefully around protruding rocks. We come out onto a small clearing with a view of the city. Boston is close as a handshake but visible in its entirety. It is the hour before dusk settles and the workers in the skyscrapers are exhaled. In the middle of the clearing is a fire pit rimmed with stones, crossed with charred branches. A surprisingly tidy affair.

This is the kind of place only kids know about, where they go to let their imaginations run and get away from us. I'm surprised Noah has found it; he's not as timid and housebound as I thought. But I always knew he was secretive.

He indicates a place under a ragged pine where we are to dig, and Thomasina and I kneel obediently with serving spoons she brought from home. After a while she tires of the task and stands apart on a rocky ledge, wisps of hair dancing around her face in a slight breeze that must be coming straight from the ocean a mile off. All this time she's been wearing her big sunglasses, as unnecessary now as they were this morning, and I see that she's not really with us at all, but adrift in private thoughts. She mouths some words and sways a bit, cradling herself tenderly in her own arms.

She's taken something, I realize. Valium or Percocet. Enough to get her through the lingering hangover and make the world seem friendly and soft.

There's a sharp drop down from the rocky ledge.

"Come back a bit," I tell her.

Noah, who had taken up her discarded spoon, glances up from his digging. "Mom, come back."

She smiles beautifully and calls us angels. Then she sits cross-legged on the ground. "Do you remember when *you* were in jail, Pirio?"

Noah gasps. "Pirio was in jail?"

"Uh-huh. At boarding school they used to make us sit in a little room by ourselves when we did something wrong. We called it jail. Pirio was in there a lot."

Noah turns to me with wide eyes. "You were?"

"I can't deny it."

"How long did you have to stay there?"

"Oh, a few hours, I guess."

"Longer than that. *Much* longer," Thomasina says with admirable restraint. "I used to go down in the middle of the night and talk to her through the door so she wouldn't be lonely. Remember, Pirio?"

"Yeah, I do." Thomasina kept me sane through much of that time. Back then, she took life as it came, sailed with the breeze. I was the one who fell down stairs and walked into doors, metaphorically speaking.

"Remember when I read the *Kama Sutra* through the door? Remember those positions? The blossoming, the bird's amusement, the thunderbolt. We were hysterical, rolling on the floor."

I have to smile. There is nothing funnier to fifteen-year-old girls than detailed descriptions of sexual positions written in sacred-sounding prose.

"What's the *Kama Sutra*?" Noah says.

"Just a stupid Indian book. Old as the hills. You wouldn't like it," I say.

"Remember when I used to play harmonica? That was back in my Joni Mitchell phase. Once I started playing it in chemistry, and the teacher sent me down to Dickhead Bates. Remember the lisp? *Thomathina, Thomathina. Thurender your inthrument.* I had to hand over my harmonica. You know, he never gave it back." She laughs brightly. "I got another one, though."

"That was mean for him to take it," Noah says sympathetically.

"Yes, it was." She gazes toward the Boston skyline.

"You're not supposed to play harmonicas in school," Noah mentions.

Thomasina smiles at him wistfully. "Bless you, sweet boy."

We fall silent. Noah and I keep chipping away at the hard ground with our spoons. Finally the time comes. The grave is about eight inches deep, and the Christmas gift bag sits on its smooth edge. Noah indicates that I am to have the honors. I take out the body and place it at the bottom of the hole, wrapped in its dish towel. I try to make the process long and solemn for Noah's sake.

When I start to push some of the dirt back in, he grabs my arm in panic. "Wait. Shouldn't we say something?"

I never learned a single prayer. I could speak extemporaneously on the virtues of Jerry, but I didn't know him well enough. All I know is some Russian literature. I concentrate and manage to drag a few fragments of Pushkin out of my memory bank. Lines that describe the usual mournful sentiments: how time is fleeting, how all is dust, how our hearts are always aching for those we lost. Appropriate funeral material.

But when I look at Noah's urgent, trustful face, I know I have to come up with something different. To my surprise, a line of Yevtushenko springs fully formed to my lips, as if it had been waiting offstage all along, eager for its chance: "I was madly mistaken / in thinking that my life was over."

Noah is quietly satisfied. Although his eyes and cheeks are dry, a deep sigh reveals his emotion. I can't begin to guess what this line of poetry means to him, but it seems to have done the trick. We gently push the dirt into the little grave until the earth is flat and patted down. Then we lean back on our heels and spend a few moments in silent reflection.

Thomasina sings softly to herself as we walk home in the twilight. We stop at Christo's for pizza and laugh a lot effortlessly, but by the time we're saying good-bye in front of my apartment building, her face has grown stiff and pinched. The drugs have worn off. She seems unwilling to go home. She asks Noah if he has both my phone numbers programmed into his cell.

"Uh-huh," he replies. "But I can't find it."

"You lost your cell?"

"I don't know where it is."

"What do you mean you don't know where it is? When's the last time you had it?"

"Not for a long time." He looks worried. It's unlike him to lose things, and he feels his mother's mounting ire.

"Why didn't you tell me? What if something happened? You've got to start paying attention, Noah. You can't just leave things lying around."

"I didn't leave it lying around. It disappeared."

"Disappeared? Nothing disappears. People are careless. That's why things get lost."

Noah pats down his army jacket. "It was in my pocket."

"We'll look for it when we get home," she says between tight lips.

We're all as tense as if a bomb were ticking.

"Mom?" Noah's pleading with her, *Please be OK.*

She leans toward him. "You have to have a cell phone, Noah. You *have* to. I don't want you to go out of the house without one. Or be at home, or anywhere, without a phone. Not for one minute. You understand?" She doesn't have to say why she feels this so strongly. We all know he needs a phone on him for the next time she fucks up.

Noah's suddenly near tears. "Mom! What if I can't find it?"

"You *have* to find it, Noah."

"But I looked already!"

The desperation in her son's voice starts to drag Thomasina back from whatever hellish place she's in.

"Come on, take it easy," I murmur.

She blinks a few times, puts a hand to her forehead. Then she sighs, kneels before him. "Oh, sweetie. I'm sorry. It will turn up. And if it doesn't, we'll get you a new one. Are you OK? I'm sorry to scare you. I'm just kind of tense right now. Oh, Noah. Please forgive me." She pulls him close, and he stays quietly pressed against her for a while.

Her eyes look up, linger on mine, dull but burning. I can see how much she wants to take care of him, yet she's pleading for help.

Chapter 11

The rising elevator is rickety and industrial and smells like fish from the ground-floor processing factory. It chugs slowly past the second floor, *pings* at the third, and opens its doors onto another world: an airy, carpeted, expansive office space lit by bright lights. About a half dozen cubicles in muted beige and gray occupy the center of the room. They're all empty, although it's four-thirty on a Tuesday. On the left there are two glass-walled offices hung with semi-sheer curtains. Those are empty, too. To the right tall clean windows look down on Boston Harbor from a modest height.

I wander farther into the office space; no one stops me. I'm an unauthorized visitor here. That, and the fact that I've skipped out of my own job early again, gives me that old high school truant feeling, a mixture of guilt and thrill. When I reach a corridor on the right, I hear human voices emerging from the last doorway. I head that way, conscious of the way the carpet pads my footfalls. I tell myself I have no reason to feel sneaky; I'm just looking for information. But it's information I'm not really entitled to.

The voices blossom into a happy hubbub as I turn into the room. It's a lunchroom with a large round table and cabinets along one wall.

A refrigerator, a sink, and a cork board with various announcements pinned on it. Ten or twelve people are gathered around the table, mostly women, mostly middle-aged. There are balloons taped to the cabinets and a shiny red banner proclaiming "Congratulations, Libby!"

No one notices me. Everyone is looking toward a gray-haired woman who is holding up a plastic knife. She's wearing a pilled green cardigan that is buttoned incorrectly, leaving one side longer than the other, heavy green corduroy trousers, and big round plastic glasses. She can't be an inch over five feet. A broad smile adorns her wrinkled face. "You're too sweet. Every one of you. Too sweet!"

"Are you speaking French again, Libby?"

"Tout de suite, tout de suite!" she says, laughing. "Now I'll have all the time in the world to study French and take Jasper to Paris. He'll look so cute in a beret!"

"What else will you do?" someone asks.

"Painting classes, my dear. Oil paints. I've always wanted to learn. I'm going to become an abstract expressionist!"

"We're going to miss you, honey," one of the larger women says.

Libby's eyes fill. "Oh, my dear friends. I'm going to miss you, too."

She begins to cut a large pan cake on the table in front of her. It has chocolate frosting, pink lettering, and pink flowers. She slaps each piece onto a paper plate, adds a napkin and a plastic fork, laughingly calling out "Who wants a rose?" The plates get passed from one person to another until they reach the back of the room. One of them is thrust at me. I smile and say thank you. Why be impolite?

A tall man in a gray suit is standing beside Libby. He's a bit stooped and nearly bald, and there's a tremulous, fretful quality to his voice. "I have a few words," he says, and everyone immediately quiets down and stops moving about. The instant dampening effect he has on his audience suggests that he's some kind of boss.

"I've known Libby since I was a boy," he says. "She used to give me cookies, and later, when I was in high school, we'd talk about basket-ball. If I recall correctly, I also got some good advice from her about the opposite sex." With a burble of self-conscious laughter, his thin lips stretch into a smile.

The audience replies with a tepid chuckle.

"I never dreamed I'd be returning to Ocean Catch as owner and president. I thought it was off to New York or Los Angeles for me after my MBA. But when my father died . . . well, I guess I just had to come back. This place is home to me, and I just couldn't sell or let it go to anyone else. But taking over a fishing company isn't easy, believe me. If it wasn't for Libby here, I don't know what I would have done. After thirty-five years as my father's secretary, she knew this place top to bottom and inside out. There wasn't a practical problem she couldn't solve, and she did it all with such wonderful enthusiasm. I don't think I've ever heard her complain. She spreads sunshine wherever she goes." He turns to the woman beside him, raising a cel-ebratory paper cup. Because of their difference in height, his arm is about a foot above her head. "Here's to you, Libby Smith! The heart and soul of Ocean Catch for forty years. This place just won't be the same without you!"

"Hear, hear!" a man calls out, and Libby's colleagues start to clap and cheer.

"Now, stop," she says, blushing, her voice just audible through the applause. "Blarney, blarney. Stop already."

When things die down, the woman beside me asks if I'd like cof-fee. I'm munching cake, so I just nod. "Cream and sugar?" I nod again. When she comes back with my cup, she asks what my name is. I respond in what I think is a normal volume. The room gets suddenly quieter.

"Are you the . . . ?" The woman seems to be having a hard time finding the right word.

Now everyone's looking at me. "I'm a friend of Ned Rizzo's," I say with bright confidence, as if that fact clearly explains why I, a complete stranger to Libby Smith, have appeared at her retirement party.

"You're the woman who survived!" someone says.

I look at all the wonder-struck faces. "I got lucky," I say, shrugging it off.

People crowd around me, offering condolences, congratulations, awe, friendship—all of it mixed with a tincture of silent terror. I try to be gracious, but every time I'm reminded of that day, I smell seawater and want to vomit.

Libby Smith fights her way to my side. "Dear, I've wanted to meet you. I knew Ned for twenty years. He was such a good man. It was heartbreaking."

The owner is behind her. He pushes through, offers his hand, introduces himself as Dustin Hall.

I field questions as best I can. Eventually the thrill of meeting me dissipates, and the workers and Dustin Hall move smoothly back to the cake pan and coffee machine. I'm left standing in a corner with Libby Smith, who begins to dab at her eyes with a crumpled tissue.

"I'm sorry. It's just that I can't think about what happened." She tucks the tissue up the sleeve of her cardigan. "But look at you . . . you're here, and looking so well."

"Thank you, Mrs. Smith. It's nice of you to say that. You know, I wanted to ask you something." I mention a few general things about Noah, his mother, and how they're getting along; then I bring up the boat and the subject of insurance; finally, I say that it's come to my attention that Ned bought the *Molly Jones* from Ocean Catch for one dollar. "You wouldn't happen to know anything about that, would you?"

She seems to have frozen in place, her eyes suddenly dry. "I can't really speak about that, I'm afraid. Maybe you'd better talk to Mr. Hall." She leads me out of the lunch room to a wood-paneled door at the end of the corridor.

Dustin Hall's office is carpeted in navy blue, with heavy mahogany furniture and leather seating. Behind his desk there's a huge map of the North Atlantic.

He looks surprised to see me, but offers me a seat. Libby Smith leaves quickly. But since I know they'll probably talk about it at some point, I have no choice but to take a seat as directed and ask my pointed question again.

With remarkable adroitness, Hall manages to frown slightly and smile politely at the same time. "I can't imagine where you got that idea."

I describe the title and bill of sale found in Ned's drawer.

He says he has no knowledge of any such gift, that Ocean Catch has a fleet of trawlers and long-liners but owns no lobster boats as the company is not now, nor ever has been, in the lobstering trade. That even if they did own a lobster boat, it would be highly irregular to make a gift of it to a former employee. Nevertheless, he'll look into the situation and see what he can find, and if he gets any more information he'll be sure to let me know. That's it. A flawless wall of professionalism. It's no use banging your head against these people, because they only get more pleasant and patronizing with each parry. I thank him and leave.

I'm standing in the brightly lit office space waiting for the elevator when Libby Smith materializes beside me. The elevator doors open, and we enter the cramped space together.

"Do you like dogs?" she asks as our reflections appear in the closing stainless-steel doors. Before I can answer, she hands me a photo of a cocker spaniel. "Jasper. My baby. Eleven years old."

The dog looks like every cocker spaniel I've ever seen. Rumpled and a bit daft.

"I always walk him at six o'clock around Jamaica Pond. Do you know where that is?" she asks.

I tell her I live not far from there.

"Such a nice place to walk in the evening. You ought to join me sometime soon." She speaks with surprising force, as if determined to make me agree.

"How about tonight?"

"Perfect." The door slides open, and we get off together on the first floor and go our separate ways as if we hadn't talked at all.

The earth is falling into night, but there's still a pearly glow in the western sky. Libby Smith is sitting on a bench in front of the boat-house. She's wearing a canvas jacket with patch pockets and a multi-colored crocheted cap. Perched beside her, Jasper tilts his head with canine curiosity as I approach.

"Let's walk," she says, and we set off along the path that winds around the pond. She takes small steps in worn brown Wallabees. The pom-pom at the top of her hat bobs just below my shoulder. Jasper trots ahead of us on the end of an embroidered leash.

"As of today, I'm a free agent," she says with tired gaiety. "I don't know what I'll do tomorrow. Maybe sleep till noon and take my coffee at a café." She offers me a wry, collapsing smile. "It's awful how we keep having to make the best of things, isn't it? You'd think at my age I'd have learned to just tell the truth. I'm excited, I'm happy, and I'm very, very scared. Who will I talk to now? Ocean Catch was my life, and all those people . . . they were my family in a way. Oh, we say we'll keep in touch, but you know how that goes. I'll have to get new friends now. But where? At the senior center? There's nothing but old people in that place!"

I smile at her tenderly. What can I say?

Jasper stops to do his business in the dirt. Mrs. Smith takes a bag-gie from her pocket, scoops the dog's waste and disposes of it in a nearby trash can. She pats and praises him while his brown eyes glow up at her from under a fall of fur.

"You know, Ned did the strangest thing before he left the com-pany," she says as we follow a curve in the path. "I gave him his bonus check, and he waved it around in the air, and said, 'This is my last one, Libby!'" Then he whooped like a boy and gave me a big smacking kiss on my cheek. I was delighted, but also very surprised. I knew, of course, that he wanted to leave the company, but most people don't have that reaction to getting their last check."

"A bonus check? Was that some kind of severance?"

"No, some of the men got bonus checks for extra work they did. Actually, that's what I wanted to talk about. I've wanted to tell someone for a while now, just to get advice, but I didn't know who to turn to. I was sworn to secrecy, but now that I'm not an employee anymore . . . And then you appeared at my party today out of the blue, and asked about the *Molly Jones*. I'm sure Dustin didn't tell you anything, but I started to feel very strongly that you should have the answer you're looking for. You were a friend of Ned's, and you've been through so much." She looks up at me inquisitively, as if to check if her trust is misplaced.

"I'll try to help if I can."

A circle of teens huddled around a bench stop their conversation. They're wearing bandanas and puffy jackets, and stare in aggressive silence as we pass.

"You won't tell anyone I told you this, will you?" she says.

"No, I won't."

She takes a deep breath. "You see, for years I handled the official payroll with federal and state tax deductions. When Dustin came in, he wanted to use an agency, insisted on it. 'They're more accurate,' he said. Only that's not true: they make more errors than I ever did. Oh dear, I'm already getting off track! Bear with me, please. My mind is so scattered these days. Anyway, in June 2007 Dustin started giving me a list of names and telling me to cut what he said were bonus checks, and to do it by hand. No other paperwork. No e-mails or computer entries. Just the list, handwritten. My instructions were to make out the checks, keep them locked in my drawer, and give them to the men in person when they came to me. I was never to leave them on top of my desk, or mail them, or give them to anyone but the intended recipient, and I was never to speak about the bonuses to anyone in the company. This would happen several times a year."

"Ned was receiving these bonuses?"

"He was one of the first to get them."

"How many others got them?"

"Eight, nine, ten, I'd say. The number changed each time, but not by much. They were a core group. Trustworthy, seasoned fishermen, most of them. A few young ones, not many."

"Hmm. Same amount for each name on the list?"

"Yes. Each man got the same amount, but each time I got a list, the amount would be different."

"How much, roughly?"

"Anywhere from five to fifteen thousand. Average ten, I'd say."

"Any idea what was going on?"

"No. They were silent as tombs, all of them. That in itself was unusual, but then I noticed that the bonuses were given out after they'd all been together on a particular boat, a long-liner the company's owned since, oh, 1998, I think. It's called the *Sea Wolf.*"

We are rounding another bend. The asphalt under our feet turns to gravel. Huge rhododendron bushes push their way onto the path. I start to feel uneasy. It's darker here—there aren't any people, and a few of the lights seem to be out in the iron lampposts up ahead. I'm about to steer Mrs. Smith back to the boathouse, but before I can suggest it, she hooks her arm in mine.

"Just a little longer," she says. "Right before Ned left the company, there was that business with the lobster boat. That was hush-hush, too. I took care of the paperwork, but I knew something was wrong."

"You wrote a note on the bottom of the invoice. *May the wind be always at your back.*"

"It's an Irish blessing, dear. *May the road rise to meet you, may the wind be always at your back, and may God hold you in the palm of His hand.* I felt something even then, you know. Right here." She presses her clenched hand into her chest. "I was worried about him. It kept me up at night. And then . . . well, you of all people know what happened."

Jasper sits down suddenly, ears erect. He whines, peers intently into the woods. There's a hill beyond the trees, and on the other side of it, the beginning of Boston's famous chain of parks, the Emerald Necklace, where you definitely don't want to be after dark.

"Look, Jasper hears something," Mrs. Smith says.

"Let's turn around now." I'm increasingly on edge for some reason, listening for crunching twigs and rolling pebbles, footsteps behind us on the path.

"Oh, don't worry. There's nothing to be afraid of. I'm out here every night with Jasper. These lights here are out, but there are others up ahead, and then it's just a little while until we're back where we started."

I agree reluctantly and pat the small dry hand that's resting in the crook of my arm, pull it in a little tighter.

Mrs. Smith frowns as she searches for the thread of her story. "There was something about the *Sea Wolf* I meant to say. . . . Yes, that's it. About the regular paychecks. It was a bookkeeper's nightmare. I went mad trying to figure it out. You see, when the *Sea Wolf* came back from these voyages, the haul size would be smaller than usual. Quite small, in fact. So the men's regular paychecks would be smaller, too, because their commissions would be less. But expenses for fuel and provisioning were as high as ever, and days at sea would be fourteen to twenty-one every time. That's long enough to haul a lot more groundfish than they were bringing in. I felt like calling Captain Lou and saying, *What were you doing out there, playing bingo?*"

"Captain Lou?"

"Lou Diggens. One of the core group. Captains every voyage of the *Sea Wolf.*"

"Did you ever ask him what was going on?"

"No, no. It's rude to ask a fisherman why his catch is small. Like asking a pitcher why he keeps throwing balls instead of strikes. I did ask Dustin, though. Several times. He'd get very stern and tell me there was nothing unusual about the *Sea Wolf*'s voyages. I think he forgot I know more about fishing than he does. In any case, even though the crew members' regular paychecks were small, the bonuses more than made up for it. Overall they were doing remarkably well for a relatively brief voyage."

"You think—"

"Yes, I think they were using the long-liner for some unofficial business, and paying the men with the so-called bonuses, off the record. Then they were bringing in a small haul of groundfish to make the trip look legitimate." She glances at me, feisty and complacent. "The doctors tell me that my brain has been aging, but I wasn't so far gone that I couldn't see what was right before my eyes!"

The entrance to the pond is up ahead. There are floodlights, the hum of traffic, a yellow lab and its master headed our way. I breathe a little easier. There was nothing to be afraid of: I'm overtired; that's all. It's hard to sleep in an apartment that's been broken into. I wake up and hold my breath, wondering if someone is there. On the street I find myself staring at people suspiciously. Was *that* man the intruder? Or was it *him*? Or was I just a little crazy that day, smelling things that weren't even there?

A cruiser has pulled onto the service road next to the boathouse. Joggers pass. Children play. A guy in a baseball cap sits on a bench, looking over the water. There's nothing to worry about. I offer to walk Mrs. Smith home, but she declines, so I accompany her to the crosswalk and punch the button. Cars whiz along the Jamaicaway, sliding across lanes, taking the curves. This is probably one of the most dangerous streets in America. The light turns red. The cars that didn't streak through the yellow screech to a stop, and the Walk sign flashes on the other side of the street.

"You'll find out what it's all about, won't you?" Mrs. Smith's eyes look directly into mine. "Just promise that you'll be careful. I want to know everything. Stay in touch. I'll worry if I don't hear from you."

"I'll find out. I promise."

I hate to let her toddle across four lanes of halted vehicles filled with impatient drivers, but she only smiles and says, "Don't worry. Jasper and I will be fine."

Chapter 12

It's an in-house focus group, but everyone calls it a sniff party. As I enter the conference room, I can feel the excitement and stress. A banquet table covered by a white cloth displays some packaging possibilities and advertising mock-ups from McKenzie and Ross, the outside firm that does Inessa Mark's promotions. The account executive, a man with the solid American name of John Rodgers, is sitting at the large conference table in the middle of the room with his assistant, Jay, and the four women and two men who compose Inessa Mark's in-house staff. They are drinking to-go coffee from Starbucks and Perrier from plastic cups. John Rodgers and Jay look slick, aggressive, and comfortable, as marketing people should.

At a second banquet table, fluttering like a nervous moth, is Jean-Luc Laboure, the thirtysomething half-Italian Frenchman who has created several Inessa Mark scents over the years and whom Maureen contracted to develop this new scent under her direction. He works for Moreau, a large perfume lab and manufacturer out of France, and will see no money from Inessa Mark until Maureen approves the scent, the pricing, and the manufacturing schedule. At this stage of the proceedings, Maureen has Jean-Luc over a barrel. If and when

Moreau becomes the supplier, he could conceivably dick her around, but because he wants the next contract, he won't.

Five small glass vials, each half filled with an amber liquid, each on a white china plate, are set in a straight line across the long table. Before each vial is a small triangle of note card with an identifying code: A37, 45X, #22, P-40, and #3. There's no point in asking what these elaborate alphanumeric combinations mean. Perfumers are intensely secretive about their formulas, almost paranoid, and the labels are not meant to be understood.

Jean-Luc stalks the front of the table, checking the placement of the vials exactly, straightening the little cards. For freshening the nasal palate, he has provided two small bowls filled with coffee beans, and these he moves here and there, looking for the best locations. He can't help being nervous. He is about to place his creative children at the mercy of people with more-or-less ordinary noses. What's worse is that these kinds of products are far from the elegant fragrances he dreamed of making when he was a young perfumer's assistant back in Grasse. No doubt the task of creating something "fresh and fruity" for the American teenage girl kept him up at night with migraines of despair, but everyone needs work these days.

Maureen is flitting around the room, murmuring pleasantries. She has chosen an exquisitely tailored geometric black-and-white dress à la Coco Chanel for the occasion. The homage to Coco, though it will go unnoticed by most and only embarrass her if it is remarked upon, is no accident, I assume. It says something about her ambition and self-doubt.

Maureen gets the focus group's attention and explains the process, and eight of us line up at the table. John Rodgers, Jay, and Jean-Luc do not participate. We pass down the table as if it were a buffet, taking up each vial in turn, dabbing drops of liquid on our wrists and inner elbows, sniffing, then sniffing again. We have little pads of paper and pencils to jot our notes. We circle around as much as we like. By common agreement, we do not talk much. Discussion will come later, when the choices have been narrowed down.

Milosa slips in late, as usual, and sits at the far end of the conference table. I finish sniffing and join him. Jean-Luc appears at my elbow, a nervous wreck. "It was very *difficile* . . . with the commission as she wanted it. . . . First *J'ai dit non.* . . . My company insists I must. . . . But so many changes, all new constraints with which I *could* not work. . . ."

"You did your best," I tell him. "It's a fruit scent to be sold in drugstores. Be paid for your work, and let it go."

His eyes widen. *"Ce n'est pas l'argent que m'intéresse."*

I spoke too bluntly and offended him. I hug him briefly with affection, and he gives me an injured, forgiving look.

Jean-Luc and I became friends years ago, when we were both in our early twenties, and I asked him to help me re-create my mother's private fragrance. I described the elements I thought I remembered: earthy saffron, black rose, vanilla, patchouli. The old perfumer who had worked with my mother to create it had died, but Jean-Luc was able to confirm with another perfumer in his company that Isa's Scent, as we dubbed it, had been a dark oriental chypre. Jean-Luc suggested adding tree moss to soften the intensity and black truffle to darken the rose. We changed the balance, brought the rose forward and back, mixed in lily, almond, sage, and tinkered endlessly. But with each successive formulation, I would shake my head. We only seemed to be getting further off track. Eventually we gave up. The truth is, people can't really remember smells; we can only recognize them.

Now several staff members are gathered around one young woman's outstretched arm, chiming delightedly over a particular scent. "I love it!" one of them crows. Maureen sniffs the girl's wrist and smiles. She likes this one, too. There's a buzz of merriment as a common preference emerges.

"Wait, wait. Caroline, get the tester strips. We must smell it on paper," Maureen asserts.

"Why paper?" the young woman asks, holding her wrist up.

"Because . . . ," Maureen says, losing her train of thought in the excitement. "Just because."

Soon they are dipping tabs of stiff paper into the vials, waving them in the air to dry, and passing them under their noses.

"Now I like *this* one better," Caroline says, pointing to X45.

"I'm not sure anymore," another says in perplexity.

"See, what did I tell you? Scent is very unstable; it can come across quite differently on paper than it does on skin," Maureen explains.

"Shouldn't it smell good on skin?" one of the women asks.

Maureen gives a crafty smile. "Yes, but . . . we're going to use advertising inserts and scratch-and-sniff displays to sell the product, so we need it to smell good on paper *first*, then skin. Isn't that right, John?"

"Yes, ma'am." John Rodgers stands at his full height to accept the admiration he's due.

Maureen frowns. "We'll be using a thicker paper than this, won't we, John?"

He nods.

"Something closer to cardboard?"

"Not that thick," he says.

"Poster board?"

"A little heavier."

"Well, you'll send us a sample soon, won't you?"

"Absolutely." His gaze deflects to his assistant, who pulls out a pen.

Maureen looks imperiously at Jean-Luc, whose eyes reflect haughty fear. "Jean-Luc, don't you have to put something in the formula to make the scent *adhere* . . . you know, to the scratch-and-sniff paper?"

Bloodless as a corpse, Jean-Luc repeats, "Adhere?"

"Otherwise, how will it stick? What I'm asking is, won't you need to make some chemical modifications to bring the fragrance in line with the marketing plan?"

"I will look into it, madame."

"Yes, but don't take too long, Jean-Luc. We need the formula in a week."

Briefly, John Rodgers and Jean-Luc square off, shoot subtly hateful glances at each other. Imagining that these two men could agree on anything is like imagining that the north and south poles could overcome their magnetic issues and meet for lunch at the equator.

Maureen turns her attention back to her employees with a schoolmarm's sharp clap of hands. "Girls! Girls! And you boys, too. Did we decide which one we liked?"

The women are giggling over their scent-dampened paper wands like the teenagers they're pretending to be. They quibble, pout, and exclaim. The two men look on with pleasure and take sniffs of outstretched arms. Three samples are easily rejected, but there's a fifty-fifty split between #3 and X45. Maureen tries to break the tie but can't. Her head tips back and forth—*comme ci, comme ça*—as she flutters the two competing tester strips. Finally she spies me sitting at the conference table with Milosa. "Pirio, you decide!"

She dips fresh tester strips into the vials, makes her way to where we're sitting, hands one of them to me with delicate fingers.

I bring it to my nose, inhale. The fruits Maureen wanted are there: strawberry, watermelon. By themselves, sickeningly sweet. But Jean-Luc added a few other tones that lend some depth: there's something dry like lemongrass, a dark woody coloring, and unmistakably pungent lotus. I give Jean-Luc credit for grabbing as much artistic leeway as he could, but there's no disguising that the scent's a total bust. I feel like I'm walking down a hotel corridor, passing a half-eaten strawberry cheesecake from the night before on a room service dish on the floor.

I smile halfheartedly at Jean-Luc, drooped in a nearby chair, and he shrugs as if to say, *What would you have done?*

"Not this one," I tell Maureen.

"Right. I didn't think so either." She hands me the second tester strip. "Try this."

I close my eyes and breathe. With this, Jean-Luc has given Maureen just what she wanted. Fresh summer air, strawberry shortcake, and bubble gum. It's unlayered, uninteresting, and underwhelming. It's so innocent of aspiration, so devoid of need and want, so self-effacingly nice, it makes me want to cry out with boredom. I smile and hand it back to her. "This is it. Perfect for a twelve-year-old."

Maureen beams with satisfaction. "I thought so!"

The young women crowd around Maureen, smell the paper wand, shriek with stage delight.

"Congratulations on a job well done, Jean-Luc," I say drily.

He nods in acute misery.

Milosa doesn't ask to smell Inessa Mark's new scent. He leaves the conference room as the attention shifts to John Rodgers and his packaging concepts. A few minutes later I follow him.

Milosa has a corner office at the back of the building. The windows overlook a narrow alley, a small paved area crammed with parked cars and trash barrels, and a brick wall crisscrossed with rusted fire escapes. I only know what the view is from the few times I've been in his office when the vertical blinds were open. Usually, they're closed, as they are now, casting shadows in the corners. On his massive desk, an ornate rococo-style lamp gives off a dim yellowish glow that seems to pull the walls even closer. I can only last a short time in this room before I start to feel trapped.

Milosa is at his computer, his back to me. I have to say hello several times to get his attention. He finally turns and motions for me to sit down, which I do, and, out of a habit that stopped making sense years ago but that I hang on to out of stubbornness, I put my feet on his carved black walnut coffee table.

We talk in a superficially pleasant way about the new fragrance, about a trip to Geneva he and Maureen are planning to take. Something is different about him. I noticed it before. At dinner the week before there was a glassiness in his eye that I thought would pass and didn't. Now I see it again, the dullness. A laxness in his usually tense face, a subtle easing of his carriage. It's just a shade of difference, but he comes across as less the alpha male he's always been. Though I've spent my whole life fighting with Milosa, I've always respected him as a worthy opponent. So it troubles me to sense a weakening. I wonder if he's sick, or if the depression that's always dogged him is finally catching up, or if this is just the incremental lessening that happens as people age. There's no point in asking, for he denies infirmity on principle.

It's not long before he asks whether the ship that sank the *Molly Jones* was found.

I describe the Coast Guard's anemic investigation and Johnny's conclusion that the collision was a hit-and-run. Milosa listens with his eyelids half lowered, hiding his shrewd interest. Then I tell him about the paperwork Thomasina found and what I learned from Mrs. Smith about the bonuses and unofficial voyages. At this, his back straightens and a sharp gleam comes into his eyes.

In his heyday Milosa lived on the edge: romantic passion and whoring weren't opposites because they both brought him to a sharp, raw place. Business wasn't interesting unless it involved cheating the government or screwing a competitor. My violent near drowning and crazy survival captured his imagination. And now this. A trail of clues and contradictions is just the kind of problem that makes him glad to be alive. His fingers drum the desktop excitedly.

"Obviously," he says, "the boat was a bribe to keep your friend from reporting whatever was happening on the secret voyages. And . . . have you thought of this? There was no accident. Your friend's death was murder."

"The first part may be right, but the second part is ridiculous."

"But you've considered it."

"Yes, I have. But it doesn't make any sense. Why would a company bribe an employee one week and murder him the next? Why not get rid of him right away? And there are easier ways to kill a person than to plow into his lobster boat in heavy fog." I don't say, *Then there's the problem of me. Why kill a second person as well?*

Milosa snorts. "Desperate people will do anything, *anything.* I've seen it. I lived under Stalin. I saw things that go beyond anything, that are incomprehensible. Your weakness—the weakness of your soft American life—is you think that all people are like you, that reason can explain everything in this world. You expect two plus two to equal four. But it doesn't. It equals whatever the powerful say it does. If they say it equals a hundred and eight, the mathematicians will prove it's so. If they want to make splinters of a man's fishing boat, nothing can stop it from happening."

"But there's no evidence of foul play." My voice is thin. In truth, it scares me when Milosa talks this way.

He shrugs indifferently. "You and your evidence. Tell me, how do you sleep? How does it feel in here?" He jabs the blunt ends of his fingers into the middle of his chest.

"Uneasy."

"Yes." His eyes glitter darkly. "Find the boat, the *Sea Wolf.*" His mouth clamps shut. In his mind, this is all that needs to be said.

I wish that he'd advised just the opposite. That for once he'd be a normal father and tell me to stay out of danger. But he wrought his immigrant success by fighting day after day, clawing for every inch, and he expects his daughter to act the same way. I sigh in resignation.

There are benefits to his attitude, I suppose. With a surprising flush of gratitude, I realize that I like the way he believes in me, the way he doesn't waste time.

I take my feet off the coffee table.

He offers me a cigar from a leather box. I take it. He lights mine and then his own. We have been smoking cigars together since I was sixteen. But only on very important occasions. We puff in silence. When the blue smoke is swirling around our heads and our nasal passages are filled with the hot muddy smell of Cuban tobacco, he broaches a subject I never thought I'd hear him talk about. "I've been cruel to Maureen. I see now what a crime it is to marry without love." He pauses, seeming to judge how much more to say. "Maureen's afraid of you. You have a sense of fragrance that she doesn't have, and she knows you don't appreciate her work. She worries you'll fire her when you take over the company."

"That's a possibility."

He squints at me, exhales through his nose. "She's been here for more than twenty years. This company is her life. She deserves more respect than that."

"Respect? The products she creates are crap. Sweet Surprise? It's an embarrassment."

"Her products are paying the bills."

My heart quickens, and my face gets hot. "That may be so. But Maureen has no talent and no vision for the company. She's a manager; that's all she's ever been and all she's capable of being. After my mother died, you gave her a greater role in this company than she deserved, and now she's afraid of losing what she knows was never rightfully hers."

"What could I do? What choice was there? I gave her the role your mother had, and she made it her own."

My heart right now is a violent jumble of emotion. Like someone took the top off a boiling pot. "As long as we're being honest, there's something I've always wanted to ask you. Were you fucking Maureen when my mother was alive?"

His color rises sharply; his blue eyes turn metallic. "Do you think your mother was faithful, Pirio? Do you imagine *she* was faithful to *me*?"

I feel my mouth twist. "Why should she be faithful to a pimp?"

He slams his fist down on the table. "How dare you speak to me like this? You, who had schooling, every advantage, everything money could buy. You talk of Maureen, but it's *you* who have what you haven't earned. And yet you sneer at *me*, who worked like a dog, day and night, to make your mother who she was. Who *for her sake* built the company that made her a happy woman. Shame on you for daring to speak to me this way!" He thumps the table again, this time with the flat of his palm.

I blink a few times, hard and fast. But I don't back down. "You don't deny it, then. That you were a pimp. My mother's pimp."

He stubs his cigar out in the ashtray. Fury turns his words into a staccato hiss. "You know nothing of my life in Moscow and before. You couldn't imagine it if you tried. What do you know of history, of Russian history? You Americans read your Civil War, that's all. And your glorious victory in World War II. You are smug and righteous, only because you are lucky and dumb."

"You blame everything on Stalin. And when that doesn't work, you go back to Lenin. Then forward to Gorbachev, Yeltsin, Putin. You point to everyone but yourself. And for your information, I *have* studied Russian history. Russian literature, too."

"Oh, yes," he drawls sarcastically. "Your Pasternak, your Pushkin. Romantic drivel. You and I can never know each other. *Pah*." He spits.

I'm breathless with tension, and trying to hide it. I should never have mentioned Russian literature. I showed too much of my soul, and let him dance on it.

Milosa and I stare at each other, not bothering to find words.

My parents' marriage was built on taunts and jeers. They could no more live together than a monkey and a hyena. But they couldn't part. Fighting was what I saw, what I learned, and now it's what I do, at least with Milosa. Sometimes I think it's our way of loving each other, that I would miss it if either of us ever got too nice. But I wish things were different, too.

Milosa picks up his cigar, relights it, draws out a few puffs, and leans back in his chair. "Maureen has worked hard for this company and proved herself many times over. It isn't right that she should live in fear of you, and what you might do . . . later on."

"What she fears is her business. And you can't expect me to make promises just to satisfy your private guilt."

His lips pinch together, hollowing out his cheeks. His thinning hair, high forehead, pale skin—suddenly I see the contours of the skull behind his face. "There's truth in what you say, Pirio. Maureen doesn't have your mother's talent or vision. I married her out of weakness, out of need. But you wield that truth like a heavy sword and cut down other truths, humbler ones, that you don't stop to see. Please, I'm asking you from my heart to give Maureen the respect she's earned. She's dedicated her life to Inessa Mark, and me. Don't throw her out on the street when—"

He stops abruptly. We look into each other's feverish eyes.

I'm quite sure he meant to add *when I'm gone.*

Some moments of incredulity pass.

I accuse him, but softly. "Are you dying?"

He turns his shoulder to me in an almost womanish way. "Of course not. I hope to be here for . . . many years."

That is not the Milosa I know. He doesn't speak like that—in wishes and hopes. He speaks in decisions and actions that don't leave room for doubt. A knot tightens in my stomach. "What do you mean, you *hope*?"

But he's already turned back to his computer and pretends not to hear.

I leave his office in a daze. The halls of Inessa Mark are cathedral hushed. The sniff party has broken up, and the staff has returned to their respective offices or cubicles. On my way to the elevator, I glance into the conference room. Jean-Luc is packing up his cards and coffee beans. Maureen and John Rodgers are standing close together by the window, heads bent in private conversation. Maureen looks up casually as I pass. Her eyes, when they find me, fill with anxiety.

Chapter 13

I have no idea where John Oster is likely to be on a Thursday morning. Maybe he's in the middle of the Atlantic hauling nets filled with squirming silver mackerel, or maybe he's still in bed. I call his cell. If anyone can tell me about the *Sea Wolf*'s voyages, he can.

Two rings. An uneasy memory intrudes. Milosa telling me I'm naive. But he always says that, the old Russian. Never misses an opportunity to ring the old I-am-one-acquainted-with-the-night bell. What does he know?

Four rings now. Little wan bleeps. Like the phone's anemic. *Soft American*, Milosa's whispering in my ear. My gut starts to twist. What do I really know about John Oster these days? Those birdhouses. Johnny up at four, sitting for hours by himself, hunched over. Johnny explaining to me that it was a hit-and-run. But the old Johnny would never have been satisfied with that answer.

Facts: As an employee of Ocean Catch, Johnny's probably involved in whatever's going on there. If I start asking questions about the *Sea Wolf*, he's going to wonder where I got the little information I have. Of course I'd never reveal my source, but he wouldn't rest until he'd figured it out. I'd be putting Mrs. Smith in jeopardy.

I end the call suddenly, glad he didn't answer.

Two nineteenth-century brick buildings run parallel to each other down the length of the Boston Fish Pier. Concrete loading docks empty onto the road between them; above each of the docks hangs the shingle of a fish wholesaler: Sonny's, Beau's, North Sea, Atlantic. Tattooed men glisten with sweat; plastic bins of silver fish are being pulled and hoisted; the pavement is slick with blood and guts. A couple of the men stare at me, a well-dressed woman with binoculars around her neck, strolling down their narrow road.

Googling *Sea Wolf* led me to a rock band, a book by Jack London, and an adventure cruise line—also to types of kayaks, luxury yachts, inflatable boats, and attack submarines. No Boston-based fishing vessel. I checked and rechecked. It hardly seems possible that there are things in this world that don't pop up right away on Google. So I came down here, figuring that if I walked around the commercial docks long enough I'd run into it. Not much of a plan, but it's the best I can do.

I reach the end of the pier. Six or seven fishing boats rock softly on the swells, their rubber baffles creaking against the pilings. They're grimy, battered. Steel-sided in green, black, red. Jauntily high at the bow, the middle area flat and open, rolls of orange netting on giant iron spools at the stern. I read names off transoms. *Audrey Marie. Capt'n Jack. Lucy Lou.* Mostly women and legendary men. No wolves. On the next pier, across a thin finger of water, the Bank of America Pavilion is almost deserted. Two couples and a man sit at outdoor tables. The blue awning over the picnic area droops.

Nearby, two guys are packing a small truck with plastic tubs of frozen fish. I walk over, wait a minute so I don't seem pushy, then shout out that I'm looking for a boat. One of the guys glances up, keeps working. The other wipes sweat from his face with a dirty cloth and strolls over. "Yeah? What boat?"

"*Sea Wolf.* You know the one?"

"Yeah, sure. It's an Ocean Catch vessel. Been fishing out of Boston Harbor I don't know how long. Before my time, anyway."

He looks about twenty-five. I ask if he knows where the boat is now.

"Drydock, I'm pretty sure. Came in from sea with some kind of problem. They hauled it outta here a couple of weeks ago."

"Know what the problem was?"

"No, ma'am."

I ask him where the drydock is. He says there are a few, but that I should try Drydock 3 on Drydock Ave first. As I head back to my car, I notice that the two couples who were nestled under the awning of the Bank of America Pavilion are gone, and now just one man is seated there, facing the harbor and city skyline. I take a second look. Maybe it's the way he's got his coat buttoned up, the collar raised, his baseball cap pulled down—it's not *that* cold out. I stare a few beats longer than I should, until I sense that the eyes shadowed by the brim of the cap are looking right at me. Or were. The minute I realize it, he's on his feet and walking away.

I freeze with unexpected fear. To follow him, I'd have to run to the end of the fish pier and along Northern Ave to the gates of the Pavilion. By then he'd be gone. But what am I even talking about? All the guy did was look at me and walk away. There's no law against that.

If I don't stop being so edgy, I'll end up doing something stupid soon.

Drydock 3 is brown and muddy; boats undergoing repair rest in huge wooden cradles that look like dinosaur ribs, their hulls scaled by ladders. Rusted parts lie around like scattered bones: bent railings, warped propeller blades.

I find the *Sea Wolf* near the entrance, looking healthier than its neighbors but none too pretty. I walk around it a few times, gazing up at the massive hull—the black below-water section, the white waterline, and the red steel sides dotted at intervals by black portholes small as pigs' eyes. The stern is built up with a two-to-three-story structure, while the front two thirds is flatter. There's an irregular notch, about ten feet by ten feet, cut in the starboard side from the deck to the waterline. From where I'm standing I can't see much more than that.

A man emerges from the manager's office and strolls over. A hunched back, stringy hair, a heavy beer gut over short legs, clothes the color of tar and rust. He looks as if he slowly blended into his environment over the years and now belongs to it the way a troll belongs under a bridge.

"Nice boat, huh?" he says. He eyes my clothes, my face, my hair—scanning to get a read on me and not having much luck.

"Is it? I wouldn't know. It just seems huge to me."

"Not a fisherman, I take it."

"Not on anything like this."

"What's your interest?"

"Educational."

"Really?" His eyebrows shoot up; he wasn't expecting that.

"Yes, I'm thinking I might bring my fourth-grade class here, show them something about commercial fishing, as part of a unit we're doing on our state's resources and industry."

"Well, this kind of boat would be a good place to start. It's a real workhorse, a big producer. One hundred and sixty-seven feet, over a one-million-pound capacity. One of the few freezer long-liners around. Most of the big commercial fishing vessels coming out of Boston are trawlers."

"My fourth graders aren't going to know what any of that means."

"A long-liner uses hooks strung on lines. That's why they're called . . . Well, you get it. The hooks are baited automatically, like,

131

thousands per day. A trawler tows a big net and hauls the catch up the stern ramp. You see, this boat doesn't have a stern ramp; it hauls the catch up the side, there." He points to the cutout area on the starboard side.

"Any way I can get on it?"

"No. The owner wouldn't go for that. I'd recommend you go down to the fish pier if you want to board a commercial fishing craft. Somebody'd let you on, I think. Long as the kids were well behaved."

"Angels, all twenty-two." I pause. "What's this boat doing in dry dock anyway?"

"Fracture in the hull."

"Oh, yeah? What causes . . . something like that?"

"Could be anything."

"Like what?"

He looks a little wary. "A collision, running aground, motoring too fast through ice. Or sometimes a crack just appears. Age, stress in the metal. It's hard to say. Anyway, it's all fixed up now. Be back in business soon."

I walk over to the bow and look straight up, craning my neck. "Where was the crack?"

He doesn't move to join me. "Why do you want to know?"

"Just curious. I don't see any evidence of repair here."

"It's been repainted."

"Really? Before you painted— I mean, when it first came in, you didn't happen to notice any chips of paint around the fracture, did you?"

"No. There were no paint chips," he says stiffly. He knows better than to answer that.

"Must be hard to tell."

He's glaring now, all friendliness gone.

"The red's nice," I continue. "Got sort of a brownish tinge to it, like clay. What color was it before?"

"Same color."

"Red? Isn't that unusual?" At this point I'm thinking that this wasn't the boat that rammed the *Molly Jones*. It's too small, and it's the wrong color. But I'll ask a few more questions to be sure.

"Red's the safest color on the ocean. Most visible. A lot of people think all boats should be painted red or orange."

"The paint chips would have been white," I say, letting the words sound nonchalant, but looking into his eyes carefully for any flicker of confirmation.

He squares off, hands on hips. He's decided he doesn't like me. "Look, I don't know why you can't just come out and say who you are. It's not like I don't know what you're doing. You people are down here all the time, crawling around. At least the other ones don't lie."

I don't get what he's talking about right away and ask a little stupidly, "Who do you think I am?"

"You're a claims adjuster, claims investigator, whatever you people call yourselves these days. Looking for a reason not to pay. Proving negligence or criminal activity would get you off the hook. Jesus." His tone is angry, but there's also a gleam of satisfaction in his eye; he's proud of having figured me out.

"Right." I see no reason to correct him.

"I don't have anything more to say about the *Sea Wolf*," he continues firmly. "I just do repairs. You want to know what happened, ask the owner. That's his business, not mine." He turns and begins to stride back to his office.

I watch him go, then I think of something and jog after him. "Wait a minute. You said there were others. Was anyone else here recently, looking at the *Sea Wolf*?"

"Sure was. Don't remember his name, but he asked the same questions a week ago."

"About the chipped paint?"

"Yeah, and a lot of other stuff, too. If you really want to know, he was a lot smarter than you."

"What kind of questions?"

He stops, turns, looks at me with disgust. "I don't know, lady."

"Was he here before the hull was repainted?" •

"Not sure. Can't remember back that far." He enjoys the taunt.

"What'd he look like?"

"You're a real pain in the ass, aren't you?"

"Look, I'm new, just learning the business, and I came all the way out here. Give me something to take back to the office. Can't hurt, can it?"

He sighs heavily. "Medium height, brown hair, glasses." He shrugs with indifference.

"Did he have a lame arm?"

The guy blinks without comprehension.

"His right arm, was he holding it close to his side?"

"Let me think. I guess . . . yeah, I think I remember something like that. He didn't move it much. Kept his hand in his pocket, as I recall."

"Did he say who he worked for?"

"Jackson Hartwell Marine Insurers. You know, the big one." His eyes narrow. "Who do you work for?"

"Myself. Freelance."

A mirthless laugh. "You don't stand a chance."

A kid running, trailing a balloon. A mother pushing a stroller, yelling for him to stop. Women with briefcases, dressed incongruously in skirts and sneakers. A guy leaning on a pretzel cart.

I'm strolling along the harbor boardwalk that passes before the high, glassy palace of the federal courthouse, taking in the sights and thinking about that guy who was at Ned's memorial service, Larry What's-his-name, wondering if I still have the slip of paper he gave me, when my cell rings.

"Hey, you called. I was hoping you would. Want me to come over?" It's Johnny.

"Uh, no."

"No?"

"Yeah. I mean, no."

A pause. "What'd you call me for?"

Got to think fast. "It was a misdial."

"Really? Sure? You got my number programmed in your cell? I'm flattered. Maybe you wanted to see me, got cold feet. Maybe I can still talk you into it."

"I don't think so."

"Where are you now?"

"Out, walking."

"Down at the harbor?"

"Uh-huh."

"What are you doing down there?"

"Like I said. Just going for a walk."

"I could meet you for lunch."

"I already ate."

"All right, Pirio. I'll let you go this time. But you can call me again, you know. Anytime. Misdial, whatever. I don't care." He takes a drink of something, swallows. "I'm taking the wife and kids out to Michigan to see her family in a couple of weeks. I fucking dread it. Ten days of hell. Landlocked, boring as piss. The in-laws looking me over like I'm carrying disease."

"What are you trying to say?"

"I need you, too. That's what I'm trying to say."

"I never said I needed you."

"I never believe what I don't hear."

"You're wasting your time, Johnny. It's not going to happen."

"No one would have to know. Just you and me, babe, our own private thing."

Some little tug occurs inside me. It could be lust, the automatic kind that happens when you randomly hear someone talking about sex, or when your eye happens to fall on a very handsome man or a billboard of a very handsome man. Or it could be something far more dangerous: the need for love.

Goddamn. I plunk my sorry ass on one of the benches along the boardwalk and try to figure myself out. But, no, it's not the raging need I used to feel; it's just a tattered little hope like the one that lives stubbornly in the bottom of Pandora's box—still there after the war, famine, and pestilence fly out. There's no way in hell I'm going to let that little ghost of hope attach itself to any part of John Oster. That would be sick.

"If things are so bad at home, why don't you get a divorce?" I say.

"Not that easy. Kids and shit."

"Yeah, I've heard that before." I shift the phone to the other ear.

"Hey, don't hang up. There's something I want to ask you. That guy ever get in touch with you? That Larry guy?"

Funny you should ask. "You mean the one we talked about?"

"Yeah. Has he tried to get in touch with you?"

"You're pretty interested in him, huh?"

"Did he call?"

"No. What's going on?"

"I just want to have a little talk with him. The dude's hard to find. Let me know if you hear from him, OK?"

"Sure, Johnny. Hey, how'd you know I was at the harbor?"

"Seagulls."

"Right. Take care."

"You, too, Pirio. Misdial that phone again real soon."

I stuff my phone in my pocket and watch waves of Bostonians striding by. They look normal and pleasantly busy. Most of them are probably married. I have to face the facts: I'm thirty and alone. A subtle fear that has started to haunt me recently is that I'm quietly going invisible, inconsequential in the world's eyes.

Don't think too much; just live, I tell myself.

A teenage boy streaks by on a skateboard. Reckless, wearing headphones, plaid shirttail flapping in the breeze. I stand up and walk briskly after him toward the city. Come to think of it, I'm pretty sure that Larry What's-his-name's phone number is still in the pocket of the coat I wore to the funeral.

Wozniak. That's the name scrawled on the slip of paper.

He answers on the second ring.

"Why didn't you tell me you're an investigator for Jackson Hartwell Marine Insurance?"

A pause. "Who's this?"

"Pirio Kasparov. The woman you met at Ned Rizzo's funeral. The survivor."

"Oh, yeah. I remember. How're you doing?" He speaks slowly, the way people do when they're thinking fast.

"I'm curious. I'd like to know why you wanted to talk to me about the sinking of the *Molly Jones* that day."

A longer pause. "How'd you find out I'm an insurance investigator?"

"A little bird told me."

The pause is so long this time that I start wondering whether he's still on the line. "Maybe we ought to talk."

"I thought that's what we were doing."

"In person, I mean." All in a rush now, he gives me the address of a coffee shop, and tells me he'll be there in half an hour.

I'm impressed. This is the fastest, most personalized service I've ever had from an insurance company.

Everyone in Café La Roche on Beacon Street looks like either a spy or a wannabe creative genius. It's the kind of place where the cups are small and no one eats cake, where even the children are absorbed in serious-looking books.

Larry Wozniak's already there, sitting at a table along the wall.

He's wearing an old gray sweater and black jeans, and he's got the hip black glasses on. His curly hair is combed back, graying at the temples. He stands as I approach and asks what I'd like. I request a large latte, double shot of espresso, unsweetened.

He goes to the counter to place the order, and I take a seat. He stands and waits for the coffee. He tries not to stare at me. I try not to stare at him. It's all rather arduous.

"How'd you find out I'm an investigator?" he asks, placing two cups on the table.

"I'll tell you how I found out you're an insurance investigator if you tell me why you wanted to hide the fact," I say.

"People think that all insurance companies want to do is find reasons to deny a claim." A bit of woundedness has sneaked into his eye. The poor, misunderstood insurance man.

"Forgive me, but that's true."

He reacts with a sharp blink and continues as if he didn't hear. "If people know you're investigating a claim, they clam up. Like you did."

"I didn't know that's what you were doing. You didn't tell me, remember? I didn't discuss the collision with you because I was emotionally exhausted after the funeral and didn't feel like dragging out my personal trauma to satisfy a stranger's curiosity."

"I thought we'd gotten to know each other a bit."

"You mean you were chatting me up, hoping to get me to talk."

He produces a suitably embarrassed expression. "Sorry."

"*Sorry?* You crash a funeral, hit on a woman to get information to deny an insurance claim, and all you have to say is *sorry*?"

He shrugs. "What are my choices?"

"I can think of a few. Like you telling me who's filing the claim in the first place since the owner of the boat, the likely policyholder, is too dead to do it."

"I can't tell you that."

"Bullshit. Why should that be private?"

"Sorry. Again. See? Not that many choices."

I sip the coffee. I wonder whether Phyllis is trying to collect on the policy, presenting herself as nearest of kin, doing an end run around Thomasina and Noah. I wouldn't put it past her. "Are you aware that Ned Rizzo has a ten-year-old son? If somebody's going to be getting a payout for the loss of the *Molly Jones*, it ought to be that child. Be careful you're not participating in a fraud."

Larry Wozniak looks away, purses his lips. Finally he says, "We have more in common than you realize. You could help me a lot if you let me ask you a few questions."

"Like what?"

"Like why Rizzo left Ocean Catch."

"Funny, I'd like to know the same thing. I know why *I* want to know, but why would that information be useful to an insurance company?"

"Did he ever say anything to you about why he left? Ever mention what he was doing there?" He's had practice interviewing: it's nothing to him to answer a question with a question.

"If I had that information, I'd want to know what it would be used for before I passed it on to anyone."

"*Do* you have that information?" His eyes seem to have grown smaller, harder to read.

"No. I don't have a clue why Ned Rizzo left his job."

He looks down at his cup, frowning.

I take a closer look at his wide face. Dark eyebrows, nicely arched. A blunt nose, the kind a child might make with clay. A tense, strong mouth; a forgettable chin. It's the kind of face that slides by in a crowd but gets more interesting the longer you sit across from it.

"I do have *some* information that might interest you," I say. "But the only way you'll get it from me is if you tell me what I want to know first. If we have interests in common, why hold back?"

He wags his head a little. Not a no, not a yes. He seems to be at a loss, as if he didn't expect the conversation to go this way and doesn't have a backup. Then he picks his lame hand out of his lap and drops it on the table. It lies there looking like a sorry plastic replica of a hand. If this is a play for sympathy, he's got the wrong woman. But I am curious.

"What happened?" I ask.

"Accident," he says.

"Boating?"

"Motorcycle. I was a stupid kid."

"Is that why you got into the insurance biz?"

He laughs awkwardly. "Never thought of that." But he's not giving up on getting what he wants from me, only circling for another try. "Look, if I told you that all the information you gave me would be used for good purposes, and promised to disclose in due time what those purposes are, would you consider telling me everything you know about Rizzo and the *Molly Jones*, and every detail you can remember about what happened out there?"

"I told you: either it's an even exchange of information, or it's nothing. But I'm willing to compromise a little. You can keep your client's identity secret if you tell me why you were looking at the *Sea Wolf* in drydock last week."

He looks startled. "You know about the *Sea Wolf*?"

"I asked you first."

"How much do you know?" He's turning white.

"A lot," I lie.

His eyes are piercing, quizzical, disturbed.

I blink, swallow. I've never made it past a few hands of poker—the minute I get scared it shows up on my face, and I'm scared now, suddenly. Because he's scared. I realize I'm sticking my toe into some kind of slimy pool, that I'm half afraid of getting pulled in and half afraid of being left alone on the muddy bank, and that either eventuality is bad.

Larry gives a long sigh of apparent capitulation. "The *Sea Wolf* came in from a voyage with a fractured hull. I was trying to find out what might have caused it." It's obvious he's not telling me anything more than what I would have heard from talking to the drydock manager.

"You learn anything?"

"No."

"Why were you so interested?"

A smirk of impatience. "Come on. Let's stop playing games. You and I both know the fracture could have been caused by a collision at sea. We're both thinking the same thing, aren't we?"

"No. You're thinking that the *Sea Wolf* was the boat that destroyed the *Molly Jones*. But you're wrong."

"What do you mean?"

"It wasn't the *Sea Wolf*."

"How do you know?" He's genuinely surprised.

"The boat that hit the *Molly Jones* was bigger. Much bigger. And it wasn't red."

He frowns. "You can't be sure of that."

"I'm sure."

He sits back in his chair, folds his arms, and stares at me like I'm a vexing but predictable problem. "You know how bad eyewitness testimony is? Woman swears the guy who attacked her was five-foot-six and wearing a sweatshirt; turns out the guy was actually six-foot-two and wearing a T-shirt. Happens all the time. No one believes in eyewitness testimony anymore. It's practically a joke. You think you know what hit you? You don't. You were in the middle of the Atlantic, scared shitless, trying to stay alive. How would you know what color the boat was? In the fog, how could you accurately judge its size?"

"I was cold and wet, not blind. I know what I saw. And don't pretend you really think eyewitness testimony is worthless. If I told you it was red, you'd believe me because it's what you want to hear."

"Come on, Piria."

"Pirio."

"Pirio, Pirio. Come on. Listen, I'm not the bad guy here."

"Really? Who is?"

"You've got to trust me. I promise—"

I hold up a hand to make him stop talking. "Wait. That phrase. *Trust me.* It's almost always a bad sign. And you want to know a phrase that I find just as troubling? It's *I promise.* That one never works out well." I start to scribble my number on a napkin. "I don't trust you at all, Larry Wozniak. You're mixed up with something not right about the *Molly Jones*, and you're trying to screw Ocean Catch out of a legitimate claim by linking the *Sea Wolf* to a tragedy it wasn't actually involved in. Those are pretty bad things to do." I slide the napkin over to him. "But I'll tell you what—if you ever want to get honest about why you're so interested in all these things, you can call me. And then we'll see if there's anything we can do for each other." I walk out.

Beacon Street is noisy with cars. The sky has darkened, and the wind has picked up. A tan car was behind me when I drove over here—a beat-up American model. It followed me through a couple of turns, parked about a block down from the café. It's still there, but there's no one inside. I walk past and see that the meter is paid. My car's across the street, headed in the opposite direction. I've got one eye in the rearview as I drive away. Two blocks down, I make a U-turn on a side street, park on the corner, and watch.

A cop who looks like Danny DeVito is writing a parking ticket. A group of teenage girls jaywalk like stopping traffic is their God-given right. The tan car doesn't pass. There are no suspicious characters anywhere. No baseball caps, no buttoned coats. Nothing, really, to worry about.

The next morning finds me at my kitchen table, frowning into my before-work coffee. I'd promised Johnny I'd let him know if I talked to Larry Wozniak. Maybe I should give Johnny a call, describe the crazy conversation I had with the insurance agent. It would be interesting to know why Johnny doesn't like him. It's obviously more than the fact that Larry crashed Ned's funeral.

I hold the mug with two hands, let it warm my fingers. *Think.* I don't know how Johnny connects to the *Sea Wolf* any more than I know how Larry connects to Ned. At this point I'm pretty sure I'm not going to be getting the full story from Johnny, just as I didn't get it from Larry. Maybe there's a way to play one against the other. Maybe if I tell Larry that Johnny's looking for him, and threaten to call Johnny, I can get Larry to open up. It's devious, but what the hell. I have nothing to lose.

He doesn't pick up at the number I called before, so I ring Jackson Hartwell on the dot of nine, ask to speak to Larry Wozniak.

The receptionist says she's very sorry, but Jackson Hartwell does not employ anyone by that name.

I ask if she's sure—perhaps he's freelance? A hired investigator?

No, he's not on the roster, never has been. She's sure.

"Oh, I see. Is Ocean Catch one of your clients?"

She's very sorry, but she cannot give out the names of individual policyholders or insured vessels. She hopes I have a nice day.

I put down the phone. Experience a bit of pre-nauseous whirling. The rabbit hole just got longer. *Trust me,* he said.

Not that I did. But still.

I google his name and get this:

Mr. Larry Wozniak WINSTON-SALEM—Lawrence Brian Wozniak, 30, of Garden Valley Drive, died Monday, July 21, 2010, at WFU Baptist Medical Center after a sudden illness. He was born June 27, 1980, in Greenwood County, S.C., to Ronald E. Wozniak and Katherine Bryant Wozniak. He attended Mars Hill College and Wake Forest University. He was a medical technologist at WFU Baptist Medical Center. Memorials to be directed to the Liver Transplant Memorial Fund at Duke University Medical Center.

No wife. No kids. The right age. A good identity to steal.

Chapter 14

"Pirio!" Thomasina greets me like I'm an old friend she lost track of years ago. When I follow her into the kitchen and see who's standing at the counter, this reaction makes more sense. It's Max, the guy from the funeral party. He's shirtless and shoeless, mixing up pancake batter. He gives me a charming smile. Thomasina goes over and rings his lean torso with her arms, turns a pleased, bashful face to me. "Pirio! You remember Max!" There's an air of festive domesticity and good happy fucks. Even the Saturday-morning sunlight streaming through the window seems especially bright.

The whole thing makes me feel like a dour spinster, since my first reaction is incredulity; my second, suspicion; and my third, doom mongering. It doesn't help that I've stopped by to share news about suspicious payments, secret voyages, and a fraudulent insurance agent. Not to mention what I forgot to tell her about the U.S. Navy and me.

I greet Max as politely as I can.

Thomasina pulls out a chair. "Sit down, by the way!"

Oil is sputtering in a frying pan. Max turns off the heat and slides the pan onto a cool burner. Noah's bedroom door is closed.

"Look!" Thomasina sits next to me and shows me a delicate pendant she's wearing around her neck, holding up its small diamond between two fingers for me to admire. "Isn't it beautiful?"

I tell her it's lovely, even though we both know that she has more impressive jewels in her box, and that the diamond solitaire pendant necklace is not an object she has ever coveted. Until, apparently, just now.

"We're dying to go away together. Aren't we, Max?"

He has disappeared into her bedroom, and reemerges in a few seconds, pulling on a T-shirt. He looks healthier than he did in the thick, jaundiced atmosphere of Murphy's Pub. High-cheeked, ruby-lipped, he's the kind of man whose appeal lies in a feminine face set on a taut, muscular body. He and Thomasina are the same height, which creates a sibling impression.

"Don't we want to go away together, Max?" She seems to have an urgent need for Max to corroborate this fact. As if it will somehow cement them as a legitimate couple in my mind. Or hers. Or maybe his.

He says he'd love to get away, hasn't taken any vacation days all year. He smiles haphazardly.

"Just the two of you?" I say, wondering where that would leave Noah. But the answer's obvious: with me.

Thomasina charges into the breach. "Well, we'll have to see. It's still too early to make plans. Max doesn't have the time off yet anyway. For now we were just thinking of something simple, like maybe a weekend at Foxwoods." She gives him a brilliant smile.

He murmurs a vague, passive assent, and I'm struck by the inexplicable chaos of coupledom. Thomasina hates gambling. She was dragged into casinos by a gambling-addicted father who dolled her up and sneaked her in well before she was twenty-one. Before he could pass her off as an adult, he left her alone in hotel rooms with an array of oversized stuffed animals that were supposed to keep her company.

A place like Foxwoods is about the last place she'd want to go. But suddenly she's gung ho on the idea, and appears to be convincing Max, who seems like just the kind of guy who'd normally be dying to experience the high life there.

Thomasina pours me coffee, and Max resumes cooking the pancakes and bacon. He tells me he works at Massport: basically, he's a harbor cop. Knew Ned for years and is good friends with John Oster. "We're a tight group, us water rats," he says jokingly. He wields the spatula, flips the pancake discs with flair. I'm guessing Thomasina told him about finding the title of the *Molly Jones*. She's not good at keeping interesting factoids to herself. Max slides the plates across the table and sits down. Thomasina, making a show of dazzlement, leans over and kisses his neck, summoning a blush.

I pick up my fork. "Is Noah going to eat?"

He ate earlier, I'm told.

The conversation shifts to television drama. Max and Thomasina, looking urgent, tell me in virtually a single voice that the fall lineup is one of the best in years. He recounts a lengthy plot involving desperate characters. Complications abound.

"Positively Dickensian," Thomasina murmurs. I scan her face for irony, and find none, so apparently complete has been her transformation into this man's better half.

A respite from the charade opens up at the end of the meal when Max goes off to shower and dress. Then Thomasina resumes recognizable qualities. "Please, Pirio. I know you're disgusted—you show it, too, by the way. No wonder Max is dying to get out of here—he won't say it, but I can feel it in his body language."

"Sorry. It's a bit of a shock. You've known this guy, what? Two weeks?"

"The time doesn't mean a thing. When you're older, you know what's out there and exactly what you're looking for." She leans close, whispers, "You better get used to him. 'Cause I think he's the one."

"Oh, God. Cut the shit, will you? Get sober, see where that brings you. Jesus Christ."

Her eyes flash. "I'm sober right now. Do you see? I'm sober." She sticks her hands under my face so I can see they're not trembling. "I'm sober, and I don't care what you think. I want to get married, and why shouldn't I?"

"*Married?* Did you say *married?*"

"People get married all the time. It's a normal thing to do. Why shouldn't I try it?"

"Try it? You don't *try* being married. It's not a fucking outfit. And for that matter, you tried it already. Remember that?"

"What do you mean? Are you talking about Ned? You know we were never married. We didn't have a thing in common. He was all wrong for me. Max is completely different. He has a college degree and a good job. He can talk about books. You heard him."

"He was talking about TV."

"So what?"

"So what? So what's the difference between TV and books? Is that what you're asking?"

"Pirio, for God's sake, what difference does it make? I meant he's *literate*, OK? He can talk about things. He knows about the world. He's not boring." She doesn't say *like Ned*.

"He's completely average, Thomasina. He'll bore you in a month. You're ten times smarter than he is."

"I'm not. I'm not!"

We both remain silent while that dainty, love-soaked lie floats to earth.

She holds her balled napkin to her forehead, gives a few rapid sighs, like she's fighting back tears or trying to find them. Finally, she speaks in a sort of angry, pleading anguish. "Noah needs a dad. Boys need fathers. What do I know about raising a boy? They need fathers—a woman can't raise a son alone. They need someone to teach them things like . . . hunting." She looks so doubtful.

"Are you insane?"

"Don't say that to me. I'm trying, aren't I? Do you see what I'm drinking? Diet Coke. Look, I'm serious. That's *Diet Coke.*"

She's pointing to her glass, full of the amber soda. Still full.

"I haven't had a drink or even a Percocet in a week, ever since the funeral for Noah's hamster. Max understood right away; he went through the apartment with me, helped me get rid of everything. He says to call him anytime; he comes over after work. He's giving me a new life, Pirio. Come on, when's the last time you saw me smile when I wasn't high? I know you're pissed about the shit I've been pulling. So am I. I want to be a good mother to Noah. He deserves so much more than what I've been giving him. And Max just makes me feel . . . I don't know how he makes me feel. . . . Just *better*. Like, maybe not well but better. Like I *could* be well. Normal, with a normal life. You know, go to the mall on Saturdays, soccer games, pizza nights with friends. . . ." Her voice trails off. "Thanksgiving," she says vaguely. "It's coming up."

I resist making a remark about Norman Rockwell, because that would have been her line. Ten years ago, it would have been on the tip of her tongue. Instead, I blurt that Noah doesn't even play soccer.

"He could learn," she insists. "He'd join a team and have friends like all the other boys. Because his mother wouldn't be a drunk anymore." Her face is hot; her lips are trembling. "She'd be married—we'd live in a real house. He wouldn't have to be ashamed." She sips the Diet Coke gingerly, trying to like it.

My eyes fill. It's true. She's drinking Diet Coke, not a morning mimosa or Bloody Mary, and she doesn't seem hungover. She *is* trying. My anger slowly deflates, and I regret everything—myself, my hard line, what I think I know about anything. I blink back tears, but my heart won't stop churning. "Jesus, Thomasina," I say finally.

She softly says, "I know."

When Max returns, damp and clean, Thomasina and I are staring in opposite directions, trying to collect ourselves. The astringent, lime-patchouli scent of Old Spice aftershave wafts off him. It's the noxiously familiar odor of too many generations of dull American men. I wish he were wearing anything else.

"Max, dear," Thomasina says, turning a composed face to him. "Pirio and I have been friends forever. Since high school. We're like sisters almost."

He understands immediately, says it's time for him to be off. Says it was nice to see me again, blah, blah, and is gone.

Thomasina gets up to do the dishes; the stiffness in her back is armor against my skepticism. I don't offer to help. The kitchen's small, there's not much to do, and I want to give that stiff back the space it's asking for.

There's a lime-green iPod nano propped in a Bose speaker on the scarred wooden table, twenty or more jars of spices grouped haphazardly on the counter next to the stove. Manila folders are stacked along the windowsill, Thomasina's rudimentary filing system. Back when we were roommates at the Gaston School, she was the detailed one, always writing notes to herself and keeping track of events in a weekly planner. She also kept diaries, scribbled her thoughts and feelings daily and copiously, seemingly on fire with the urgency of making a complete record of herself. What I assume to be her present diary—a leather-bound book with an ornate medieval-looking clasp—is on a shelf next to an incense burner. I imagine her up at midnight, engrossed in getting down all the intimate details that no one else in this world cares about. Why wouldn't she want a real person to confide in, instead of a blank book?

Having rinsed and stacked the dishes, she pours me more coffee and sits down at the table with a purposeful thud that indicates she will not be easily moved. "Please be happy for me, Pirio. Please."

"Sure. I'm happy," I say woodenly.

She drops her voice to a low, confidential level. "You know how I know he's the one? I drew the Empress at Madame Jeanne's."

Oh, no. This is worse than I thought.

Madame Jeanne is Thomasina's muse and mentor, her spiritual guide. On Wednesday afternoons she sits in the window of a trendy café on Newbury Street and gives fifteen-minute tarot readings for ten dollars. Thomasina brought me to the café once several years ago, and, when I sat down across from Madame Jeanne, a cold wave of aversion passed through me. I didn't like the powdered web of wrinkles at the corners of her eyes, or her blue eyeliner, or the brownness of her large, flaccid lips. She was old, but it wasn't her age that bothered me, or even her cheap costumey clothes. It was her aura of emotional collapse.

"The Empress is the arch feminine," Thomasina says. "She's all about love, sexuality, and fertility. A really positive card. I've always wanted to get it but never did, never thought I would. Then I met Max, and I started to feel just a tiny bit like these things might be possible for me. So I went to Madame Jeanne, hoping in the back of my mind to get this card, and—can you believe it?—it turned up in the second row.

"But that wasn't all. I also got the Wheel of Fortune and the Nine of Cups. The Wheel of Fortune is about a really big positive change about to take place. And the Nine of Cups? Well, that's just about the best card there is. Riches, success, fulfillment—it's all predicted in just that card. Getting these three together in one reading is unbelievable. It's like all the stars lining up and the whole world suddenly transforming into a better place. Funny thing is, I always thought it would happen for me this way—that someday my life would just change. Years of going nowhere—and then one day I'd wake up and everything would be different, better—the way it always *ought* to have been. Madame Jeanne kept asking me what was going on, and the only thing different in my life was Max."

I've never seen her so delusional. And that's saying a lot. "What you're describing isn't love. It's not even romantic love."

"What's romantic love anyway? Isn't it just the same as hope? A crazy hope?"

"No." It can't be that. But I'm not sure. "Are you really happy with Max? With him and no one else?"

"I can see why you might be skeptical. I know I'm getting ahead of myself right now. But if I believe in what I'm doing, believe whole-heartedly in this choice and give it my all, then who's to say in five years' time it wouldn't have become love after all, and then everything would have turned out all right?"

"But how is it *today*, Thomasina?"

"Max is good for me. I haven't dated anyone like him for a long time." She picks up the Diet Coke, sips at the rim like a determined ten-year-old. Avoids my eyes.

The problem with alcoholics is that it's easy to think you make them do it. That my raining on her love parade is the simple hex that will cause what actually is inevitable. That could even be what she'll end up telling herself, at moments anyway, in her future hours of bitter, lonely stupor, which are prophesied in the white-knuckled fingers that clasp the glass, and her oddly twisting mouth.

Noah's room is filled with a bed, a desk, a rocking chair, an aquarium, and a turquoise lava lamp. There are posters on every square foot of wall, and every square inch of horizontal surface is covered with books, projects, artifacts, stuff. The shades are drawn; dirty blue curtains droop from their rods. Noah, fully dressed, is lying on the rumpled sheets of his bed, lost in a comic book.

"Has he gone?" A tone of patient sufferance.

"Yes." I take a seat in the rocking chair.

Noah slowly turns a page, only the top of his head visible. "I like Mighty Thor better than this. The Hulk's getting stupider."

"Really? Why?"

"He says dumb things."

"And Thor doesn't?"

"Not *as* dumb."

"Oh."

He closes the comic book. "Want to see a box I found?"

"Uh-huh."

He scrambles to his feet and kneels by the bed, pulls out a wooden box, and puts it on my lap. There's a faded flamenco dancer painted on its top—dark hair piled high, two blotches of rouge on her cheeks, castanets in her bent wrists. She is whirling, showing a saucy profusion of white petticoat under her red dress. He takes pains to show me how the top is fit into a groove that slides open noiselessly, letting a wisp of sweet, dirty tobacco odor escape. Inside are only a few wood shavings.

"What are you going to put in here?"

"Nothing." Noah turns the box upside down and shows me how to spring a false bottom by pressing down in one corner until the opposite edge slowly lifts. The workmanship is ingenious and precise; the secret space is the size of a pack of cards. It's also empty.

"What are you going to put in *here*?" I ask.

He shrugs nonchalantly, avoiding my eye, a man about his business. "Don't know yet. Maybe money." There's something rough and mechanical in his movements as he closes up the box. Playtime over.

But Pirio the Good Fairy Godmother isn't going to let him get away with that—reality may be harsh, but a secret compartment is still a secret compartment. "Money is good," I say. "Treasure is better."

His eyes find mine, the same heartbreaking gray as Thomasina's, and his pursed mouth relaxes a bit. "What kind of treasure?"

"Rubies, turtle shells, bark of a mango tree."

He nods, giving judicious consideration to my list. Then he tells me that if you light methane gas it will explode. "Cows fart methane, just like us. It makes global warming worse."

I tell him that if we could harness the power of methane gas, we wouldn't have to burn coal or have nuclear plants. The problem becomes the solution.

"Right." He's excited now, and way ahead of me. "We'd put all the cows in a big building and cover it in, like, some kind of plastic thing, and then we could suck the gas out with fans"—he holds his nose with clothespin fingers—"and make all the gas go in tubes to the city, and then light it on fire."

As he talks he bends forward, elbows on the arm of the rocking chair, then slides into my side nonchalantly, like he's just leaning, and a minute later he's on my lap. Little Noah again, with the fine-as-silk, sweet-smelling hair.

We draw some pictures of possible methane-collection apparatuses that would probably burden the animals with no more indignity than what they presently suffer at our hands.

"Wait," Noah says. He crosses the room on quiet feet, slides open his desk drawer, and removes something that fits into the palm of his hand. He comes back and opens his fingers slowly, showing the object to me. It's the whalebone. "I'm going to put *this* in the secret compartment, so no one can find it but you and me. I'm not ever going to let *him* see it." He tips his head in the direction of the door.

We go into the living room, where Thomasina is camped out on the couch with a cup of coffee and the *Globe*. It feels OK. Sunlight. Saturday morning. The apartment clean, Thomasina sober. Noah jumps next to her, leans against her arm.

"Hungry, sweetie?"

"No."

Mother and son smile at each other. Thomasina puts her arm around him, and he snuggles. They've been through a lot together, and when they find each other, they're home.

Time for me to go. The shady dealings I wanted to talk about don't seem important right now.

The phone call from Thomasina comes that evening. "Max and I were thinking maybe next weekend. Foxwoods, I mean. Just two nights. But only one if you'd rather. That is, if you can do it." A pause. "You'll take Noah, won't you, Pirio? He won't stay with anyone else."

"Yes, of course."

"Oh, thank you, thank you. I'm so grateful—you have no idea."

Chapter 15

Murphy's Pub on a Saturday night draws a motley crowd of tired-looking singles. The men are in flannel and dirty denim; the women wear tight jeans and a lot of eyeliner. The jukebox is carrying on with the eternal golden oldies, and the television above the bar is showing the Red Sox playing the Orioles in Baltimore. A few guys on stools are staring up at the screen. I take a seat between two of them and order a draft beer from a friendly, burly bartender. Finally one of the guys notices me, and as soon as we start talking, the guy on the other side of me checks me out and joins the conversation. Turns out the first guy, Ron, works construction and the second, Tim, works at Ocean Catch. It isn't long before they figure out that they're sitting next to the Swimmer. This wakes them up a bit; they move in closer, innocently excited, eager to tell their own miracle tales that they readily admit can't compare to mine. There's friendly sparring between the two gentlemen. They scan my face for approval, nearly blush when they get it. The boilermakers keep coming—all free for me—and soon the worn-out pub starts looking kind of sparkly and magical.

After about an hour, when we're three best buds and pleasantly looped, I turn to Tim and casually say, "I was down at dry dock the other day. Saw one of your boats with a cracked hull. Like, that must be kind of scary, huh? You're out in the middle of the ocean, the hull cracks. What do you do?"

"It wasn't as bad as it sounds. Stress fracture, that's all. We made port in time."

"You were *on* that boat?" I say incredulously. "The *Sea Wolf*?"

"Yeah, sure. Was a hell of a trip."

"I'll bet. Where'd you go?"

"Oh, no place special. Same old, same old. But I'll tell ya, I saw one thing on that voyage I ain't never seen before. Captain and the fishmaster almost came to blows. I swear, I thought Lou Diggens was gonna toss the little Jap overboard. Lou's a damn good captain, but he's a hothead. Not good to be on Lou's bad side. Thank God the Jap backed down. Or else it would have been sayonara for him."

"No shit," the construction worker says, nodding solemnly. He asks what they were fighting about.

Just then I happen to twirl a bit on my bar stool—I'm about half sober. Or less. A young skinny guy is standing in the shadows beside the doorway of the pub. He's got slack dirty-blond hair and a face shaped like a beaver tail. There's a weird, unhealthy twitchiness to him. More disturbing, I'm sure that his vivid black eyes—all pupil, no iris—were just boring a hole in my back. There's a couple of seconds of lag time, then he slips out the door so fast I'm doubting he was really there.

"Hey, Ron, Tim. Did you see that guy? The one who just left in a hurry."

"Nope," says Ron, not even turning around.

"Who? What guy?" says Tim, glancing over his shoulder.

"Never mind. Go on with your story."

"So the cracked hull, that's where it came from," Tim explains. "The fishmaster insisted on top speed. Captain Lou went along with it at first, but when ice floes appeared, he said no way. Jap said do it.

157

Lou said no. Then we hit a sunken floe straight on, and Captain Lou just about threw the little guy overboard. I heard Lou went to Dustin Hall afterward and said he'd quit before he'd work with another ignorant Soga bastard."

Ron asks what a fishmaster is.

"He controls the fishing operations. Which fishing grounds to go to, where to set the hooks or nets, how long to stay in an area. He's not supposed to control the ship itself. That's the captain's job, and the captain has seniority. Always. No one goes against the captain."

"So why was this guy being such a prick?" I ask.

Tim swigs his beer. "Why do you think? He wanted a bigger catch. Doesn't give a shit about anything else. Those guys aren't even supposed to be on our boats in the first place. There's a law that says American commercial fishing vessels have to be under the control of American citizens at all times. That's to keep foreigners from buying American vessels and fishing in our waters."

"Soga?" I repeat, to be sure I remember it.

A shadow passes over me, and a heavy arm is laid across my back. "*There* you are. Tim, you met my girlfriend. She's a sweetheart, isn't she?"

I shrug Johnny's arm off my shoulder. "Where'd you come from?"

"Where'd *you* come from? This isn't exactly your side of town anymore."

"I missed the place. Anything wrong with that? And I wanted a beer."

"Yeah? Looks like you had a few." A look passes between Johnny and Tim. Tim gets off his stool and disappears without a good-bye. Ron disappears, too. Maybe they think I really am Johnny's girlfriend.

"You sure you weren't looking for me?" he says, shooting me a rare, guarded smile.

"It's date night for marrieds. Where's your wife?"

He leans in too close. I can smell his breath, see the pores in the skin on the side of his nose and the pink stubble on his upper lip. I'm so uncomfortable that I don't even hear what he's murmuring in my ear.

Obviously, it's high time for the likes of me to be heading home. I slide off my bar stool. The floor's closer than I thought it would be. Johnny catches my arm before I fall.

"Hey, careful now. Sit down over here for a minute," he says, leading me to a table. "You and Tim had a nice conversation, I take it. What were you talking about?"

"Lots of things: swimming, cars, his lard-ass ex."

Johnny's face is impassive. He's trying to figure me out.

Then it comes to me: I'll play the traumatized drunk. It won't be hard since I'm already halfway there. I let a disorganized torrent of emotion gush from my mouth. The accident, the flashbacks, the nightmares. Why did it happen? Why haven't the bastards been caught? And who the fuck makes fucking life rafts that don't fucking inflate? My voice rises in outrage and breaks soulfully in the appropriate places. I nearly cry. Usually, a performance like this is enough to make a guy like Johnny run for cover. But he's hanging in, studying me harder than he ought to be, without much sympathy.

I demand another shot of whiskey and another bottle of beer, and when they come, I tip the shot glass into my mouth, swallow the whiskey in one gulp, and slap the empty down on the table. "My father always told me—he's a bastard, in case you didn't know—he always said . . . *Get back in the saddle, girl!* That's the only way to cure the fear when you've been thrown by a horse. If you don't crawl right back into that saddle, you'll be horse shy forever! That's what he always said."

Johnny blinks. This is just the kind of macho hogwash he believes in himself. "Does that mean you want to go fishing again?"

"Sure. I gotta be free, don't I?" My hand wraps clumsily around the beer bottle.

He pries it from between my fingers. "Let me take you home. You shouldn't drive."

At this point, I'm pretty sure he's satisfied that I'm an authentic emotional mess. That I came down here to get drunk like I used to in the good old days and ended up harmlessly bending Tim's ear with my neurotic survivor needs. I burp for good measure.

"Nah, don't bother, Johnny. I'll take a cab."

"You won't get a cab down here. I'll take you," he repeats.

"Well, you're not coming in!" I announce.

"Not tonight anyway."

"Not ever, Johnny. You're a married man. Four kids. Fuck it. Shame on you."

The car ride's quiet. He pulls up outside my apartment. I fumble with the door handle, and he reaches across my lap to open it. But before he does, he leans some of his upper body weight on me, brings his big square face close to mine.

"Stay uptown from now on, Pirio. I don't want you getting hurt."

"Why would I be getting hurt, Johnny?" I drawl.

"Go home now. Go to bed."

There's no home page for Soga Fisheries, but I find two news stories on the web. One says that in addition to buying millions of dollars' worth of fish from around the world for distribution to Japanese retailers, Soga Fisheries operates its own fleet of six fishing vessels. One of these was caught trawling in a twenty-five-mile Hoki breeding ground on the west coast of New Zealand's South Island last summer. The company forfeited a $2.4 million ship named the *Soga Maru No. 8* and a catch worth $85,000. Another story reports that the company lost another of its ships, the *Soga Maru No. 1*, when it capsized off the northern coast of Russia. Twelve of the thirty-six crew members died, and the Japanese Coast Guard accused Soga of inadequate safety measures.

OK, so Soga Fisheries cuts corners. Interesting, but not unusual.

I return to the top of the article and realize that in the very first sentence Soga Fisheries is described as a subsidiary of the Jaeger Group.

The Jaeger Group's Website reveals that it's a conglomerate composed of forty international companies involved in real estate, manufacturing, and fisheries. It has offices in New York, London, Moscow, Tokyo. The home page is crisp, glossy, and polished, with revolving photographs of breathtaking forests, oceans, city skylines—the various worlds of Jaeger are bathed in clean sunshine pouring out of cloudless skies. I click around the site and discover that there are relatively few pages, that information is scant, and that the copy is mostly self-congratulatory. The Jaeger Group sponsors a scholarship program for young scientists and is dedicated to community involvement and social responsibility. Its commitment to global environmental sustainability is repeatedly emphasized.

I fall into bed with an authentic boilermaker headache and no answers.

It's Sunday and a special exhibit, so the Museum of Fine Arts is crowded. I happen to be occupying the choicest spot in a small group of viewers clustered around a self-portrait of Henri Toulouse-Lautrec—jaunty, mysterious, smug. A woman with a large handbag jostles me. Apparently, she thinks I've been studying the artist's self-portrait long enough.

Moving out of reach of the woman's handbag, I scan the crowd. Mrs. Smith's low gray head is bobbing among the patrons. She insisted on meeting me here when I called her this morning. She sees me and waves. Today she's wearing a fun-loving purple trench coat. Her canvas tote shows a stylized cat's face over the words "Walk for Animals."

"Let's go someplace quieter," I say.

I steer us out of the crowded hall, through the gift shop, down a long corridor of nineteenth- and twentieth-century European art. We find an empty bench of tufted velvet in the last hall, before the massive painting of Gauguin's *D'où Venons Nous? Que Sommes Nous? Où Allons Nous?*

"What do you know about Soga Fisheries?" I ask her.

"Soga Fisheries? They're Ocean Catch's best customer. They buy about seventy-five percent of the company's fish."

"Is there any reason they'd put one of their employees on an Ocean Catch vessel?"

"I don't see why. They're a wholesaler. They buy from us and other American companies, and sell to Japanese retailers."

"Seems like a long way to come to get fish."

"It's a global market now. The wholesalers go wherever they get the best price. And there's a big demand for the flounder and halibut that come out of the North Atlantic."

"They must be getting a good price from Ocean Catch."

"I'm not sure what they get. It would vary with market rates. But I'm sure they do well enough. Dustin's very loyal to Soga. If it weren't for them, we'd have had a hard time keeping our head above water when the new fishing regulations went into effect a few years ago."

"I heard there was a Soga fishmaster on the *Sea Wolf*."

"Hm, can't imagine why . . ."

"What about the Jaeger Group? Know anything about them?"

"Jaeger Group . . . Jaeger Group . . . I don't think so. Oh, unless you mean Bob Jaeger? He used to call Dustin once in a while. I was always supposed to put his calls through right away. I never met him, but Dustin went to New York for meetings with him a few times."

"Do you have any idea what they talked about?"

"Dustin acted like they were personal friends."

"Really?" Fretful Dustin Hall doesn't seem like the kind of guy who'd fit in socially with billionaires.

I pull out my phone. "Give me a minute, Mrs. Smith. I want to look up Bob Jaeger." As I'm searching the Internet, Mrs. Smith gets up and wanders over to the Gauguin. She stands a few inches away from the far right side of the painting, and begins looking up and down the canvas, squinting as if she's attempting to decipher a vertical hieroglyph.

There are a lot of entries for Bob Jaeger. I click on the first link—an article in a golf magazine. Apparently, Jaeger and a partner won first place in the Pebble Beach National Pro-Am tournament this year. But an attentive golf official noticed that Jaeger had submitted a greatly inflated handicap that had given him an unfair advantage, so he was stripped of the title.

The next link goes to a tabloid newspaper. Headline: "Fairy Tale Over for Billionaire and Princess Bride." Turns out Jaeger's wife was diagnosed with schizophrenia after she set fire to their house, and went off to a life of close supervision in a mental hospital.

The rest looks like boring business stuff. I put my phone away. Mrs. Smith has made her way to the left side of the Gauguin by now. She is staring at it with rapt attention and finally breaks away to rejoin me on the bench.

"I hope Dustin didn't play golf with Jaeger," I say.

"Really? Why?"

"He cheats. Mrs. Smith, think. What else can you tell me about him?"

She frowns. "Let me see. Uh, no . . . I'm sorry. If I remember anything more, I'll let you know."

"I need to find out where the *Sea Wolf*'s been going. There's got to be a way."

"Well, you obviously can't ask Dustin or Lou or any of the crew members. The only other way would be to get ahold of the ship's logs."

"Where would I find them?" But my heart's sinking even as I ask the question. If reports do exist for the *Sea Wolf*'s voyages, it's not likely they'd be accurate.

"In Fred Jacobsen's office. He's the director of operations. Third floor, next to Dustin. There's a file cabinet in the corner. I used to file the logs in there according to vessel."

"Aren't there electronic versions?"

"Oh, no. The logs are always written by hand on board ship. I know it sounds old-fashioned, but fishing is a very traditional business. The only changes fishermen like are ones that have to do with safety or productivity."

"What does Fred Jacobsen use them for?"

"If he ever consults them at all, I'd be surprised. The logs are just archival information. Even so, they seem to be the heart and soul of the company. The story of every voyage, kept for posterity."

Mrs. Smith and I leave European Art and pass through the rotunda. I'm wearing a black cowl-neck sweater dress with a green suede belt and a houndstooth newsboy cap. My hair is gathered in a clasp at my left shoulder and falls loosely to my waist. A lot of people look at me, especially men. No one looks at Mrs. Smith. They look past her, through her, around her, to get to me. She doesn't notice, of course. The curve in her back is not too pronounced, but it keeps her head angled down a bit, failing eyes on the humble floor.

It occurs to me that I haven't asked why she's seen fit to offer me so much possibly incriminating information about a company she still seems loyal to—that, in a way, I haven't noticed her either. As we step into the crisp late-September afternoon, our light coats draped over our arms, I ask.

She looks up and smiles when she hears my question. "One doesn't ever really know, does one? Why we do things? But I can say that, with this business, there are things . . . , I mean, *ways* . . . No, there are *things* . . ." A sigh. "Oh, blast it. The truth is, one holds on to what one can. One learns to cherish what's left. Of ourselves, I mean, when the rest is stripped away."

She looks at me for confirmation, and I try for a neutral expression, though what I'm feeling is a vague alarm at her confused and confusing answer.

My expression doesn't fool her. "I'm sorry, dear. I'm not all here anymore."

I nod, and she pats my arm reassuringly, as if I'm the unfortunate one.

"But don't worry," she continues briskly. "I don't leave pots on the stove or go walking through the streets in my pajamas. I just . . . well, sometimes I'm not sure exactly where I am. Or why. The doctors don't tell you how much you've lost. They just keep an eye on you. I try to exercise my memory to keep up what I've got left. But it doesn't seem to go very far. All the people I used to know—I'm not sure of their names anymore. Men I loved—and let me tell you, I had my loves. . . ." She drifts off. As her mind wanders even further afield, she smiles ruefully to herself and whispers, "Those were memories I would like to have kept."

I wonder now if anything she told me about Ocean Catch is true. And as far as memories of men go, I wonder if she'd like to take mine.

"But what I meant to say is that, now that everything is going from me, I have learned to treasure what I think I know."

I wait a beat. Two beats. "Which is . . . ?"

"Which is what you'll find out. If it's there to be found. If I'm not an old fool, and still count for something. Wait. I'll give you something that will help." She rummages in her canvas tote, pulls out a pencil, and tears a strip of paper from an address book. She holds the pencil over the paper for six, eight, ten seconds—frowning deeper all the time. Finally her eyes pop open—the tight, dry eyes of terror. "You see? I've forgotten it, the password to the alarm system. It's gone."

"I'm sure there's some way—"

"No, there's no other," she insists. "They'll never give up the logs if you ask. You have to go at night when no one's there, and simply take them. If I had that password . . ."

As we walk down the museum steps, I take her hand and realize she's trembling.

"Eventually everything will go this way, won't it? I mean, my mind," she says.

"Please, Mrs. Smith. I'm sure . . ." But I stop, tongue-tied.

"God bless you for doing what I can't," she whispers.

Mrs. Smith lets me drive her home to Jamaica Plain. She lives on the first floor of a three-decker with concrete steps and an old glass-paned door in which a sweet lace curtain hangs. I hear Jasper greeting her with happy barks as she steps inside.

Twenty minutes later, I'm listening to her voice on my message machine. "Twice a month the Bay State Cleaning Company cleans the processing area and the offices at Ocean Catch. They've got a team of five or six, I think, who work most of the night. They have their own set of keys to a basement door on the side of the building and to all the offices. They come the first and third Wednesdays of every month. So the next time they'll be there is this coming Wednesday, October 2. Ha! I remembered that!" I can almost hear her smiling. "Good luck, Pirio."

Chapter 16

The morning after my sudden departure from Panama City, Eileen had called in a dither about the aborted experiment that was supposed to have taken place that Monday. I had apologized, citing a family emergency. She asked when I was going to return to complete the most important part of the test. I said I would when my family matter was resolved. She called my office on Wednesday right before the sniff party. I said things were still up in the air. When she called again the following morning, I had the office assistant tell her I was in a meeting. I didn't get around to returning her call, having more pressing matters on my mind. The truth is, I'd blocked out the whole Navy thing at that point. (Excuses: worrying about Noah, getting Thomasina out of jail, finding mysterious boat, uncovering false identity of so-called insurance investigator. Oh, and this one: not crazy about freezing to near death.)

But Commander Audrey Stockwell is not one to let a test subject get away, especially one that's already taken up a fair amount of the Navy's time and money. So Friday morning she herself called my home, office, and cell to invite me back to her emerald-oceaned city. Seeing caller ID on my cell, I didn't pick up, so she left a voice mail.

Her manner was friendly, but her voice was a tart three-to-one blend of vinegar and sugar, and I got the feeling that if I didn't agree to show up at NEDU soon, armed enlisted men would appear at my door in the middle of the night, a black car idling in the street below. So I took a deep breath, dialed her direct number, got bumped to Eileen, muttered something not-untrue about having to attend a sudden funeral (for a hamster), and we got through the awkwardness. A half hour later Eileen e-mailed travel arrangements.

I'm leaving for Panama City today at noon, coming back tomorrow night. Two more days off work. Maureen's been handling my sick days and half days without complaint. She asks me endlessly how I'm feeling, whether I'm up to this or that perfectly ordinary task. I get the impression she'd be in favor of my taking a long PTSD sabbatical.

My flight's not for several hours, so I have some time to catch up with myself. Laundry, cleaning—that sort of thing. I don't dislike it, actually. The results are so lovely. Fresh smells, folded clothes, clean sheets. The toothpaste tube squeezed from the bottom, its top on, lying peacefully next to the toothbrush. Order and comfort have always been closely linked in my mind. What catastrophe can occur when there are fresh flowers on the table, beautifully arranged in a crystal vase?

I start in the living room—stack magazines, plump pillows, pull seat cushions off the couch. In the crease at the back where the pencils and crumbs hide, the edge of a metal object gleams. I pry it out a bit anxiously, because I knew as soon as I saw it that it wasn't mine. But it's nothing bad—just Noah's missing cell phone, which must have fallen out of his pocket when he came back here after Taffy's that day to play dominoes. I toss it on the coffee table, and make a mental note to call Thomasina to tell her I found it.

Tuesday, 7 a.m. A room in the Paradise Hotel. Not the one I was in before, but it might as well be. I put my toes on teal pile carpeting that feels like recycled plastic, shuffle to the bathroom, and observe my pale face under fluorescent lights that chronically pop and hum like mumbling schizophrenics abandoned in an insane asylum. Maybe I'm overreacting to the lights, I don't know. I'm terrified. The toothbrush shakes at the end of my hand, and my mouth feels dry as chalk, even when I'm brushing. I put on the Speedo Eileen gave me yesterday when she picked me up at the airport, then regular clothes over it, and tuck the green bathing cap into my purse. Still no flip-flops. It actually upsets me. It's easy to lose perspective when you've got a date with a tank of forty-degree water in an hour.

Eileen is waiting in the lobby to drive me to NEDU, but she is not nearly as friendly as she had been on my first visit. Her mouth is a stationary dash not more than an inch and a half wide. I am not the ideal test subject anymore, just the one she's stuck with.

Eight a.m. The gang's all present and accounted for at the Experimental Test Pool. There's a medical doctor, the sports scientist, a guy at the monitoring station, and a couple of people who are hanging around for undisclosed reasons. There's a Navy SEAL there, too. In a wet suit. I'm thinking he's my rescue squad. I'm 115 pounds, so one rescuer ought to be enough. He eyes me hungrily, not with sexual interest, more with ambition. Maybe he's eager to demonstrate his search-and-rescue capabilities to the top brass. I look around but don't see Commander Stockwell. I feel a bit hurt by that, as if it's my birthday party and the most popular girl in school decided not to come.

Eileen stands with me by the side of the pool. I've been fitted with a belt and harness that hold a round metal transmitter snugly against my chest. With a wan smile, I ask if I really have to don the bathing cap, and she looks at me as if I'm an idiot who should know better than that. So I put it on. I figure the cap will prevent my hair from clogging the filters as I lapse into shock or prolonged excruciating pain.

The water is darker than I remember it. No happy turquoise here. My toes curl over the concrete edge of the tank. Tender as pink flowers, homely and unwitting, they look like a line of plump toddlers who forgot their bathing suits. I suppose my toes are getting all my sympathy because I don't want to think about what's going to happen to the rest of me. I take Eileen's advice and do not dip any one of them in the water to test the temperature.

The sports scientist, a short brawny guy in a polo shirt, asks if I am ready.

I nod, inhale a shallow breath. I tell myself I'm back in Boston at the Y, that this is just a normal workout. I dive.

The water feels like a dozen jackhammers and a thousand pins. My brain contracts, as if running in terror from my skull. My fillings seem to expand in my mouth—bursting silver ice cubes along my aching jaw. The shock is exactly what I felt on September 7, except this time my head is filled with a different, more corrosive kind of fear. The kind that comes from knowing what I'm really doing to myself.

In seconds I'm disoriented. What world is this? I manage to get over to the float in the middle of the tank, grab hold of it, try to even my desperate gasps. It is hard to keep my right hand around the rope because my fingers are rapidly losing feeling. A long way away my bloodless feet dangle. My left hand slaps about ineffectively. Through the greenish water, my skin looks pickled and flayed.

When my breathing stabilizes, my fear abates a bit. I concentrate on drawing deep, even breaths, though my lungs feel as thin as tissue paper behind my ribs. My eyesight is curiously dim. The people on the edge of the pool seem to be miles away. They are facing me in a line, short and hunched, like penguins on an ice cap. Or seals, sea lions— I'm searching for the category of marine life they belong to. As if the fish in me is emerging and I only know how to recognize other aquatic creatures.

I don't know how long I hang on there until I experience a strange warming sensation. Like hot oil spilling from my core. I want to weep, I am so grateful. I am special! My body is fighting back! The grandiose impulse to swim comes over me. Letting go of the float, I roll onto my back, roll again like a revolving log, stroke down under the gentle waves I've made until I touch the bottom of the pool. Going up again, emerging into the air, my head butts forward, my shoulders and arms slope down.

The warming sensation was temporary. Violent shivering takes its place. I get myself back to the float somehow, barely keeping my flapping, chattering jaw above water. It feels as if my neck is trying to shake my head off. A strange compulsion to undress comes over me. I jerk off the bathing cap, and try to pull the strap of the Speedo off my shoulder, but I've got the harness and belt on and, in any case, my limbs are not coordinated enough to carry out this task. I do manage to wiggle one arm free, though. The people on the edge of the pool are gesturing and yelling to me, but I can't hear what they're saying.

My loosened hair floats around me like dark seaweed. This calms me for some reason, and I go a long way inside myself, to a restful place. My imagination begins throwing a lot of things my way. I am a worm in a wormhole pushing up through dirt, a leopard making crunching footfalls across a gleaming crust of snow. Then I'm a snake, armlessly contracting. There are other snakes around me, and they're all asking, *Where's the wind?* Strange, the lovely freedom that comes over me. To live instinctively like an animal, to be one among many, the burden of consciousness repealed.

Now the husky, unearthly barking of seals comes through my open bedroom window, and the thick, gauzy odor of drying stalks of Labrador tea wafts in from the kitchen. My bare feet pad across warm wood floors, turn a corner into a bright room. She looks up, smiles, pushes aside what she was doing. Folds me in her arms, sweeps me up to the sky, holds me close. I am special, loved. *Yes,* my heart replies. *It is so. Thank you for this life.*

Then it all goes black. No mother, no flowers, no barking seals. I'm all grown up, cold and alone, sick and weak. Around me shadows darken, lengthen, coalesce into jerking human shapes. Terrible peo-ple, cruel people. Encroaching from every angle. There, in the center. Someone I've met. *Mother? Isa? I'm frightened. He's here.*

I come to my senses on a bench by the side of the pool. The shiv-ering is so violent that I'm afraid my ribs will crack. I lurch to a stand-ing position and am pushed back, told to sit. A great deal of talk and commotion is happening around me. Things are being moved and pulled across my back. I am lifted, and my suit is pulled off; hot water bottles are shoved under each arm. A bathrobe is thrown around me, but it's not enough. I groan for more. A rational, well-regulated voice speaks to me in clear sentences: The test is over. I am not in danger. I have come through with flying colors. They will warm my body slowly so that the temperature of the blood in my extremities does not rise too quickly. In a little while I will be given heated water to drink. Then a shower. It has been decided that I don't need intrave-nous fluids.

Relief spreads through me. I want to hug everyone I see.

Eileen looks shaken. Maybe she's forgiven me. The terry-cloth robe feels luscious against my naked body, but my feet are still bare.

"Hey, am I ever going to get those flip-flops?" I say.

Several hours later, after a few more medical tests and a compli-mentary lunch consisting of a ham sandwich, cheesy corn puffs, Chips Ahoy!, and bottled iced tea, I'm ushered to a conference room on the second floor. Beyond the windows, sparkling sunlight pours onto a bright green lawn. Birds chirp, flowers bloom, palm fronds sway. It's hard to take war seriously in a geographic location such as this. But the Navy flag and the United States flag are standing together in a corner of the room like close fraternal twins, and three of the people at the table—Commander Stockwell, the medical doctor, and the sports scientist—are in uniform. There's a fourth person, too—a woman roughly my age in civilian clothes. She's introduced as Trudy

Flanagan, a psychologist. There are folders at each place, donuts and coffee on a side table. I take the only empty seat.

The medical doctor begins. He is long and thin, as quaint as a Victorian lamppost with a big bulb of head on top. He goes over some of the things Stockwell already said. Reactions to cold vary widely among individuals, and all that. Some people's bodies start breaking down right away; others succumb to hypothermia at the normal rate; a select few are able to keep their core organs warm somehow. They're the ones who make it to the top of Mount Everest. My physiology, he informs me, is at the Mount Everest end of the spectrum.

He passes around a handout with the data. But before he goes over the results, he tells me sternly that I was not supposed to dive into the tank; I was supposed to enter the water carefully, so as not to dislodge the data-gathering equipment. As it turns out, the transmitter worked anyway, but that was luck.

Some people believe that postevent scoldings are their virtuous obligations. Those people are assholes who deserve cold, stony looks.

The data: After 20 minutes my temperature had slipped to 94°F—mild hypothermia. At 60 minutes I was at 90°F, shivering violently, and my extremities were blue. At this point, while my body's cooling was taking longer than normal to occur, I was still reacting as expected. At 90 minutes and a temperature of 82°F, pulse and respiration rates slowed significantly. I had entered the danger zone. They were just about to haul me out when something strange occurred. My temperature began to rise. Slowly. They checked the instruments, waited, conferred, made a judgment call. They decided to keep me in. Fifteen minutes later I was back at 94°F, still cool, but showing no signs of stress. In fact, I was calling the Navy SEAL perched on the edge of the pool a sissy for needing a wet suit.

Everyone has a nice chuckle over that.

The doctor smiles with the lower half of his face. "The physiologic process actually reversed itself. We have no idea how that happened. We've never seen that in a human before."

I shoot a tiny smile back at him. I have no idea what to make of any of this.

The young sports scientist steps to the front of the room. He's as hip as you can be in a uniform, with an endearing cowlick at the crown of his short-haired head. He dims the lights and pulls down a screen. Of all the film clips I expect to see projected on it, about the last is a dozen Siberian huskies tethered to a stationary sled, barking uproariously and straining against their harnesses, obviously eager to run.

"The human body is constantly burning through its reserves of glycogen and fat. The harder it works, the faster the stores are depleted. Some of us call this process *exercise*." He smiles to let this ray of light-heartedness sink in. "As energy is depleted, we feel fatigue, and it becomes increasingly difficult to continue exercising until glycogen and fat stores are replenished. We've always thought of fatigue as one of the ways the body protects itself, a necessary biological process common to all living things. Then someone noticed a curious thing about the dogs who run the annual Iditarod sled race in Alaska. *They didn't get tired.* They ran eleven hundred miles across difficult terrain in freezing temperatures, and when they got to the end, they'd turn around and want to do it all over again.

"Researchers decided to measure their metabolic rates at different stops along the trail. At the start of the race, their bodies behaved in ways we think of as normal. But within twenty-four hours, their metabolic rates had slowed to the level you would expect to see in resting subjects. That's right: *slowed.* While they were running about a hundred miles a day and keeping it up for ten or twelve days in a row.

"It made no sense, had never been observed before, and went against everything we thought we knew about the mammalian body.

But there it was. Everyone could see it happening. Somehow the dogs were managing to stop—and even reverse—the fatiguing process.

"Since then we've been trying to find the biological mechanism, or switch, that the dogs are using to reverse the physiology of fatigue. It's entirely possible that humans have the same capacity. If we can find this switch, and learn to turn it on and off, we could teach our soldiers to overcome fatigue in strenuous situations such as combat. Unfortunately, our research so far has been inconclusive. But now you've come along and shown us something very similar in the case of thermal exposure."

He smiles broadly, like a man meeting his beloved. "So now we have a whole set of different questions to ask: How are you similar to a sled dog? How are sled dogs similar to you?"

I smile back, not so broadly. What I love about scientists is their vast imaginations and endearing social clumsiness.

Commander Stockwell leans across the table toward me, speaks in a clandestine voice. "What if someday we could program these twin metabolic functions, or train people in them? Imagine a fatigue-free soldier who could survive extremes of temperature. We almost wouldn't need troops anymore, just a few well-trained individuals. It sounds like science fiction now, but almost every medical advance and technology we rely on today sounded like science fiction when it was first considered."

There's silence at the conference table. I sense that I'm supposed to say something. But what? The whole thing feels weirdly invasive—all these people taking an interest in my body for reasons I didn't know until now and could never in a thousand years have guessed. I need time to sort it out, fit it into my identity somehow. *Pirio the Bionic Woman* doesn't sound right. But that's sort of what they're telling me.

I need a donut. I get up and walk to the side table, where there's an untouched assortment. I pick a chocolate, a glazed, and a jelly. This is no time to count calories. I bring the paper plate back to the table and start in on the chocolate.

Dr. Gas Lamp gives me his tepid smile. "Your physical was completely normal, as were all your labs. You're perfectly healthy, Ms. Kasparov. Nothing seems out of the ordinary. Yet you warmed yourself somehow in a situation that ought to have eventually killed you. We'd like to know more about how you did that."

"The psychological aspect needs to be investigated, too," Commander Stockwell asserts in a dry voice that sounds like a concession.

Flanagan takes the opportunity to chime in. "There could be personality traits that contribute to your resilience. Even attitudes and beliefs can play a part. Testing would give us a more thorough profile." She smiles, determined to establish trust. "The self-knowledge could be valuable for you, too."

The chocolate's a bit dry and crumbly, so I try the jelly. The people in this room smile way too much.

The psychologist's eyes brim with sympathy. "This must be a lot for you to process right now." She reminds me of the Empath on *Star Trek*, with her big pooling eyes and cushion of bosom.

"Yes, it is." In fact, echoes of the words I've heard are reverberating in my brain. *Sled dogs. Biomarkers. Fatigue-free soldiers. Science fiction.* I think I liked being a miracle more than I would enjoy being a specimen. A miracle is wondrous and powerful, but a specimen is small and brainless. It exists at the wrong end of pointed implements such as pens, tweezers, and microscopes.

"We would very much appreciate your cooperation for one more day," Commander Stockwell says.

Flanagan offers a coaxing smile. "Our battery of psychological tests is quite sophisticated. It could fill us in on mental survivalist traits that can't be discovered any other way."

"Sorry. I don't do psychological tests."

"Really? Not at all?" She wobbles a little regretful smile that promises best-friend status if I concede.

"Not on your life."

Flanagan looks startled, can't conceal a glint of anger. "May I ask why?"

I purse my lips to keep from saying what I shouldn't. In my mind's eye, I see a fat manila folder with my name on it sitting on Dickhead Bates's desk. It's crammed with tests, reports, notes, and analyses from the psychiatrist at Children's Hospital, the psychological testing service, and the therapist at Gaston. Hundreds of pages of pseudoscience to rationalize locking a girl in a room not much bigger than a walk-in closet for twenty-four hours at a time. A brilliant, benign, necessary, air-tight diagnosis that in the end was just a way of not taking an innocent, troubled child at face value or giving her what she most needed: the benefit of the doubt.

"It's personal," I tell Trudy Flanagan.

Flanagan begins shuffling papers clumsily. Commander Stockwell frowns.

I address my next remarks to her. "You have my DNA, CAT scans, MRIs, and bodily fluids. I swam in cold water for you. I think that's enough."

Stockwell regards me patiently. She's pleased with today's results and doesn't need to push for more right now. "You might reconsider when you've had more time to think about it. Your country is grateful for your service, Ms. Kasparov."

She slides an envelope toward me. Inside is a five-hundred-dollar honorarium and a complimentary ticket to Ripley's Believe It or Not! Museum.

"Maybe they'll put me in it," I say.

I have a few hours to kill before my flight, so I visit the museum. A big hardcover compendium of believe-it-or-not facts catches my eye in the gift shop. I buy it for Noah and read it myself on the plane. Dancing ants, fainting cats, a blind photographer winning awards. *Strange doings,* I think, *are business as usual on planet Earth.*

Chapter 17

It's just past two a.m. A harsh floodlight illuminates the Bay State Cleaning Company van parked near the entrance of the Ocean Catch processing plant and corporate headquarters. Two other cars are parked near the van—an old Corolla and a Chevy Impala that looks like it should have been scrapped years ago. There's a sharp bite of salt in the air from the ocean a few blocks away, and the creeping toxic odor of broken tar from potholes.

To avoid any security cameras, I left my car in a lot a few blocks east and picked my way along a narrow, rutted service road that runs parallel to the main street. The door Mrs. Smith told me about is just ahead, down a few concrete steps, lit by a single bulb overhead. It's standing about a foot ajar, probably propped open at the bottom. For five or ten minutes, I stay in the shadows, watching the door. No one goes in or out. I pull my wool cap lower over my face and scoot inside.

A basement storage room. Empty, bright, just a clean smooth gray-painted floor, and cold, dehumidified air. I pass through a door on the far wall into a hallway that has recently been cleaned with ammonia. At one end is a closed metal door, at the other a door with a red Exit sign above it. It opens onto a stairwell.

At the first landing, I stop and listen. The high whine of a vacuum cleaner reaches my ears. I proceed past the second floor and pause at the door to the third floor, where the administrative offices are. All's quiet, so I slip into the carpeted corridor. An elevator is directly across from me. To my left are four doors. Three are closed; the last is open, spilling light onto a yellow molded plastic cart stuffed with brooms and mops and cleaning liquids. To my right there's a bathroom and Dustin Hall's office.

Mrs. Smith said that Fred Jacobsen's office was next to Dustin Hall's, but it's obviously not. Who knows what other errors her misfiring brain has made? Maybe the whole ship's log thing is a fantasy. At least she was right about the cleaning company. I try the first door on my left. It opens smoothly, and in the same instant the room springs to brilliant life. It's the staff kitchen with a motion-activated overhead fixture where Mrs. Smith had her retirement party.

I open the next door, and this time the room stays dark. I enter, close the door gently behind me, and flip the wall switch. The office is small and crammed with furniture—desk, small couch, armchair, coffee table. A beige vertical blind covers the window. A metal file cabinet in the corner is stuffed so that the drawers don't close, and there are stacks of paper all over the floor. Looks like the digital age missed this room.

The diploma hanging above the desk among some framed family photos was awarded to Frederick Prentiss Jacobsen by Northeastern University in the Year of Our Lord Nineteen Hundred and Eighty-Two. I realize Mrs. Smith was right after all. Jacobsen does have the next office to Hall's; it's just not the next room. Jacobsen himself, if he's the guy holding up a trout in one of the photos, flanked by two boys roughly thirteen and fifteen years old, appears to be in his early fifties. Stout, with thinning blond hair, pink flaccid cheeks, and sweetish liquidy eyes.

A vacuum cleaner starts up in the room down the hall. I lock the door. I twirl in Jacobsen's imitation leather chair a few times like a kid. I can't deny there's a thrill in actually being here, undetected (so far), with (I hope) some answers close at hand. I rummage through the desk drawers for the perverse fun of it, but the contents are dull.

I move to the filing cabinet where Mrs. Smith said the logs are kept. I find invoices, engineering records, bills of sale, mechanical specs. The information dates back ten years. I scan for names of vessels, voyage reports, anything that might be a euphemism for a ship's log. Nothing. Maritime charts, reports from the EPA, and Fishing Commission documents fill the next two drawers. The bottom drawer's more of the same, except for a bottle of Jack Daniel's hiding out in the back with two shot glasses wrapped in paper towels.

The vacuum cleaner shuts off, leaving the floor preternaturally quiet. I have no idea what I would do if someone tried the door. The cleaning staff would be surprised to find it locked, since it wasn't before. I'm going through the stacks of paper on the floor when I hear the soft pneumatic whoosh of the elevator door. I freeze. A man's voice calls out for Nanda in a charming Indian accent—part clipped British, part dusky subcontinent. A woman's voice answers melodically from down the hall. A few seconds later there is joyful, bubbling laughter just outside Jacobsen's office. She must have rushed to meet him, and now, not more than ten feet from where I'm sitting, a passionate reunion is taking place. It is heartening to think that the long, lonely nights of a cleaning woman can be enlivened in this way.

I listen because I have no choice. It's impossible to pay attention to what you're doing when people are consuming each other sexually within earshot. And I can't exactly bang on the wall and tell them to get a room. I try not to follow where the sounds are taking me—back through the past to my own wild nights, which eventually became the last wild night, which segued into long, cold nights of Russian novels and decaffeinated tea. There's no place you can go in this world, no time of the day or night, that will let you forget about love. Finally, just when it seems the happy couple is on the verge of falling to the carpet to consummate their passion, they manage to drag themselves to the office at the end of the hall, leaving me to get back to what I was doing.

That's when I see the portable plastic file cabinet on the floor a few feet from the desk. It's got a handle on top and a clasp that's partway open. A little sticker under the handle says "Logs" in blue marker. I open it. The files are arranged alphabetically by vessel. The *Sea Wolf* folder is second to last. I pull it out and scan the contents. The most recent report is three years old.

I spread the other folders across the desk and quickly flip through them. Each one contains reports that are no more than a few months old. The company's entire fleet has been submitting detailed descriptions of its voyages to the director of operations in handwritten, stapled pages that are chronologically filed, the most recent on top. The entire fleet, that is, except the *Sea Wolf*, which hasn't filed a report since 2010. Despite how busy it's been.

Again, the elevator doors sigh and ping. I wait, expecting to hear someone get out, perhaps a supervisor to ruin things for the lovebirds. The doors close; I hear nothing. It seems no one got off, but then I sense a quiet step on the carpet outside Jacobsen's door. I'm thinking I must have imagined it when I see a gleam as the doorknob slowly turns, stopping when it hits the lock. Whoever is on the other side of the door pulls and pushes it a little, gently.

A woman's voice rings sharply, but with a genteel Indian cadence. "Can I help you, sir?"

I have no idea where she came from. I'm pretty sure she's not the young woman who's most likely being blissfully ravished down the hall.

A male voice answers—an American voice, low, muffled. The two converse briefly. I can't make out the words. He seems to be explaining something. She gives a friendly laugh. A jingling sound follows.

There's a metal clicking in the lock. She's got a set of keys and is about to open Jacobsen's door.

I can't go under the desk; it's too obvious. I fly across the room and manage to squeeze behind the armchair as the woman finds the correct key and turns the lock. I'm crouching down as the door swings open. Silence as they enter. The man thanks her, says he usually has his key. He—Jacobsen?—says something in a joking way about forgetting to shut off the lights. The woman asks if he still wants the office cleaned. He says it won't be necessary, and she leaves. Who the hell goes to the office at this time of night?

When I peek out from behind the chair, it's not the man in the fishing photo that I see, but the man who stole Larry Wozniak's identity. I don't know his real name, so for now I have to be satisfied with his borrowed one. He's sitting at Jacobsen's computer, and if he looked up he would see me, but he's too busy inserting his thumb drive into the USB port one-handedly. He's got his hair in a negligible ponytail; the lenses of his glasses flash in the computer glare. When the download's finished, he stands up and stuffs the thumb drive into his jeans pocket. The ship's logs are on the desk where I left them, a spread of nondescript manila folders. He doesn't touch them. He doesn't bother with the cabinet either, doesn't investigate the portable file box on the floor. A second later, he's out the door, leaving it ajar.

I crawl out from behind the chair. At the door I pause, listen. There's a three-way conversation taking place at the end of the hall. From the civil sound of it, I'd say the lovers were dressed and dutifully dusting when the woman with the keys arrived. I don't hear a trace of Wozniak. I look out. The corridor is empty. I've probably got only a few seconds before the supervisor comes back this way. I ought to jump into the stairwell, but I'm convinced Wozniak is still on this floor, and I want to know what he's up to.

I step lightly to Dustin Hall's door and touch the doorknob. Crazy, but it feels warm. And the door gives. Gently, I push it an inch or two, until I can see a corner of Hall's desk, illuminated by a lamp. I dare not open the door any more for fear of drawing Wozniak's attention, if he's there. But I know he is. And I can't help it. I swing the door open a little wider, until I see the sleeve of his brown leather jacket resting on the gleaming mahogany.

I retrace my steps and slip into the stairwell, race down three flights. Opening the door to the basement, I practically fall into a young, dark-skinned woman carrying a large carton with several rolls of toilet paper stacked on top. Her startled look quickly turns into alarm. She's not sure who I am; she only knows I'm not supposed to be there.

"Good evening, miss. I'm from the home office, sent to inspect your crew's work. I have to say I'm impressed. Very, very impressed. The carpets are fresh, not a speck of dust anywhere. Empty wastebaskets, spotless bathrooms. With your high standard of professionalism, you are a credit to the Bay State Cleaning Company. You can be sure I'll be giving your team an excellent report."

Her magnificent brown eyes have widened considerably. She's shocked, disturbed, flattered, delighted. She thanks me sincerely, letting a few toilet paper rolls fall off the carton in her excitement. I pick them up, balance them on top of the carton again.

"Carry on with the good work, miss," I say.

The moonless night is a relief after the building's manic fluorescence. The van and the two cars I saw before are still in the parking lot. I'm jogging to the dark corner that leads to the service road when I see another car, a red Honda CRV, that I'm pretty sure wasn't there before.

It's got to be Larry Wozniak's. I go over to take a look. The passenger door is unlocked, so I slip into the seat before I even know what I'm doing. Then I realize where my instinct is taking me. His car registration will give his real name.

The glove compartment is locked.

I try it several times, in case it's merely stuck. My frustration mounts. I feel like smashing the lock with something blunt, but I probably wouldn't have much luck. There's a waver of light in my peripheral vision. It's Wozniak crossing in front of the floodlight, making his way to his car. If I get out now, he'll see me. I dive into the backseat, try to lie down across the floor. First I have to push aside a pair of muddy hiking boots and some empty water bottles and Dunkin' Donuts coffee cups. The backseat is covered with folded maps and rolled nautical charts. There's also a small cooler and an alpine anorak. I feel like I've stumbled into a Boy Scout den. I quickly pull the anorak over me.

The thud of hard, fast footsteps heads toward the car. Wozniak gets in and sparks the engine. We do a one-eighty; the tires bump woozily across some broken pavement by the gate. He drives pretty fast—at least it feels that way to me—along the wide avenue that leads away from Ocean Catch.

From the change in the floor vibrations and the humming of metal, I can tell when we cross a bridge. Pretty soon we're taking a left. What street is this? I can't be sure. He puts on the radio and starts humming along to a Stevie Nicks tune. At one point he actually sings, not quite in tune. Given the hiking boots and maps, I'm starting to worry that this trip may be a long one. Out to some godforsaken suburb or, worse, the country. I'd hate to end up in a place where a person can't hail a cab.

"Shit," he says suddenly and emphatically. "Damn it, get off my ass." I feel the car brake, then speed up again. Brake, and speed up. He's being tailgated and, as some males are wont to do, is perversely trying to make a point. I take the anorak off my face and see headlights bouncing on the ceiling of the car and across the backs of the front seats. The car behind isn't backing off. Now the hum of a passing car makes me wonder why so many people are driving around the usually deserted waterfront district at this time of night.

"Fuck!" he erupts. "Watch it, will you?" The CRV swerves sharply to the right and stops with a jolt. He's out the door, slams it behind him. I hear his voice raised in anger, then other slammed doors—one ahead, one behind the CRV.

If these were cops, I would have seen blue lights.

Wozniak falls silent. I hear no other voices. Then two more car doors slam. One ahead, one behind. In addition to Wozniak, it sounds like at least four men have stepped out of cars. My blood slows to a crawl. A low, droning voice speaks for a while, then stops.

"Fuck you," Wozniak says, his voice carrying clearly in the cold air. Then his sharp footsteps are returning to the CRV.

The car is rocked by a heavy thud against the driver's door. Wozniak cries out. More thuds follow—thick, dull, rhythmic. I hear Wozniak's low groans. The blows, falling like rocks, follow him away from the car, until I can no longer hear them.

Sick with horror, I throw off the anorak and crawl into the driver's seat. The window beside me is spattered with blood. Wozniak has fallen to the ground in the middle of the road and is being kicked and beaten with pipes by three men who make a hunched circle around him, under a streetlamp that sheds a pallid light.

The CRV is still running. The headlights illuminate a black sedan not more than five feet off the front bumper, and a man in a down vest standing beside it.

Fuck. It's Oyster Man.

He doesn't see me. No one has seen me.

I shift into drive and jam the accelerator pedal to the floor.

The CRV crashes into the sedan, not a foot from where Johnny's standing. I'm slammed forward as the air bag inflates, hitting me in the chest and face, bouncing me back, breathless and stunned. I shift into reverse, stomp on the accelerator, and smash the car behind me.

I shift into drive, crash again. Can't see a thing with the air bag all around me, but it doesn't matter.

Shift into reverse, crash.

Shift, crash.

Shift—

Through the side window I see the thugs running to their cars before I manage to destroy them. I press the air bag down enough to see out a portion of the front windshield. Johnny isn't where he was. Before I can crash into the sedan again, it speeds off. The car behind the CRV swings out and follows it, passing a hairbreadth from Wozniak, curled like a fetus in the middle of the road.

I blink, draw a breath. I push the rest of the air bag out of the way and get out of the car. Wozniak's good arm reaches up, as if to hail a passing ship, and falls again. He rises on an elbow as I walk over, raises a ghoulish bloody face. "Who's that?"

"Pirio Kasparov."

"Oh, you." He's groping flat-palmed on the ground around him.

I pick his glasses off the pavement and put them in his hand. "Welcome to the land of second chances."

He puts on the glasses and peers up at me. "Pirio Kasparov. Sure enough."

I help him to his feet. One arm around my neck, he hobbles to the car and attempts to enter it on the driver's side.

"Oh, no. I've had enough of your driving." I steer him around the front of the car, heading toward the passenger side.

He stops midway, looks at the considerable damage. "What the fuck did you do to my car?"

"Nothing a body shop won't fix."

"Will it even fucking drive?"

"We'll see."

It does drive, though haltingly. Part of the wheel well has collapsed onto the right front tire, so forward motion is retarded by the friction and accompanied by an unpleasant scraping sound as layers of rubber are peeled away. Also, a sort of whining shriek is coming from who knows where.

He starts giving me directions, presumably to his house. We

bump along Summer Street, grind right onto Atlantic Ave, continue on Cross Street, hang a right onto Salem, and go six or seven blocks. The passable part of the road is narrow, the brick sidewalks are narrow, the brick town houses are narrow. Everything in the North End is narrow. We stop in front of number 180, just past the Old North Church. Parked cars are crammed end to end along one side of the one-way street, and anywhere else they can fit, except for in front of the church, which is a no-parking zone.

"The parking here is fucked," Wozniak explains.

"You don't have to say *fuck* in every sentence, do you?"

"Sorry. I'm about to spit my teeth out." He sticks a finger into his mouth, and it comes out bloody. He sighs. "I really don't feel like driving around looking for a space, so just pull in front of the church there and I'll risk getting a ticket. Who knows? I could get lucky. This time of night, it's a fifty-fifty chance, I'd say. What do you think?"

"Your call."

He nods judiciously. "What the fuck were you doing out there anyway?"

"I was lying on the floor in the backseat of your car."

He laughs maniacally. "Of course. Where else would you be?" He points behind him. "The church is back there on your right."

I throw my arm over the seat and back up slowly because one of the wheels keeps making a loud weird clunking sound. "Do you know who those men were?"

"Not a clue."

I step on the brake. "You mean you don't know who's trying to kill you?"

"No. Do you? Did you see them?"

My jaw clamps shut. I can't say his name: John Oster. He's still my friend, sort of. He was Ned's friend, definitely. And who, by the way, am I talking to? An insurance investigator named Wozniak? Better to play dumb. I don't think Johnny would have killed Wozniak anyway.

He's a fisherman, not a killer. He and his boys finally caught up to the funeral crasher and were teaching him a lesson, Boston style. That's all it was, I think. But I don't know.

"Let's not hang out here in the middle of the street in front of the church, OK? I don't need the whole neighborhood knowing I'm about to park illegally," Wozniak says.

"I think they're mostly asleep."

"Ha. That's what you don't know about the North End. This town has eyes."

I back into the space and shut off the car. He sighs with exhaustion, thanks me for driving, opens the door to get out.

"Wait. What about me?"

"You come, too." He's smiling, his bloody teeth pink in the glow from the dashboard.

Chapter 18

"One car pulled out behind me about a block away from Ocean Catch," Larry Wozniak's impersonator says. "I don't know where the other one came from."

He shuts off the tap at the kitchen sink. His mud-spattered glasses are on the counter. He's been splashing water over his face and neck for the last few minutes, washing off blood and dirt, soaking his T-shirt. At one point he stuck his whole head under the faucet, and some blood on his scalp rose and streamed through his ropy curls. Now his face is clean and chalky, except for a bruise sliced by a thin red cut that's blooming on his cheekbone. He's bent sideways a little, like a broken puppet. All the way from his car, along the sidewalk and up four (very narrow) flights of stairs to this apartment, he was hunched over, favoring the right side of his torso.

At this point in my life, no power on earth could turn me into a nurse. It's a well-established Kasparov trait. When I was a kid with a scrape or bruise—even, one time, a broken arm—Milosa would point out that the word *sympathy* is in the dictionary between *shit* and *syphilis*. When I reached my proud teenage years, I told him defiantly that I didn't see why a little sympathy should be so hard to come by. He looked at me as if I were a buzzing gnat and explained his position: "Emotion is like money. Once you spend it, it's gone. So don't waste your emotion on things that aren't worth it. A bruise heals, so what's to feel sorry for? A broken bone gets stronger. If someone hurts you deliberately, save up your self-pity and spend it on revenge."

"*It* is not a bruise; *it* is *me*," I told him, piping up.

This enraged him. "What? Who are you? Your flesh? Your tiny cut? Pah. Your body is nothing; it sickens and dies. If that is Pirio, I say good-bye to you now." When he got like this, you had to keep your mouth closed and let him rant. He might go from Gogol to perestroika to the American stock market to a son-of-a-bitch mule-beating uncle named Lusvin whom he hated with all his might. It all proved his point somehow, though the point itself usually remained elusive. In any case, if you wanted a Band-Aid, you had to get it yourself. A lousy excuse for why I don't jump up to dab at Wozniak's cuts with rubbing alcohol or insist that we rush off to the emergency room to have his ribs x-rayed.

Wozniak rinses off his glasses and dries them with a towel, slides them onto his nose. He starts rubbing his damp hair with the towel, and sits across from me at a tiny white formica table pressed against the wall of a galley kitchen.

I ask if he knows any reason someone would want to hurt him.

He asks what I was doing in his car.

I remind him that I saved his life.

He sighs. "I came across evidence of a . . . let's say, *unusual* relationship between Ocean Catch and a Japanese wholesaler called Soga Fisheries."

I tell him to go on.

"Ocean Catch used to sell its product all over the world, to whoever was the highest bidder. Then about three or four years ago, it started selling almost exclusively to Soga. Now about seventy-five percent of its catch—that's millions of pounds of fish each year—goes every week by air freight directly to Tokyo, packed in ice. Soga pays top dollar for it, well above market rate."

"Sounds like a good deal for Ocean Catch."

"It's more than that. The company was a few months away from bankruptcy when Soga stepped in. Basically, Soga's business prevented Ocean Catch from going under, and it's been single-handedly keeping the company alive since then." Some of the color has come back to his face. He tosses the towel on the kitchen counter. "See, the entire groundfish industry has been shrinking steadily for the last decade or more, and in the last few years fish companies have been going out of business left and right. Ocean Catch was on the verge of cashing in its entire fleet to a federal buy-out program. But somehow, pretty quickly, the company got turned around and started operating in the black."

"So maybe Ocean Catch is doing something else for Soga, besides supplying fish. Any idea what it could be?"

"That's what I'm trying to find out."

He's got a perfect poker face: bland, inscrutable. But I'm pretty sure he knows more than he's saying, and if by some slim chance he doesn't, he soon will, because the flash drive containing both Hall's and Jacobsen's computer files is most likely still tucked in his pocket. This is as good a time as any to call his bluff.

"By the way, I know you don't work for Jackson Hartwell, and I'm pretty sure your name's not Larry Wozniak."

He gives the casual half smile of someone who's been caught doing something that he thinks isn't so bad. "Sorry. Russell Parnell, journalist. Most people call me Parnell."

"First a friend of the deceased, then an insurance man, now a journalist. I'd be crazy to believe anything you said. That counts for the *sorry*, too. Which I'm pretty sure I've heard you say before."

"Google me when you get home."

"Will there be a picture?"

"Yeah, probably."

"OK. So tell me how the *Sea Wolf* and Ned Rizzo fit into this business with Soga."

"Rizzo worked almost exclusively on the *Sea Wolf* during the last few years. He and the same small crew used to go off on voyages, returning after two or three weeks with a fraction of the haul they should have brought back. Then he left the company unexpectedly, ended up dead in a freakish collision at sea, and the *Sea Wolf* returned to port right around that time with a cracked hull. Need me to connect the dots?"

"I told you the *Sea Wolf* wasn't the ship that hit us."

His mouth purses with impatience, but he keeps it shut. There's a bit of dried blood at his right ear.

He still hasn't told me anything I didn't already know, but he hasn't said anything false either. I don't know if I should trust him. I get up from the table and go off in search of more information about the man who now says his name is Russell Parnell. The adjoining living area is dark, but the window shades are open. Looming outside, brilliantly lit by spotlights in this inky dead of night, the steeple of the Old North Church rises like a ghost of America's past. I switch on a gooseneck standing lamp. Blank walls, no coffee table, no television. Just a bookcase holding a lot of papers and about two dozen books. An Apple laptop open on a small desk, a dozen notecards scribbled on in big, rough handwriting. A cubist couch in urban black, probably from IKEA. Actually it looks like everything in this room came from IKEA. Instant apartment for small change. Two steps above transient, one step above college student.

I check out the books on his shelves: *Planet in the Balance, The Vanishing Arctic, Hiker's Guide to the White Mountains, The Elements of Style, La Cocina de Mama: the Great Home Cooking of Spain.* There's also a big glossy hardcover about whales lying flat on a shelf. The environmental books are persuasive, but the book that makes the strongest case for his not-evil character is *The Elements of Style*. What bad guy would give a shit about the difference between *which* and *that*? And the fact that he was just beaten pretty bad by Oyster Man and his morons does make me feel a little warmer toward him.

The shock of seeing Johnny tonight still hasn't left me. His snub-nosed profile and buzz cut, thick arms folded across his down vest, just above his bump of paunch. The cold-blooded way he merely watched, keeping his hands clean for the delicate work on his bird-houses.

Johnny didn't follow me to Ocean Catch tonight. The streets were so deserted at 2 a.m. that I would have seen a tail. And he was waiting outside the company parking lot, not where I left my car. He must have finally discovered the funeral crasher's address and had a few of his guys staking out the apartment. They followed him to Ocean Catch, where Johnny met them. Johnny was unwilling to enter the building when he saw the cleaning van. He waited on the street outside the gate, where he could track Parnell (I might as well call him that for now) leaving and ambush him.

Parnell—smaller, one-armed, nearsighted—is no match for John Oster. When he was talking just now, trying to act tough, I noticed that his voice was tinctured with the startled terror he's trying to suppress. I'm willing to bet that tonight's violent events are not a regular feature of the world he hails from. Which adds up to this: Whatever Johnny wants from the alleged journalist, he will eventually get.

When I glance back to the kitchen, where Parnell has started making coffee, compare his dead hand to his working one, and see the tension in his drained, pulpy face, some actual human sympathy starts bubbling under my crust. *Shit, syphilis,* I remind myself. But it doesn't work.

I go back to the kitchen and tell him everything I know. I explain the secret bonuses, the company's gift to Ned, and what I heard about the argument aboard the *Sea Wolf* between the captain and a Japanese fishmaster. Then I inform him that his chief assailant was a guy named John Oster, a good buddy of the deceased fisherman Ned Rizzo, and a longtime employee of Ocean Catch.

"How do you know?"

"Hard to mistake an old friend."

He blinks. Not sure what to make of that.

"I'm not one of them, if that's what you're thinking."

He spoons coffee into the coffeemaker while he mulls this over. Finally, he says, "I thought you might be one of them when we first met. You were on the *Molly Jones* when it went down, so you were obviously working with Rizzo to some extent. But when you were hitting me up for information in the café that day, I realized you actually didn't know that much."

"So why don't you tell me what I don't know."

"Look, it could be dangerous. These people . . . they're—"

"Come on. You think I don't know? I just watched what they did to you."

He disappears into the living room, comes back with the glossy book about whales, and hands it to me. The cover photo is of a black whale rising majestically out of the ocean. The whale appears to be turning slightly in the air, showing its white underside. The crown of its massive, rectangular head is disfigured by dingy white and pale gray wattles that look like clustered barnacles or the scabrous growths of a strange disease. Not far from the corner of its fearsome maw, a tiny black eye is nestled in blubber.

"The North Atlantic right whale," he says. "It was on the brink of extinction a decade ago, along with its cousin, the southern right whale. After the international ban on hunting, the southern right rebounded successfully, but the North Atlantic right hasn't come back at all. There are only about two hundred and seventy-five of them left in the world. They're closer to extinction now than they ever were.

"Some people think ship strikes are killing them as fast as they breed, which seems possible, since their migration routes directly cross the shipping lanes. But due to public pressure, traffic was rerouted a few degrees in the Bay of Fundy, where the whales live most of the year. Ship strikes were reduced significantly, but the population is still low.

"Now people think it might be fishing gear. We know the whales get caught in nets and lines because we can see the marks on the bodies of the ones that break away. Others may be drowning or dying of skin infections from the slices. There's a move to make fishing lines out of different, softer materials. But the truth is, no one really knows what's happening out there."

He stares at me with dry eyes and pursed lips. The coffee's stopped percolating, but he doesn't make a move to serve it. I'm getting an idea of where he's headed, but it's hard to believe.

"Whale meat's a delicacy in Japan," he says.

"But the *Sea Wolf* can't be taking that many whales, can it?"

"I have no idea how many whales would have to be killed to keep the population from rebounding. I don't even have any hard evidence that that's what's going on. But I suspected Ocean Catch and Soga were colluding somehow, and now I know I'm onto something." He pulls out cups, milk, and sugar with jerky one-handed anger.

Suddenly I realize that he must be the one who broke into my apartment. He probably did it to download my hard drive like he did Hall's and Jacobsen's. While he was there, he must have tapped my phone as well. He no doubt heard the message Mrs. Smith left on my machine about the cleaning people at Ocean Catch. That's how he knew which night he could get into the offices easily, and why he still hasn't asked me how I ended up in his car. He knew I might be there, too, and was taking his chances on meeting me. But I doubt he knows that I was in Jacobsen's office, watching what he did.

"You tapped my phone," I say.

"No, I didn't."

"You did. You broke into my apartment and tapped my phone because you thought I was working with Ocean Catch. You probably stole my computer files, too."

"I didn't, I swear."

"Then how'd you know you could get into Ocean Catch easily tonight, when the cleaners were there? You heard the message on my machine."

"I did. That's true. But I didn't break into your apartment. You gave me your phone number at the café. . . ."

"So?"

"I got remote access to your answering machine. It's easy to do when you know how."

"So you heard the message from Mrs. Smith."

"Is that her name? She sounded old."

"What else did you hear?"

He looks embarrassed, and I try to recall how many times the Married Guy called and what nonsense he might have talked. It's a stupid thing to worry about right now. But still. A bigger worry: if Parnell didn't break into my apartment, I still don't know who did.

He pours the coffee, and I wrap my fingers around the mug. It's cold in the apartment, and the warmth feels nice. "You're not safe here. You have to move. John Oster won't quit until he gets what he's looking for. Take my word for it. He'll be back."

He sits across from me, showing no reaction to what I just said. "What about you? Did he see you tonight?"

"I don't think so. The high beams were blinding him, then the air bag was covering me."

"How much does he know about your involvement?"

"Not that much, actually. I went to him and asked him some questions when the Coast Guard couldn't identify the freighter involved in the collision. I was frustrated with all the bureaucracy. He said he'd done his own private investigation and was satisfied that the collision was a hit-and-run." I sip my coffee, rack my brain for more details. "Come to think of it, he did ask about you, pointedly—more than once, in fact. Luckily, I couldn't remember the last name you were using. I think he was satisfied that I didn't know you. Since he didn't see me tonight, he has no reason to suspect that you and I have talked. And unless he got access to my answering machine as well, he'd have no way of knowing that I've spoken to Mrs. Smith. We only met privately on two occasions, and I doubt anyone saw us."

I give Parnell a sly smile, pleased at the idea that I'm flying under Johnny's radar. "As far as John Oster's concerned, I'm just a woman he used to know who happened to be fishing with Ned that day, and the only reason I was asking him questions at all is that I'm easily annoyed with bureaucracy." I stretch my legs. It feels like a long time since I've moved my body freely. "He must have found you somehow and followed you over there tonight."

"Yeah, I guess," Parnell says grudgingly. He's not about to give Johnny credit for anything.

"He knows where you live. Which means that you've got to get out of here."

He shrugs with apparent indifference, but I can see that he's trying to get his head around the idea of moving out.

"What else do you think he knows about you?" I ask.

"Not sure. The whole time they were assaulting me, they kept asking who I was working for."

"What did you say?"

"Nothing."

"Who are you working for?"

"No one."

"What's your interest in all this?"

"Like I said, I'm a journalist."

"You're going to a lot of trouble to get a story."

"It's my job."

"Right." It's hard to believe that journalistic ambition alone would motivate someone to break into an office in the middle of the night. But what do I know? Maybe he fancies himself an ecological Woodward or Bernstein. Outside the narrow window, a milky bone of light is lying on the horizon. This night is ending, finally. It's been a long one. I want to go home and vegetate in total undisturbed quiet, but I'm also very hungry, so when Parnell asks if I want something to eat, I say yes.

While he's frying eggs, I look through the whale book, rife with four-color photos and informative captions. I learn that the species' Latin name is *Eubalaena glacialis*. Early New England whalers called them right whales because they were considered the right ones to hunt. They're huge: forty to eighty tons of bone, warm blood, and blubber, with a maw that can swallow entire schools of fish. But toothless, nearly blind, and strikingly unbeautiful as whales go. A caption tells me that the purpose of the unsightly white crusts on their heads is unknown. Apparently, they like to press their crowns into the sea floor, and the scaly patches may actually be scabs. Why do they do it? I wonder. Self-destructive urges? Itchy scalp? Repeated fruitless attempts to bury themselves in a whale's game of hide-and-seek? Their strange behavior makes me like them, the way you like a helplessly eccentric friend.

Parnell is holding a plate of fried eggs and toast in front of me. I close the book and, when I lean down to put it on the floor, its paper jacket slips off. I open the cover to slip it back on and find myself looking at a pasted bookplate on the otherwise blank first page. In the middle of the bookplate are the printed words *From the library of . . .* The name handwritten in blue pen under that is *Jaeger*.

I nearly fall off the chair.

"You all right?" he asks.

"Fine," I say, sitting upright.

"You like over easy, I hope." He slides the plate in front of me.

There's a din filling my ears. I mumble something about having to get home.

"Right now?"

"I have to."

"Can I give you a ride?"

"I'll take the T."

"Sure?"

"I like the T. And your car doesn't work." I sound idiotic.

"At least eat first," he says.

I nod moronically, scarf down the eggs, stuff the toast into my mouth, chew like a crazy woman, smile insanely, and gulp the last of the coffee. As I'm stumbling out the door, he hands me the whale book. "Here. Take it with you. And thanks for saving my life."

"Oh, it was nothing. Glad I could be there." Now we both sound idiotic.

My heart is hot and pounding as I run down the flights. I can almost hear Milosa laughing. *See where sympathy got you? In bed with the enemy, your brain and everything you know about the situation picked over like a bone.*

I get to the marble vestibule that leads to the street. High ceilings, old brass mailboxes, a gilt and crystal chandelier. If a person happened to be cornered in this small space, she wouldn't have anywhere to run. Johnny and his pals hightailed it out of the seaport district, but who's to say they didn't circle back to follow us and are waiting outside now?

A narrow stairway leads to the basement. I hurry down it. A damp smell, washers and dryers, a racing bike padlocked to a heating pipe. A back exit to an alleyway. Two minutes later I'm walking along a cool, quiet street, headed toward Haymarket Station. There are chrysanthemum pots on the stoops. The aromas of coffee and fresh-baked bread come from the open window of a café.

Chapter 19

The first thing I do when I get home is google Russell Parnell. Six or seven identities pop up. One is a journalist who's published about twenty articles in places like *Vanity Fair*, the *New York Times*, and Salon.com, as well as smaller newspapers, magazines, and Web sites. Most of his work appears to be travel essays, but he's also covered medical developments—genetics, psychiatry, microbial pathogens, SARS—and there are a few environmental pieces on such things as the clear-cutting of the Amazonian rain forest and the cleanup of the Gulf of Mexico oil spill.

I check Images and get four pretty good photos: a distant image of him with close-cropped hair and a pencil-thin black tie, shaking hands with someone at the podium of a journalists' organization; an author photo from the contributors' section of a hip new magazine; a head-on shot of a guy in a bike race in the desert, his face hidden by a helmet and highly reflective diamond-shaped sunglasses, but the chin the right shape to be his. The fourth photo is unexpected: a staged engagement shot in which he's positioned over the shoulder of a saucer-eyed, full-bodied brunette. They're neither good-looking nor bad-looking, and can't be more than twenty-two. Both are smiling with the openness of psychologically healthy young adults. I find the image touching, and sad. Did she die? Are they divorced? More cyber-sleuthing leads me to a professional site for networking journalists, where I discover that he went to San Luis Obispo High School and Columbia University, and that his full name is Russell Alejandro Parnell. I google *Parnell* and *Jaeger* simultaneously and get nothing.

I slog through a busy day at work on autopilot. In the evening I go over Parnell's articles one by one. For several I can get full-text versions by subscribing to the publication. I do, which takes a boring hour of filling out required fields and creating passwords. I make coffee while the articles are printing, and finally sit down on the couch to read about the disappearing rain forest, the alarming spread of antibiotic-resistant pathogens, and modern-day treatment of the severely mentally ill.

About three-quarters of the way through the article on mental health, I run across a case history of a young Hispanic woman who married a prominent American businessman. A year into the marriage, the twenty-year-old woman set fire to their house. She spent several months at a privately owned mental hospital on Cape Cod before being transferred to a supervised group home where she lived for two years. Here, her medications were closely monitored, and she received help with the chores of daily living. She was re-admitted to the hospital whenever her symptoms became unmanageable. Her husband assumed the financial support of her immediate family members, who stayed in close contact with her and saw to all her needs.

She had agreed to be interviewed on the condition that she remain anonymous. Then twenty-four, she told Parnell that she was grateful for all the care she had received. She was lucky to have the support of a devoted family and a generous, protective husband. So many people with her terrible disease had much harder roads. Her life was simple but satisfying. She lived with a sister in a small house in Falmouth.

Her sister drove her to appointments and made sure she took her meds. She worked at a Falmouth thrift store weekday mornings, and enjoyed reading in her spare time, although the medications she was taking made it hard for her to concentrate for very long. She regretted setting the fire that put her and her husband's lives at risk. The allegations she'd made at that time were completely false, she told Parnell. "Everything I said then was just a symptom of my disease."

Parnell's article concluded with the good news that her story and other stories like hers offered hope to thousands that one of the world's most frightening diseases could be brought under control.

I toss the pages on the table with some dismay. At least Parnell's other articles were interesting. This one's pretty bland.

My coffee's cold, so I go into the kitchen to refill my cup. It's ten p.m., too late for caffeine, but I didn't sleep at all last night and am so tired that there's not much chance the caffeine will keep me up. I toast a bagel and slice a cantaloupe. You can never have too many breakfasts. When I'm done eating, I take a shower, put on sweatpants and a clean T-shirt, braid my wet hair so that when it dries it will be wavy, and water the African violet on my windowsill. I'm thinking, but I don't know what. My sluggish brain just keeps turning over the same words: *Fairy tale. Princess bride.* Then the neurons connect.

I go back to my computer, and in a few keyboard strokes, I've pulled up the tabloid story I saw before about Bob Jaeger's schizophrenic wife, and linked to a local news video from June 2009.

Now things get more interesting. Apparently, Jaeger's wife, Caridad, had spent the first months of her treatment in a Cape Cod psychiatric hospital insisting she was sane. Her appeals to the hospital administration, the Physician Review Board, and the governor's office went unanswered. Her immigrant parents were unable to marshal effective support. Still, her entreaties continued. She managed to call a local television station from a hospital pay phone. The TV crew that showed up at the hospital was denied admittance, but she was spotted in a third-story window, banging on the panes, and ten seconds of video were recorded before she was led away. The station ended up doing a short news segment that juxtaposed color photos of her lavish society wedding, stark pictures of the fire-damaged mansion, and a dark, grainy image of her contorted face behind the hospital window's safety bars. Her husband refused to comment; her doctor could not be reached.

The tabloids ran with the story, adding paparazzi photos of the husband relaxing on yachts and golf courses. His conglomerate's international holdings were listed in a sidebar, along with estimates of his wealth. Soon after, he issued a public statement: the medical record showed conclusively that his wife had been diagnosed with acute schizophrenia. She was receiving the best, most humane treatment available. It was a tragic and deeply private family affair.

At this point I'm willing to bet that the patient featured in Parnell's recent article and Caridad Jaeger are one and the same. I need to know how and why he chose her, and whether his connection is only to her or also to Bob. Which Jaeger does the whale book belong to? Is Russell Parnell somehow part of Jaeger's team?

My one lead: a thrift store in Falmouth, Massachusetts. I search and discover that there's only one thrift store in Falmouth. Driving time: 1 hour, 27 minutes. I call my office, leave a message explaining that I won't be in tomorrow, and set two alarms for 6 a.m. so I'm sure to wake up.

The Heavenly Afterlife is housed in a former barn not far from the town center. Just inside the wide doorway, a mannequin greets visitors, hips canted, hand raised in a Queen Elizabeth parade wave. The mannequin is wearing a mink stole, elbow-length white gloves, and a pillbox hat with a peek-a-boo veil. Nothing else. Clustered around her are a John Deere lawn mower, a vintage snow sled, and a four-foot inflatable Easter bunny with fat buck teeth. Maybe not the best work environment for a person trying to keep a grip on reality. But what do I know?

Inside, four or five aisles stretch from a bright front area into a shadowy back. Used lamps and blenders, tattered books and games, cracked statues, and God knows what are stacked on tables. Rugs, furniture, and kitchen appliances are stockpiled in the rear. It looks as if a good portion of the "ten thousand things" that Lao-tzu wrote about have been gathered here. An obese woman with an incongruously elfin face is sitting behind the cash register, following me steadily with her eyes. Another employee is working about halfway down the wide center aisle, unpacking crockery and arranging it on a table. Midtwenties, small-boned, about thirty pounds heavier now than she was in her wedding pictures. Caridad Jaeger.

I smile at the cashier. "I'm looking for plates."

She nods toward the middle of the store.

A few feet from Mrs. Jaeger, I stop to pick up a thirties-era creamer. It's so sweet, I actually might buy it. I hold it up. "Do you have the matching sugar bowl?"

She frowns, comes to where I'm standing, surveys the table. "I thought we did. Let's see." She begins sifting through some old dishes and serving bowls. She's maybe an inch shorter than I am, with hair as black as mine. It's greasy, pulled back, with stray pieces curling behind her ears. Her eyelashes are long and sweeping, and her nose is perfectly formed. Tiny gold hoops in her ears, the kind little girls wear.

"I thought we did," she repeats. "But I don't see it."

"I'm looking for a refrigerator, too."

"I can show them to you."

"Please."

She walks to the rear of the store very slowly, as if to underscore the fact that there's no need to rush in the Afterlife. At the end of the aisle, we turn a corner, moving out of visual range of the cashier, and she stops in front of a green Frigidaire.

"Interesting color," I say.

"It's avocado."

"I was thinking of white."

"Oh." She takes a few steps along the row. "Here's one. A Maytag."

She's wearing jeans and a gray hooded UMass sweatshirt a few sizes too large. Her thumbs fit through holes in the cuffs of the sleeves, making a kind of half glove. Her fingers are dirty; her shoulders slump.

"They're usually thirty or thirty-six inches wide," she says. "What size were you looking for?"

"I'm not sure. I'll have to go home and measure."

"You're supposed to leave an inch on either side. And you have to decide whether you want the door to open on the left or the right."

Her eyes are acorn brown, listless. She's not really present. Whether it's disease, medication, or defensive numbing, I can't tell. I only know that I'm flooded with a deep, cold sadness. Too many people leave this world before their lives have even begun.

She's uncomfortable with the way I'm looking at her. "Do you want something else?"

"I'm also interested in whales."

"What?"

"The North Atlantic right whale. Would you happen to know anything about them?"

"What?" Her lip is trembling. I see now that her mouth is full and tender.

"I was looking for a book, actually," I say. "I have this one, and I'd like to find another like it." I remove the whale book from my satchel.

Her eyes go wide, as if she's received an electric jolt. She puts a hand on the Maytag door. Doesn't open it, just holds the handle. The other hand reaches for a small gold cross at her neck.

"Where'd you get it?" she asks.

"Russell Parnell."

"Oh." She releases the refrigerator door and pushes her hair behind her ear self-consciously. "Did he give it to you?" Her casual voice betrays her disappointment.

"It's just a loan." I place the book on a table, as if to disown it somewhat.

She puts her hand on the cover, fingers spread, a gesture both tender and resigned. "It was supposed to be just for him. For something we talked about, just us."

"So the nameplate—" I open the front cover to show it. But I already know the answer.

"I always put my name in my books. Because they're mine." She sighs. "This one was my gift to Alejandro."

"Alejandro?" Then I remember Parnell's middle name from the Web site.

"He was so nice to me. He believed everything I told him."

Something clicks. "Others didn't believe you."

"Of course not. I'm very sick. My sickness tells me lies, and I tell them to others. I don't even know what's true."

"But Alejandro believed you."

"Yes." Her beautiful mouth relaxes into a smile. "He's one of the angels. I pray for him every day." She drifts for a few moments, then her chin juts out belligerently. "Who are you?"

"I'm a friend of Alejandro's. We were talking about . . . about these whales. And a company, a fish company that's . . . Well, it's doing some suspicious things." I'm not sure how much to say. "He showed me the book, and when I saw the nameplate with just the last name, I wasn't sure whether the book had come from you or—"

"No. Don't say his name." Her eyes dart up the aisle. "He's everywhere, like the devil. He'll make you crazy, give you shocks." She lowers her voice and raises a dirty, delicate hand. "If you listen, you can hear him buzz."

I listen quietly and hear humming fluorescent lights.

She rears back, her eyes suddenly wide and frozen at the sight of something behind me.

I whirl around, half expecting to see Bob Jaeger himself. But it's only the dumpy cashier standing at the end of the center aisle. "Caridad, what are you doing?" She pronounces it *Carrie-dead*.

Caridad's face goes slack. With a strange sinewy motion, she turns her back to the woman as if she didn't hear.

"I'm remodeling," I tell the cashier with a quick, businesslike smile. "A cottage on the beach. I need an entire kitchen—all the appliances and so forth. This young woman is being very helpful."

The cashier's sweatpants are pooling around her ankles. Her feet seem impossibly small under the wide inverted rotunda of her hips. She grunts, hitches up her pants, and leaves.

"Is there somewhere private we can talk?" I say to Caridad.

"About what?" Sullen, like a punished child.

"Please. I think we could help each other."

She presses the gold cross between two fingers, murmurs, "How is Alejandro?"

"He was fine when I saw him last night, but he's in danger. Some people are looking for him. I want to help him, but I need to know more about what's going on with the whales. He won't tell me, and I know now, after meeting you, that it's because he doesn't want you to be hurt."

She says nothing, just takes it in, all the while worrying the cross, pulling it from left to right and back on its chain. Finally she says, "My sister will pick me up soon and take me to the house. She has the big bedroom; I have the small one. I leave the house at night sometimes alone. But it's dark, and I don't know where to go. She's not my real sister. I'm a child of God." She wanders down the aisle to a stove, places her hand flat on the burner. "Do you want a stove?"

"No," I say, following.

She waltzes a few more feet to another stove, opens the door on the front, which squeaks on a rusty hinge. "An oven?"

"No, thank you."

"No. You wouldn't need an oven." She closes the door slowly, with something like regret.

We stand in the aisle looking at each other. I have no idea what's going on in her mind. "You don't have to tell me, Caridad. I think I know. A few years ago, you made some allegations against your husband, and it was discovered that you were sick. Alejandro came here to do a story on your treatment. He met you and guessed that what had happened to you was not so simple. It wasn't so simple, was it, Caridad? You were trying to say something. Something true."

"I don't know. I can't remember anything." Her eyes are quickly filling with tears.

"Think, Caridad. What you said about your husband. Did you talk to Alejandro about that?"

She wipes her tears before they fall with the back of her hand. "He said he'd find out if it could be proved."

"I think that's what he's trying to do. I wasn't sure exactly why until now. If he can show that what you said was true, you'll be vindicated, right?'

"I wish he'd come back soon."

"Where can we go to talk?" I say.

Her head drops as her eyes slide sideways. It's a sly, unattractive gesture, the mark of a person who has shameful secrets, or who is trying to hide her chronic contempt. I run back to the refrigerators, retrieve the whale book, stuff it in my satchel, and follow her. In the back corner of the building, near a door marked Emergency Exit Only, she stops. The area is poorly lit and empty but for some folding banquet tables stacked on end, leaning against the wall.

"Bob took me to India on our honeymoon," Caridad says. "Far out in the country. Four or five other couples were there. We stayed in tents with native people cooking and getting firewood. The men played soccer in the evenings. During the day we went in jeeps through the forests on narrow roads. I didn't know where we were exactly. But it was beautiful, like being in a secret part of the world where no one had ever been. We found an elephant herd and followed it for days. Every day the men shot two or three. Mothers, babies—it didn't matter. The elephants would roar. Scream just like people do, and stampede right into the guns. But the jeeps were faster, and we always got away. Everyone would be laughing with their mouths wide open, the women, too.

"After a few days, I stayed inside the tent. I could barely move. I kept seeing the elephants in my mind, hearing the sounds they made. When I went outside the tent, the Indians pointed at me, yelling *Sanaki, sanaki*. Crazy. I wanted Bob to take me home, but of course he didn't. Men like him don't listen to anyone. I didn't know marriage would be like that. I thought it would be better." She sighs briefly at her own naïveté, stiffens, continues her story. "He came back to the tent at night smelling of blood, and wanted me to make love to him. I couldn't, and he said I was worthless. I had no one to talk to."

She cranes her head as if she sees someone coming. I look, too, but no one's there. Caridad crosses her elbows across her chest. "I hate that woman. Carla."

"The cashier."

"Yes. What time is it?"

I check my watch. "Ten to twelve."

"My sister will be here soon."

"You have time."

She leans back against the fire door. I'm worried she's going to pop it open and set off the alarm, but I don't say anything. Her head tilts up toward the ceiling, and she continues her story in a monotone. "I found out that Bob and his friends went on safaris, hunting trips, whatever you want to call them, all the time. They called themselves something . . . some kind of club . . . I forget the name. There was scoring, and betting, and money involved. They didn't always go together.

Sometimes just two or three of them would go somewhere. They took movies and showed them at our house.

"Then Bob came up with the idea of hunting whales. He talked about it to his friends a lot. He owned a company. Sagga, Santi—I don't know." She's looking over her shoulder at an artificial Christmas tree.

"Soga."

"Maybe. Anyway, I went to the police to tell them about the elephants and whales. They said they'd look into it, but weeks went by and nothing happened."

"What about the fire, Caridad? The fire you set."

"Oh, right." She laughs hollowly. "I don't remember setting it. I only remember waking up and all the smoke in the bedroom. Bob wasn't next to me. I ran out to the living room—flames everywhere, right to the ceiling. I got outside, and Bob came—he put a coat around me—we watched until the fire trucks came. Then an ambulance arrived, and I was put inside it and taken to a hospital. I told people again and again what was happening to the animals, but no one cared."

She steels herself and smiles slightly, coldly. "Tell Alejandro to do what's best for himself and not worry about me. Tell him I'm fine. My loving God takes care of me."

"Are you being treated badly?"

She blinks rapidly, as if she doesn't understand the question. "They tell me I'm OK when I take my meds. I want to go home, but I don't have one. When is Alejandro coming back?" She presses the cross hard into the base of her neck.

Chapter 20

I'm back from Falmouth in time to pick up Noah from school so that Thomasina and Max can have their long weekend at Foxwoods. Thomasina packed pajamas for him, but he goes to bed on the living room couch wearing his dirty school clothes minus the pants. I figure it's not my job to make him wear certain things, or eat certain things, or think or feel any particular way. This attitude is why I would be either a horrible mother or a really good one. With any luck, I won't find out.

At seven on Saturday morning I slog sleepily to the kitchen for coffee, expecting to tiptoe through the living room so as not to wake my young guest. The first thing I encounter is a black snake of meticulously placed dominoes stretching across the floor. It begins in the middle of the raised slate platform in front of the fireplace, extends to the edge, resumes on the hardwood floor, travels parallel to the Turkish carpet, undulates down the hallway, makes several sharp geometric shapes as it enters the dining room, and (I follow it to see) branches out into paired trails that crisscross several times before merging into a tight double strand that ends in a spiral four or five circles deep under the table.

The dominos are kept in a trunk next to the bookcase. For Noah's amusement I have been adding to them for years and have amassed a staggering number. This particular design must have come close to using them all. It's one of his best. He must have been up for several hours in the middle of the night, and now he's conked out on the couch with the pillow on the floor and the sheets and blankets helter-skelter as if a small gale blew through.

I go into the kitchen, start making French toast. In a few minutes, I turn from the stove to find him standing in the doorway.

"Nice work," I say.

"You want to do it?"

"You want to eat first?"

He shakes his head.

I turn off the stove, and follow him into the living room. We stand ceremoniously before the first domino on the lip of the fireplace. I'm worried about the bumpiness of the slate, the precipitous drop to the floor, the right-hand angle as the trail enters the dining room. The energy will have to flow at exactly the same rate along the paired lines in order for them to merge without incident, and one domino slightly out of place will stop the tight spiral in its tracks.

Coolly, like a pilot preparing for takeoff, Noah asks if I'm ready.

"Ready," I say.

Gently, he pushes the first domino with his finger. The plastic tiles fold at a steady pace; each makes a distinct click, which flows into the next to make a rapid-fire *rat-tat-tat*. There is a split second of silence while the domino at the end of the fireplace falls precisely onto the edge of the domino on the floor, then the efficient clicking resumes. Noah and I can't take our eyes from the spectacle of controlled collapse that is proceeding without apparent agency across the room. We follow the motion into the foyer, then the dining room, until the last domino is flattened and the clicking suddenly stops.

Noah breathes a happy sigh of accomplishment, and I beam with pleasure. The start of a good day. I serve the French toast; he gobbles the first helping and asks for more. He downs two glasses of orange juice, belches, and gives me one of his rare and glorious smiles.

I know better than to ask why he, who's spent a mere decade on this earth, much of it below the age of reason, was awake and obsessively lining up hundreds of little black squares for hours in the dark of night. We all have our methods for getting through this life. Noah's defenses may be more elaborate than other children's, but then they have a lot more work to do. After a long discussion of the probability of life on other planets, and another about the challenges of building tunnels underwater, after a banana, hot chocolate, and a game of hangman, he goes off to lose himself in his laptop.

A few minutes later, he's back. "You found it!" He's holding up his cell phone.

"Oh, right. It was in the couch cushions. It must have fallen out of your pocket the last time you were here. Sorry. I meant to call."

"Now I can tell Max I was right. It *was* here!"

"You told Max you left your cell phone here?"

"Uh-huh. He kept asking. He's a wicked control freak."

"Control freak?" Odd to hear this term from a fifth grader.

"That's what Mom says."

"Really? She says that about Max?"

"No, *I* say it about Max. She says it about anyone she doesn't like."

"Oh, I see. I guess you don't like Max. Why?"

"He takes a long time in the bathroom, and my mom acts weird when he's around. Plus, he smells bad."

"Yeah, I noticed that. All three of those things, actually." Pause. "Is he nice to you?"

"I guess."

"I wonder why he'd care so much about your cell phone." The minute the words leave my mouth, I recall that he was talking to Noah about his cell phone at the funeral. What could he have wanted? Then I remember something else—Noah's whalebone. I can't believe I didn't think of it as soon as Parnell showed me the whale book. Is it possible that the story Ned told his son was true, at least in part?

"Noah, you didn't show Max your whalebone, did you?"

"No way. I hid it in the box, remember? And I'm not going to show him my pictures either."

"What pictures?"

"The ones my dad sent me. Look, they're really weird." He presses some things on his phone, hands it to me, and hovers over my shoulder while I look.

There's a grainy, gray, indistinct image on the screen. I peer closely and see that it's a beach shrouded in mist. A scattering of smoothly mounded boulders half-submerged in wet, dark sand. No people, no landmarks. Just a bunch of white things sticking up. Some straight, some warped. Some come to a point on the end; some don't. I can't judge height because there's nothing in the frame to compare them with. I have no idea what they are. Best guess: leafless birch saplings planted in rows—a grid, actually. I count seven across, but that's just how wide the camera angle is.

"From your dad, huh?"

Noah nods. "From his cell phone camera."

"Any more?"

He shows me two more that are substantially the same. I can't make out any details that would help explain the images. But there is a date—August 7. That's shortly before Ned left Ocean Catch. The photos were snapped a few seconds apart.

Some weird, random things hook up in my brain, and drag me toward a question. "Noah, when you say Max smells bad, do you mean he smells like Old Spice? Or something else?"

"What's Old Spice?"

Of course he wouldn't know. But I want to, right away. "Let's go to the pharmacy. Come on, get your coat. I'll buy you a hamburger on the way home."

"I just had French toast."

"Oh, right. Then let's just go."

At Walgreens, I grab the iconic buoy-shaped bottle off a shelf, pay for it, open it in the car, stick it under Noah's nose.

"Euuii," he says, and waves his hand under his nostrils.

"Max?" I ask.

"Yeah. That's him in the morning. The really gross smell is at night."

"A different gross smell than this?"

"Way different."

Looks like our Max is a two-cologne man. "One more stop, then. You up for this? Think your nose can handle it?"

He laughs. He's having fun. "Sure, Pirio. Let's go smell things."

There's an essential oils shop in Allston. A long, narrow place with a bead curtain to a back room, New Agey posters on the walls, and shelves of little glass vials containing oils from all over the world. I visited the place once when I was trying to reconstruct my mother's private fragrance. The oils were cheap, probably diluted. Some clearly past their prime. But they're good enough for this venture.

The proprietress behind the counter is wearing purple velour pants and a tank top. She has the aura of someone who has spent years trying to be spiritual, but has nevertheless failed to even slightly alleviate her constant irritated disgust with the entire human race. I say that my friend and I are interested in sampling four different oils: rosewood, sandalwood, oud wood, and oak moss. There's enough similarity here to make discrimination necessary, enough difference to make identification by the untrained possible. The woman sets the vials on the glass counter about four inches apart. Pulls out the corks and gives me a look that says she's not enjoying the game.

"Is Max in one of these?" I ask Noah.

Dutifully, he brings each vial to his nose and experiences his reaction. A shaking of the head, a nose scrunch, a second sniff, a frown or smile. At the third vial, he says, "This is him." I ask him to take his time, to be sure. Dutifully, he sniffs the fourth vial, goes back along the row. "It's definitely this one," he says. Oud wood.

Great. Now I know. Max is the one who broke into my apartment, leaving a trace of his heavy-on-the-base-notes cologne. No doubt he was sent by Johnny, who knew exactly where I'd be for an hour or so. No wonder Johnny was so eager to invite me to his home. But Max didn't find the phone, and now it's in my possession, and only Noah and I have seen the photos stored on it—evidence of I don't know what. I'm guessing that in the process of tracking the phone, Max stumbled across Thomasina and her trust fund, and decided to dally.

I try not to act alarmed, but I can't keep the urgent edge out of my voice. "Come on, Noah. Let's go home."

"Wait. Can I smell some more?"

"Yeah, I guess. I mean, of course you can." He deserves a little fun for his patience, and a few more minutes isn't going to make much difference at this point.

I manage to smile sweetly at the proprietress. "Can we sample a couple of florals? Maybe rose and jasmine. And some fruits—grapefruit, orange, mango. How about patchouli, balsam, vanilla? Oh, and do you have any civet?"

The proprietress sullenly proceeds to assemble the throng.

Noah smells thoroughly and deliberately, like a connoisseur tasting wine. He's probably never fully experienced his nose before. Each scent gets a little nod. When he picks up the civet, his head snaps back. "Oh, geez!"

I smile. "Want to know something crazy?"

"Yeah."

"That's from the anus of the civet cat."

217

"Anus?"

"Bum."

"Whoa!" Noah's eyes widen.

"No kidding, huh? It's a common ingredient in perfumes. Just think, all the fancy ladies dabbing Shalimar and Chanel No. 5 behind their ears are really dabbing cat bum."

"Cool!"

The proprietress, nearly snarling, begins hastily recorking her bottles. But for Noah learning this arcane factoid has made the trip a huge success.

At home, I pour hot chocolate into two mugs. Noah dumps a handful of tiny marshmallows in his mug. I ask if I can send the pictures to my computer and delete them from his phone.

His eyes darken. "No, they're mine."

"OK. Right." Noah doesn't insist on his own will very often, but when he does, he's hard to budge, especially when he's right. The pictures were sent by his father. Of course he doesn't want to give them up. Better for me to duck and circle back later. Luckily, he changes the subject himself, though not to safer ground.

"Why did you want to know what Max smells like?" He touches the rim of his cup, but doesn't drink. He likes to wait for the marshmallows to get sticky.

"I guess . . . hmm." I'm caught off guard, not knowing what to tell him. He's probably going to see more of Max, and I don't want him to be scared.

"Why, Pirio? Why did you want to know?" He's ramrod straight like Thomasina gets when she's about to blow.

I don't see a way around this. "I smelled his cologne in the apartment. I think he came here looking for your phone once when I wasn't home. That's why it would be better if we took the photos off it and sent them to my computer instead."

His head dips away. He puts his mouth to the cup and slurps. The cocoa splashes onto the table. He's blowing bubbles in it, buying time. He knows there's a lot I'm not saying. He also knows that I can be stubborn, too. Direct questioning probably won't get him very far, and there are too many questions anyway. He doesn't know where to begin. He seems to come to a decision, picks up his head, drives to the question he really wants to ask. "Is my mom going to marry him?"

"It's hard to say. They've only just met. Sometimes grown-ups get all excited at the beginning of a relationship, then it peters out."

"She keeps asking if I like him. Says he's really nice and I have to give him a chance. But I don't like him. I want him to go away." His hands are clenched, but there's a catch of vulnerability in his throat.

"Oh, Noah. Right now everything's a mess. There's a lot that has to get sorted out. With Max, with your mother. With all kinds of stuff that's going on. We have to take one thing at a time right now. The pictures, for example. Would you please let me take them off your phone and put them on my computer, where you can see them anytime you want?"

"They're mine! They're *mine*!"

"I'm sorry, Noah. Yes, they are."

"You're not telling me what's going on! What are those pictures of? Why won't you say? Why doesn't anyone tell me anything? Everyone has secrets, and nobody cares about *me*!"

"Oh, Noah. I do care. I care very much." I want to hug him, but he's too angry. His eyes are burning, and his voice is hoarse from the deep place it's coming from.

"You don't! You don't, Pirio! You don't care about me!"

"Please, Noah."

"Why won't you let me live with you? I can sleep on the couch. I'll clean up my stuff, and I'll be really quiet, I promise. I *promise*, Pirio!"

"Oh, Noah." My eyes are brimming. "Oh, sweetheart."

There's a silence, unearthly. His eyes are naked, full of hurt and hope. My stomach is twisting at the hard words I must say. "I'll always be your friend, Noah. And I hope you'll always be mine. I want us to be the very best of friends for as long as you want to be."

He draws a sharp breath into his nose and holds it, his chest puffed out. Then with his entire arm he sweeps both cups of hot chocolate off the table. They smash against a lower cabinet and shatter. Broken porcelain in a spreading pool on the floor, spatters of chocolate everywhere.

In his eyes I see Thomasina's passion. And something solid, honest, and brave. Like Ned.

"I love you, Noah." The words are out before I can stop them, the words I didn't want to say. And all the words that come after them— that *must* come after them if they are to be true and meaningful—are right there in my throat.

"Pirio, I love you, too." Then he's in my arms, and we hug and rock together quietly.

I push his hair out of his eyes. "Noah, listen. I promise I'll take care of you if anything . . . ever . . . happens."

There. It's done. The promise made. No going back.

He goes still and quiet, as if he didn't hear me. But I know he did. A peace settles over us both.

That night, when he's asleep, I call Thomasina's cell phone. About twenty times. I leave five or six messages urging her to get back to me and reassuring her that Noah's fine. Finally I call the hotel. They've checked in under her name, which seems odd, until I realize she's probably paying. No one answers in her room, so I leave another message with the concierge.

I take Noah's phone into my bedroom and e-mail the photos to my computer and my iPhone. Then I delete them from his phone. Tomorrow I'll tell Noah what I did. I'll explain that I'll give the pictures back once I find out what they're of. Until then, we can't run the risk of Max finding them. I'll say I'm pretty sure that this is what his dad would want us to do. I hope Noah will be OK with that.

Close to dawn my cell vibrates with an audible buzz.

"Pirio, is that you?" Her voice is frail and distant.

"How's the roulette wheel treating you?" I say groggily.

"I'm not there anymore. I'm home."

"You're home? When did you get back?"

"A few hours ago."

Dread starts in. A few seconds is all it takes anymore. "What do you mean?"

"Is Noah sleeping?"

"Of course he's sleeping. It's five a.m. He's on the couch in the living room."

"How's he doing?"

"Fine," I say tersely. It's bad, the trouble she's in. "What's going on?"

A deep sigh, with a cry bubbling up from the center of it. "I fucked up. Real bad."

I listen as she softly weeps. I feel angry, though I'm not sure why. And tired.

"Please, Pirio. I know what you're thinking."

"Do you want to come over?"

"I don't want Noah to see me." Again, the tiny voice, the stifled sob.

"Where's Max?"

"He fucked me over. Oh, Jesus, did he fuck me over."

The pit of my stomach wants to crawl away from this conversation. The crown of my head wants to fly away. I'm thinking how warm my bed is, and how I'm not going to be in it again this morning.

"He's not with you, I take it." She seems pretty sober now. Sick sober.

"If he was, I'd rip his heart out and shove it down his throat."

This is where I start to lose it. Saccharine pity and vile sarcasm vie for control of me. The pity wants to cry out, *Oh, Thomasina, why do you keep doing this stupid shit to yourself? Like your life is one slow elevator ride to the bottom.* The sarcasm fills my mouth with no particular words, just the bitter taste of itself.

Wearily, I ask what happened, and Thomasina tells me her story. It is lengthy, convoluted, self-justifying, and probably partly false, since it's being assembled and packaged for my consumption after a fog of booze and the sour shock of humiliation. I want to resist being swept up in the drama—*just the facts, please, ma'am*—but I'm drawn in anyway. I still want to believe in her, still want to see her crawl out of her dark cave and win. Hope still trumps experience, though it's been battered pretty badly. This everlasting hope of mine may be friendship, or it may be denial.

Long story short: Thomasina got tipsy, took ten thousand dollars out of her checking account to buy a silver Aphrodite dress and some cool accessories. She laid down the rest at a high-stakes poker table. Won, lost, won, lost. Walked away with roughly the same amount she started with in her slender satin clutch. Feeling pretty good about herself. No fool, her. Daddy's little gambling girl with her speedy microprocessor of a mind and just the right amount of moxie. At which point clever Max got her soused, slipped something in her drink that made her go all haywire. He had to practically carry her back to the room, where she passed out on the bed. When she woke up, the satin clutch was open on the dresser, only a lipstick inside. Max's clothes were gone from the closet. She called his cell. Turns out he was already back in Boston. Told her that she'd gambled away all her money in a blackout and gouged his face with her fingernails when he tried to drag her away from the table. Said she was a sick, dangerous woman and he never wanted to see her again.

I get out of bed and go into the kitchen quietly so as not to wake

Noah. I still have the phone pressed to my ear, though there's nothing but alternating bursts of self-justification and self-pity coming from the other end. In truth, I'm relieved. It's only squandered money, not a hit-and-run or a drug arrest. I pour myself a glass of milk and take some mint Girl Scout cookies out of a box.

Thomasina clears her throat and asks if I want to know the truth.

"Yeah, sure." *This ought to be good.* I bite off a piece of cookie.

"The bastard stole my money. I even checked under my finger-nails to be sure, and there wasn't any flesh."

I shake my head at this. An ingenious girl.

"Do you believe me?" she asks in a small but demanding voice.

I brush away some crumbs, sip the milk from its cool glass, and put it down on the kitchen table. Do I believe her? Thomasina is more than capable of gambling away ten thousand dollars in a blackout, or even just while decently stewed. If Max escaped with nothing more than a gouged face, he's lucky, considering what I know she can do. But Max is no angel either. He's been lying to her all along. If somehow in the course of whatever shady business he's involved in, he did develop genuine feelings for her, then he's stupid as shit, because what sane person would want to be with a woman who routinely vomits before breakfast? Unless, of course, she keeps you in booze and drugs and snazzy gambling duds. And if you married her, you'd have access to all the money her trust fund sends her monthly, half of which just accumulates in her account so that a ten-thousand-dollar withdrawal is no big deal. Fact is, Thoma-sina's always been begging the world to exploit her.

"Pirio? Are you there?"

"I'm thinking. I'll call you back." I end the call and go out to check on Noah. He's sleeping on his side with light exhalations, dark eye-lashes resting on pale cheeks. I return to my room, sit on the bed, drink the rest of the milk, eat the last cookie. I take a shower, get dressed, and call Thomasina back.

"What the hell do you expect me to do with all the fucking information you just gave me? I don't give a shit about your money or your stupid little affair! I'm sick of you fucking up. I've had it; I'm done. Goddamn it, Thomasina! Next time, call someone else!" I jab the end button and feel like hurling the phone against the wall.

It vibrates two seconds later. "OK, OK. I deserved that. You have every right to be mad. Please, go ahead, scream at me. Tell me I'm a worthless whore."

"Why? So you can feel sorry for yourself and drown in more booze?"

"You hate me now, don't you? I've lost your friendship. You hate me now just like everyone else."

I don't rise to the bait. I don't hate her. I can't. I just miss the old Thomasina, the one who seemed destined for something good.

"Don't withdraw, Pirio. That's what you always do. You get so cold, so distant. I feel like I'm being sent to Siberia. It's much worse than screaming. Please, yell and scream if you're mad. Pound the table, anything. I deserve to be abused."

"Give Galahad some more time with you; I bet he'll step up."

"That was cruel."

"You had it coming. That and more."

"You're the only person I can talk to."

"Really? Where's Madame Jeanne?"

"I hate how sarcastic you get."

"Me? Oh, right. Let's talk about me. First I'm cold. Now sarcastic. You'd think I was the one with the problem."

"I'm sorry. I'll go to AA."

"Fuck you will."

"I will. I stopped drinking for ten days. I did it, and I can do it again. For Noah's sake."

"Not for Noah. For *yourself*. Because you're fucking better than this, and you know it. You do it for yourself first. *Then* for Noah."

"Yes, you're right. For me." Her voice is small, trying out self-respect. A pause, then an attempt to backpedal. "I didn't really drink that much when I was at the poker table. Only a coup—"

"Oh, please. Stop right there. If you finish that sentence, I swear I'll never speak to you again."

"Oh, God. I'm sorry. Can I come over?"

"Yes."

A pause, a sigh. "I'm worried I can't do it, Pirio. I've tried so many times. And everyone hates me now. I hate myself. . . ."

The call ends while she's still talking, but I'm not the one who hangs up.

I sit at the kitchen table and wait for her.

When Thomasina's in her cups, she's ludicrously emotional. It's awful, of course, but not alarming. After all, it's only drunkenness. The condition she's in right now, though—this is different. This sick-sober-hungover state, when she's conscious of her bathos and sane enough to feel humiliated by it, when she needs forgiveness that she knows she doesn't deserve, when, desperate for clarity, she enlists her perfect logic to blame the entire world and understands full well that she is lying—this is when bad things can occur. I don't want to think about what those bad things are. I just hope she gets here soon so I can stop worrying and move on to being glad when she leaves. A paradox anyone can understand.

Noah appears in the doorway. Barefoot, skinny-limbed. Hungry, no doubt. More proof that I'm ill-suited to parenting is the fact that merely feeding a child three times a day seems like an onerous job to me.

I make toast and pour juice. While he's eating, we make up a story about a boy gnu. The plot involves fantastic characters and situations that I have a hard time keeping straight. Conventional me, I expect the story to end with the boy gnu getting rich as a sheik and marrying the best-looking girl gnu, but Noah steers the plot in a different direction. The gnu builds an enormous machine that can do "everything"—which mostly means of a lot of warfare and some mining. He draws it. It's got steel arms and legs, inlaid winches, antennae, and a square robotic head. A machine like that is a horror to me, but to Noah it's a pinnacle of evolution. He probably imagines himself inside it, inviolable.

Thomasina arrives with modest, downcast eyes, wearing her voluminous black cape. Noah gives her a happy hug and tells her excitedly about the anus of a civet cat. She smiles, pats his hair, doesn't say too much. I'll call her later to tell her about Max and Johnny and the pictures Ned sent to Noah's phone. Maybe it will console her to know that her former boyfriend really is a low-life scumbag.

We order Chinese, have it delivered, split the bill. Noah loves that it's Sunday morning, and we're not having breakfast food. Thomasina stuffs a fat wad of extra tip into the delighted delivery boy's hand. The gesture upsets me, but I don't bother wondering why.

Chapter 21

I've been standing in the cramped vestibule of 180 Salem Street for ten minutes, pressing the buzzer for number 4. Now it's just a matter of accepting the fact that he's not home. But I came all the way here, and I want to see him, badly. So I press again. Still no answer. His phone is no longer in service. If he got a new number, why hasn't he let me know? I pace the marble floor, unwilling to leave. The heavy glass door to the street shuts out sounds. Cars drift by soundlessly like fish in an aquarium. A watery image rises in my mind—of Russell Parnell being hauled through this foyer in the middle of the night, taken to a deserted lot behind an abandoned factory, bludgeoned to a pulp, and thrown into the harbor.

I jam my thumb onto the buzzer and lean into it as if the added pressure will make a difference. I press notes in Morse code gibberish—dash, dash, dot, dash, dot. A minute or so later, I calm down.

There are four filigree brass mailboxes set into the wall. They're so old that the edges of the letter slots are worn to dull gold from all the mail that's passed through them. I try to get two fingers inside the number 4 mailbox, predictably without luck. Irrational anger rises. Even his mailbox is denying me admittance. I press the side of my face against the wall and try to see diagonally inside the slot. What a ridiculous thing to do. I tear a piece of a Lost Cat poster off the wall, scribble my name on it, and stuff it into the mailbox. At least he'll know I was here.

On the way home I stop at Quincy Market and pick up a few things I need: warm socks, rubber-soled shoes, rain gear. Godiva chocolate and a short cigar. Ray-Ban aviator sunglasses. Leaving the store, I predict how quickly I will lose them, and go back for another pair. Then I hump my packages a few blocks west to a camera store on Tremont Street, where I select a Minolta SR-T 102 that fits like a small apple in the hollow of my hand. After talking to the salesclerk at length, I add an ultracompact, completely waterproof Kodak PlaySport, with full HD recording capability and a memory card so tiny you can stash it anywhere.

He calls that evening, to my relief, but not because he found the note. He took my advice and left the Salem Street apartment, preferring to avoid another run-in with Johnny and his gang. He changed his phone number, too. He's at an old rooming house in Charlestown, he says apologetically. Temporary shelter on short notice, no car required to get here, he explains. There's something charming about his slight embarrassment at his low-rent digs.

I tell him I talked to Caridad Jaeger. "She told me everything."

A pause. "Can you come by tomorrow morning?"

"Tomorrow after work," I say, remembering my job.

It's an enormous old home, formerly spacious and elegant, now cut up, sectioned off, and beaten down, like a Moscow mansion the Bolsheviks took over. The manager wears a yellow turban, sits inside a little room behind a barred window. He's working a crossword with a stub of pencil while a talk show host excoriates pompously from an old television set. I'm about to speak to him when a figure appears in my peripheral vision. It's Parnell, moving quietly as a cat. He leads me wordlessly out the back door, across a parking lot, to a diner down the street. We slide into a booth at the back. Sticky red vinyl, the tears covered with duct tape. There are a couple of beefy guys at the counter, and an Asian woman in a red wool coat. The waitress comes, takes our order for two coffees, and shuffles away.

First thing Parnell says is that he bought a handgun. Slides it under his pillow at night, straps it to his ankle during the day. He says it's a .38-caliber Colt Mustang with an overall length of about five inches. With a loaded magazine, it weighs less than a pound. He gives a bland shrug to acknowledge that these details aren't really important; he's just making conversation. But there's a new edge to him: a stubble of beard darkens the lower half of his face, and there's a wild look in his eyes. He's out of his depth, and he knows it.

Curious, I ask if I can see the gun.

He tips his head, and I go horizontal on the vinyl bench. Under the table, he's pulled up his pant leg. The gun is black and silver and so small it looks like a toy.

I sit up. I want to say, *Don't worry so much. I know John Oster. He's not a killer. Asshole, yes. Fucked-up crazy man, yes. Into bad moonlighting gigs chasing whales on the North Atlantic like Ahab, yes. But not a killer.* That's what I want to say. But I don't know if it's true.

The waitress brings our coffee. We both take it black, so there's nothing to do with our three good hands. My eyes stray to Parnell's left-hand fingers curling around his porcelain mug. It's almost too intimate to look at this part of him. A hand with living fingers, a hand that can touch. I tear one sugar packet, then another.

"We need evidence," I say.

He doesn't balk at the plural pronoun, but doesn't carry it forward either. "Yeah, I know. But how do I get it? That's where I'm stuck. I need places and dates. Everything, all the players, the whole story. I got nothing so far."

"Somebody has to get on board the *Sea Wolf.*"

"I thought of that. But they know me now." He doesn't add that his hand would disqualify him in any case.

"I'll go."

"What? You?"

"Why not?" I push the spilled sugar into a little mound.

He looks stiff and embarrassed. "You're not a fisherman."

"I lobstered, didn't I? I think I'm ready for bigger prey." I try to sweep the mound of sugar into my hand, but most of it falls on the floor.

"They'd never let you on."

"Sure they would. There are some women on the boats."

"You don't have any skills." A cool glitter in his eye. He thinks he has me on this one.

"I can cook." Sort of. "And processing can't be that hard."

"Come on. Why would your friend there, this John guy, agree to take you on his secret voyages?"

"I'm an old friend. He likes me. We go way back."

Parnell scoffs. "That's not enough."

"It will be when I add that I know what's going on. I'll say Ned spilled the whole story to Thomasina before he died, and she finally broke down and told me. Johnny'll have no trouble believing that Thomasina would blurt out Ned's secrets. I'll tell him I want to go whale hunting because I'm bored and need some excitement in my life. He'll have no trouble believing that either. Come to think of it, I already told him I wanted to get back to fishing as a way of conquering my posttraumatic stress disorder. But he won't be questioning any of this too deeply, believe me. When I said he likes me, I meant he likes me *a lot*. In fact, I'm pretty sure he'll grab any excuse to take me along."

Parnell's eyes flicker shrewdly as he considers the merits of my idea. "If you're wrong?"

"I'm not. Johnny has no reason to suspect me. I've been through it all in my head a hundred times."

Glancing out the window at the sunny morning and the busy street, I flash on an image of the guy at the Bank of America Pavilion, the tan car parked near the café on Beacon. But I never saw that guy again; the tan car was driverless when I walked by, and didn't follow me. Nerves, that's all it was. Creeping, creeped-out uneasiness. The same feeling I had walking around Jamaica Pond with Mrs. Smith, only there wasn't even a particular car or person to be suspicious of that night.

I turn back to Parnell and state what neither of us wants to say. "If he did suspect me, he'd take me along anyway, just to keep me from talking to the wrong people."

Parnell pushes his mug away roughly. "So you'd be trapped on a boat with a guy who wants to get rid of you." He leaves the rest unsaid.

"Yeah. But I don't think that's going to happen, and I don't see any other options." I know exactly what the risks are. My heart has fairly stopped at the prospect of becoming, once again, a lost human speck on the surface of the ocean, my waving arms visible for a little while, then gone. I vividly remember how black it is underwater, how unearthly cold. In fact, nothing terrifies me more than the thought of what Parnell is suggesting. Yet I can't stop thinking about being on the *Sea Wolf*, can't run away from it like a saner person might. Ever since the collision, I've harbored the stubborn conviction that there's more out there on the ocean for me to do, and the feeling's grown stronger every day. Something deep inside me is pushing me back to the sea.

"You told me yourself this guy is dangerous," Parnell is saying sternly. His sternness feels sweet.

"Anyway, I have pictures."

"Pictures?"

I pull out my phone and start pulling up the photos. "One of Johnny's friends, a guy named Max, broke into my apartment. I'm pretty sure he was looking for some pictures Ned sent to his son's phone just before he died. Max didn't find the phone, but I did, later. Nobody but me and Noah, and now you, know that the pictures were taken off Noah's phone and stored on my computer and my phone. Look. These three photos were taken on a beach somewhere."

I slide my phone across the table.

He hunches over and stares like he's going blind. "Where is this? What are those things?"

"I have no idea."

"What about the other two pictures?"

"Same. I'll send them to your phone now. Johnny doesn't need to know that I haven't got a clue what they're of. And this way, if I don't come back, you can publish them when *you* figure them out!"

Parnell shakes his head at my misplaced enthusiasms. His lips are pursed and pouty. He looks like a scruffy boy unfairly barred from Little League, who has to watch the girls' game instead. He gives me his new number and stares moodily at the screen on his phone until my message appears in his inbox.

"Oh, and another thing—Ned gave Noah a piece of whalebone and told him that he'd been hunting whales."

Parnell's eyes spark with the first excitement he's shown today. "OK, now we've got something: Rizzo thought taking rich guys whale hunting was fun and games for a while. Then something changed his mind, and he tried to get out of it. Dustin Hall didn't like that. He had Jaeger to please, and couldn't afford a leak. He probably tried to convince Rizzo to stay. Maybe Rizzo threatened to go to the authorities or maybe not. In any case, Hall gave him the *Molly Jones* to buy his silence and then killed him in it."

"I'm with you up until the last part."

"All right," he says briskly. "We'll leave that an open question for now."

"They're all open questions."

"You're really going, aren't you?" He's thunderstruck, but knows me well enough at this point.

Suddenly we've run out of things to talk about. I realize that I don't want to say good-bye. I'd like to spend another hour or two with him, walking in a park somewhere, having the kind of easy, wandering conversation people have when they're getting to know each other. But I can't think about that.

"You ought to leave before me so we're not seen together on the street," I say.

He glares and abruptly, wordlessly, complies.

The minute he's gone, I wish I hadn't sent him away. His coffee cup is still half full. And I'm alone. Why am I so often alone? But I can't think about that either.

I motion to the waitress. Order the turkey plate special with extra cranberry sauce and gravy. The Asian woman gets up and starts buttoning her red coat. Now there's only one beefy guy at the counter. I didn't see the other one leave, which bothers me. I have to start paying better attention to these things. To everything.

A dark, hushed lounge on the first floor of a hotel. Little candle flames flickering on low tables. No music, thick carpeting, a perfect indoor temperature of about sixty-eight degrees. A handful of men and women in dark suits are scattered about, sipping after-work cocktails. An upscale watering hole in the heart of the financial district is about the last place you'd expect to find the Oyster Man. Maybe that's why he picked it.

His red hair fades to auburn in this light. He's wearing clean jeans, a tucked-in black T-shirt, and a leather belt. This is how he dresses up. A nylon jacket is laid neatly across the arm of an adjoining chair. He's got a grip on a bottle of Amstel Light.

"Watching the weight," he explains when he sees me glancing at it. His face reddens as he hears himself. So middle-aged. Has he become a bore? Have the diapers, the mac-and-cheese, the skateboards in the hallway killed his manly swagger? He leans back into the cushioned chair. Gives half a smile, and crosses one leg over his knee. Says he's glad I called. But this time he doesn't mean it. He's blinking too much, and his face is stiff.

My gut tells me I ought to turn around immediately and head right back through the hotel's ritzy doors. But I sit down and hear myself smoothly ordering a glass of sparkling water from the waitress. Maybe I'm just too stubborn to heed my gut's warning. I've got one hand to play, and I'm going to play it. Game is on.

After a few pleasantries, I give my spiel. Act naturally, throw in some laughs and a couple of heartfelt sighs. The logic of my proposition unwinds smoothly. My various motivations are progressively revealed. I take care not to overexplain. Johnny doesn't expect me to be sensible, doesn't like sensible people. He's always grabbed license to heed whatever calls to him, be it women or whales, and he understands others who want to do the same. But he's nobody's fool.

When I'm done, he says with a crooked smirk, "I knew you liked fishing, but I got to admit, I didn't see this coming. But, hell, I'm not surprised. Still crazy after all these years, right? Who said that? Bob Dylan?"

"Paul Simon."

"Yeah, right. Never liked him. But you, you're something. More balls than half the guys I know. But come on. You really want to do this? You sure?"

"That's why I'm here. You can work it out for me, right?"

"Absolutely." He nods straight up and down to emphasize his power. "Some of the guys might be surprised to see you, but I'll tell them you were tight with Rizzo, I've known you from way back, and so on. We had a woman up until a few months ago. Big dyke named Abby who moved down to Florida. Flabby Abby, we used to call her. You can cook, right?"

I nod. I'm wearing very tight jeans, very high-heeled boots, and a very low V-neck sweater. This is the closest I can get to cheesy-seductive without wanting to throw up.

"What about Dustin Hall? Doesn't he have to agree?" I ask.

"Nah. He leaves the operational shit to me. All of it, especially crew. I know who can be trusted and who can't. My guys are loyal to me, even Captain Lou. They don't give a shit about Hall. He's too busy sucking up to Jaeger and the so-called guests. Hunt club, they call it. Like a bunch of pansy Brits. Wait till you see them. Not one of them is normal, like how you or I would define the term. They don't give a shit about Hall either. They're superrich; he's just sort of rich. Us guys on the bottom, we're all the same. Room for everyone where we are." He swigs some beer, rubs his mouth with the back of his hand.

I have a feeling there's more to follow, so I wait.

"Hall, man. That guy has no business being at sea. The minute the swells are over three feet, he goes green. Keeps a bottle of Dramamine in his pocket, and pops pills when he thinks no one's looking. I wish he'd stay off the boat when we're working. He just gets in the way. Always checking up on me: *How's it going, Oster? We on schedule? We find whales yet?* I'll tell you, I'd rather be a fucking untouchable than that sorry bag of floating turd."

Years ago Johnny took courses at Harvard Extension School but never finished a degree. He painted for a while and burned his canvases while drunk. A section of one of his abstracts looked like a guy hanging from a noose. *Is that a guy hanging from a noose?* I asked. *What the fuck? It could be fucking anything,* he said, glad to be found out.

He glances around the shadowy room, finds the waitress, swings his beer bottle from two fingers to show he wants another. "You'd think they'd give you peanuts or chips," he says. He shifts, crosses his other leg over his knee. A heavy, muscular leg. Old Nike sneakers, the laces grimy.

I sip my sparkling water. This whole thing feels wrong. Johnny's trashing Hall instead of flirting with me. His eyes are swooping around the room, resting on me intermittently and then taking flight again, as if they made a mistake. Maybe he's found a hot new mistress and doesn't want me anymore. More troubling than that is the fact that he acquiesced so easily to my request, taking me into his confidence without so much as a pause. Maybe the whole operation is a lot looser than Parnell and I thought.

"You're lucky," he says. "No spouse, no kids. Get up and go whenever you want. I envy that." The waitress arrives, and as she puts his fresh beer on the table, his eyes travel up her slender arm to her face. "What took you so long, sweetheart? A man could die of thirst."

He waits for her to leave. "Who else knows about the whales?"

"No one. Me and Thomasina, that's all."

"You sure?"

"Yeah."

"Don't lie to me."

"I'm not lying, Johnny."

He picks carefully at a piece of lint on his jeans, and I'm reminded of the tiny things he makes at home. "Rizzo should have kept his mouth shut. But I'm not surprised he didn't. I'm pretty sure a couple of other guys have talked. Thing like this, you can't keep it secret for long. Too many people involved. But it doesn't matter at this point. The whole thing's going to come apart pretty soon anyway. I can feel it. Jaeger's getting flashy, and his boys are getting too slick, too comfortable. Taking too many risks. Hall wants out, but he doesn't have the balls and is scared of the company going under. Some weird stuff has happened lately, people showing up in weird places. What's that law they talk about in physics? The one that says everything goes to shit?"

"Entropy."

"Yeah." He laughs. "That's the one. Hey, you explained it to me once. Remember that? Think you can do it again?"

"You just said it, Johnny: everything goes to shit."

"Right. The law of entropy. Something I always suspected. Sort of makes it official when it gets a name." He reaches over and grabs the

new bottle, but doesn't drink from it. "So right now our little operation is on the entropy side of the equation. I'm thinking, after this
voyage, it's time to cash out. Got to know when to fold 'em, right?
Who sang that? Johnny Cash?"

"Kenny Rogers."

"Damn. Could have sworn it was Johnny Cash."

"It might have been. I don't know."

"So why'd you say Kenny Rogers?"

"I thought it was him. Yeah, actually, it was him."

"But you're not sure."

"I don't know, Johnny. Who gives a fuck?"

"Don't act like you know if you don't know. That's all I'm saying."

"OK. I hear you."

He tents his fingers in front of his face. "You ever tell anyone what
we're doing out there, you'll regret it. You know that, right?"

"Yeah." I hold his gaze, try not to let my feelings show.

There's something eerily calm about him, as deeply settled as a
sunken galleon, as if we've finally reached the dark, hidden part of his
heart.

"I mean, you'll seriously regret it, Pirio. That's all I'm gonna say.
You know what I'm talking about, right?"

I nod.

"I need you to tell me that you heard what I said. Say you heard it
for sure. Say it in words."

"I know for sure, Johnny." The back of my shirt is damp with
sweat.

"Good. Now if we ever had a disagreement, you couldn't pretend
you didn't know." He snaps a dry smile at me. Swigs long and hard
from the bottle. "You're all excited, huh? You're thinking it's going to
be better than *Moby Dick*."

My hair is loose, twisted over my shoulder. I'm stroking it like it's
a cat. I try to smile. "I don't know. What's it like, Johnny?"

"You mean the killing?"

"Yeah."

"Well, you are a bloodthirsty little bitch. You don't mind me saying that, do you? I mean it affectionately." He's starting to act drunk, but he can't be drunk on two beers. He must have had a few before he arrived.

"What's it like?"

"It's like nothing, darlin'. Hate to disappoint you. A whale's just another animal, a big one. Big as a bastard. You'll see. And the blood, warm blood, lots of it. Maybe for you it'll be some big experience. Like the rich boys finding their inner cavemen, and getting all sticky about it. They take videos and show them to each other; it's fucked-up. For me, it's just a job. I do it so I can pay the mortgage and buy iPads for my kids. And to help my employer through a hard time, I suppose. I'm a loyal company man." He laughs at his own falseness, looks over at the bar, lets his eyes fall on an elegant woman sitting there.

I start thinking about my new Minolta. I've been practicing with it, and it's captured my heart. All I need is a few minutes of slaughter in the same frame as some of the ship's identifying marks and, if I can get it, a face or two.

"You look like you've got something on your mind," Johnny says.

I smile, pick the lemon wedge out of my glass. "This keeps away scurvy, right?"

"There won't be any scurvy on this cruise, sweetheart. I promise you that."

"When do we leave?"

"We? No, just you. I won't be going on this one."

"What?" I balk. I didn't see this coming. "I thought you'd . . ."

He looks quietly amused at my confusion and, I might as well admit it, my distress. I realize that I thought that Johnny being on board would be some kind of safety net for me. An obviously foolish idea, but the kind you cling to anyway without even knowing it's there.

"Oh, right," I say casually. "I guess you're going to Michigan to see your in-laws."

"Actually, that trip has been postponed. I've got some business to attend to right here in Beantown that can't wait."

"Really? Sounds important." *Is it tracking down Russell Parnell, I wonder, or something innocent?*

"Oh, it is. I assure you. Don't worry; you'll be in good hands. You leave Friday, five a.m., from the fish pier. I'll arrange it all." He signals to the waitress for another beer and turns back to me with a boyish smile. "By the way, you're in for a surprise."

"Not sure I can handle too many surprises, Johnny."

A quick wink. "No worries, Pirio. You can trust me."

My shirt is now soaked with sweat, and the blood pounding in my ears sounds like a stampede. "What's the surprise, Johnny?"

"You'll see."

"OK. Thanks for the drink." I've got to get some air.

"Gotta go? So soon?"

"Yeah, I gotta be somewhere."

"Feeling OK?"

"Fine." I stand up.

"Wait. Let me look at you." His gaze is long and empty.

"What are you doing, Johnny? You're acting weird."

"Good-bye, Pirio."

Outside I squint painfully at the headlights of cars, the neon signs. I draw a deep breath, but I don't relax. I walk past a brightly lit glass foyer, where a clock on the wall says ten past ten. How many hours and days will there be until all this is over? I don't know. But I can hear time ticking. It's as if, somewhere in the accelerating cosmic entropy, an hourglass with my name on it was just turned upside down.

Chapter 22

The gorgeous strains of Mozart's Piano Concerto no. 21 waft through the closed doors of Milosa's study. It's the end of the famous andante movement—elegiac, heavenly. If there is a God, he poured this melody directly into the mind of Mozart. I figure Milosa is hanging on the last beautiful notes, so I wait for their echoes to fade before knocking.

He's sitting in his leather wingback chair, which has been turned slightly to face a window framed by velvet drapes. The room smells of cigar stubs and oily furniture polish and Milosa himself—dry, dense, spiced with something like anisette. His expression is sadder and more tranquil than I've ever seen it. I feel like I've come upon him in a deeply private moment and mutter that I can come back.

"No, come in. I want to see you."

The chair across from him is also tilted toward the window. When I sit down, I notice his shoes. Ugly utilitarian shoes with thick laces. Russian shoes. There's a wool blanket heaped on the floor next to his chair. He probably had it wrapped around his legs and tossed it aside when I knocked.

Hesitantly, I ask if he's well.

"Very well." He gazes out the window at the autumn afternoon. Dusk is approaching. Burnished sunlight splashes into our laps like daytime's final gift.

Then why do you seem changed? I want to ask. But I'm no braver than he is, no more honest, for all my complaining. I head for the safety of our usual turbulence by asking a question that's been on my mind since our last talk.

"Why were you so worried about the way I might treat Maureen?"

"Oh, that." He lazily touches the iPod on the table next to him to lower the volume. "You're impulsive, Pirio, and you're still holding a childish grudge against her. But you'd be a fool to push Maureen aside. She knows more about Inessa Mark than anyone else, including you and me."

"Wait. Are you saying you don't think I could run the company without Maureen?"

The orchestral third movement of the concerto is swelling softly through the speakers. He touches the iPod to pause it. "You're too much like your mother. She couldn't have run a company."

"She did, though."

"She had me."

"People like you can be hired."

He chuckles dimly. "Oh, I see. I was dispensable. Is that it?"

I think about it. "More or less."

"Ah, there it is. The stubborn pride. I used to admire that quality in Isa—it made her exciting. But it was also just blindness, and got tiresome in the end."

I feel my ire build. There he goes again with the gratuitous criticisms of the dead. "I don't care what you think about my mother's character. Or mine."

"Bravo! She would have said the same. It's uncanny to see you grow more like her, despite not having her around. Like you, she was indifferent to other people's opinions. She treated me badly when I met her. Nineteen years old, in a cheap cotton dress. Scornful and aloof. I thought she'd change, grow softer, but she never did. It's strange to look back and see everything so clearly—there I was all those years, an atheist waiting for a miracle. I believed in love. Did you know that about your old man, Pirio? *I believed in love.*"

It chills me that he's talking this way. I say the only thing I can get my head around. "My mother wasn't indifferent, and neither am I. She wasn't scornful and aloof. Maybe to you, but not to me."

"Of course. You were her child. She saw herself in you, and loved you all the more for being difficult."

I want to hurl a sharp retort. *Difficult children, lonely children, remember love from those who give it.* But I need these moments of honesty so badly that I manage to hold my tongue.

"Why are you saying these things now, Milosa?"

A smile so fleeting that it fails to become one. "I'm dying. Didn't Maureen tell you?"

I think I may have misheard him, so loud is the rush of emotion that fills my heart. I suspected it, of course. But I denied it, too. Milosa dying? Was that even possible? I believed every legend he ever told about himself, every posture of strength he adopted. I never saw him sick, never fearful or uncertain, never even slightly diminished until recently. I'm angry, as though he's been tricking me all along, making himself out to be larger than life. Then I wonder how he'll die. Not placidly. I think he'll die raving like a lunatic. It scares me to imagine it. Like imagining an enormous, jagged-peaked mountain sliding thunderously into the sea.

I steady myself with some effort and manage to ask him what he's got. By which I mean, what disease.

He laughs like I've told a real knee-slapper. And doesn't answer.

OK, so it's obvious. He's got life, a human body. Organs programmed to screw up. One or two cells forgetting how to do their jobs is all it takes. What difference do the details make when the end is the same? I want to ask if he's sure that he's dying, but he wouldn't have used that word if it wasn't accurate and earned. I won't bore him by asking him to describe what the doctors can and can't do.

"I'm sorry," I say finally. No gush of sympathy, no tearful scene. Because I know that's what he wants. He accepts my simple comment with something like pain clouding his eyes. But it isn't pain; it's vulnerability, need. Our eyes see each other's emotions—a moment horrifying for both of us. He turns to the window, remarking that he always liked the view.

"Yes, it's beautiful," I say quickly.

We are looking down on a small yard and flagstone terrace. A sparrow flits among the wet branches of the apple tree, flicking off sparkles of recent rain. I used to gaze out my bedroom window onto just this view, envying the birds their ability to fly away. I was raised with beauty and luxury, and only wanted to escape. Now I'm sitting here, heavy as a boulder, and Milosa is leaving. The room already feels emptier.

"I've always loved the second movement of this concerto," I say.

"Oh, yes. The Elvira Madigan theme. It's very famous. But the one that was just playing, the third, is the one I prefer. Mozart unleashes himself in that movement. It's as if he gave himself permission to apologize for nothing, cater to no one, and obey no rules. The tempo is allegro vivace assai, which means 'play it as fast as you can.' The pianist has to be a real virtuoso—only real risk takers, high-wire performers, dare to take it on."

I tell him I'd like to hear it again. I suddenly want to go where he goes, hear what he hears. Be close however I can.

"I'll start it at the beginning," he says with pleasure. He fiddles with the iPod; the music begins; he pauses it immediately to explain something. "The orchestra introduces the first theme. The piano opens with a solitary G above high C, followed by a fermata or dramatic pause. The first musical phrase—all played above high C—is E,

F, F-sharp, G. . . . Oh, what am I saying? This doesn't mean anything to you."

"Wait. How much of it do you know?"

He closes his eyes. "E, F, F-sharp, G, A, G, F-natural, E, D, grace note E, D, C . . ."

"You know the actual notes?"

"I used to play before you were born," he says impatiently.

"I never knew that. Why didn't you keep it up?"

"I was no good."

"But you can't believe that."

"Of course I can."

"You couldn't have been *that*—"

He waves away the blandishment. "No. Listen. *I was no good.* Now you'll hear someone who *is* good." He presses play and closes his eyes.

I want to love it, really want to love it, but my attention wanders. There are pictures of my mother all over Milosa's study. Isa in Paris, wearing a prim hat and double-breasted suit by Dior, seated in pale hauteur at a drugstore counter next to a gray wolfhound with limpid, bulging eyes. Isa running through Central Park toward the soaring New York skyline, wearing a short flounced dress by Bill Blass, her legs long and almost shapeless. There are candids, too—Isa at different ages, in different moods, yet always riveting, diffusing her tragic, playful, provocative light.

The photos are too familiar to be enchanting. But I keep scanning their surfaces, keep trying to see around and through and behind all the silver frames. I haven't engaged in this particular form of self-torture for years. The news of Milosa's mortality must have made me regress. Because suddenly I'm a child again, wide-eyed and faithfully searching, wondering why in all this monumental glory there isn't even a snapshot of me.

I find Maureen at her computer. A shelf of binders above her, stacks of paper on the desk. Reading glasses perched on her nose, gemstones flashing as her fingers fly across the keyboard, making the insect music of rapid rhythmic clicks. Her dress is cream and pink, a boat-neck, small stripes, and some kind of floppy belt. It looks as if it started out in the morning for a 1912 steamship, took a detour to a 1950s garden party in the suburbs, and ended up in a 2013 online catalog.

"What does he have?" I say.

She stops typing, gives a deep, defeated sigh. Exits her document and swirls to face me. "Kidney disease."

"What kind?" It makes no difference, but I still want to know.

"Glomerulonephritis, also known as Bright's disease. They've been treating it with drugs, but his reaction has been poor, and recently his doctor told him he would have to go on dialysis. He's refusing." She gives a hollow laugh. "Of course."

"How long have you known?"

"A few months."

"Why didn't you tell me?"

"He didn't want to say anything at first. He thought he'd get better. Instead, he's gotten much worse."

"He said he's dying."

"He will if he continues to refuse dialysis."

"Why is he refusing?"

"You know your father. It's all or nothing. Life or death. A machine that cleans his blood means he isn't alive on his own. Also, on the practical side, he says that being treated for a disease that's going to kill him anyway is a waste of time."

She gestures toward an array of medications on a silver tray on a side table. "He's supposed to take pills five times a day. But I suspect he's throwing them away. I think the only reason he doesn't refuse them outright is that he's afraid I'll grind them and put them in his food."

I pick up a caramel-colored plastic vial. A white cap with directions: *Open—Push and turn—Close*. The name of the pharmacy emblazoned in red. His name in square black letters: Milosa Kasparov. A patient. It looks odd printed that way. The name of a mortal man.

Maureen joins me, pointing to each vial in turn. "Enapril, for high blood pressure. Calcitrol, a form of vitamin D. Phoslo, a phosphate binder. Procrit for anemia, and Lasix, a diuretic."

There's one left. I pick it up and read the name. "Halcion. What's this for?"

"Sleep."

"He has trouble sleeping?"

"He's been ranting in the middle of the night. He gets up and wanders around, going on about Russia. I hear him talking to his mother and father and other people he must have known back there. Then he plays music, symphonies, loud, and when I go into his study I can see he's been crying, but he screams at me to go away."

Her face is taut, brittle. Milosa is taking his toll on her, as always. Yet she soldiers on, keeping everything going, a corporate and domestic sergeant, forever on duty and at attention.

I briefly think about staying here to help, but I would only get in her way.

"I'm going on a trip. Leaving Friday. Two or three weeks—I can't be sure. Will he be here when I get back?"

"He ought to be. The doctor said a few months."

"You won't be able to reach me for much of the time. I'll call when I can."

Her dry lips form a line. She wasn't expecting help from me.

I think about what Milosa said, about her being afraid of me and me being too hard. "Thank you for taking care of my father, Maureen. For everything you've done."

She looks confused, hurt. "It's nothing to be thanked for. He is my husband, isn't he?"

The question hangs in the air, drawing attention to itself.

"Thanks for covering for me at work, too. I know I've been taking a lot of time off recently. But after these next few weeks of vacation, I'll be back and ready to buckle down."

She shrugs as if my absences are unimportant. "A vacation is a good idea. It's been a while since you've had one."

I find Jeffrey in the kitchen, unpacking groceries. The television on the counter is showing an episode of *Brideshead Revisited*. Jeffrey watches the entire miniseries—about eleven hours of film—once a year. I used to watch it with him when I was home from Gaston, so I immediately recognize Charles and Sebastian, and sink down into a chair to witness the end of the heartbreaking scene in Venice. When it's over, Jeffrey points the remote, and the screen goes black with a tiny pop. He throws together a celery, carrot, and hummus plate with pita triangles.

"I have a favor to ask. It's about Noah and Thomasina," I say. Back in high school, Thomasina spent a number of Thanksgiving and Christmas vacations at our house, rather than riding them out by herself in the deserted halls of Gaston when her parents couldn't be bothered with her. Jeffrey always asks about her and Noah, whom he's babysat several times.

"Of course. How are they doing?"

"Noah's OK for having just lost his father. Thomasina's not so good."

I explain her struggle with addiction, and Jeffrey nods without surprise. I describe her failed attempts to get sober, how she's become even more unreliable lately. I mention her night in jail and a bit about the Foxwoods fiasco.

"Noah's always been able to call me if he needed anything. He called me the night his mother didn't come home. But I'll be out of town for a while—I'm leaving Friday for a few weeks—and I'm worried. Thomasina promised she'd go to back to meetings, but she doesn't have a very good track record where that's concerned."

Jeffrey snaps a celery stick between his teeth. "I think I know where this is headed."

"Noah really likes you, Jeffrey. He still talks about the day you took him to the science museum and sat through the Imax movie about dinosaurs twice."

Jeffrey chuckles. "I didn't mind. He explained the parts I didn't get."

"He knows that you raised me, and that I think the world of you, and of course Thomasina's always loved you and trusts you implicitly, so—"

"So you want to bring me into the picture, just in case."

"Do you mind?"

"Of course not. Tell them they can call me anytime. Give them the home phone and my cell."

"Great. I'll give you theirs as well." I jot down the numbers on a notepad. "Maybe you could give them a call before I leave, just to say hi. I want Noah especially to feel OK about calling you if he needs anything."

"I can do more than that. I'll take him to the museum again so we can renew our bond."

"You will? You're the best, Jeffrey."

He grins, accepts my bear hug, then holds me at arm's length. "Now tell me where the hell you're going."

"On a cruise."

"I didn't know you like cruises. Where to?"

"The Bahamas."

"Well, I hope you have good weather." He looks at me thoughtfully, as if he senses something off. "Be careful, will you, Pirio? Some of us love you, you know."

There's nothing to bring me to his doorway. Nothing more I need from him, nothing I want to know. But I'm here anyway.

I park on the street and walk down a dirt driveway to a cottage on the outskirts of Rockport, a quaint seaside village thirty miles north of Boston. He left the rooming house in Charlestown and moved here a few days ago. It's got WiFi and a view of the harbor, he said. A train goes into Boston.

It feels late, though it isn't. Only nine o'clock. The sky is pure blackness, no moon or stars. A thin mist, too delicate to be called fog, swirls in the halo of the light above his door.

I'm leaving on the *Sea Wolf* tomorrow morning. My duffel bag's packed, zipped tight as a sausage, secured with a small combination lock. The cameras are inside, wrapped in fleece sweatshirts; an extra cell phone is stuffed into a wool sock. A backpack holds my laptop and some books, including Aksyonov's *Generations of Winter*, a modern Russian saga that I've been meaning to read for some time. In case there are a lot of empty daytime hours or, more likely, sleepless nights. It's all sitting on the floor next to the door of my apartment, waiting to go.

If I were home right now, I'd be pacing like a lunatic. Fear is easier to bear when you're physically in motion. But there are different kinds of fear, and as I mount the two wooden steps to his front door and gently knock, a more subtle kind takes hold of me.

The door opens soundlessly. He's standing there. We are silent, and the air feels thick around us. I ask if he'll teach me to cook.

His face darkens; he turns away. Now he knows I'm really going.

I follow him into the kitchen, where he starts opening and closing nearly empty cupboards in a flurry. Says he doesn't think there's a cookbook, but he knows what he saw his mother do. Says you don't need any special instructions to cook on board a vessel like the *Sea Wolf* anyway. The men are likely to be starved and grateful, meals, sleep, and pissing being their only breaks from work. "Whatever you do, make a lot," he counsels. Recommends carbs: pasta, rice, pancakes for breakfast. Things like that. Says frozen meatballs are probably a good thing to have on board. And sausage, home fries, tomato sauce, syrup. Says fish is best seared for a few minutes in a hot pan or baked in the oven with breadcrumbs. Beware of overcooking. He gives an ironic arch to one eyebrow. They won't be lacking in fresh fish, right?

Then he asks me when, by the way, I'm leaving. There's a gravelly edge in his voice.

I say tomorrow morning at five.

"Right," he says emphatically, and bangs around a few more cabinet doors. "In that case, the boat's already been provisioned. You'll just have to get creative with whatever's there." He leans back against the counter, folds his left arm over his right, stares at me without pity. Cooking lesson concluded.

If tomorrow wasn't tomorrow, I might wish I hadn't come. I sigh deeply. I do it again. The sighs are loud and completely involuntary.

He pulls a bottle of wine and two glasses off the counter, goes into the living room. I follow. It's got matching plaid furniture, knotty pine tables, a braided wool rug. A wall hanging featuring a deer in a forest and small woodland creatures. Lamps with faded shades.

He opens the bottle by sitting down, squeezing it between his thighs, working the corkscrew with his good hand. I don't dare offer help. He pops it somehow, pours one glass. Before he pours the second, I tell him I don't want any.

"Oh, great," he says sarcastically, as though that just takes the cake. "What are you, an alcoholic?"

I tell him that if I had one glass of wine, I'd probably have several, and probably get drunk, and probably still be drunk at three-thirty when my alarm went off, and so might end up, as they say, missing the boat. That if I was an alcoholic, I probably wouldn't be sitting right where I am, stone-cold sober; I'd be back at my apartment tossing back shots of vodka or gin.

I do have a bit of an exercise habit, however, I explain. Over the last few days I've swam for hours and hours, trying hard to catapult myself into that blissful, high-endorphin zone. But my breath and kicking never synchronized. I just got dog-tired and dragged myself out of the pool. Oh, and I also have a small shopping issue, I admit. Recently I spent an entire evening online, had a lot of stuff shipped overnight express, and when it all arrived, I didn't even feel like opening the boxes. I did open them, though, and for a while I played around with all my new stuff like it was an only child's pathetic Christmas morning. I inflated the pricey rubber survival suit to see if it really worked and ended up puncturing it with the Swiss Army knife.

I smile lopsidedly. "So that's my addictions lineup. None of them work very well."

Not entirely true. I omitted last night's cigar and the pleasure it gave me. But I wouldn't be a real addict if I didn't keep something back. Besides, sometimes a cigar is just a cigar.

I perform the stogie ritual just as Milosa taught me: I snip the end and lick the bitter brown paper, spiral fully half of it in my wet mouth. I light a wooden match, watch it flare, hold the fire steady, and puff. Short coaxing puffs until the leaves crackle and I see a steady glow of red. Until smoke streams internally down the length of the cigar, fills my mouth fully, and eventually leaves it to swirl around my head. Smoking stogies is hardly a trip to Nirvana, but it's a few stops down the line. As always, it's the smell that matters: a thick, brown, dirty odor that clobbers your pretensions, coaxes your brain to release its store of natural opiate, cradles you in a hot, dry, unbearable presence, like a desert wind you would willingly lie down and be baked in, becoming smokable yourself. Cigars work wonders for me.

But right now Russell Parnell and I both know that the substance I really want, and what I'm really here for, is love. That cliché, that pop-tune staple, that stingy old hermit in the hidden cave who has stubbornly refused to show his face to me, though I've clambered up his mountain path countless times to prostrate myself before his pile of stones.

Maybe I'm unworthy. It's crossed my mind. I don't know how to wait, bide my time. Maybe it's because I'll settle for sex. And have, too many times. But who can help it? Need is sharp and raw. It bores a hole in your chest from the inside and pulls you into rooms like this one, where you are forced to awkwardly refuse or accept glasses of unnecessary seduction wine.

I've been around too long to believe that what might happen here tonight is likely to be anything more than transient. But tomorrow I'm leaving on a possible death trip, so what is that to me?

Parnell and I sit facing each other in the small room, tension between us. Electric, dense, warm. He wants me. It's in the set of his jaw, the level gaze of his eyes. In the way he moves the fingers of his good hand, as if the sinews are about to pop.

What would it be to be folded in those arms, my face in the roughness of his sweater, my face looking up to his? What would it be to touch his face and run my fingers across his lips to let the blood rise into them before they're kissed? I want him, too. I want to feel what our love might feel like if it was real.

But my body doesn't move. I see it traveling between us, crossing that short distance, but it doesn't go. It's leaden, heavy. This is not my choice—it's simply what my body is insisting on. Not to go. Wisdom or betrayal? I ask myself. But the body doesn't answer abstract questions. It simply doesn't walk the four steps between Russell Parnell and me. I sit there without a wineglass in my hand, feeling dumb as a fat tree, as if my feet have sent long, ugly tendrils underground to root me to the spot.

He sees what has happened, and his own desire slips gracefully away. No hard feelings.

I leave the apartment soon after that, stomp petulantly down the dark driveway to my car. I'd like to know what my body thinks it's doing. Which, in its wisdom, it won't say.

Chapter 23

I'm standing on the dock in inky blackness, my luggage at my feet. The taxi that dropped me off rolls quietly away. I check my watch. It's 4:43 a.m. I'm early. Usually I'd be wary of hanging out alone and carless in the dark in this section of town, but I figure the muggers and murderers are still in bed. Floodlights shine on a few gently bobbing fishing vessels. The *Sea Wolf* isn't one of them. Also, and not incidentally, there are no people around.

Wrong day? Time? Place? But I swear I heard Johnny right.

It's cold, an hors d'oeuvre of what's to come on the mid-October Atlantic, if I ever make it there. I shrug my shoulders under a jacket that already feels too light. It's high tide—I can tell from the sound of seawater lapping against the pilings just a few feet below the dock. A police car cruises down Seaport Boulevard; the pudding-white face inside stares at me as it passes. Maybe he thinks I'm an outdoorsy prostitute; maybe he doesn't give a damn. I stomp my feet, feel the icy air in my lungs. Was I duped? Am I being tested? A water rat scurries across the pier.

An old red Corolla pulls into the lot and stops in front of the dock, leaving its headlights on. The trunk pops up. A man gets out and walks toward me. He's in his midthirties, hair neatly parted and combed flat. He grabs my gear. "This way," he says, heading back to the car. He tosses my duffel bag into the trunk, slams it, and slides behind the wheel. I hesitate, then get in the car.

"Where's the *Sea Wolf*?" I ask.

"Change of venue. More your style." He looks me over smilingly. "Name's Brad."

"Pirio."

"I know. You're the Swimmer. Nice to have a celebrity on board."

"I'm hardly that."

"You don't get to choose."

"Ned Rizzo saved my life."

"So I heard. I knew him well, worked with him for years. But you, you're something else—" The way Brad looks at me, I almost glance over my shoulder, thinking Mary, Mother of God, must be favoring him with a visitation.

"Where are we going?"

"You'll see."

We're headed south on 93, passing gas tanks and billboards and empty lots and scattered tall buildings and three-deckers set next to one another with no room to spare. My heart is pounding so hard I'm surprised I can't hear it. Brad seems like a nice enough guy—they mostly are, these local fishermen—but that doesn't change the fact that Johnny's already played me for a fool. There I was, standing on the dock like well-behaved bait, and now I'm being taken to an undisclosed location. I can hear Milosa in the background laughing. (I always hear Milosa in the background laughing.) Yet there's no choice now but to stick with the plan and act normal, even though every movie I've ever seen featuring abduction, imprisonment, and torture is playing in my head at once.

Somewhere in Dorchester we get off the highway and head east along a wide, flat road that looks like it's on its way to nowhere. It dead-ends at a marina. Boats all around, many of them sailboats. There's a pink seam of light at the eastern horizon, and trickles of sunlight are creeping across the water, making it glow green like tarnished copper. I open the window to the screech of gulls and the clang of halyards.

We drive behind a warehouse, and there in the near ocean, in a space all to itself, floats a luxury yacht, brightly illuminated inside and out. Two hundred feet probably, sleek, white as sea foam, with a needle-sharp bow. I count four levels, stacked like the tiers of a wedding cake, with a lookout and a lot of sonar stuff spewing out the top. It's a nautical Taj Mahal in a neighborhood of huts.

Brad wags his head like a kid arrived at Disney World. "Will you look at that? It's something, isn't it?"

"Whose boat is this?" It obviously doesn't belong to Ocean Catch.

"Bob Jaeger's. Named the *Galaxy*. This is its maiden voyage. Jaeger's girlfriend got sick of the *Sea Wolf*—not exactly luxury accommodations—and when it got that crack in its hull, she said she wouldn't set foot on it again. Convinced Jaeger to get a superyacht, and he did. The boys say the damn boat's got every damn thing you can think of. Even the toilet paper's extra soft. Have to say, I'm disappointed I'm not going on this trip. But it's just as well. It's not something a guy like me can get too used to. Still gotta go back and haul flounder, you know?"

He looks at me a bit apologetically. "I know Johnny hired you as cook to take Flabby Abby's place. But we just found out last night that Jaeger brought along some of his own people for the hospitality end of things: supposedly, he's got a crackpot chef, a waiter, and a lady who takes care of everything. So I don't know what they're gonna do with you."

He parks, and we take my gear out of the trunk. He carries my duffel up the gangway. A man in a navy sweatshirt meets us before we board. He's in his forties, thinner and more stooped than you would expect a fisherman to be. He offers me no greeting, acts like he has better things to do than be a host. He and Brad exchange some muffled words, and Brad goes back to his car.

The man maneuvers my duffel down a stairwell, carries it along a narrow corridor, and drops it in front of a door. This I take to be my cabin in the yachting equivalent of the low-rent district. There are three other doors on the hallway, all closed. The din of engine noise, not too loud, rumbles through the steel floor into the soles of my sneakers.

"You're the last on board. We'll be leaving soon. You're supposed to report to Zorina in the galley right away," he says and walks off.

Zorina. My new boss. We already have weird names in common. Maybe we'll get along.

I enter my cabin. It's amazing what can be done with a seven-by-nine-foot space. There's a cozy bunk, a tidy formica desk with an easily accessible outlet, a slim built-in closet and stack of drawers. Even a chair for a visitor and an oval mirror attached to the back of the door so I can stay looking my best. Starched sheets and a nice woolen blanket are tucked around the mattress. A steerage-size porthole offers can't-get-much-closer-than-this ocean views. A good place to die or write or pray, though I'm not going to do any of those things. Right now I'm more inclined to take an unguided tour of the environs.

I retrace my steps and find the stairwell when, lo, I notice an elevator next to it. Imagine that. I take it to the fourth floor, enjoying its Fifth Avenue ambience (red carpet, gilt-edged mirrors veined with gold), and step out into a big lounge decorated in contemporary blues and grays. Coffee tables, lamps, and cozy club chairs are arranged around a huge, wall-hung TV screen. Sleek windows offer a panoramic view of Neptune's watery world. I do a double take, surprised to see the skyline of Boston shrinking with alacrity into the horizon. The yacht's so huge and stable, you can't even feel it move.

I make my way through sliding doors onto an open deck with a bar, a dining table with seats for twelve, and a covered Jacuzzi under a blue retractable awning. Three or four steps lead up to an area near the bow populated by lounge chairs.

I'm having too much fun to wonder what Zorina meant by *right away*, an admittedly relative term despite its flavor of urgency, so I take the elevator down to the third floor. What greets me when the doors slide open is an eye-popping grand salon straight out of Versailles. Tasseled brocade drapes, velvet settees, a huge chandelier with about a dozen crystal tiers. A grand piano, a black Yamaha, sits on a plush red-toned oriental rug the size of a small skating rink.

So far I haven't met anyone. I'm starting to think I'm on a ghost ship, but when the elevator doors open on the second floor, I hear distant voices: male, angry; female, commanding. Running water and the clanging of pots. I pass through a small library into an empty dining room. The next room is obviously the galley. A skinny waiter emerges carrying a tray of upside-down wineglasses. His hair is shorn in the back and spiky at the crown, with a long swoop over one side of his face. He glances my way, doesn't seem surprised to see me, and begins setting the table.

I'm not ready to make anyone's acquaintance, so I hop back on the elevator and descend to the first floor, emerging into a hallway softly lit by frosted wall sconces. There are six closed doors, three on each side—the staterooms, I figure. I've only taken a few steps on thick Berber carpeting when the door I'm passing opens and a young woman walks into me.

"Gosh, I'm sorry," she says. "I should look where I'm going. So clumsy." Attar of rose, carnation, a hint of woody moss. A gorgeous scent—classic, French, extravagantly feminine. Like an elegant Parisian grandmother with a wealth of romantic secrets to impart.

"That's more self-flagellation than is really called for." I am, in fact, trying to be kind.

She smiles. "I wish you were a parrot I could put on my shoulder."

"Thank you."

With this, I feel we've established a certain bond.

She says, "I didn't see you last night, but I don't like parties and went to bed early. Now everyone's sleeping, and I'm awake. What are you doing up?"

"Looking for Zorina."

"Oh, *her*. Bob won't leave home without her. She remembers all his appointments, dates. God knows I can't do that. She hates me, let me tell you. She'll probably poison me before it's over. Not that I'm anyone to be jealous of. Middle class all the way. But we were *urged*, shall I say. I played harp and went to Bryn Mawr. Where'd you go?"

"UMass Boston."

"Oh. Too bad."

The young woman is dressed in a loose nightgown and flowing robe, the fabric delicate, nearly transparent. Only the diaphanous folds afford some modesty. Her face is a pale oval of classical beauty. Red hair falls across her shoulders and down to her waist. A siren-red gloss has been freshly and heavily applied to her lips. Interesting that, though it is but six in the morning and she is barefoot and barely clad, she did not leave her stateroom before using lipstick and daubing scent behind her ears.

"By the way, do you know where we're going?" I ask. I feel as though I can ask her this question, and she'll forget my notable ignorance instantly. Like one of the nymphs of Maxfield Parrish, she seems to be not entirely real.

"To the north pole, I think. Someplace like that. *Arctic* is what I was told. Only with Bob you can never be sure. He changes things so fast. The only thing you can count on is that at some point we'll be forced to stand on the upper deck looking through binoculars at animals. We might see polar bears, he said. Walruses, maybe. Sea lions. Silver fox.

Doomed things. The ice cap is melting, and we've got to get photos before it goes. That way, when Bob and I are released from our cryogenic preservation tanks, we can tell our new space-age friends, 'Look, there we are standing on a glacier back in the good old days when planet Earth was cold.'" A pause. "You think I'm kidding, don't you?"

"Not sure."

"You'll see. This is your first trip, huh?"

I nod.

"I'm Margot. Who are you with?"

"I'm not with anyone. My name's Pirio, and I'm crew."

"Really? Why aren't you wearing one of those, um, T-shirts they all wear?"

"Haven't got it yet, I guess. Got to find Zorina first."

"Well, pity you. She's probably in the galley, screaming 'Off with her head.' I'm headed there for warm milk and honey. Out of pills, but they don't work anyway. Can't sleep. Never could. Don't know why I bother trying. If I read, I'd be unbearably brilliant by now. I knit sometimes. Baby booties. Of course it doesn't help that Bob snores. I wish you'd told me you were staff. I wouldn't have gone on so much. Self-disclosure is like a disease with me."

"It's OK," I say, following her down the hall.

"For you, sure. Why should you care?"

She seems to have decided that I don't, and it seems to hurt her. I'm guessing she's frequently hurt.

The sealed cabins we pass are quiet as tombs, sleeping revelers inside.

As we enter the galley, a woman I assume is Zorina, barely glancing up from some paperwork spread before her on the counter, announces to a round-bellied Asian cook that a guest is in need of warm milk. Her face is strikingly narrow, her features crammed onto it in a straight line down the middle: close-set eyebrows; close-set eyes; high, flared nostrils; and a small round mouth. She's wearing what looks like a flight attendant's uniform, cinched tight at the waist by a big brass button. Her figure is generous, but she holds herself stiffly, and comes off as uptight.

Rather suddenly, she addresses me. "You're late." She throws a T-shirt at me. Navy and white nautical stripes in cheap polyester. A horror.

"You'll be serving, cleaning, doing laundry. Can you bartend?"

"Yes."

"Then tonight you'll be behind the bar in the small salon from nine to midnight at least, probably later. Wear something nice."

"Not this, then." I hold up the T-shirt.

"Something sexy, but not too. Don't look better than the female guests."

Margot laughs at this, lightly amused.

"I didn't bring anything nice," I say.

Zorina sighs, oppressed with the varieties of incompetence she is forced to contend with. "I'll drop something by your cabin later."

"Where's Mr. Hall?"

"Why do you want to know?"

"Shouldn't I check in with him?"

"You don't need to do that. Mr. Hall supplies the technical crew and oversees the boating operation. He has passed you off to me because you apparently have no skills he can use. God knows why I have to take you, or, frankly, what you're doing here at all."

Margot emits another peal of tinkly laughter.

The pot-bellied cook puts a mug on a stainless-steel counter. Margot takes it and begins to sip, addresses him with affection. "I ate an entire loaf of French bread last night, didn't I, Katsui? With scads of butter. The urge for bread comes over me when I least expect it, and I simply must give in." Katsui nods in solemn respect at the mystery of gustatory needs.

Zorina's eyes accost me, heavy with the burden of keeping order among such cretins. She takes a small black device, a beeper, out of a drawer and hands it to me. "You'll carry this with you at all times. When it goes off, call immediately on one of the house phones located in any of the main rooms. Press zero to reach me. Brunch is served at eleven on the upper deck. We have an afternoon smorgasbord in the library for those who want it from two-thirty to four. Dinner at eight in the grand dining room. You're on call for room service, housekeeping, laundry. When I call, you come. For all your duties, except bartending, you wear the striped shirt. You'll eat in the crew's dining room one hour before the regular meal is served. At all times you're to keep a professional demeanor. No loitering, snacking, sloppiness. You're not to be seen speaking to other staff members except on matters pertaining to your duties. Don't speak to a guest at all unless spoken to. And then reply concisely, calling the guest *sir* or *ma'am*. If by some unlikely chance you find yourself with time on your hands, don't be seen above the first level. Stay belowdecks." Zorina pauses. "I think that's all."

Margot, looking on in doe-eyed wonder, gives me a sympathetic shrug. "Pity you." She yawns, placing two delicate fingers over her mouth, and puts the mug back on the counter. "I think I can sleep now. Unless he's still snoring, the pig." She wanders off.

With an arched eyebrow, Zorina watches her go, waits until the redhead is out of earshot. "Margot will try to make a friend of you. But that, of course, is not allowed." She unbuttons her jacket, which seems to let out some stuffy air in her torso, and tells me I can go.

Back in my cabin, I make a cell phone call. His voice sounds refreshingly normal: *Hi, this is Russell Parnell. Leave a message.*

I tell him what I know so far: I'm on a luxury yacht named the *Galaxy* that belongs to Bob Jaeger. John Oster is not on board, but Dustin Hall and some other crew members from the *Sea Wolf* are. We're leaving Boston Harbor headed north, possibly to the Arctic Ocean. I'll tell him our exact destination the minute I find out.

As we're setting up for breakfast, my fellow server (as we're called), spiky-haired Andrew, gives me the backstory of each male guest as he steps off the elevator onto the upper deck and takes his place at the table. There's a smugness in the way Andrew possesses the men's public stories, a malevolent glee in the way he passes on the outlandish rumors that swirl through the news clips and articles about them that he's obviously assiduously read. He seems to love hating the guests (as they're called).

Soon they're all seated—six men and three interchangeable bimbos. Margot is not among them. Presumably she's catching up on sleep sans Jaeger's snores. Andrew and I pour coffee, display the pastry tray, take orders. Omelets, French toast, or yogurt and fruit. There's something inescapably maternal about serving food. If I squeeze my eyes partway closed, it's possible to envision each man as a darling twelve-year-old.

Bob Jaeger's seated at the head of the table. According to Andrew, he has a fondness for helpless girl-women such as Margot, to whom he insists that his divorce is only a matter of time. Well over six feet, with a flat square face, narrow eyes, and chiseled chin, he looks more like a Ken doll than a global mover and shaker.

Next to him is Yevgeny Petrenko, aka the Diamond Man of Russia. He made his first fortune twenty years ago in plastic bags (a commodity so scarce in the former Soviet Union that people washed and reused them), his second fortune in Siberian diamonds, and his third in the Internet. As a young man he was jailed for eight years on charges of fraud and embezzlement, and now is fond of quoting gulag graduate Solzhenitsyn, who famously admitted he got his real education in the convict world. In a business suit and buttoned-up pink shirt, Petrenko holds his jaw up and forward like the shovel on a dump truck. His big belly, proof of good living, occupies half his lap.

In loose khakis, slippers, and wire-rim glasses, Hollywood producer Alan Stempel exudes low-key American chic. An art collector and music aficionado, he's known for a series of blockbuster movies pandering to popular tastes, but the bulk of his wealth comes from fertilizer, pesticides, and weapons. He has ties to several governments (U.S., Israeli, Libyan, Jordanian), and a stated desire to bring peace to the Middle East. Charges of espionage never stuck. Handsome, gleaming bald, with a sly, self-effacing manner, he has seven children and is on wife number four.

Richard Lawler, a ruddy Scotsman with a halo of frizzy blond hair, is an international commodities speculator. His famous manias lead him to yell incomprehensibly in public, go on wild purchasing sprees, and capriciously fire employees. At regular intervals he retreats to his estate in the highlands, where he abides with a spinster sister, herds of sheep, and a gaggle of border collies. He's boyishly single, sexually skittish. His erratic buying and selling binges always manage to escape the effects of market downturns. His every move is followed closely in the investment world, despite speculations that he is in fact mentally ill.

Next is a young Swede named Jorn Ekborg, whom Andrew knows less about. Ekborg meets my eye when requesting more coffee, dives to retrieve a dropped napkin in a show of helpfulness. Occasionally he gets up and wanders to the windows to drink in the glorious, unbroken spectacle of the Atlantic, and I note that his eyes slide in my direction to see if I'm watching. With his strong elegant body, delicate face, and imploring dark blue eyes, he could play the romantic hero of a Viking saga. Or a serial killer with an MFA in poetry. Andrew says he's into phones and social media.

Last is Dustin Hall. He's downright fidgety, and seems oddly tardy in all his movements, like a klutzy hanger-on who's mimicking what the cool kids do. This morning he's sporting a stiff Harvard baseball cap that sits too high on his forehead and a zipped-up navy blue jacket with the Brookside Country Club logo of crossed golf clubs. He doesn't rate much airtime from Andrew.

As I'm pouring coffee from a silver carafe, Hall notices me, nods anemically. I assume he remembers me from Mrs. Smith's retirement party and knows that I'm Johnny's new hire. I nod back just as anemically. Awkward, to say the least. I'm glad when Andrew takes Hall's order, leaving me to work the other end of the table.

The guests dine slowly and eventually begin to leave. Finally there are only two diners left, Jorn Ekborg and Yevgeny Petrenko, who sit among the drained coffee cups and dirty dishes still on the table. Their conversation is punctuated by hearty, deep-throated laughs.

As I'm clearing their plates, Ekborg stays my hand. "Come, come, put those down. Join us for coffee. Surely you're allowed to drink coffee? No? But you must! It's the national drink of Sweden, and if you refuse I shall take it as an insult to my country. Wait, I'll pour it for you!"

Charmingly, he jumps up to get a cup and saucer from the service cart, sets them at an empty place next to his. I sit down while he jogs back to find a spoon. He pours from the carafe still on the table while Andrew, stacking dirty dishes nearby, looks on with envy and disapproval.

"Yevgeny and I are good friends. Can't stop talking, can we? Isn't it odd? A Swede and Russian, three decades between us. But that's the nature of true friendship. The usual boundaries disappear."

"Oaf!" Petrenko says. "When have I heard such nonsense? Be careful, young woman. He's impressing you with his poetic soul!" He smokes with wet lips and yellowed fingers.

"You see how he loves me? Like a brother," Ekborg says. "We met in a survivalist camp in your state of Montana. You are American, aren't you? Of course. I can tell before you open your mouth. You American women have such a . . . bluntness about you."

Petrenko roars. "Bluntness! You know how to talk to a pretty woman, Jorn. I should take lessons from you!"

Ekborg turns to the Russian. "Yes, why not? I'll give you a master class, which will be lost on you, Yevgeny, I'm afraid. You've already made an important mistake. Never call a woman *pretty*. It's too common, demeaning. *Beautiful* is the word to use."

"But you're saying this right in front of her! Do you think she's deaf?"

"This woman is not seducible," Ekborg declares, regarding me with a smug, affectionate smile. "She has a strong character. You can see it in her face. She takes a man on her terms only. You must wait until she comes to you."

"Pah. I see no such thing. Only a pretty woman, and I'll call her that." Petrenko exhales smoke through his nostrils.

Ekborg leans toward me. "Let her speak for herself, then. Which would you prefer to be called—pretty, beautiful, or strong?"

"Are you really such an idiot?" I ask. "Or are you only pretending to be?"

He smacks the table with his open palm. "See? What did I say! Now listen, Yevgeny, you must *never* call a woman like this beautiful. Unless you're prepared to have an ax sunk in your forehead while you sleep!"

Petrenko catches my eye and winks, his double chin doing a little jiggle. "You're right to insult him. Who does he think he is? He treats me like a backward man who can't compete with his suave charm. But if I call you pretty, it's no offense to you. I say no more than what is obviously true, and so I earn your trust. If I were a young man and not so fat, it is I who'd be walking off with you on my arm."

"Tell me about your survivalist camp," I say.

Ekborg smiles and leans forward eagerly. "We learned basic skills for surviving a nuclear holocaust, earthquakes, meteor strike, anything that might cause a mass extinction. A lot of us have camps in remote places, with runways for small planes, two generators, canned foods, a five-year supply of water stored in barrels. Books to teach our children, medical supplies. Guns, of course, and agricultural tools.

With the right tools and the right knowledge, we can maintain a decent lifestyle for our families while the planet regenerates itself."

"That's fine for you, but what about the rest of us? Wouldn't it be better to put your resources into preventing these kinds of disasters?"

"My, my. You *are* American," Ekborg says teasingly. "You think such things can be prevented with—what's the word—ingenuity?"

"Ingenuity!" Petrenko says, as though he loves the word's sound. "But you Swedes are more American than the Americans." Another wink at me. "I only say that to egg him on."

"Yes, ingenuity," I say. "Along with science, resolve, cooperation."

Ekborg sits back and studies me, as if searching for just the right path of logic that will open my dim democratic mind. "I know what you're thinking. You're thinking that we survivalists are in it only for ourselves. That we don't care about humankind. But you're wrong. We care so much that we'll do anything to keep it going. Isn't the survivalist instinct what brought our species this far already?"

"Your logic is self-serving and dangerous," I say. This is why I never did well in school. I get too emotional and simply pounce.

Petrenko hoots. "With this fine lady, you won't get an ax in the forehead while you sleep, my friend. You'll have your tongue cut out at the roots while you speak!"

"Dangerous? How is it dangerous?" Ekborg asks in a tone of hurt and challenge. I can see that he's pleased to have drawn me into an argument.

"First, tell me how hunting fits into your scheme."

"Ah, yes. That's what we're here for, isn't it?" He pours himself more coffee. "You're not one of those bleeding heart liberals, are you, Miss—"

"My heart doesn't bleed for anything. Or else it bleeds all the time. And my name is Pirio Kasparov."

"A Russian! I knew it!" Petrenko crows. "Russian women are strong as tanks."

Ekborg smiles slowly and graciously, as if it's been decided that my rough edges will not preclude our being friends. "It's human nature to kill, just as it is to survive. One flows from the other. Does that offend you, Miss Kasparov? It shouldn't. We have only to look at history to see how bloodthirsty we are. During the twentieth century millions were slaughtered simply for the pleasure of it."

"Pleasure? No, it was for power," Petrenko says, still enjoying the conversation.

"What power was given to the Communist henchmen or Nazi soldiers who murdered their neighbors? Genghis Khan and his hordes wiped out ten percent of the entire human population at that time. They didn't care about power, only killing. They did it as sport."

Ekborg goes on with sad, contented resignation. "We're all murderers, and the most dangerous among us are the ones who won't admit it. Hunting is the least destructive of the forms that murder takes. There's no politics involved, no hate. And animal populations replenish themselves quickly for the most part. Think about it. If more people were allowed to kill game, there might be less need for war. But it has to be prey that truly challenges a man's abilities and resourcefulness. Ducks and squirrels don't do the trick."

Petrenko stubs out his cigarette on his plate. "Jorn is a master hunter. We have a video of him in Africa. If you want to see it, he'll show it to you tonight, I'm sure. He's got his eye on you like he did on that lion. He's a wild man, this Jorn. I'm telling you, watch out for him."

"I'd love to see it," I say, finding a plastic smile for Ekborg.

"Then you shall, Miss Kasparov."

"Tonight I'll be bartending in the small salon after nine."

"Perfect. That's where we show our videos," Ekborg says.

The elevator doors open and Zorina storms out, looking like a glass bottle rocket ready to explode. Andrew, I notice, is gone. I feel the reflexive guilt of the employee caught loafing, then fear that she'll be so mad she'll take me off bartending tonight and make me scrub latrines instead. I jump up, start stacking dirty dishes.

"Gentlemen, excuse me, but I need Ms. Kasparov," Zorina says with cold geniality, coming over to the table.

"Don't punish the young lady, please!" Ekborg crows while Petrenko looks on with amusement. "It's all my fault. I forced her against her will to neglect her duties and drink coffee with us instead. Both Yevgeny and I tried relentlessly to seduce her, with no luck. She's a paragon of virtue, this woman."

"I'm sure she is, but I must have her now. I'm sorry to take her away."

"Madame, you do an impeccable job," Petrenko says. "The service is first-rate."

Zorina smiles stiffly, refusing to be buttered up.

Petrenko presses forward with the distracting blandishments, designed, I suppose, to get me off the hook. "I'm looking forward to our little adventure. With my friend Jorn on board, we'll be twice as busy as usual in Baffin Bay."

I freeze, my hand gripping dirty silverware. Baffin Bay. A huge body of water between Canada and Greenland. Remote, untraveled, its distant shores populated only by sparse Inuit settlements. A perfect place to hunt whales.

Zorina grabs my elbow and pulls me aside, drags me over to the bar, where she can harangue me without being overheard. I'm carrying a tray heaped with dishes and almost drop it on her feet.

"Listen, Ms. Kasparov. You need to watch yourself, do you hear? The guests may want to talk and flirt. Fine, if that's what they want, you go along. I won't even stop you if you're inclined to give them more. But never forget that you're an employee who's being paid to forget whatever they tell you or show you, and whatever you see or hear on this voyage. I trust Mr. Hall went over these rules with you."

"I was told, yes."

"And please don't be stupid enough to think they would ever care for you. There are no fairy-tale endings here."

"I didn't think there were."

"Good. Now finish up here and come see me in the galley." Zorina sweeps off and, when I return to the table with my empty tray, the men are gone, leaving balled napkins and Petrenko's crushed empty pack of Dukats.

Chapter 24

Each of the staterooms has a bathroom, there's an extra bathroom on each level, two in the crew's section, and one on the bridge. Altogether, thirteen bathrooms. Maybe a few more Zorina forgot to mention. Enough bathrooms for hundreds of residents of Calcutta or a couple of families from La Jolla. Zorina circled their locations on a deck plan, and handed me a canvas bag filled with cleaning supplies. I was instructed to respect Do Not Disturb signs and to yell *House-keeping!* before entering a stateroom. Thoughtfully, she folded the deck plan and put it in the bag so I wouldn't get lost. But I can't promise not to get lost. It's such a big boat. So many doors.

On my way to the stairwell I pass the elevator, which I was told crew members are not allowed to use. It wouldn't do for one of the guests to have to share that lovely box of polished wood and mirrors with people like us. *Invisible* is the word Zorina used to describe what we're supposed to be, and my fellow employees seem to have taken this directive to heart. In the half day I've been aboard, the only workers I've met are Zorina, the cook, and Andrew. But I've been told there are twelve of us. With the ten guests—six gentlemen, three bimbos, and Margot, who's in a class by herself—there are twenty-two people aboard. On a boat this size, I suppose it's not surprising that the salons and corridors feel sparsely populated.

It only makes sense to tackle the lavatory on the bridge first. It's likely to be small, just the right amount of challenge for a beginning latrine artist. And, not incidentally, the bridge, the brains of the boat, is where the captain is likely to be.

It's on the third level, a curved room at the bow. Cold, gray, devoid of charm and imagination, just what a good frontal lobe should be. Dozens of gauges and switches are set in panels under a bank of windows. In the center of the room stands a metal wheel with a protruding lever—a contraption that looks like it could have come from a Model T Ford. It's distressing to think that our lives could rely on something so low-tech. The captain is there, consulting a chart. He looks up with a trace of annoyance. I'm wearing the striped T-shirt with the *Galaxy* logo; there's a toilet brush sticking out of the bag I'm carrying. This prompts him to yell across the room, "Oh, no! What kind of trouble are you?"

But he hasn't seen into my soul; it's just a friendly tease. I explain my mission. He points to the lavatory door. "Let me not keep you from your appointed rounds."

He's short, thick through the middle, decked out in a navy jacket with some yellow stuff embroidered on the shoulders and cuffs. Obviously more of the mandatory boat garb, since he doesn't look like the kind of guy who'd willingly don a wannabe Sergeant Pepper blazer. His face is pasty and bloated, capillaries blooming like purple rhododendron bushes on his cheeks. A lock of sparse sandy hair falls along one side of his face. The way it's combed reveals a bit of delusional studliness on the part of a man who might be pushing sixty.

"How are we set for icebergs?" I say, because I want to start a conversation, and it's the first thing that pops into my head.

"Not to worry. Gotta get farther north before we have to start thinking about those little darlin's."

"Right-o. How far north?" There's a tiny, unintended yelp of fear in my voice.

His pouchy eyes register amusement. "Don't tell me. You saw *Titanic*. Good movie, huh? What'd you think of Leonardo? Reminds me of myself at that age." He burbles a bit of laughter. "That's a joke. But listen, sweetheart, don't you worry about icebergs. I've had a lot of experience in these northern seas, and you can rest assured that I'm not a horse's ass like the captain of the *Titanic* was. You're safer here with me than you would be driving on Route 93."

"Still. What if—"

"Did I tell you not to worry? Were you listening? Gotta do what the captain says, right?" He winks with flirty pleasure in his own authority. "You can call me Lou, by the way. Or Captain Lou, but I don't insist on it."

"Lou Diggens, right?" The captain who got into a fight with the Japanese fishmaster on the *Sea Wolf*'s last voyage.

"Two points for you."

I tell him my name and set down my bag.

"Oooo-weee. Yes, ma'am. Your reputation precedes you. You got a nickname already, you know that? The Swimmer, we're calling you." His face darkens. "Shame what happened to Ned Rizzo, huh? Used to work with us."

"Yeah, I know. He saved my life." I no longer expect a reaction.

Lou turns back to his chart. "He told you what we're doing out here, huh?"

"Uh, yeah."

"And you couldn't wait to join the party."

"Uh-huh. So when do we get to Baffin Bay?"

"Who said we're headed there?"

"Yevgeny Petrenko."

"That fat Commie wouldn't know Baffin Bay if it bit him in the ass. I'd be careful of him, by the way. He likes the ladies. Zorina's had to beat him off, not that I can see the attraction. Did you meet the redhead yet? Jaeger's mistress? She's actually a very sweet girl."

"I met her." It feels good to be offered so much gossip in so short a time. Makes me feel socially accepted. "What's Jaeger like?"

"Hell if I know. He was in here this morning to look over the charts, make sure we're not headed to Australia. Got a face like stone. Richer than God, apparently. But you can't hold that against him, can you? I mean, we'd all like to be him. And he's pretty damn generous with his cash. There's a nice trickle-down, shall we say."

"If we're not going to Baffin Bay, where are we going?"

Lou picks up a pen and starts writing something on the chart. "Don't ask too many questions. Everybody just does what they're told here. We're all better off that way."

I glance over his shoulder. "Can't hurt to show me, can it? I hate not knowing where I'm going. It gives me nightmares."

He surveys me top to toe, as if to be sure he's got me correctly classified. I try to look infantile. "All right, I'll show you. Because we don't want you screaming in the middle of the night, do we?"

The chart is about three feet square, its edges slipped under clear plastic arms to keep it flat. There's a lot of white landmass: the southern reaches of the Canadian Arctic Archipelago, with probably a thousand or more miles of coastline flayed into tiny strips like machine-shredded paper. Greenland, also white, is cut off on two sides and stuffed in the upper right corner. Mostly there's a lot of blue.

"It's an easy-as-pie voyage, navigation-wise," Lou says. "Most of the time we'll be in sight of land. We're about here right now." His dirty finger lands on a spot in the Gulf of Maine. "We'll head up the east coast of Nova Scotia, hang a left at the Cabot Strait, follow the western shore of Newfoundland through the Strait of Belle Isle. Probably stop for some R&R at Makkovik, then north along the Labrador coast, across the Hudson Strait, bear left here, after the Hall Peninsula, into Cumberland Sound."

"Cumberland Sound?"

"Right. That's where we're headed. But you can call it Baffin Bay if you want. Or anything else. The guests don't know the difference. You could dump them in Greenland, tell them it's Canada, and it'd take them a day to figure it out."

"When we get there, do we just, uh . . . float around, or do we stop at a port somewhere?"

"There aren't exactly ports up there. There's a little settlement the locals call Pang snuggled next to a really spectacular fjord. But we're going past that, through some of these islands up here." He sweeps a finger northwest up the sound. "There's a certain place we drop anchor to have our fun."

I peer at the map. "Where?"

"What does it matter? It's all remote. The land's uninhabited. No supply ships where we're going, I can tell you. Closest people are the Inuit down at Pang."

Lou's a glib, sleazy guy, but he's also likable. I'm wondering how to get more information out of him when I hear a scraping sound behind me. A tall, limp young man is pulling up a folding aluminum chair and sitting down. He's got a sallow face and stringy hair, and there's a nervous jump in his legs, now stretched out behind me within tripping distance.

"Meet my stepson, Troy," Lou says drily, "up from the bowels of the engine room."

"Hello, Troy," I say.

"She's the Swimmer," Lou says with less enthusiasm than he had before.

Troy's eyes glimmer, but he offers no comment.

The conversation turns personal. A bit too personal. Basically, Lou used to be married to Troy's mother. After the divorce, he inherited the care and feeding of her troubled son, got him involved in fishing as a way to keep him off the streets. Not that it worked. All this is told with heavy sarcasm by Lou, who seems to want credit for his non-biological altruism, while at the same time distancing himself from the obviously pathetic outcome.

When Lou stops talking, Troy nods in the direction of his stepfather and says, "This guy taught me everything I know."

"Didn't teach you how to break and enter, assault police officers, sell drugs, and keep getting caught, did I?" Lou says angrily.

"No. Just how to suck up and bend over." Troy looks at me like this is a good joke that he and I could laugh over easily if we wanted to, and I see Lou's neck redden under the collar of his blazer.

I feel like I'm watching Lou and Troy play themselves on reality TV.

"This is the Swimmer's first day. Let's not scare her off," Lou says tightly.

"She's not scared of sailors out to make a few bucks. Especially when she's one of them."

Lou glances at me nervously and apologetically, then his eyes scoot away. His stepson seems to have bested him. When his side-swept lock of sandy hair falls over his face, it's like watching the curtain come down on a cheesy one-act. Troy is sitting with his legs spread wide, staring at me like I'm an empty beer bottle on a fence and he's bored white trash.

These are some family dynamics, I think as I pick up my bag of cleaning supplies and head back the way I came.

"Hey, what about the lavatory?" Lou calls after me.

"Later," I say.

Troy gives an ugly laugh.

I've got to let Parnell know where we're headed right away. My cell phone isn't going to work forever out here in the Gulf of Maine. But we're still close to land, so there's a chance we're in roaming distance for my network.

I tear down three flights of stairs to the bottom level. There's a constant hum on this floor, a vibration in every surface, and a rhythmic thumping that I don't understand. I don't expect to meet anyone, so at first I'm merely surprised to see two men coming out of my cabin. Then I notice that one of them has my laptop under his arm and the other is holding my new Minolta. They head in the opposite direction.

"Hey, wait a minute!" I yell.

They turn. One is bulky as a linebacker, with a placid face. The other is the unfriendly stooped guy who took my bag this morning. They're both wearing navy sweatshirts with the *Galaxy* logo.

"Where are you going with my stuff?"

"You're not allowed to have these devices on board. You'll get them back at the end of the voyage," the second one says.

"But I've got my life on that machine," I say, pointing to the laptop.

"You shouldn't have brought any of this stuff with you. No computers, phones, or cameras. Those are the rules."

"Come on. Give me a break."

He shrugs, and the two walk away, leaving me standing in the corridor.

I go into my cabin. My duffel bag is open on the bed, and my clothes are strewn about. I check around and discover that they took my iPhone and the Kodak PlaySport as well. They even got the pay-as-you-go phone I packed in case of emergency and stuffed in a wool sock.

I sit on the cot among my scattered things. Without my phone and laptop, I feel naked. Without the cameras, there's no point in my being here at all. Now what do I do?

By ten o'clock there's a rowdy little crowd in the small salon. Bob Jaeger, Jorn Ekborg, and Richard Lawler are deep in conversation. Lawler keeps wagging his great blond head excitedly, a loud peal of laughter occasionally breaking forth. Margot half reclines on Jaeger's left, looking wan and listless. Yevgeny Petrenko's got his arm around a woman I haven't seen before. She's older than the others—early forties, round and placid, with poufy bleached hair. He's caressing her bare elbow, rubbing it obsessively, while she blinks lazily like a contented cat.

The salon's cozy by *Galaxy* standards: there's a round card table in a corner and two couches facing each other in the middle of the room. Against the far wall, a projection screen's been pulled down, and there's a laptop open on the table. Subdued lighting makes everyone look good.

I'm shaking and pouring behind the polished rosewood bar, grabbing glasses and tossing maraschino cherries and lemon and lime wedges into whatever drink looks like it could use a little color. It's been a while since I did this, and I know I'm getting proportions wrong, but so far no one's complained.

After a while, Margot detaches herself from the group and comes over to perch on a bar stool. "It's nice to have another reasonably intelligent woman on this boat. You've no idea how bored I get. With Bob, it's business, business, business. Half the time I have no idea what he's talking about. We've been together a couple of years. All I do is travel and go to parties and events. And sleep, of course, when I can. I don't have any friends."

I have no idea how to respond to this deluge, so I take refuge in the obvious. "Can I get you something to drink?"

"Champagne."

She stares at the fizzing bubbles as I pour, touching the stem of the glass lightly with long plum-colored nails.

"How many of these voyages have you been on?" I ask.

"This is my third. I'm so glad we have decent accommodations finally. I was the one who convinced Bob to get this boat. I couldn't stand that other one."

Again, I have the sense that I could ask Margot anything without rousing her suspicion. And that even if she did suspect me, it wouldn't make any difference to her.

"What do they do with the carcass—I mean, after they kill the whale?" I ask in a neutral tone.

"*The* carcass? There's more than one. Hundreds."

"Hundreds? Really?" She's even ditzier than I thought.

Margot's eyes look vaguely affronted. "The bodies fall to the bottom and decay. Piles of them. A mass grave. What did you think?"

"I didn't know."

She sips her champagne by childishly bringing her lips down to the rim of the glass where it sits on the bar. "Jorn is after you. You can tell by the way he's trying to ignore you."

It's true. He hasn't looked at me all night. But the way he keeps his back to me, shows me his profile, stands in a dominant position over the others on the couch—all this seems to include me most particularly.

"Most people would say that was a contradiction, but I know what you mean."

She smiles, accepting her due. "Do you like him?"

"He makes me uncomfortable."

"Naturally. He makes all women uncomfortable. He's very handsome and insanely rich."

"Speak of the devil."

"Ladies," Ekborg says cordially, taking the stool next to Margot, "are you ready to see my footage?" There's an appealing lilt in his Swedish accent. You think of brisk air and elderberries.

"I've seen it, Jorn. Isn't this the third time you've shown it?" Margot says.

"Don't be silly. I shared a bit of it last night with you and Bob, but the others want to see it now. Including our friend here." He nods in my direction, still without looking at me.

"You mean this bartender?"

"Miss Kasparov."

"I'm sure it will impress her. It's not every day one gets to see a lioness being slaughtered by machine-gun fire."

Ekborg laughs indulgently. "Not a machine gun, Margot. Please. You make it sound so brutal. There's an art to it, like bullfighting."

Margot cocks an eyebrow at me ironically. "Oh, toreador!" She slips off her stool and wobbles to Jaeger's side, carrying her champagne flute aloft like a torch.

"She's fragile," Ekborg says to me confidentially. "Like his first wife, I hear."

"I think he's still married to the first one."

"Is he? I wouldn't know. And you— are you married?"

"I haven't had that pleasure."

"A woman so lovely. I'm surprised."

"What about you?"

"I tried it years ago. We weren't right for each other. I knew it at the time, but I lacked the courage to say no to her, to follow my heart. You look surprised. But knowing yourself, knowing how to love . . . these things take time."

His face is so handsome that I can see how a woman might fall into helpless awe.

An order is shouted for several more drinks. I make them, put them on a tray. Ekborg serves them for me in a happy, connubial way.

"Let's see the film," I say when he returns, just to get him to stop gaping at me with those limpid, marine-blue eyes.

Ekborg looks pleased by my request. He goes to the laptop, leans a shoulder against the wall, and clicks through a menu with a remote. A dry, brown land that is clearly Africa rises on the projection screen. Jiggling in the camera and the rumble of a noisy engine indicate that the person holding the camera is riding in a car. There are voices in the background; I think I hear some native accents among the hard English consonants. The camera sweeps lazily across a grassy plain dotted with clumps of brush and tall trees whose branches are etched against a searingly blue sky.

Ekborg provides the voice-over, mimicking a carnival man. "Here we are, ladies and gentlemen, on the lush wetlands of Botswana's Okavango Delta. That river you see in the distance is infested with crocodiles, and you will see in a minute—yes, there they are, you can just make them out—the lioness and two cubs swimming across it. One of the cubs is slower. Watch how she drags him out of the water and tosses him up the bank. They've just made their way back from Duba Island, where there's a herd of buffalo—fierce animals, those, with huge slashing horns—and now she'll have to take her chances against rival prides and, well"—Ekborg gives a modest chuckle—"with the likes of us."

"Hurry up, my friend. Some of us were there with you. We don't need a science lesson!" Petrenko calls out.

Ekborg shoots me an apologetic grimace at the way the Russian is ruining the experience. "You can wait, Yevgeny. I want to set the stage."

"What stage?" Petrenko calls back. "Look, there you are!"

Ekborg looks quickly back at the screen and says excitedly, "Yes, that's me. There I am."

The jeep has come to a stop, and now the camera is being held rather still. Ekborg has appeared at the right of the frame, making his way toward the tall grass. He's wearing a green do-rag on his head, a grimy muscle shirt, and long khaki pants. He's tanned, perspiring heavily. He's got some kind of heavy gun slung over his shoulder, yet he moves with athletic grace and appears elated.

"The camera loses her here, but I know where she's slunk off to. She's still close to the river, making her way toward the plain. I know she'll smell me soon, and she is quick, so I'd better watch out! A quick cat. But I am quicker." He laughs.

"Look at you! A Swedish fool," Petrenko chortles.

Lawler and Jaeger ratify this with approving grunts.

The salon grows quiet. In the video Ekborg has stopped, frozen. He raises the rifle, puts it down, raises it again, takes a few more steps. You see a quivering along the top of the grasses. Then, slowly, the lioness grows visible among the stalks, like a hidden picture emerging. She's yellow, and steps onto the plain without hurry. A cub darts in front of her. The other tumbles after it.

A shot rings out, and she folds, dropping first onto a shoulder and then collapsing straight down. It's a shock to witness the finality with which another inch, another step, another breath has been denied her. How, in an instant, her body is transformed into an unmoving pile.

The cubs keep cavorting across the plain.

Ekborg stops the video. The whole thing has taken only a few minutes, but it feels much longer. There's a heaviness in the room, almost a numb satiety, as if something truly profound has happened. And it has. I begin to grasp a deep, ugly source of the hunter's joy: killing is eternal. It leaves a permanent mark.

The party goes on until midnight, then Ekborg, the last to leave, approaches the bar where I'm cleaning up, preparing to load glasses into a small dishwasher beside the sink. He left me alone after showing the video, perhaps to give me time to absorb the depth of his prowess.

He wastes no time. "You intrigue me, Miss Kasparov."

In my hand is a nearly full glass of scotch and soda and melted ice, left by one of the others. Before I can stop myself, I toss the drink in his face.

Ekborg gasps, shakes his head, rubs his eyes with balled fists. With a napkin, he dries his cheeks and dabs at the front of his black cashmere sweater where the liquid is coursing down.

He tosses the napkin on the bar, stares at me coldly for a few seconds, doesn't speak. I am not worth anything to him now, not even words.

With a blasé attitude, he strolls out of the salon.

Chapter 25

It rains for the next few days—sharp, fine drops that prick the surface of the ocean like millions of small pins. The windows of the *Galaxy* are so spattered and streaked that the effect is one of partial blindness. A torpor descends inside the yacht. Impossible to be this close to the weather and remain unaffected by its moods. Only the gulls outside are brash and noisy: swooping, scudding, keeping up a raucous cawing that can be heard in almost every location on board. When the rain stops, fog creeps in, spreading close across the surface of the water, distorting sound as well as sight. Time seems to have slowed down: the minutes feel unbearably long; the hands of clocks seem to barely move.

Jorn Ekborg pays me no more attention. I've not just slipped into disfavor; I've ceased to exist. Yevgeny Petrenko has no more words to spare for this American of Russian descent. While waiting table or bartending, I feel Dustin Hall's eyes on me, but he says nothing. Margot offers me inviting, conspiratorial smiles. In the evenings in the salon, she perches at the bar and happily bends my ear with her opinions and regrets. To the other guests I am as Zorina wished—invisible.

The crew is even more frosty to me. Conversation dies down when

I approach. At one meal the strongman who took my stuff looks straight through me as he picks his teeth meticulously.

No doubt word of my confiscated items has spread. I tell myself that it's still possible they don't suspect me of anything. The items were removed from my cabin in a routine, casual way, as if they were no more than oversized bottles of shampoo at airport security. Checking a new crew member's stuff for contraband items may simply be routine. And I'm pretty sure there's nothing incriminating on the phone or computer. Before I came on board, I erased my search history, emptied the trash, and took Noah's photos off both devices. If questions are put to me, I can hide behind honest ignorance. John Oster never mentioned that cameras and electronic devices weren't allowed on board.

Still, nothing feels right. For one thing, Troy keeps popping up. At the end of a corridor, in the doorway of a salon. Appearing and disappearing like an apparition. It gets eerie, nerve-racking. With each successive vision he seems more and more like a black bird of impending doom, dredged from my own unconscious. At night in my cabin with the door closed and bolted, I feel the gentle depression of steps outside my door. Once, then again. Stalking. I suspect it's him. Under these circumstances, I don't dare try to get word to Parnell. I wouldn't know how to get through to him with the ship's radio, anyway.

We arrive in Makkovik, halfway up the Labrador coast, on a clear night. I must have my sea legs, because I can feel the calmer surface in the deepwater bay where the *Galaxy* drops anchor. The town is nothing more than a few sparse, yellow lights some distance off. From the talk in the salon, I know the population's about four hundred, mostly Inuit. It's got an airport and a little inn that, with advance warning, will serve a very good meal. There's a small museum, and to the north an American radar base that was dismantled in the sixties. That amount of information appears to exhaust the subject of Makkovik.

Still, there's a sense of excitement among crew and guests at the chance to walk for a distance on firm ground, to be less coddled in luxury for a day. The bimbos will purchase something if it's humanly possible. And I intend to quietly make my way to the Makkovik community center, which, I overheard, offers phone and Internet service to the public.

In the morning the guests head to shore first, spiffed up and smiling, crowded onto a motored skiff the town sends out to welcome us. The crew will complete its work on board, then have a few hours on shore from late morning to late afternoon. Zorina tells me that now's the time to thoroughly clean the deserted staterooms. As I am walking down a corridor with my canvas bag of cleaning products, the two crew members who raided my cabin appear at the other end. They approach, stand very close to me—so close that I can smell the cold sea air emanating from their sweatshirts—and instruct me to come with them.

They lead me to the elevator—apparently, it's not off-limits now. We sink in gilded luxury to the ship's lowest level. The whole time I'm thinking that this was bound to happen. I shouldn't be surprised. They want to ask me a few questions about my cameras and so on. I breathe deeply, imagine myself giving clear, sane responses that show how completely innocent of any wrongdoing I am.

When the elevator doors open, I'm sandwiched between the men, one ahead and one behind. We make our way along the corridor to the hot, clanging, cavernous engine room. We cross to the far side and enter a smaller room filled with electric panels, a generator, and valves. In the center of the room there's a metal chair and metal table, empty but for four sets of handcuffs.

I turn heel and run. One of the men bars my way. Then the two of them pick me up under the arms and transport me, feet dangling, to the chair. In seconds, I am seated, and my hands are cuffed together behind my back.

Dustin Hall enters. He's got on the navy jacket with the logo of crossed golf clubs. It's zipped up tight to where his slender neck rises like a pale stalk to his tulip-shaped head. The two crewmen assume positions beside and slightly behind him, standing tall as columns.

"Pirio Kasparov," Hall says musingly, as if my name were an interesting riddle. "I had you followed and hired a private investigator to look into your background. I've got a dossier on you the FBI would be proud of."

"Yeah. I bet you know every book I ever bought at Amazon and the location of all my favorite ATMs."

"Your mother, a famous fashion model, died when you were ten. Your father and his new wife sent you to boarding school, where you were a consistent underachiever and disciplinary problem. Apparently, you had a psychiatric condition, and possibly still do. You went to UMass Boston and are presently employed at your family's perfume company, which you're going to inherit someday."

"Not bad. Can you see into the future? I'd like to know if I marry a prince."

"I suppose it's possible. This is a pick-your-own-ending fairy tale. Here are your choices: One, you tell me what I want to know and carry on with your life. Or, two, you die today, and your body is never found."

"Hmm. Don't think so. Those options are kind of dull, and way too obvious. A really good ending is the one you don't see coming. So we'll just have to wait and see."

"You're awfully clever for a person wearing handcuffs."

Hall glances at the crew member to his right—the big one with piggish eyes, pumped-up muscles, and tiny hands—and a very bad feeling comes over me. I watch in horror as the guy comes around the table and holds up his fist briefly, as if to examine it. Then he punches me in the stomach, hard. Before I can get my breath, he does it again. An experience that gives new meaning to the phrase *puking up your guts.*

"Really, Ms. Kasparov. Can you afford to be uncooperative? Look around. Think about where you are. You can't seriously believe you stand a chance."

When I can wheeze audibly, I say, "I suppose you're right. It'll save time if you kill me now." There's a loud ringing in my ears.

"First I want to know who you're working for and how much you know."

"I'm working for you. Ned Rizzo told me what you were doing before he died, and I wanted to be a part of it. So I asked John Oster, and he hired me, or didn't he tell you that?"

"You really thought you were brought on board this boat as an employee?"

"Yeah. I was supposed to cook."

Hall's eyes remain expressionless. "We know that you're working with a Mr. Wozniak, Larry Wozniak. How long have you known him?"

"Wozniak. Was that the guy at the funeral?"

"You made a call to someone named Russell Parnell after you arrived on board the *Galaxy*. What did you say?"

"I said . . ." Oh, God. I forgot that the cell phone would have shown Parnell's number. "I said, *Oops, wrong number. Sorry to trouble you.*"

"What was Larry Wozniak looking for when he broke into the Ocean Catch administrative offices?"

"I have no idea."

"What information did you receive from Mrs. Smith?"

My heart nearly stops. *How does he know about Mrs. Smith?*

"You look startled, Ms. Kasparov. I'm aware that you and Mrs. Smith talked on two occasions. At length. What were you talking about?"

"Dogs. Dog lovers never run out of things to say."

"Do you own a dog?"

"No, but I always wanted a St. Bernard."

"I'd hoped you'd be more cooperative."

Hall comes around to the side of the table and perches on its edge. I have a mental image of his bony, flabby, naked haunch sporadically studded with bristling pink hairs. If this man has a wife, I don't see how she can bring herself to touch him.

"Hmm. Pirio Kasparov. A lonely woman with a lonely life. Friendless but for a drunken whore."

"That's one more friend than you have."

"What's your relationship to the United States Navy?"

Again, I'm startled. Did they follow me all the way to the doors of NEDU? "The Navy was wondering if I'm bionic. Turns out, I am. Cool, huh?"

"You have a vivid imagination, Ms. Kasparov."

"Funny, that part is true. Exaggerated, I guess. But basically true."

"I see. Are you sure you're not a government agent?"

"I'm very sure."

"Is Mr. Wozniak working with the Navy, too?"

Suddenly, just like that, I run out of clever things to say. When did they start following me? Since the day I talked to Johnny in his garage? Or since Mrs. Smith's retirement party? Or was it even earlier than that—since the collision? I feel sick as the realization washes over me that I jeopardized Mrs. Smith and Parnell just by talking to them, being seen with them. I may have put Caridad Jaeger in danger, too. Hall has put the facts together, but he's overinterpreted them, decided that Parnell and I are government agents, tipped off by the company whistleblower, Mrs. Smith. He's not going to be talked out of this idea. It all fits together too perfectly in his mind. Tidy stories make the brain snap shut. I'm thinking I might be better off admitting to being a Navy spy. That way I could make him think I have more power than I do, which might provide some protection to my friends. It's possible that I could even pry apart Hall's loyalty to Jaeger, who blithely holds a little Boston fish company hostage to his entertainment needs. I could make a deal, promise Hall and his crew amnesty. But it's all coming at me too fast. I need time to think.

Before I can say anything, Hall rises from the table, nods to the strongman, calls him Brock. What a name. I try to steel myself, to blot out what's about to happen. Brock takes his time, seems intent on damaging every one of my internal organs with his fists.

Milosa once said that you can overcome pain through mental discipline—that is, unyielding focus on something other than the pain. So, as the blows fall, I bring every ounce of brainpower I have to the task of remembering the choice Russian swear words he taught me when I was just a little girl. When Brock is done, I've got a mouthful of pulpy blood, and my eyes don't focus right. But I've retrieved what I was looking for, and I can't help sharing it.

"*Yob tvoyu mat.*"

"What?" Brock says with some alarm.

I obligingly translate. "Fuck your mother."

He whirls to Hall. "What language was that?"

Hall's eyes have narrowed. "Russian."

"Careful. She could be with Petrenko," says the stooped, shrewd-faced minion on the other side of Hall.

"No, I don't think so. Oster would have said something," Hall mutters.

It's nice to see the faith he has in his employees.

I dimly make out Troy slipping into the room with a laptop tucked under his arm. He slithers down the wall, sits on the floor with hunched shoulders, like a tardy schoolboy hoping not to be noticed.

Hall glances at him sharply. "Did you get in touch with him?"

Troy nods.

"Is it done?"

Troy tips his head again.

Hall perches on the desk once more, leans over for an intimate chat with me. His demeanor is weirdly paternal.

"Libby Smith, our dear friend," he says gently, "was found at dawn by a driver on the Jamaicaway. Victim of an apparent hit-and-run. Dressed in her bathrobe and slippers. She was most likely killed instantly, we were told. But there's no way of knowing that, is there?" He shifts his weight slightly, pulls on his earlobe. "It happened early this morning. Needless to say, people at the office are very upset. She'd been with us so long and was very well liked. But everyone knows that her dementia was progressing rapidly. She should probably have gone to a home. It's dangerous for people with dementia to live alone."

Hall sighs. He asks if I would like to tell him exactly how much the Navy knows about Bob Jaeger and Ocean Catch.

I can't speak. Won't. Silence is all I'm capable of now.

Hall asks his minions to find something with which to wipe the blood from my face. This creates some confusion. They're patting their pockets, shaking their heads. Brock offers to take off his T-shirt, but you can tell he'd rather not. Finally, the smarter one volunteers to get a towel out of the bathroom. It's ironic. I put the towels there myself this morning. At least I know they're clean. There is utter silence in the room until he returns.

"I brought two," he says, demonstrating thoroughness.

"Thank you, Dennis," Hall replies.

Hall gives the order, and Dennis, frowning in concentration, begins to dab my face. He has coarse black eyebrows and bad breath. Every time he touches my face it hurts.

"Get around her eyes," Hall says.

Dennis smears the towel back and forth across my left eye, then my right. He leans back to assess his progress. It must not be great because he starts in with the towel again. Hall tells him that's enough.

"I have something to show you, Ms. Kasparov," Hall says. "I want to be sure you see it clearly. It has many implications, which I'm sure you'll grasp. A woman as bright as you doesn't need things to be spelled out."

He motions to Troy, who brings the laptop over and opens it on the desk with the screen facing me. Troy clicks to an archived video.

Sunlight is glimmering through branches of elm and oak. Thomasina and Noah are walking to school. Noah has his backpack on; Thomasina's hair is loose and shiny, freshly washed. They're on a sidewalk; the street's not busy. It's one of the well-kept residential neighborhoods near Thomasina's apartment. The camera is following from a distance of about thirty feet.

The scene shifts. Noah is standing on a busy corner outside the school in a group of children, all wearing backpacks. It's afternoon. He looks tired. There's noise from children and cars. A crossing guard stops the traffic and directs the children to cross. Most of them proceed blithely. Noah hesitates, checks left, then right, then left. In case the crossing guard got it wrong and a renegade driver is bearing down. Noah knows better than to rely completely on the judgment of adults.

In the next scene he's walking alone through the same residential neighborhood. The camera is following closely, too closely. Noah doesn't even turn around. I'm stricken with panic. I take a few deep breaths.

"Do you want to talk now?" Hall asks.

"I don't know. You've given me a lot to think about."

"It is a lot, isn't it?"

"I need to know that he's safely at home with his mother. I won't talk until you prove that to me."

"That the child is safe for now is something you will have to take on faith."

"I'd be a fool to take anything you say on faith. I need some kind of proof and a guarantee that he won't be hurt. Then I'll tell you everything. And if I find out you lied to me, or if a hair on his head is ever touched by you or anyone you know, I'll hunt you down and kill you in cold blood. I promise you that."

Hall stands up, a thin post of bone and sagging muscle. "You don't make the deals here, Ms. Kasparov. You'll either talk to me now or later tonight, after you've had some time to think about it. Your choice."

I stare at him, closemouthed.

"So be it. I'm going to leave you with Troy for the rest of the evening. Say, five or six hours. We'll be back later tonight to see how you're doing."

I snap my wrists against the cuffs. "Take these off."

Hall smiles. "I'm way ahead of you on that."

My cuffs are quickly undone by Brock, but before I have time to shake some feeling back into my newly freed wrists, my hands are cuffed to opposite legs of the table. My arms are stretched so much that my right cheek is pressed into the tabletop. I can't even turn my head. Then my ankles are cuffed to the same table legs. I'm spread out, flattened like the Road Runner when he runs into a wall. It hurts like a bastard. If they kick the chair away, my body weight will dislocate my shoulder and hip joints.

Luckily, they don't do that. I hear the key clatter onto the table about six inches from my head. The door opens, filling the room with the din of engines, and closes with a quiet click.

There's no point in trying to scream through the engine noise, and no one who would help me anyway. I gingerly try to adjust one of my shoulders to see if I can make it more comfortable in its socket, and immediately pain shoots up my neck and down my arm. My face flushes, and I start to sweat.

The smell of tobacco reaches me, then a sour body odor. I hear a person slide down the wall to sit on the floor. The crinkle of cellophane, the click of a lighter. Wafting smoke.

"Hey, Troy. Are you there?"

"Yeah. What do you want?"

"Can you take these off?"

"No way."

"Please."

"No."

I take this as progress—his denial shortened from two words to one. He's not loyal to Hall: he's not loyal to anyone. It's written in his body language. Every gesture speaks self-absorbed alienation. It's possible he's never cared about anyone but himself.

"What are they going to do to me, Troy?"

"They're gonna kill you. What do you think?"

"Is there any way I can get out of it?"

"Nope." He puts a little pop on the final consonant.

"Not even if I tell them what they want to hear?"

"Nope." He likes this word. "Don't make no difference if you talk or not; don't make no difference what you say. This is your last day on earth."

He smokes. I try to stay calm. I know the key is lying on the table, and I know Troy is corruptible. There's got to be a way to make those two facts work together.

"Great. The last day of my life. Do I really have to spend it like this? It hurts, Troy. It really fucking hurts. Why should you care if I'm cuffed? I'm a hundred and fifteen pounds. They beat the shit out of me. My fucking ribs are broken. I probably can't walk, and I'm gonna die anyway. So have a shred of mercy, will you? I can't spend five or six hours like this. Even prisoners on death row get a last meal, don't they? I wouldn't mind having a cigarette. Just one lousy smoke. You can hook me up again before they get back. Let me sit down and bum a cigarette from you, Troy. It's my last fucking day on earth."

Silence greets my proposal. A denial shortened from one word to none.

"Troy, what are you doing here anyway? You're no fisherman. This isn't your kind of gig. It's obvious they're using you. I know you're the one who was following me. I saw you at the Bank of America Pavilion. And you were in the tan car, weren't you? That day on Beacon Street. How many boring hours have you spent watching me? How much did they pay you? Minimum wage? Or did they just promise you something, like a big payoff at the end? Which, if you think about it honestly, you're never going to get. They think you're shit, Troy. They're not gonna give you anything. Not a dime. Smell the coffee. You're smarter than they are. Take the cuffs off. Please."

He moves, smokes. "You're rich, aren't you? You drive an old car, but you got a house on Beacon Hill."

"It's my father's house."

"Yeah, I know. How much you think he'd pay to see you again?"

"How much do you want?"

"A million dollars."

"He can do that, Troy. Cash. No questions. I just have to ask."

"How fast can you get it?"

"Faster than fast food. Get me a phone, and tell me where you want him to leave it. Brown paper bag, whatever. We'll do exactly what you want."

Silence. The cigarette smoke is tickling my nose.

"Take the cuffs off, Troy. We've got to get out of here."

"If anything happens, I'll kill the kid."

"Let's leave him out of it. Nobody needs to die. You're doing me a big favor. You'll be my hero after this. We'll both get what we want."

I hear him pick the keys off the table. In a few seconds, I'm released.

I carefully reassemble my scattered limbs, put them in the correct relation to their respective joints. It makes me so happy, I could cry.

Troy slides back down to the floor, sucks a drag of tobacco, and stubs the butt out on the bottom of his shoe. His knee thumps, and his hand is shaking. He's red around the eyes, jumpy as a hyperactive kid. Scared shitless, probably. It's a big risk he's taking, reckless as hell. It makes me sort of like him. He's sitting between me and the door.

"When it gets dark in a few hours, you and I will take off," he says. "There are a bunch of dinghies tied up at the stern for people going back and forth to shore. We'll get in one, row to town, disappear, head back to the States. When we get to Boston, we'll call Daddy. No calls till then. He doesn't need to know his baby's in trouble until we're right there on his door. You can talk to him, tell him what to do, and if he doesn't have the money in an hour like you said, I'll kill you. Until then, we're gonna stay real close. I'm gonna keep these"—he dangles the cuffs—"and I've got a gun." He pulls aside his jacket to reveal a handgun in a shoulder holster. "In case you're wondering, this is what I was going to kill you with."

My blood runs cold. "Why were they going to make you do it?"

"I do all the shit work around here." He closes his jacket.

"What will happen when they find out we're gone?"

"Nothing. They won't do shit. They have to stay with the ship. Can't afford to tip off Jaeger that something's wrong. If he ever got wind that we had a Navy spy on board, things would get ugly for Hall real fast. Hall's scared shitless of Jaeger. He'll keep quiet to save his own ass, and get Oyster Man to deal with us. He's the one to worry about. He'll be after us right away, but he's more interested in you than me. My guess is, he'll stay in Boston, knowing you'll show up there eventually. I'll disappear for good as soon as I get the money. Someplace warmer than this."

Troy rubs the side of his nose with a vengeance, scratches his neck. His bent leg is thumping the floor. He's not just jumpy; he's about to blow apart from stress. Then I get it. The teeth like burnt timbers. The yellow, blotchy skin. He's a meth addict. Yeah, it fits. All that petty crime Lou Diggens told me about was going to support a habit. Now, thanks to his stepdad's less-than-illustrious connections in the fishing world, it's forced detoxification on board a supposedly drug-free yacht. Troy's not with the program, never has been. He can't wait to jump this ship. Getting back to his dealer with a fat wad of cash in his hand is his only true and heartfelt dream.

"You'll get your money, Troy. You can leave Johnny to me." I sit on the floor next to him and hug my legs together, wrap my aching arms around them.

He nods heavily, like he's relieved.

We sit in silence, waiting for dark. I'm crazy with stress, thinking that Hall and his serfs will return early. Troy keeps consulting his watch.

"How much longer?"

"A couple of hours."

"No way. I can't wait that long."

"Who asked you?" He must take some pity on me, though, because he produces his pack of Winstons and slides one out.

When I refuse, he looks offended. "You said you wanted a cigarette."

"I actually don't smoke."

He rolls his eyes.

"Troy, I'm curious. If you guys—Johnny, you, Hall, and the others—were onto me this whole time, why did you take me on this voyage at all? Why didn't you question me a week ago, and kill me then?"

"How? That was the question. How would we kill you? The old lady, you can run her over, and nobody suspects a thing. You, it's harder. Healthy, prime of life. Hall and Johnny—they didn't want violence or anything that could be traced." He picks a piece of food out of a gap in his teeth. "On a boat, everything's easier. People fall overboard, disappear. International laws, or maritime law, I guess—I don't know what it's called. Basically, no one's watching too closely, and no one really gives a shit."

"But why wait till now?"

"So they can tell the guests that you quit in a huff, and headed back to the States the first chance you got. Everyone knows you're crazy as shit. Throwing drinks in people's faces and getting into arguments. So no one will think twice about not seeing you around. And if the question ever comes up, everybody'll be telling the same story—

last seen in an Inuit settlement in Labrador, Canada. No forwarding address."

He stretches out one skinny leg. He's relaxing a little, telling his cozy story.

"We were going to keep your body hidden until we were out in the Labrador Sea again, then dump you overboard. With enough weight on you, you'd sink to the bottom and stay there forever. No body, no murder. It was a pretty good plan."

"Who was the mastermind?" But I already know.

"Oyster Man. Who else?" Troy smiles with something like affection for the legendary one.

Johnny knew all this in the lounge that night. That's why he didn't want to go to bed with me. He already thought of me as dead. I guess he still has a shred of humanity—draws the line at screwing a woman whose murder he has planned. He joked it up pretty good, though. A better liar than I was. Milosa's in the background of my thoughts, not even laughing anymore, just shaking his weary head.

"Come on. Let's get out of here," I say.

"No, someone will see us. We gotta wait until it's dark."

I can't believe how insane this is. "Listen, Troy. You just described my impending death in loving detail. If you don't get me out of here right now, you won't get your million dollars and feel that sweet, sweet drug in your veins."

He looks worried, slides the Winstons into his pocket. "OK, OK. How 'bout a quickie first?"

"A what?"

"A quick fuck for the road."

"Oh, God. Tell me I didn't hear that. You want to get paid, or don't you?"

"Yeah, OK. Maybe later, huh?"

"Never."

He nods as if he's been denied a donut. "OK. Let's go."

Chapter 26

Dusk is brief in autumn in the north. The sun drops to the horizon fast after a short, understated slide across the sky. The *Galaxy*'s main deck is empty. The running lights gleam dimly across the polished teak, the service bar, the chaise longues and the potted plants. The guests have not yet returned from shore leave. A dinner was planned for them at the Tungortok Inn, which the crew will join, too. That's where Hall was headed with Brock and Dennis, Troy says.

Troy glances up at the windows on the second and third levels that have a clear view of the main deck. Even if Hall and the boys have left already, someone will still be on board. He repeats that we should have waited until dark, but I'm too afraid to care. All I know is that the handcuffs are behind me, and the salt air filling my lungs is making me feel human again.

There's a flimsy ladder down the side of the yacht to a dinghy tied there, bobbing gently on the black water of Makkovik Bay. I go first. Troy uncleats the painter and begins to descend after me. I imagine yanking the line out of his hand and heading across the bay on my own. But in the next moment he's stepping carefully into the dinghy, and the opportunity's gone. Hunched over to keep his center of gravity low, he moves to the back where the engine is, while I, seated on the center bench, scoot over to let him pass. I could push him overboard while he's next to me, unbalanced, but again the moment passes too quickly.

My mind is racing to figure out how to get away. I have no intention of returning to Boston with Troy while the *Galaxy* continues its journey north. He can return to Boston by himself and wait for his money until I arrive. I'll work around Milosa's likely vengeful reaction and make sure that Troy gets paid. I'll do it for Noah's safety mostly, but also because a deal's a deal. The next problem, how to deal with Johnny, is going to take some thought.

The whine of the motor spreads across the quiet bay. A violet fog blurs the outlines of the two or three low, flat buildings on the shore ahead. Glancing back, I see that darkness has gathered over the Labrador Sea. The superyacht rises from its black surface like a luminous glacier—tall, massive, gleaming white. I watch it fade like a bad dream.

Troy cuts the motor as we approach Makkovik. Next to a makeshift pier there's a paved roll-on, roll-off ramp for freight boats. The shore is rocky. There's no other place to land. Several dinghies are already tied there. We tie up, too, and disembark, splashing through the shallow water.

One main road, unpaved, leads inland past a few more squat buildings, painted pink and blue. The terrain on either side is a moonscape of smooth black bedrock, outcrops of shale, sparse scrub, tufts of grass, impassable bogs. Low hills rise to the north and south, gently mounded by harsh winds, treeless but for a singular, anomalous copse of spruce on the northern slope.

The town is quiet; it seems uninhabited. Then I dimly hear the unmistakable, urgent guitar chords of Clapton begging Leila, coming from a row of small identical houses built back from the road. A rising *slap, slap, slap* causes me to whirl around. It's a little girl with a lime-green jump rope windmilling her way toward us, wearing a lovely frown. She sails by, uninterested in visiting strangers. We follow her, walking in plain view on the road because there's nowhere to take shelter. I recall that Makkovik is at the tip of a narrow peninsula.

Up ahead the wooden sign for the Tungortok Inn hangs from the low roof of a lopsided porch. A Buick and a couple of motorcycles are parked haphazardly on the front lawn, and there's a Range Rover in the narrow driveway. Apparently, the Tungortok has more customers tonight than just the *Galaxy*'s guests and crew. The inn itself is painted bright blue, two stories, long like a shoe box, without shutters or adornment of any kind. There's warm rosy light inside and festive voices coming through two front windows that open onto the porch.

I have no idea how far away the highway is. It could be fifty miles, or ten, or two hundred. In nothing but my bloodstained *Galaxy* T-shirt, jeans, and wet sneakers, I'm shivering. I'm also hungry and very tired. I need to get to the community center, which is nowhere in sight, and by now probably closed, to get a message to Parnell. If he can bring some video cameras and meet me up here in Labrador somewhere, we can make our way together to the Cumberland Peninsula and take it from there. But before that, Troy and I have to get past the Tungortok Inn without being seen, and find somewhere to lie low until morning.

I feel Troy tense, quicken his step. "Do you see that?"

"What?"

"There." He points. There's a key in the ignition of an old silver-bellied Honda.

"Wait," I say warily.

He doesn't wait. He sprints ahead, swings his leg over the bike. "Come on. Let's go!" He stomps the accelerator pedal, and the engine roars to life, loud and sudden as a detonating bomb in the still air. He steers the bike onto the road—headlight on, muffler spitting exhaust— and idles there, waiting for me. "Hurry up!" he yells over his shoulder.

I take several steps forward as the front door of the inn opens and two men come out. They look like native Inuit. "Hey, what're you doing?" one of them calls out in a not-unfriendly tone. Troy revs the engine. I slip back, behind the Range Rover. Troy's in a fix now. He'll never be able to explain what he's doing here, stealing a motorcycle, and once Hall finds out I'm missing, Troy won't ever be safe again. I scoot down the driveway along the side of the inn. There's yelling and commotion as more people come onto the porch, then a scream of acceleration as Troy races away. Within seconds, other engines ignite—what sounds like both remaining motorcycles and a car— and set off in pursuit. The whine of the vehicles grows progressively quieter until arctic silence is restored.

What now? I'm in the middle of nowhere, on foot, without a dime. I don't dare return to the road, and if I head out across the uneven, rocky terrain without a flashlight, I'll end up with a sprained ankle or broken leg. Not to mention lost. The back entrance of the Tungortok Inn is just ahead, up a few unpainted steps, illuminated by a bare orangeish bulb above the door. Most everyone seems to be at the front of the inn, talking loudly about the theft.

The door's unlocked. I enter a dark mudroom where a couple of bulging trash bags emit the putrid odors of decaying fish and garbage, quickly pass a brightly lit kitchen on my left, and come onto a gloomy hallway covered in frayed red carpeting. There's a pay phone on the wall, an old cigarette machine, and two doors bearing dandyish stenciled signs for Gents and Dames. I'm ready to slip into the Dames' room when I see a narrow stairway farther along. I sprint up it, and emerge in another hallway, hushed and seedy. Thin blue carpeting, peeling wallpaper of gold medallions on blue, several closed doors with round brass knobs. An overhead light at the front end illuminates a wider staircase that descends to the front of the inn. I'm terrified someone will step out of a room and see me, so I try the closest door, which opens with a quiet creak. The room is small, square, low-ceilinged. Light from the hall throws out shadows from a double bed with no headboard, a pine dresser, a straight-back chair. I see no luggage, no signs that the room's being used. But it's the trapped damp and mustiness that suggest I might be safe. The single window in this room hasn't been opened for weeks.

I shut the door behind me, wincing at the creak. It locks with a simple button that a bobby pin on the other side could pop out. Right there and then, I collapse on the floor in the darkness, curl into a fetal position. I lie that way for a while, trembling all over, riding out the day's accumulated terror, too overwhelmed by it to think. One floor down, at the distant front end of the inn, the guests and crew of the *Galaxy* are enjoying a well-cooked meal of local delicacies. Some people have all the luck.

I finally pick myself off the floor and go to the window. Millions of stars swirl in milky bands across the jet-black sky. It crosses my mind that Van Gogh was not so demented after all. But enough about art. I have to find a bathroom. There's none in the room, so I peek out the door, then skip across the hallway into a common bathroom, large and clean and windowless, and lock myself inside. I pee hot urine and peel off my bloodstained clothes. When I look in the mirror, I see a small, squashed, pulpy person with a multicolored face, delicate white breasts, pretty pink nipples, and bruises everywhere else. I start to laugh uncontrollably at the thought that my woman parts were cordially omitted from punishment.

I shut up and freeze. There are people coming up the stairs, a man and a woman bubbling with playful conversation. As their voices become more distinct, I recognize the clear lilt of Jorn Ekborg's smug tenor voice. Then, if I'm not mistaken, I hear Margot, breathless with self-importance and tipsy seduction. They enter a room farther up the hall and close the door.

I want to take a shower, but I don't dare with people so close by. I grab one of the guest towels, wet it, and sponge off the blood that Dennis didn't get. My face looks a little better now, though a few of the bruises are beginning to swell. I could probably pass for someone who was in a car accident or fell into a hornet's nest or had a severe allergic reaction to shellfish and walked into a door.

The distant rumble of motorcycle engines grows increasingly loud, until the inn's wood frame is reverberating with the din. The door of Ekborg and Margot's room is flung open, and a man's heavy footsteps descend the stairs. It seems that the lovely Margot holds less appeal for the handsome Swede than a hunted-down thief does. I wonder if she's surprised.

Confiding in Margot poses an obvious risk. I have no idea how she'll react or who she'll squeal to. She could march straight to Jaeger himself. But I'm willing to take that chance. Because for the last few nights she's been lingering on a bar stool in the small salon after everyone else leaves, pouring out her secrets to me, her sympathetic bartender, her tongue loosened by generously flowing champagne. Why do people always assume that bartenders are discreet? In any case, Ekborg is just the latest dalliance, one anyone could guess. The other male on the ship who regularly receives her favors, Captain Lou Diggens, is a more surprising choice. Bob Jaeger, for one, would be shocked to know of it.

I bundle up my clothes and sneakers, wrap a towel around me, slip out of the bathroom, and enter her room. A small blue lamp on the night table is on. She is lying across the bed in an unbuttoned shirt and a raised-to-the-waist long white skirt with adorable tulle fringe, a freckled forearm flung across her eyes. "Oh, Jorn. I can't. I'm so dizzy—everything's spinning. And Bob will kill me if he finds out."

"Margot. It's me, Pirio."

She picks up her heads, squints. "Pirio? Why are you wearing a towel?" She rises to one elbow. "What happened to your face?"

"I need your help."

"What?"

I explain that I'm a friend of an Ocean Catch fisherman, that I found out about the hunting and came on board to film it, that I was found out and beaten up by Brock, with Hall and Dennis looking on. That I might have been killed had young Troy not set me free. He stole a motorcycle outside and was followed, while I escaped into the inn.

"Oh, my God! You poor thing!"

"You can't tell anyone you saw me."

"No! Of course not."

"I need help to get away."

"Oh, my God! Where will you go?"

"I'm not sure. But I need clothes and money."

"I don't have any clothes but this"—she flounces the skirt—"and a cover-up. I spent all my money this afternoon at the craft fair at the Moravian church."

"What did you buy?"

"A hand-knit sweater. Beautiful gray and blue with, like, little seals or something walking across the top."

"Can I have it?"

"Really?" She gives a wounded grimace, then apparently thinks it through. "Of course you can. But what are you going to do about your face?"

"Money, Margot. What about money?"

"I have a few dollars left, that's all."

"What about Jaeger?"

"Bob's always got money."

I give her a meaningful look.

"You want me to . . . ?"

"Would you?"

She sits up on the side of the bed, smooths her skirt, begins buttoning her blouse. "I guess I could. You really need it. I don't see why not. I mean, it's not like he needs it."

"Thank you, Margot."

She gives me a wobbly, embarrassed smile. "Jorn's a self-absorbed narcissist, don't you think?"

"You got that right."

"I could feel his dick through his pants. It's tiny."

"Not surprised."

She stands, sweeps her gorgeous mane of red hair off her neck, lets it fall heavily down her back, and shakes it out. "I can't wait until we get back to civilization. I get so sick on these voyages, and all I can eat is bread. But Bob doesn't care about anyone but himself. He has a tiny dick, too."

"That can't be very satisfying."

"It isn't. Let me assure you." She strides to the door. "I'll be right back. This won't take long."

I tell her I'll be in the room at the end of the hall. "One more thing, Margot. Food."

She returns in about twenty minutes with some bread slices wrapped in a napkin. I was hoping for something more, but I'm not in a position to complain. I start tearing the bread with my teeth as she tosses the sweater and a wad of cash on the bed. Her eyes are gleaming with a sharper light than I've seen in them before. "I told Bob that I needed everything in his wallet to pay the nice ladies at the craft fair who refused to take plastic, that I'd promised to leave money for them at the inn."

I count almost three hundred dollars. I put on the sweater and my jeans. I ask Margot what's happening downstairs.

"Everybody's talking about what happened. They caught the guy, Troy, who stole the bike. Well, they didn't catch him, actually. They said he was driving crazy, going way too fast. A tire blew and he skidded off the road, rolled down a gully. The bike landed on top of him somehow."

"And . . . ?"

"And he died. When they got there, they said he was dead."

"Who said that?"

"The guys you talked about. Brock and Dennis. They were on the other bikes."

"Of course." It's convenient that Brock and Dennis were the only people who saw the accident and can describe Troy's sudden death.

"Captain Lou is really upset. He's crying, actually. He says Troy never listened to him. Apparently, he was in a lot of trouble with drugs."

"Yeah, that's what I heard. Poor Captain Lou."

"It's sad, isn't it? That he should feel responsible. He's really a very kindhearted man. But it's not like you can fix someone else's problems." Margot sighs, sits on the bed. "What are you going to do now?"

"I don't know. How far is the highway from here?" I want to get out of Makkovik as fast as I can and meet Parnell somewhere safer than this.

"No idea. Wait. There are maps downstairs."

She leaves and comes back shortly with the rudimentary black-and-white map, about the size of a placemat, that the innkeepers provide for their guests. I sit on the bed to look at it. It shows the important buildings of Makkovik—police station, store, health clinic (doctor available once a month), and the airport about a half mile west of the inn. The coast up to Nain is jagged with narrow inlets and peninsulas.

"This is crazy," I say. "Where's the highway?"

Margot sits down and looks over my shoulder. "I don't think there is one. Or, look, there's one. But it only goes from Happy Valley west."

"There have to be some roads that just aren't marked."

"I don't know. In winter, they'd all be impassable anyway. People get around on snowmobiles up here. Where do you want to go?"

I'm staring at a town on the map, halfway between Makkovik and Nain. Hopedale. It takes a minute for the name to register, then memories flood back. Hopedale is where my mother and I spent a month every summer, picking flowers and making fragrances. Where, if nothing's changed, the house we rented from the architect stands empty from September through May.

"Go downstairs, Margot, and ask the innkeeper if you wanted to get to Hopedale from here how you would do it."

She catches the urgency in my voice and hops up. At the door she pauses and looks back at me with a solemn expression. "Pirio, I'm helping you because I can see from what they did to you that you have to get out of here. I could never forgive myself if you were hurt again or, God forbid, killed. But I don't want Bob to get in trouble either. I mean, I know what he's doing isn't strictly legal, but he tells me there are a lot of whales out there, and it doesn't matter that much in the long run. He's not a bad person; he's just . . . well, adventurous. You know, men used to hunt whales all the time, and they didn't die out. You would see that for yourself when we got there. There are still a lot of them around. Plenty, in fact."

For a few seconds we just look at each other.

"I love Bob, you know. Even if I do things I shouldn't. I'm just bored. I don't mean anything by it."

"I won't tell, Margot, and I'll never forget that you helped me."

When she comes back, she's flustered. "I have to hurry. They're all leaving now, and Jorn is still after me. Like I'm not supposed to have noticed that he dumped me the minute he heard the motorcycles. I told Bob I have a headache and was lying down. He doesn't expect me to eat anyway. So I went out back and asked the innkeeper how to get to Hopedale like it was just a typical tourist question. He's a really nice guy named Yoskolo. He said if I didn't want to take a boat, I could fly. I asked him to look up the flight times, and he said there's one leaving tomorrow morning at 8:55 a.m."

"Thank you, Margot." I'll take my chances in this room tonight and leave quietly as soon as it's light.

"Good luck, Pirio. Take care of yourself." Then she's gone.

I step to the window. No moon has risen, but the myriad stars are close and glittery. Low on the horizon, a wide emerald band slowly swirls and undulates. In its eerie glow, I feel as if I'm standing at the edge of the known world.

What is it about death that makes us look to the sky? I imagine Troy out there, riding the spreading, bucking waves of the northern lights, and hope it's better than a fix.

Chapter 27

The plane is a De Havilland Twin Otter with large windows for observation and thinly cushioned seats for nineteen passengers. This morning there are only five. Myself, an Inuit mother and child, a white man with an air of scientific detachment, and an elderly woman with greasy, unkempt hair. No one talks. A young Inuit stewardess takes our tickets while the captain can be seen through the open door of the cockpit, flipping switches, doing preflight checks. I was awake all last night—first listening to a few guests settle into rooms at the front of the inn; then, when everything was quiet, watching out the window for the early sunrise to provide enough light for me to get out of there. Once we're in the air, I try to sleep but fail. Exhausted, I stare out the window at the craggy brown terrain, unbroken by roads, and the sunlight gleaming off the silver wing. Hopedale appears on schedule: the runway a black slash gouged into a rocky hill, the town no more than a sprinkling of low buildings on the edge of a vast sparkling bay.

I walk down the hill into town, past a school and tired playground, and a two-story red inn with a tin roof. Around a bend in the road, I spy the store where my mother and I shopped years ago. It looks exactly the same. I know that just beyond it is the one-room town library, where I'm hoping I can get access to phone and Internet.

It's an airy, yellow-painted room with potted plants on the windowsills. A large corkboard propped on an easel is studded with community announcements. There are no patrons at the tables on this Thursday morning, and when I approach the main desk, a young man looks up from a computer. He asks how he can help me—he seems to intuit that I'm not looking for a botany book or novel—and after some discussion he offers me the use of the phone at his elbow to make a few calls.

The first call is to Thomasina's landline. It rings and rings. Doesn't anyone answer their home phone anymore? I leave a message in which I urge—no, order—her to take Noah out of school immediately, go to my father's house, and stay there until I tell her it's safe to leave. *Jeffrey will know you're coming,* I say. I call her cell and repeat the message. Before I left, I told her about Max and the voyage I was going on, so she'll know better than to second-guess.

Next call goes to Jeffrey, who, thank God, picks up immediately. I don't go into the specifics: I'm conscious of the young librarian, who can't help hearing everything I'm saying. But after a few questions Jeffrey realizes that the situation is serious, says he'll keep trying to get in touch with Thomasina, and will go with her to get Noah out of school.

"Will you explain to Milosa and Maureen?" I ask.

"You better do it."

I decide to bypass Milosa and go straight to Maureen. She and Jeffrey take care of the house guests anyway, and for the time being I'd like to avoid Milosa's impatient, probing questions. When I get Maureen on the phone, I make it short and sweet: my friend and her son are coming; they'll be staying for a few days in the guest room; her hospitality to them will be much appreciated.

"Of course. We're always happy to help." She volunteers that there's been no perceptible change in my father, and I feel guilty for not having asked.

The last phone call will be the hardest. I can feel my throat clotting with what appears now to have become my primary emotion: fear. Fear of the bad guys; fear for Noah, Thomasina, and my father; fear of drowning; fear of love. I pick up the old-fashioned receiver one last time, but my finger stops in midair, hovers over the numeric keypad. I can't call him. I don't know his number. It was programmed into my iPhone, not committed to memory. I'm half insanely frustrated, half relieved.

"Internet," I say to the young man. "May I?"

He stands up, gestures for me to come around the desk, pulls out the chair. I take a seat on the still-warm vinyl. Parnell's e-mail is easy to remember: rparnell@yahoo.com.

I explain where I am, ask him to meet me with a zoom lens and tripod. Also a Kodak PlaySport. And my passport, which I left in my top desk drawer, assuming I wouldn't need it, but do now—presuming (hoping) I'll be going back to Boston. He has to come right away. I tell him I'll e-mail my super, ask him to let Parnell into my apartment, and will leave a note for him at the general store here with directions to where I'm staying. I hesitate while signing off. Should I say *Love* or *Thanks* or *Best wishes*? I settle on my initial, and make it lowercase: *p*. Then I call the super, whose number is listed, and he says he will let Parnell in. Tomorrow I'll return to the library to get Parnell's reply.

I thank the young man and walk back to the general store. The same bell jingles when I open the same battered door; the same odors assault me—dust and peanuts, cigarette smoke, astringent cleaning products doctored with fake meadow smells, and stale, fan-circulated air. No one's behind the counter, where an old gentleman is waiting patiently. I pass aisles of junk food, processed food, candy, cases of soda. Refrigerated units on the far wall hold beer, cheap wine, more soda. The origins of most Western diseases are efficiently packed together on these shelves. At the end of the far aisle, in the very back corner, it's possible to put your hands on milk, eggs, wilted heads of iceberg lettuce, and bruised bananas. On my way back to the counter, I grab some toiletries.

Now a middle-aged woman in a pink Gap sweatshirt is behind the cash register, ringing up the old man's canned peaches and instant coffee.

"Just get in?" the woman asks as the old man leaves and I put my items on the counter.

"Yeah. Just now."

"Fly?"

"Uh-huh."

"Not tourist season anymore, but it's still a pretty time of year. Soon the bay will freeze all the way across, and the snow will pile up. It's pretty then, too. Everything quiet and white. Staying long?"

"A few days."

"Over at the inn, I guess."

"No, I'm headed out to a rental north of town, on the bay." I remember the road there very well—its dust and ruts and the way the architect's house looked when we came around the last corner and saw it outlined against the sea.

"By yourself?"

"Yeah. Just me."

"Oh." She nods as if this is a strange but oft-observed habit of the Caucasian visitor. "You must be writing a book. Had a guy here last winter, stayed three months in a rental by himself. Turns out, he was writing a book. A fiction story, he said. Real nice guy. Said he never drove a snowmobile until he came up here, and now it was his preferred mode of transportation. *Preferred,* he said. I got a laugh out of that." As her fingers have been punching buttons, her black eyes have been taking me in, assessing my unwashed hair, hand-knit sweater. No jacket, no purse. My face. "You had some trouble, huh?"

"Yeah. Gotta get away for a bit. Clear my head."

"Uh-huh." She nods wisely. "You take your time now. It's safe around here. A woman doesn't have to do anything she don't want. Freedom's the best thing."

"Somebody's going to come here asking about me in the next few days. He's my friend; his name's Parnell. You'll know it's him because he's got a bad arm. If anyone else asks about me—which I'm not expecting—you don't have to say."

She smiles, showing dimples and short teeth. "I'm glad you have a friend coming. As for any others, I don't know a thing. I'm Sukie, by the way. Either me or my daughter Charlotte are usually here."

When my purchases are packed in two brown grocery bags, she sees me hesitate.

"I walked from the airport," I say.

She smoothly comes to my rescue by saying that Charlotte will drive me if I want. I accept the offer, and ten minutes later Charlotte and I are jostling along the rutted road in an old jeep with spent shock absorbers, out to the architect's house. Her son, Nicky, seven years old, is in the backseat, standing on the wheel well with his arms around his mother's headrest, and his delicate face peering curiously at me. His quiet patience seems entirely natural, a result of either his Inuit temperament or the gentler lifestyle of this part of the world. He makes me miss Noah, who I think would like it here.

I find the key to the house just where it always was, hanging on a nail in the shed. The cathedral ceiling and the scarred kitchen table are eerily familiar, though smaller than I recall. The whole house seems smaller, and a bit dingier. The cedar deck where my mother and I spent so many hours is empty, the chairs having been put away for the winter. Slender yellow birch leaves are mounded like wind-blown refuse in the corners.

It's chilly inside. Charlotte helps me start a fire in the woodstove; then we carry in more logs and kindling for the fireplace from the woodpile outside. There's a stack of *New Yorkers* and the *Economist* on the bookshelf next to the fireplace, along with *The Thorn Birds* and several historical romances. Nicky runs excitedly from room to room, perhaps trying to understand why a house this big and bright should go uninhabited for most of the year. When they leave, I make eggs and toast with tea. And shower, and make the bed, and lie in it, and finally sleep.

Late afternoon finds me up and eating again—pasta and salad—trying to regain my strength and some kind of emotional equilibrium for the next part of the journey. There's floating pack ice in the bay—I saw it as Charlotte and I were driving here. She said a gale's predicted. Fifty-knot winds, huge swells. Suicide for small boats. The *Galaxy* will ride it out, no problem, but it will be slowed down. I figure it will take another few days at least for the yacht to make its way up the northern Labrador coast into the Cumberland Sound. I got a nice head start traveling here by plane. But now I've got to wait for Parnell, and I can only hope he will come as fast as he can. Then we've got to get to Cape Chidley and somehow meet the challenge of crossing the Hudson Strait.

Sometimes the best way to solve thorny problems is to ignore them for a while. It's as if, when they realize they're not commanding your hysterical, anxiety-laden attention, they agree to shrink and become more reasonable. That's why I take the time to get a nice blaze going in the big stone fireplace, open up *The Thorn Birds*, and curl on the couch like a vacationing princess, letting the afternoon hours simply pass.

I'm engrossed in Meggie's troubles at Drogheda when I hear a soft knock on the front door. I open it to an Inuit man in his midthirties. About five feet seven, strong, with a wide, deep chest. Wearing jeans and an old green parka, unzipped. His face is round and thick, but also pleasantly angular in the straight nose and high cheekbones. A relaxed smile and something almost bashful in his eyes quell my urban suspicion. Then, without quite knowing why, I feel a smile starting. I know him from somewhere, I think.

He tells me his name is Martin Naggek, that he was driving home from work, saw smoke coming from the chimney, and thought he'd stop by and see if Mr. Collins needed anything. I tell him I'm a former renter who's in the area unexpectedly and staying a couple of days with Mr. Collins's blessing. (At this point, I'm not going to sweat telling a white lie or two.) We both agree that Mr. Collins is a very nice man.

In a careful voice, Martin says, "My father was friends with a woman who used to come here in the summers. He always kept an eye on the chimney, in case she came back. Since he passed on a year ago, I've been keeping an eye on it, too. Family tradition, I guess."

I explain to him about my mother and me, how we spent a number of Julys here more than twenty years ago. I invite him in, feeling a bit unnerved.

"My father used to collect ambergris for this woman. He'd keep it in our shed and give it to her when she came."

"Yes, that would have been my mother. She used ambergris oil in the perfumes she made."

Martin smiles broadly. "I remember her. You, too." He waits. "Don't you remember me?"

Looking hard at him, I start to make out an older version of the boy I used to play with—the one with the laughing voice and shiny black hair.

"You were just a kid. I was a few years older," he says. "My dad and I would come for dinner, and you and I would play on that deck out there and climb those trees on the other side of the inlet. There were always flowers hanging all over your kitchen, and my dad brought *pitsuk* from home."

"I remember *pitsuk*." Memories of salty dried fish and bright summer nights flood back. "Now I remember you! You ran faster than me, which I hated. I used to stomp my feet and throw sticks at you. Or rocks, handfuls of dirt. Whatever was handy."

He throws his head back and laughs. "I tried to teach you to sneak up on the seals. You were so bad at it."

"Not *so* bad."

We laugh. "Long time, no see, Pirio." His eyes twinkle gaily. To a pure childhood bond, twenty silent years is nothing more than a refreshing nap. He touches along his cheekbone. "Got hurt?"

"Yeah."

"Accident?"

"Uh, no."

His gaze sweeps across the living room and into the part of the kitchen he can see from where he's standing. "You alone here?"

"Yeah."

"You feel OK? Safe?"

I nod, moved by his concern.

"Labrador tea will help those bruises."

"Tastes awful, as I recall."

"Not the way my wife makes it. Come for dinner tonight."

I'm suddenly elated at the prospect of dinner with friends.

Martin Naggek lives in a one-story yellow house with a red tin roof on the northern edge of Hopedale. It's an unassuming rectangle with evenly sized rooms. In the living room, a large window opens to the bay, which is so close that you can see the smooth black rocks along its shore, and scattered clumps of gold and brown seaweeds that disappear and reappear with the flux of the tides.

Martin's wife, Tiffany, greets me warmly, joking about how few new people she gets to meet. I can tell she is full of questions about my life, but is holding off for now. A baby girl named Matilda sits regally in her arms. With a finger, the proud mother gently lifts the baby's top lip to show me two tiny teeth. Matilda responds with gobs of drool and a jolly gurgle. A feathery sprout of hair is gathered at the top of her head in a pink bow.

Over a dinner of pasta and thin strips of dried caribou meat, Martin tells me that he's a seal hunter as his father, Roger, was. Since a recent European Union ban on the importation of seal products, business is sluggish, even though seal products from Inuit hunters are supposed to be exempt from the law. He's earning sixteen dollars per pelt compared to the one hundred dollars per pelt he used to bring in. He talks about money this way, without self-consciousness. Low prices, he says, have caused the local seal processing plant to stop production.

When Martin's face darkens, Tiffany seamlessly takes up the story, explaining that she has turned their kitchen into a hair salon. The women sit at her table and wait their turn for a wash and cut. They tell stories in Inuktitut while eating bannock and drinking tea. Tiffany says that she enjoys her work, and that Matilda in her playpen in the corner loves the busy atmosphere.

Between the two of them, says Martin, they're doing all right.

After dinner, Tiffany, as promised, serves Labrador tea. She also dampens the leaves to make a poultice, which I press dutifully against one side of my face, then the other, not quite believing it will help. The smell of the raw leaves brings me back to the cool subarctic days of my childhood. I find myself describing how my mother worked in the kitchen of the architect's house, using the flowers' dried petals to make a scent that was later synthetically manufactured and sold as a fragrance called L'Amour du Nord. I promise to send Tiffany a bottle when I return home.

I noticed that Martin and Tiffany exchanged several private glances over dinner, and now they do so again. They have a secret they're not hiding very well. Emboldened for some reason, Tiffany nudges his elbow. "Go ahead. Give her the box."

Martin drops his eyes in embarrassment. "Tiffany, please."

"There may not be another time," she urges.

"I said *no*."

Tiffany sits back in rumpled distress. Martin remains silent, apparently bracing for what she will say next. A strained minute passes.

Tiffany finally says, "Think of your father, Martin. What he would want you to do."

Martin continues staring at his plate with a reddened face, a tense jaw.

"He would want you to give her the box."

"It isn't for her. It's for her mother."

"Her mother hasn't been back for a very long time. Pirio can deliver the box to her. It's what your father wanted, Martin. He said it specifically."

A dull ringing in my ears makes me feel separate and alone, far from this loving marital struggle. I almost wish I could slip away from the table before the conversation goes any further, because I've already put some pieces of a stubborn old puzzle together. Seeing Martin Naggek again after all this time stirred up a welter of memories, emotions, and intuition that has been turning and tumbling inside me for the last few hours.

Roger Naggek was the man who sometimes drove us places, and trekked with us through forests and fields of wildflowers, helping my mother find the things she wanted. He often came for dinner, either alone or with his son. A sturdy man with unkempt black hair, weathered skin, a flat face, and a long straight nose, I remember him as surging with vitality. Everything about him seemed to be in some kind of natural, irrepressible flux. His hands were sure and quick. His eyes twinkled intelligently, and his lips bubbled laughter. He sampled my mother's essences and oils with a smile that revealed a chipped tooth.

I hated him because he took my mother away from me for long evenings during the one month of the year she was supposed to be entirely mine. And because he played four square with me while dinner was cooking, and sometimes succeeded in making me laugh, and

made up crazy stories with me, expressing lots of disbelief and wonder, just the way I make them up with Noah now. I hated him because,
after all that pleasure, all the opening and sharing of our hearts, he
walked out the front door into the dark night, leaving us alone.

Which was fine with me. Being alone with my mother was all I
really wanted, but, after Roger left, it felt all wrong. For a period she
would be pensive, distant, falsely cheery when she remembered I was
there. I could see that a special light inside her had dimmed, a light
that only he controlled. I hated him for making it glow, and then not
tending the fire. I hated the happiness he brought her, and how she
had to stitch it back inside her heart again when he was gone.

That was Roger Naggek. My mother's lover.

"It's all right. I think I know," I say. I won't cry—I won't.

A trace of sadness comes into Martin's eyes. "My father passed a
year ago."

"I'm sorry."

"He had cancer. A few days before he died, he put some things in
a box for your mother. I was to give it to her if she ever came back."

"My mother died twenty years ago," I say with some coldness.
"Didn't he know?"

"No." Martin looks shaken.

"He must have had an address."

"He said she never wanted that. They were to be together only
while she was here."

That sounds like Isa. The conditions and withdrawals, the games.
She wouldn't risk becoming love's victim, though it always seemed so
clear that she was.

"Surely he could have called the first summer that she didn't
return," I say without mercy.

"Who? Who would he call?" Martin is angry now, too, though he
controls it with effort. "He just kept watching the house."

We sit in heavy silence.

"Where is *your* mother?" I finally ask.

"She left when I was a child. My father raised me alone."

"There was no one else?"

"Only her. One month a year. Then she returned to your father, leaving my father alone," he says in a bitter voice, and I realize that we both feel cheated somehow.

Matilda in her high chair is dropping pasta on the floor and leaning over to see where it went. Tiffany is studying her plate.

"So." Martin heaves a deep concluding sigh, though nothing is really over. He places his palms on the table and pushes himself to his feet. "So I'll give you what he left."

I'm about to say I don't want it. That I shouldn't even have been told. That I don't want evidence of whatever was between them. That what was meant for my mother should not come to me. That Isa and Roger have both moved on, and so should we. That reaction is cowardice, of course. Fear of actually learning the deeper truths about my mother's heart that I've always wished I could know.

Tiffany disappears to put Matilda to bed, and Martin and I move into the living room. He takes a box off a bookshelf and places it on the coffee table in front of me. It's a red cedar box with a black fitted lid. A fish silhouette and a bird's stern beaked face are painted on its sides in black and green. Martin sits across from me as I open it. Inside is a folded note, old photos, a whittling knife, and a small brown vial. I unfold the paper with trembling hands. *Dear Isa, I waited, but you didn't come back, and now I have to leave. You are the greatest gift I was given in this life. Keep my love close by your side, believe in it with all your heart, even when I'm gone. Love always, Roger.*

I swallow a few times and pick up the photos. Kodak black-and-whites with creases and tears from a lot of handling. Names and dates written on the back. The first is of Roger himself, head and shoulders, in his early twenties, smiling broadly out of the fur-trimmed hood of a parka. Snow flurries and diffuse light obliterate the setting. His skin is smooth and supple, his lips are full, and he's growing a little mustache. He looks happy and kind. It's before he chipped his tooth.

The next is of Roger and Isa sitting on the front steps of the architect's house. They are smiling bemusedly, their thighs gently touching, seemingly caught by surprise by some visitor's camera. My mother's wearing old clothes and no makeup. Her skin is glowing, and her eyes are warm and kind.

The next picture shows Isa and me in a wooded area. Isa's wearing a jaunty scarf tied under her chin and big sunglasses. Her smile is confident; her posture is light, athletic. I'm about five or six, in a T-shirt and shorts that reveal sturdy, dirt-covered legs. I'm scowling pugnaciously at the camera, with a hunk of flowers in my hand.

"I don't know what to say," I murmur.

"It's a lot to take in."

I put the pictures back in the box.

"You can have them," Martin says.

"I don't know. Let me leave them with you for now." Those pictures in my pocket would feel too foreign, too heavy. I still have so much to do before I can give myself over to what I've learned. I squeeze Martin's hand, and he smiles back. It's funny, but he feels like a brother now.

Tiffany is standing in the doorway. I don't know how long she's been there. I motion her to join us, and she sits quietly beside me on the couch.

"I need your help," I say. I tell them almost everything, from the collision that sank the *Molly Jones* to the *Sea Wolf* to Caridad Jaeger and the *Galaxy*. I leave out Noah, Mrs. Smith, and Troy and give the briefest explanation of my bruises and my escape. "They're headed to Cumberland Sound near some islands and a settlement called Pang on Baffin Island. A friend will be meeting me here with some cameras in a day or two, I hope. I want to get up there as soon as possible."

"The only way is to fly," Martin says. "You'll be crossing the Hudson Strait. Past Pang, the land is uninhabited. If there's fog, you may not find the yacht. If it's clear, there's still the problem of where to land and how to get close without being seen."

The way he says all this knocks the air right out of me. He took what I said at face value and jumped to the solution right away. I wonder if decisions are always this easy for him. If so, I want what he has.

"You sure about the location? It doesn't make a lot of sense if they're after whales," he says.

"That's what the captain said. He talked like they'd been there a few times before."

Martin gives a curt nod. "OK. I have a friend who can take us in his Piper Cherokee."

"Us?"

"I'm going with you."

I look at Tiffany, and she nods without hesitation.

I'm insanely happy. In fairy tales, helpers appear at the very last moment, which is the moment after the hero, certain that she's alone, commits herself to the impossible task anyway. Martin is my helper, my free gift from the gods.

I wish I could call Milosa. Hearing of Roger and Isa's love has made me sharply miss my difficult, betrayed father. It's not pity, more like identification. We were both left in the dark. Then I realize I can call him. I'm so used to being out of touch that I didn't even notice the phone on the table next to me. The Naggeks agree to let me use it.

Maureen answers and puts me through to Milosa, whose voice is noticeably weak. He listens to a thumbnail of my *Galaxy* adventure without comment. I know he's thinking about what he can do to help, but all he says is *Come over for dinner when you get back and bring your film.* I want to ask, *Will you promise to still be there?* But I don't.

I call Thomasina, and this time she picks up. "Why aren't you at my house? You should be there by now."

"We're going as fast as we can. Jeffrey's here, and Noah's packing some things."

"Don't let Max or anyone around Noah."

"I know, I know. Be careful, Pirio. And whatever you're doing, hurry up."

I wish I could talk to Parnell. I want to hear his voice.

Later that night, Martin takes me back to the architect's house in his pickup. We stop at the end of the rutted driveway. The headlights illuminate a clump of birch trees between us and the dark mass of the sea.

"Can I tell you something, Martin?" I still haven't accepted my ocean survival and the results of the NEDU tests at face value, as things that simply happened to me. In fact, though, those experiences seem less strange here in Labrador than they did in the States. It's as if this remote place, in its simple modesty, is somehow better able to accommodate the world's most unlikely possibilities.

When I've finished describing my experiences, he continues looking out the windshield without speaking, as if by simply listening he's done his part.

"Have you heard of anything like that before?" I prompt.

"I've heard of lots of things. Few years ago, a hunter got caught under the ice and came up at a seal breathing hole a good distance away. He pulled himself onto the ice, took off his wet sealskin coat, and walked back to the village without freezing. Others drown— maybe from cold or exhaustion, or being sucked down by the weight of their clothes. Why some return and others don't is a question that doesn't get asked much around here. There are no answers for it, at least not ones that we can know."

"I survived," I tell him urgently. "I'm one of the ones who survived."

He looks at me tenderly and simply nods.

Chapter 28

There are four of us in the droning single-engine plane. Russell Parnell and I are thigh to thigh in the cramped backseat. Martin's up front, next to the pilot, Jimmy, who is thin, toothless, and grinning like this is the most fun he's had in a long time. A screw-cap silver flask peeks out from under a pocket flap of his canvas jacket. Since Jimmy smells OK and Martin seems at ease, I decide to ignore what would be cause for criminal charges in the States. We have no luggage other than the cameras Parnell brought, a cooler, some sleeping bags, and a small tent Martin stowed in the back.

Parnell replied to my e-mail, giving me his cell number and the flight he would be coming in on. We embraced when we met at the airport, then stepped back and said hello awkwardly, realizing that we'd gotten the order of greetings wrong. It was overly nice to reacquaint myself with his tense smile and restless eyes, and feel the strength in his good hand when he decided to cover over the embrace by squeezing my shoulder in a companion-like way. There's a lot for us to say, but we're hushed at the moment, watching the sharp peaks of the Torngat mountain range passing beneath the plane, and the shimmering Labrador Sea expanding eastward to a gently curved horizon.

Small ice floes dot the brilliant water, and the distant sun bleeds a cold yellow stain.

"There it is," Martin says, and Parnell and I peer out the front window at Baffin Island, a huge misshapen gray-green mass. Its mountaintops are snowy; their slopes plunge to fields of grass, rock outcrops, and sparkling streams. Jimmy heads the plane northwest along the Cumberland Sound, low enough that the crash of the surf against the cliffs is audible over the engine drone. He says we're lucky because the island is often shrouded in fog. Today the settlement of Pangnirtung is visible to the north, a scattering of low buildings huddled along the shore. Jimmy says that some of the buildings are rooted to the ground with steel cables because of the harsh winds. There are a couple of ships in port—a supply ship and some kind of fishing vessel.

In a few minutes we're approaching the offshore islands Captain Lou showed me on the chart. They're gentle green mounds in the blue water. As we come over the top of the largest island, the *Galaxy* appears below us, gleaming white, its anchor line taut in a current flowing between the two landmasses. Two inflatable orange dinghies are bobbing off the stern, and two kayaks that must have been brought up from a storage area are lying on the deck. I don't see anyone on the yacht or nearby shores. If anyone hears our small plane, they'll probably think it's only a local pilot out for a sunny-day spin. Still, I lean my face away from the window.

We pass over the yacht, bank eastward over an inlet that has a rocky mouth, a low cliff on its northern side, and a sandy beach at the far end. The plane climbs higher, heading out across a vast tundra, a steep mountain rising to the south. Jimmy glances at Martin and asks, "What's the game plan, boss?"

Martin looks back at me.

I say, "Let's land out of sight of the yacht and head back along the inlet on foot and find a place where we can see what's going on."

"OK. But we can't land here," Martin says.

"Over there." Jimmy nods toward a lake with a smooth wide shore nestled at the base of the mountain.

"Looks good," Martin says.

Soon we're stretching our legs on damp gravel in the chilly shadow of Mount Duval. The lake is glassy, pristine. I'm told the water is OK to drink. Martin and Jimmy say they'll stay back to set up camp, so Parnell and I grab the cameras out of the back, ready to trek across the uneven ground to where the *Galaxy* waits. It looks like about a half mile, and I'm suddenly eager to get there. It's one o'clock in the afternoon. Martin says the sun will set at around a quarter to five.

We hike along the cliff on the northern side of the inlet. At the end, we are able to look down with relative security upon the *Galaxy* floating calmly in the protected water between the offshore island and the mainland. Now there's some more activity. Bob Jaeger is leaning against the stern rail, gazing across the water. Margot stands beside him, wearing big sunglasses and a mauve scarf wrapped loosely around her head and neck. Jorn Ekborg and Richard Lawler sit at a table, conversing in an animated way.

More time passes. Nothing happens. I'm getting restless. What if we're waiting here for days? By three o'clock Parnell and I are seated on the cold ground, our backs to a rock face, out of reach of a brisk wind. Martin and Jimmy still haven't joined us. I'm dozing with my head on Parnell's shoulder and the coat Tiffany lent me buttoned up to my chin. Suddenly he rouses me. "Listen to that."

It's the chug of a motorboat coming down the sound.

We scramble back to our lookout. On the yacht's deck, Yevgeny Petrenko, overdressed in a fur-trimmed parka, is chatting with Jaeger. Margot is gone, and no bimbos are in sight. The usually reclusive American filmmaker, Alan Stempel, has appeared and is seated at a table, sipping a glass of wine. He has his eyes on the horizon in the direction of the approaching motorboat. Brock, Dennis, and another crew member stand at the rail. The two kayaks are now in the water, tethered to the stern of the *Galaxy*. Ekborg and Lawler are in the two orange dinghies, floating close by.

Now the motorboat rounds the north edge of the island: it's a sleek fiberglass about twenty feet long with an Inuit man at the wheel and another facing backwards, binoculars around his neck. This man gestures with a wide sweeping arm. Jaeger turns with excitement and gives the same signal to Ekborg and Lawler in the dinghies.

The Swede and the Scotsman spark their engines. Dennis and Brock lower themselves into the kayaks and paddle out to join them. The third crewman is pulling another rubber dinghy onto the dock. This one is compressed into a large, ungainly square. He unfolds it until it is full size, lying flat, and begins to inflate it with an electric foot pump whose cord snakes behind the service bar.

Petrenko claps Jaeger on the back. Stempel gets up and stands beside them. Their heads turn toward the motorboat and the flotilla of small craft.

I hear a scrambling behind us and turn to see Martin at last. He says Jimmy decided to stay with the plane. I wonder if this had anything to do with the flask in Jimmy's pocket.

So far no one on the *Galaxy* has looked up to where there are now three of us clustered among the rocks at the top of the cliff. I grow bold and set up the tripod at its shortest height. Parnell has the handheld camera ready. The sun is low, casting a rosy light, and the ocean has darkened and become choppier in the wind. Far out in the sound, ice floes drift by like misshapen swans, and flat pack ice close to the shore gives off a pale blue gleam.

Martin, scanning the horizon, shakes his head. "There aren't any whales up here."

The Inuit man in the back of the motorboat has his binoculars trained up the coast. Now he raises his right arm hesitantly to the sky. He pauses, brings his arm slowly down, and firmly points in the direction of whatever he is looking at. The motorboat, orange dinghies, and kayaks spread out across the water until they are positioned about thirty yards apart in a curving line that leads from the sound into the sheltered bay. The third orange dinghy has been inflated and lowered into the water. It's occupied by Alan Stempel, who is paddling to a position farther along, at the mouth of the inlet.

It is impossible to see what they're waiting for. Parnell, Martin, and I are stiffly silent.

Finally there appears a dark roiling under the water in the sound, and the Inuit man signals again. The motorboat's engine commences screaming at its highest pitch, but the gearbox is obviously in neutral, because the boat doesn't move. Ekborg, Lawler, and Stempel take up their dinghies' aluminum paddles, plunge them into the sea, and begin banging them with short metal pipes. The roiling veers to avoid the boats and enters the bay, where it slows and seems to stop, becoming a great black underwater mass that creates a chaotic pattern of bubbling waves around the *Galaxy*.

As the roiling near the *Galaxy* becomes denser, what appear to be man-sized twisted toothpicks pierce the surface of the water at different angles, some low to the water, some as high as ninety degrees. They point in different directions, rising and sinking without apparent agency.

"Narwhals," Martin says, his voice a mixture of certainty and disbelief. "Their fall migration. They move from coastal waters into the deep ocean. There can be hundreds in a pod. Even more, I've heard. Sometimes thousands." Martin is agitated. "Narwhals do everything through echolocation. Those engines and banging tubes will be deafening to them. I guarantee that all they want to do right now is get the hell away from here. But they can't turn around. There are too many following."

So they go in the only direction left to them—up the inlet. A continuous, churning surge of them passes below our cliff. They swim fast, bodies jostling, nearly touching. They're white, black, gray. Mottled and patched. They have short snouts and sleek shoulders. There are calves among them, squirming to keep abreast. The huge tusks of the males shudder in the refracting water like so many sunken Excalibur swords. I've got my camera trained on them, and Parnell is sweeping his across the bay and inlet, to where it dead-ends at a flat brown gravelly beach like the one we landed on.

"They could overturn those kayaks in a second," Parnell says, sounding frustrated that they don't. He's right. The largest whales are probably sixteen feet, two tons of muscle and blubber. The largest tusks are long as men and thick as lampposts, swirling and narrowing to honed points.

"They won't, though," Martin says. "One of the things narwhals are really good at is staying away from humans. They're not going to change that behavior now. My people have been hunting them for thousands of years, usually during these migrations, when they tend to pass by the same places at roughly the same times. We're allowed to take a thousand a year total. Each village has a quota. But there's no one to police it, obviously. I'm guessing your friends paid these local hunters to show them this place and teach them how to do it."

"They're not our friends," Parnell says bitterly, to which Martin makes no reply.

We fall silent, watching.

"Incredible," I hear Martin whisper behind me. "Look over there."

The narwhals are still coming, a wide coursing river of them, pouring into the sheltered bay from the Cumberland Sound. They fork at the *Galaxy*, flowing on both sides of it, following the others. Petrenko, leaning over the rail, turns his head this way and that, as if he can't decide which direction to look in first. Jaeger's filming the spectacle from the deck of the *Galaxy*.

I grab my camera and tripod, ready to head to lower ground and get closer, better footage, whatever the risk.

"Watch it, Pirio," Parnell says in a warning voice. "Don't fuck this up."

He's right. There's nothing we can do. The whales, stuck in the inlet, will perish in any case. I need to keep my head, and focus on getting what we came for.

Ekborg in the orange dinghy is riding right among the whales, almost on their backs at times, looking like a Swedish film version of a primitive hunter, his face gloriously alive. At the mouth of the inlet he breaks away to sidle next to Stempel's dinghy. He takes a rolled fishing net out of the bottom of his boat and passes one end of it to the American.

By now the first narwhals have reached the end of the inlet, where they are unavoidably beached in the shallow water. The migration keeps coming. The fast-moving whales collide and crush one another like cars in a gruesome pileup on the highway. The water is not deep enough to allow them to dive, so some of them ride right over smaller whales in front.

The air fills with a cacophony. Clicks and grunts. Sounds like hammers knocking, squeaking doors, the rattling of a dozen sticks dragged along a dozen picket fences. Human sounds like cranky babies' cries and high, imploring questions. All of it running together and swelling into a chaotic din.

The last of the migration pours into the inlet, and as the creatures jam together, it stops being an inlet at all and becomes a blubbery road of living narwhal meat, with tusks sticking out all over the place.

Ekborg takes his end of the net and crosses the inlet, about fifty feet. Ekborg and Stempel drop the net in tandem, closing off the inlet's mouth.

"That's a seal net," Martin says. "It goes pretty deep. The kellies anchor it to the bottom, and those cork buoys float on top. They don't really need a net, though. Those whales won't swim back to humans, even if they could turn around."

Jaeger and Petrenko are yelling encouragement from the rail of the *Galaxy*.

The three dinghies and two kayaks assemble in a line beyond the net. The men in kayaks reach along the narrow bows and unclip something. The men in the dinghies pick something off the bottoms of the boats. Harpoons.

Chapter 29

The only way to handle what's about to happen is to think of it as a job, to keep my eye behind the lens, and to try not to see the blood. The camera feels heavy in my hand, reliable. Ballast against the horror.

I film the floundering whales, the floating phalanx of harpooners, the spectators on the superyacht anchored in the bay.

"Damn. The yacht's facing the wrong way. I can't get the name painted on the stern," I say.

"The numbers on the side are enough to identify the boat," Martin says.

"I want to get closer, down to that beach at the end," I say.

"Forget it," Parnell says. "Use your zoom."

Ekborg's motorized dinghy crosses the submerged net and moves up the inlet into the churn of whales. The skittish narwhals manage to separate, opening up a shallow path. Stempel follows Ekborg. Lawler is next. Brock and Dennis bring up the rear.

Eventually Ekborg has to stop. The whales at the end of the inlet are beached and can't move. He shuts off his motor, gets out of the dinghy, crawls and then walks across their blubbery backs. He's wearing rubber boots that come up to his knees, holding his harpoon aloft. He strides with a deep bend in his knees, as if on a tight trampoline. He manages to get to a strip of beach on the south side of the inlet, splashes across rocks in the shallow water, and turns back to egg on his comrades. Stempel pushes himself up from his boat, rises on wobbly legs like a baby learning how to walk. Less sure of himself, taking cautious, measured strides, he follows Ekborg's trail. The ungainly Lawler unfolds himself from his dinghy and gives whale walking a try. Using his harpoon for balance, he causes bloody gashes as he goes, slipping several times but managing to stay on his feet. Ekborg and Stempel, standing on the shore, hurl taunts like frat brothers at a hazing. Brock and Dennis float quietly in their kayaks, awaiting their turns.

Soon all five men have clambered and splashed their way to the wide beach at the end of the inlet. They gather in a tight group to confer. Then the two crewmen retreat to boulders at the back of the beach, where it meets a slope of tangled scrub. Dennis lights a cigarette behind a cupped hand. Apparently, they are letting the honors go to the paying guests.

The harpooning begins. It goes on and on. The water at the end of the inlet turns pink, then red. In time the sand at the water's edge is stained a deep maroon, and the sea froth is the color of wine.

Like all jobs, killing has its tedium. And its challenges. Ekborg, Stempel, and Lawler have to wade in deeper and deeper to reach still-living whales. Their rubber boots don't go high enough. They shouldn't have left their dinghies where they did.

After some conversation, the two crew members head back along the rocks and narrow beach to collect the abandoned craft and maneuver them closer to shore. Now Ekborg, Stempel, and Lawler are able to continue the killing from the small boats.

The sun is dropping, flattening into pink streaks and a reddish band. The eastern sky has mellowed to deep indigo. Vaguely, stars have emerged.

I have not taken my face from behind my camera, or looked back at Parnell and Martin, who've both on occasion muttered swears. But eventually they fall silent, and now it seems that everything—the whole arctic world—is monumentally hushed. The eerie quiet, I realize, comes from the fact that the narwhals have ceased their clicking chatter. Even the still-living ones are mute.

Finally the hunters head back to shore, using paddles to push their way through the whale bodies, which seem to have spread out and sunk down, opening up more space. They get out of their boats, pull them onto the beach, and pause for a few minutes. Their clothes are blood-soaked, their faces and hair blood-covered. It looks as if about sixty narwhals are dead, roughly half the migration.

Ekborg strides to the back of the beach, where Brock is pulling something long and heavy wrapped in a tarp from among the boulders. The tarp is unfolded to reveal a gleaming metal saw that must have been stowed there earlier. Ekborg picks it up and points the blade skyward jauntily.

He begins sawing off tusks. Due to the animals' positioning and the changing depth of the shallow water in which he wades, he must occasionally adopt a contorted posture—one foot pressing down on a snout, or his torso curved across a melon head to reach a tusk half hidden behind blubber. The men on shore look damp, cold, and tired—less like glorious heathen, more like soft, monied vacationers at the end of a long day in a foreign city, waiting for the tour-guided bus to pick them up and take them back to a good meal in a nice hotel.

They rouse themselves to begin collecting the severed tusks. Along with the crew members, they drag the tusks onto the beach, and begin sticking them upright at regular intervals in the soft sand. Eventually I recognize the emerging shape of the strange grid I saw on Noah's cell phone.

Obviously, Ned meant for his photos to be used as evidence. He probably thought he was keeping them safe by sending them to Noah's phone. But somehow either Hall or the Oyster Man found out about it, and Max was given the job of getting Noah's phone before anyone figured the pictures out.

It is now near dark. Ekborg, it seems, does not want to share the saw. He carries on in a crazed, triumphant way, and Stempel and Lawler stand by, shuffling their feet.

Brock approaches them and gestures toward the yacht. They gaze across the water and up at the sky as if finally noticing that the sun is about to set. Stempel begins to wave his arms in wide sweeps like a man signaling a jet. Ekborg raises his head from his work, tosses back his pink-streaked hair. The men on the shore wave him in.

Ekborg complies. On the beach the long saw is rewrapped in its tarp and stowed in the shelter of the boulder. Apparently, they're planning to return.

The five men steer the kayaks and dinghies through the floating carcasses and still-living whales, to the end of the inlet and out into the bay, where the *Galaxy* floats like a tall pristine island, outlined by white running lights, all four interior levels lavishly illuminated against the encroaching dark.

"Come on. We've got to get back to the plane while there's still light," Parnell says.

"What about the tusks?" Martin says.

"Leave them."

"No. They shouldn't have the profit."

"They don't give a shit about money. They did it for fun."

Martin nods toward the ivory grid. "That's more than fun. They're planning on doing something with those tusks. If they're not going to sell them on the black market, they're going to use them as status symbols, gifts. Fucking coffee table legs."

"So we'll call the authorities as soon as our cell phones work."

"No, I don't trust them. There's too many people getting paid off around here."

Parnell heaves a sigh. "What do you want to do?"

"Wrap them in the tarp, drag them up the incline, and back to the plane. Bury them, or drop them in the lake until we can come back for them."

"Are you crazy? It's almost dark now. We don't have time for that. Besides, if they don't have the tusks in their possession, they'll just deny it ever happened. We *want* those tusks to be on board the *Galaxy* when it comes in to port."

Burning with anger, Martin strains against the obvious logic of Parnell's position. "They belong to my people."

"Oh, please. Don't start with that. Your people want to make money like everyone else. Those Inuit guys on the motorboat brought the rich white boys to this place and showed them what to do."

"Be careful what you say."

"I'll say what I want."

Martin's chest expands. He takes an aggressive step toward Parnell.

Parnell stiffens, doesn't flinch.

"This seems like a pretty bad time to be having an argument," I say in a loud, sarcastic voice. "Especially since we're all on the same side."

With slow, dramatic reluctance, the two men turn away from each other.

"I'm heading back," I say briskly. "You guys bring the cameras." I start striding down the incline toward the end of the inlet. Then I start jogging. Then I run.

They don't notice at first, which gives me time to get ahead. When I reach the steep slope that leads down to the beach, I descend too fast, stumble, fall on my ass, and begin to slide through the short scrub, setting off little avalanches of scattering rocks.

"Where the hell are you going?" Parnell yells.

"Gotta do something," I call back.

"What?"

"You'll see."

I hear Martin and Parnell's thudding footsteps on the path above. With luck, I'll make it in time. I race to the water's edge, start stripping off my clothes.

Parnell shouts, "What the fuck? What are you doing?"

"Going for a swim!" I yell.

"Are you crazy?"

"Don't you dare come after me. The temperature will kill you."

I splash into the shallow water, push my way through dead narwhals, and when I'm up to my waist, I dive. The water's cold. But not too cold. Just about the same temperature as the tank at NEDU. Which, if I'm being honest, is pretty fucking cold. I suck air, suck water by mistake, choke, suck air, and start swimming like a madwoman escaping Alcatraz. I'm in serious distress and telling myself it's a piece of cake.

I can smell the blood in the brine, and when I lift my arm to stroke, there's a pink film on it that gleams. The narwhal bodies bump against me, soft and smooth, dense and strangely buoyant. I slither through them, doing a short breast stroke in the tight places, passing lifeless pupils the size of dimes and huge gaping mouths from which the tusk, actually a front tooth, has been hacked. When I get to the deeper water, I slow down a bit, conserving strength, and sense something big near me, ghosting along, partly in my wake and partly underneath me. I look back and realize I have a companion. A gray calf that bobs its head like a colt and is merely twice my size.

I have no idea how far I've swum or how far away the net is. I've lost touch with my hands and feet, my eyes, and half my brain. If I think about what I'm doing, I'll surely lose my nerve. So I don't. I just keep stroking. I talk to the little whale. I ask if he likes stories. I think absurd things like that.

I start to sense that the whales around me are alive. Their bodies are just as soft as the carcasses, but there's living tension in them. They feel more like muscle than blubber. Can whales be angry? I wonder. And I recall the sperm whale that bludgeoned the nineteenth-century whale ship *Essex* several times with its monstrous head until it found the exact tension point that made the whole boat crack to smithereens and descend posthaste to the floor of the Pacific. Thus making an impression on the young Herman Melville, who turned around and gave us *Moby-Dick*. These narwhals, rumored to be placid, could nevertheless with one languorous roll keep me submerged until I drowned.

Not good thoughts, not good thoughts, I whisper to myself, picking up my pace until I'm stroking as fast as I do at the Y when I want to push the edge. The calf is only a few feet underneath me now. Maybe it thinks I'm its mother. Maybe that's what's protecting me.

My body is quickly deteriorating. My thoughts are sluggish, but I'm still conscious. To the best of my ability, I conjure mental pictures of Lewis Gordon Pugh and Lynne Cox. I think about his V-shaped chest, her hourglass shape. The frigid, dark blue Baltic. The sun setting over Antarctica. Ice floes like modernist sculptures. But the images fuzz out quickly in my overtaxed brain, and random words take their place. *Three hours. Four hours. Mental stamina. Body fat.* I'm not even sure what I'm muttering. *Mount Everest. Thermal exposure. Sleep.*

The face of Trudy Flanagan floats before me: *This must be a lot to handle right now.* I slap the water, drag myself through it. *No, no. Piece of cake. No psych testing. Jelly is best.* The sports scientist pops open his mouth to cheerfully report that when the huskies get to the end of the Iditarod, they turn right around and want to do it all over again. A laugh bubbles up in me. Those crazy dogs! I see their bright eyes, hear their joyous barks. Then the voice of the Navy doctor booms like a warning foghorn between my ears: *Don't fuck with the equipment.*

Fuck you, I tell him.

Shut the fuck up, he says. His bulb head lights up with new knowledge. *The data shows that the physiologic process reversed itself. Reversed. Reversed. Reversed.*

Tranquillity spreads through me. I have to believe it. We're not all the same. For reasons I will never know, this moment is my birthright, what I was made for. Nobody said it would be fun.

I swim right over the net and feel it only because my kicking leg touches its slightly submerged top. I grab the top rope, pull myself along ten yards or so to the buoy at the end.

The sun has shrunk to a red pinprick on the horizon. I watch it wobble, disappear. Instantly, the ocean goes black, and the night sky comes alive. A deep, dark, velvety blue. No moon. Flickering stars. Cold, clean air, and a sense of expectancy.

My fingers have no sensation, but with my palms I can feel the thick knot that attaches the net to the enormous buoy, which is not cork at all, as Martin said, but rubber, like a mooring, and much, much bigger than it looked from shore. There's some kind of wire involved in the fastening, and a chain like a plumb line that sinks to the seafloor and keeps the bottom from drifting up. I have no idea what to do. I want to cry out in frustration, in fury at myself. I'm naked, half drowning, and hypothermic. I certainly did not bring a knife. What was I thinking? How can I possibly move a buoy in the ocean, or a huge megapound net?

Now, with the goal so close, but impossible, I begin to shiver violently. My teeth rattle; my ribs feel like they could break. It's as if the opening of a chink in my willpower (or was it just delusion all along?) is making my body break down, too. I try, but my stiff hands will barely curl around the knot. There's nothing to be done. The net is firmly connected.

I think about everything ending here, like this, in this frigid water, and call myself a fool. So close to the bay, I feel a current pulling me.

The tide's going out, leaving the inlet. Unless I can grab hold of something, I risk being pulled out to sea.

I wrap my legs around the top rope of the net, hook one arm around the bottom of the buoy where it attaches to the anchoring chain. I will have to stay here until someone comes for me. Where are Martin and Parnell? Sweet Martin, he took me at my word. He would have told Parnell my secret by now, told him to let me go. One-armed Parnell probably can't swim anyway. If either of them tried, chances are they wouldn't make it this far anyway, much less back to the beach while dragging me. And there's no boat.

I should swim back now, before I'm even more exhausted. But the prospect makes me weak with dread. I've lost my stamina, my edge, and the way back is cluttered and dangerous.

Maybe I can get to the rock face behind me and pull myself along until I find a place to crawl up. Maybe. I can hear quiet splashes where the water meets the cliff. Or should I pull myself along the top of the net to the other buoy, and try my luck on the side of the inlet where the rock face isn't as high? Or I could let the current gently wash me toward the *Galaxy*, get myself to the stern ladder somehow, and crawl aboard. Naked and spent, a doomed fish flopping on the deck.

It all feels difficult, very difficult. The more I think, the more the choices multiply. Can one be right, when they all look bad?

When adult narwhals come up to breathe, it's only the tops of their heads that break the surface. Their eyes, nearly blind anyway, stay below. That's why something as simple as a seal net can catch them. To them it's a soaring wall.

The calves occasionally jerk their heads up when they breathe. Not yet graceful in the water like their parents, not yet well behaved. Although I can't see it in the dark, I hear flaps and slaps from the little whale that followed me, as if it's rolling and twisting around. Now, suddenly, I feel a powerful rush as its bulk passes close by me in the water. It's swimming right over the net where my body has slightly depressed it. Under its weight, the net is depressed even more. I'm dunked; the buoy's pulled down and rolls on top of me. I lose my grip, panic, grab at something floating on the surface, and realize I'm holding a loop of rope. It feels loose. Why?

Then, in a flash, I get it. The knot I felt wasn't to the net at all; it was to the chain underneath. The top of the net is hooked over the buoy with a simple loop. The loop feels loose right now because the buoy is momentarily submerged. Still underwater, I swim down and away, pulling the rope with me as the whale passes like a thundercloud overhead. The loop clears the submerged buoy, and the rope is torn from my hand as the heavy net falls away quickly through the blackness. The buoy bobs back up after the narwhal passes. I come up after it, gasping and sputtering, grab hold of it again. The net's still attached to the buoy on the other side of the inlet, but now, on this side, there's a huge gaping exit to the bay.

I look for the calf. It's gone.

A minute passes. Sounds begin: chattering, clicking, whistles, creaks.

The current seems to shift; the water churns.

The narwhals begin streaming out. The enormous bodies pass one after the other, three and four abreast; one clips me with a flipper. I hug the buoy tighter, wrap my legs around the chain to keep from being sucked along in the watery stampede.

They keep passing. Ten, twenty, more than I can count. Out in the bay, heads occasionally break the surface, glisten in starlight. Raised tusks glow white.

For a minute, I long to go with them, to fall in with that beautiful stream and swim far out to sea. Back to the place where I felt death waiting. Ever since the collision, he's been calling me back, whispering *I'm here. You know me now. You know you'll come to me soon.*

Not now, I whisper back. Not now.

When the whales are gone and the surface of the bay lies flat and unbroken, I swim slowly down the inlet toward the beach. I'm comfortable enough, don't feel particularly cold. I don't know when my body flipped its switch. I only know it did. Still, it's a great relief to get through the bumping narwhal corpses and stagger onto the sand. Parnell catches me, wraps his coat around me. Martin's got a flashlight; his drawn face is visible in its wavering beam. While I was swimming, Jimmy arrived, bringing the torches to help us get back to the plane.

My clothes are shoved at me. I'm shivering too much to put them on, so Parnell helps me, kneeling down to tie my sneakers. His back to the others, he says in a husky voice, "If I asked you never to do that again, what would you say?"

"I can't help it. It's who I am."

He nods. "Then I guess I won't."

When I'm ready to go, we head back across the tundra. I scoot next to Parnell, lean in to his left shoulder, and he puts his arm around me as we walk.

Chapter 30

We spend the night next to the lake at the base of Mount Duval. Jimmy, unfazed and grinning, produces a half-full bottle from his backpack and offers it around. Martin, Parnell, and I decline, so he empties it himself and goes off to sleep in the tent. The three of us sit in the short grass near the plane, surrounded by dark tundra, talking aimlessly about simple subjects, but with the kind of intimacy that comes from having been through something together. We have no fire, since there's nothing but grass to burn, but I'm wrapped in a sleeping bag and feel fine. I'm mesmerized by the glowing bands of green light swirling lazily in the night sky.

We're airborne at daybreak, flying south across the Hudson Strait. By midmorning we've landed in Hopedale. Martin, Parnell, and I throw our bags in the bed of Martin's pickup, while Jimmy, smiling broadly, waves good-bye from beside his Piper Cherokee. Once home, Martin strides through the kitchen, past Tiffany's breathless questions, to the phone in the living room. Soon we hear his usually supple voice, grown hard with urgency, giving the exact location of the *Galaxy* and the narwhal slaughter to the Canadian authorities. Parnell opens his laptop on the kitchen table and begins pecking at the keyboard, composing the first draft of his story. I disappear into the bathroom to shower off sand, salt, and whale blood. Tiffany lends me some clothes.

As Martin and Tiffany prepare lunch, I retreat to the quiet living room to make my round of necessary phone calls. But first I have to think, try to sort things out. I sit on the sun-dappled couch, curl my legs under me. There's a handmade purple afghan on the back of the couch and bright plastic toys scattered on the coffee table. Cheerful, mundane objects that feel comforting.

My first impulse is to call the Boston Police Department with information about Mrs. Smith's murder. But there's no evidence she *was* murdered. I'm sure Johnny covered his tracks extremely well. If I accuse him out of the blue, with no evidence to back it, I'll only end up looking like a fool.

I have no doubt that Johnny's been searching for Parnell since the night Parnell was beaten on the waterfront. It appears that Parnell has succeeded so far in giving him the slip. It's lucky that I wasn't followed to the rooming house in Charlestown or the place in Rockport. I guess I have Troy's spotty work ethic to thank for that. In any case, as long as Parnell stays away from the Salem Street apartment, he can probably elude Johnny awhile longer.

As for me: Johnny obviously considered me finished business the moment I stepped aboard the superyacht. A virtual prisoner for the first leg of the voyage, I was expected to make a lifeless journey to the bottom of the Labrador Sea. His complacency would have been shattered Wednesday night, when Hall would have let him know that I'd escaped. No doubt he's been looking for me since; today or tomorrow, when the story of Ocean Catch's involvement in a narwhal slaughter breaks, his motivation to do away with me will exponentially increase.

Johnny has no idea where I am right now. All he knows is that Hall showed me the video of Noah, so at some point I'm going to arrive in Boston to make sure that Noah's safe. I doubt that Johnny will go after

Noah until he has me in view. A missing child creates a lot of news that he would want to avoid, and he needs Noah to be available as bait. Even if he had tried to kidnap Noah at some point during the last few days, he wouldn't have had any luck. Thomasina and Noah left their apartment the day after I escaped. If Johnny had staked out the place, he would only have wasted a lot of time figuring out that they weren't actually there.

Johnny's no fool. He knows me, probably figures I called them as soon as I could. Then I gasp out loud, and my stomach falls away. *He knows me.* I'm suddenly stricken with panic at the thought that he might make the educated guess that Thomasina and Noah are at my father's house on Beacon Hill.

Forget the Boston police. My first call is to Thomasina, who doesn't pick up. My second is to Jeffrey, who does. "You've got to get Noah out of that house. He could be found there. I can't explain any more than that right now. I'll be in touch, I promise. Just take him and Thomasina somewhere, and do it soon. Right away. Now."

"Hold your horses, Pirio. I don't like the sound of this. Who are these people?"

"One's a guy named Max. Thomasina knows him. The other is John Oster, a fisherman. He doesn't want Noah; he wants me."

"Why aren't you going to the police?"

"The police won't do anything. I have no evidence, and by the time they figure anything out, Noah could be harmed. Please, Jeffrey. You've just got to believe me and get Noah out of there."

A ragged sigh. "Where will I take them?"

"I don't know. A resort? A summer house? Someplace you can get to fast."

"And you? What about you?"

"I have a friend with me. I'll be OK."

"Pirio, this is crazy stuff. You need to tell me right now what the fuck's going on."

"I will; I promise. Just not right now. I need a few more days."

"Pirio. What are you doing?"

I've heard that tone of voice so many times before. When I was five and bringing garden worms into the kitchen. When I was ten and refusing to talk. When I was fifteen and slamming doors. When I was twenty and drunk.

I hold the phone tighter, press it into my ear. "You were always there for me, Jeffrey. You took my side when no one else would. If it weren't for you, I don't know where I'd be. Please. One last time."

"Oh, crap," he says, giving in.

"Let me talk to Thomasina if she's there."

"She's helping Maureen rethink her wardrobe. It's amazing how well they get along."

"See if you can tear her away."

Two minutes into my conversation with Thomasina (basically just a repeat of my conversation with Jeffrey), I realize with a jolt that she's sober. She's irritable, focused, defeated, and grounded as hell. No bullshit, no stories, no excuses. Just two bare feet on the burning coals of reality. Even so, it's hard to gauge how much of what I'm saying she's really taking in, and I'm grateful that Jeffrey at least understands the urgency.

"I can't sleep. I have insomnia. The guest room's way too floral. I can't keep anything down. Your stepmother is emptying out her closet. And now you tell me this," she says disgustedly.

"How about a spa in Vermont? Picture a hot tub, a masseuse. Just stay away from the bar."

"Don't give me advice, OK? Do me that one favor. From now on, keep your advice to yourself."

I want to reach through the phone and hug her. "How many days?"

"What the fuck difference does it make?" A pause. "Since Foxwoods, fourteen."

"Don't let Maureen talk you into a glass of wine."

"Oh, God. I'd rather she was pushing booze on me than trying to help. She's worse than you with all the advice she has. *Did you know you could be a candidate for delirium tremens? I called AA and printed out a meeting list. The B vitamins are very helpful. I can recommend a good psychiatrist.*" She sighs. "Jeffrey's awesome. It's been nice to have his help with Noah. I've been going to two meetings a day. Whoever thinks Beacon Hill is ritzy should look to see who's in the basements of the churches around here. Pirio, nothing bad's going to happen to Noah, is it?"

"No, nothing bad. As long as you do what I say."

"Good. Because I couldn't handle that. You want to talk to him?"

"No. Just tell him I said hi." I'd love to hear his voice, but I am incapable of making cheerful godmother noises into the phone when I know that John Oster's out there, with Noah, me, and Parnell in his sights. I privately vow that the next time I talk to Noah, he'll be safe. We all will be. I have no idea how that's going to happen, but I won't rest until it does.

Thomasina continues, "Last night he watched *The Maltese Falcon* with your father. Now they're upstairs listening to Rachmaninoff."

Oh, Milosa, I think. *Please don't give him a cigar.*

We all gather round the kitchen table when lunch is ready. Matilda is placed in her high chair, where she squirms, fusses, and starts to cry. Tiffany picks up her teething daughter and holds her on her lap, rocking and humming a little to soothe her. Parnell sits next to me, and it feels good to have him near. I'm glad for the hot coffee and hearty meal, but there's a strange foreignness to everything. As if I were gone too long, or traveled too far, and now must relearn how to use silverware, drink from a glass, and wipe my mouth with a napkin. With each rise and fall of my breath, I'm conscious of the ocean, the narwhals, and a sense of freedom singing in my blood. The house in comparison feels constricting, overcivilized.

Something's been nagging me since the last time I was here, but I can't put my finger on what it is. I keep flashing to the painted cedar box with Roger's letter to my mother and the photos. After lunch, when Tiffany takes Parnell into town so that he can check his e-mail, I notice the black bird face peering down from the top of the bookcase, and ask Martin if I could look at it again.

"Of course," he says, handing it to me.

I sit on the couch and open the box, remove the letter and photos. The only things left are a pocketknife on a thin knotted rope, and a small brown vial.

I hold up the pocketknife. "Is this . . ."

"Yes," Martin says with an uncomfortable nod. "He made carvings. I'll show you some later."

"I wonder why he wanted my mother to have it?"

"Maybe it would have meant something to her. It was one of the most precious things he owned."

I replace it a little sadly, wondering about him.

Then I pick up the vial, and before I've finished unscrewing the plastic top, my heart is racing. I know what I hold in my hand.

When the cap is off, I raise the vial to my nose, inhale the escaping molecules, and it's as if she's standing in the room. No, even closer: living in the air I breathe. Flowing emotions, cascading memories—a hundred reactions fill me at once. Wonder, love, and disappointment. Anger and longing, contentment and pain. Her laugh is a bright, clear bell in my ear; her cigarette burns in the ashtray; I see her eyebrow arch. Her thin fingers, strong and warm, caress me, and the straightness of her back is what I strive to attain. I can't get enough. I hold the vial like a chalice and breathe my childhood, the wildflowers of Labrador, the cool dust of July. In a vision, she stretches lazily on the chaise longue on the deck of the architect's house, drops her book to the ground, and complains that no one knows how to write a good story anymore. Then she smiles, and there are crinkles at the edges of her eyes. As I lie in bed, she leans down to kiss my forehead, then sits up straight and whispers, *Listen. Do you hear them? The seals are barking on the rocks.*

"It's my mother's fragrance," I explain to Martin, blinking back tears. "She made it one summer up here in Labrador, and always wore it."

He takes the vial and holds it under his nose. He gives a thoughtful nod. "It's nice."

"It brings her alive again," I say with urgency, trying to explain the inexplicable. "Like she's suddenly here." *It's a highway to the unquenchable heart of me*, I might have added, if I had the courage to be grandiose. *To the place where my mother and I wrapped around each other and were one. It's the story of my childhood told in molecules that only I can understand.*

Martin tries another inhalation, holding the vial gingerly between two fingers. Frowns with serious intent. "Yeah. I like it. It's nice."

I end up laughing. I can't help it. "Martin! It's more than nice. It's perfume genius!" The emotional associations, I realize, can only ever be mine.

He looks a little upset, knowing he's come up short. Gives a third earnest sniff, which results in a flared nostril and a shake of the head. "I said I liked it."

"Sweet Martin," I say, folding my almost-brother in my arms, rocking him back and forth with joy. "How very lucky I am."

"Wait! Don't spill it!" he says, laughing. He unwraps my arms, closes the vial tightly with the plastic top, and presses it firmly, ceremoniously, into the middle of my palm, as if it were the exact wrench I needed to do some important carpentry work.

Parnell and I are in the backseat of a yellow taxi coursing through the soot-smeared Sumner Tunnel. It's Monday, midmorning. We got a flight from Hopedale to St. John's yesterday afternoon but had to wait until almost five this morning for an Air Canada flight to Boston. As we were leaving Logan, Parnell told the taxi driver, "Sumner Tunnel." Now, as the end of the tunnel approaches, and more specific directions are needed, Parnell says "North End" and I say "Storrow Drive" at exactly the same time. The driver throws up his hands in a dangerous release of the wheel. "Make up your mind!"

I turn to Parnell. "Your apartment's not safe. You can't go back there."

His eyes are bloodshot, and his face is haggard. "I need some things there to finish this story. I don't give a shit about John Oster."

"You don't get it, do you? He's a killer. I didn't believe it before, but now I know it's true. He's after you, and I can promise he's got your place staked out. If you go back there, you'll be jumping right into his net. You'll be like a fish that he catches just by waiting."

"Which is it?" the driver yells into his rearview.

Before we can answer, we miss the Storrow Drive exit, and he steers us toward the North End.

Parnell's eyes flash at me defiantly. "Did you just compare me to a fish?" He gives the driver his address.

As we wind through the narrow streets, I try to persuade him to stay in a nearby hotel at the very least. Just for a few days. He rightly points out that, if either apartment is being watched, it's more likely to be mine. Therefore, if I'm serious about wanting to evade this pathetic Johnny-douchebag guy, I should take my own advice and stay in a hotel as well.

We end up at the Bostonian. Adjoining rooms.

I sit on the bed, and try to figure out what to do. Parnell seems to have decided that the hard part of our job is over: now that the ring is busted and we've got footage and a story, we're close enough to the finish line to let down our guard. He seems to think that Johnny's just a footnote who will eventually be caught in the net of the official investigation, once it gets under way. Or maybe he just doesn't want to run anymore, and, with his handgun strapped to his calf, is willing to take his chances. In any case, he won't last more than a few days in exile from his apartment. He's only here at all because he thinks that this is what he has to do to keep me away from my apartment.

As for me, I can't wait for the authorities to nab Johnny. The investigation into the hunting ring will most likely be slow. It could take weeks before there's enough evidence to implicate him. I have to neutralize him before he gets to Noah, Parnell, or me. But how? The only answer seems to be to find a way to link him to the murder of Mrs. Smith.

I've got one advantage. Right now he doesn't know where Parnell, Noah, and I are. But that won't last very long: Parnell's not going to stay holed up in a hotel, and Jeffrey won't be able to keep Thomasina and Noah out of town forever. Whatever I'm going to do, I have to do it fast.

I call Jeffrey from the room phone. He's relieved to hear from me. He says that at this moment they're having lunch in a resort in the White Mountains. Cornbread, hearty stew. Gorgeous view outside the windows.

It's nice to know that we all have excellent accommodations.

He said they did some leaf peeping this morning, but the height of the season has passed. There's not a trace of enthusiasm in his voice. The tour manager role, less than twenty-four hours old, is already wearing thin.

"What's going on down there?" he asks tensely.

"Things are being resolved."

"Damn you, Pirio."

"Just give me time."

"How much?"

"Not sure."

Thomasina gets on the phone. "Noah wants to know when he's going back to school."

"Soon."

"I don't care if I never see another goddamn tree in my life."

"How many days now, Thomasina?"

"Sixteen. What do you think? Two more than the last time you asked me. Big whoop, huh?"

Before I can say anything, Noah's on the phone. "Hey, Pirio. You know how it says 'purple mountain majesties' in that song we always have to sing in school? Well, the mountains here really *are* purple. So why do they call them *white*?"

"I can't answer that. But it's nice to hear your voice."

"I'm missing a lot of school. We were going to do electricity in science, and I think I missed the whole thing."

"Electricity will always be around."

"This is a weird time to have a vacation."

"It's good to be different sometimes."

"But we're not having any fun."

"Vacations are like that more often than you think."

"Your dad was teaching me to play chess, and that was better than this."

"Did he show you how to smoke a cigar?"

"I'm not supposed to say."

"You'll be back soon, and then you can finish learning chess."

"It's hard, but I like it. Your dad said I could play with him whenever I wanted."

"That sounds nice. But I'm warning you: he won't let you win."

"That's just for little kids."

"I have to go now, but I'll see you soon."

"Good-bye, Pirio. It was nice to talk to you."

"Good-bye, Noah. It was nice to talk to you, too."

Sunlight is pouring through the room's sliding glass door. I step onto a balcony overlooking Quincy Market, where people flow in every direction, and a breeze tugs the last stubborn leaves off the sidewalk-planted trees. Chrysanthemum pots are everywhere. More flowers wrapped in cellophane stand in buckets of water outside a shop, and two men perch on a bench, strumming Spanish guitars. I want Noah to have a world like this. Safe and bright. But those worlds don't happen by themselves.

Reentering the room, I catch sight of myself in the mirror over the dresser. My bruises have turned various colors—blue and purple, but also the yellow of summer squash and a froggy green. I'm not sure if these changes have anything to do with Labrador tea. Completing the rainbow effect is my outfit: Tiffany's pink sweatshirt and navy sweatpants. I can't go anywhere looking like this.

I'm about to pop out the door when I realize I don't have a credit card or even an ID to make a withdrawal. The money Margot gave me is long gone. Parnell put the plane tickets and hotel rooms on his card. I go out to the hall, knock on his door. When he opens it, I explain and tell him I'll pay him back.

He accompanies me across the street. We go in and out of various stores while I buy clothes, makeup, sunglasses, bubble bath, and shoes. At the inside food court, he orders a ham sandwich to go. I get a dozen raw oysters with horseradish. We sit outside to eat on a granite bench on a lovely historic cobblestone plaza, and try to feel like everyone else. It doesn't work. Every square-faced, red-headed man who walks by is John Oster until I blink and look again. Parnell looks none too happy himself. We end up lunching like we're on speed, toss our trash in a receptacle, head to the Apple store in Back Bay, and purchase an iPhone. I program Parnell's number and the ones I know from memory. He gives me some more cash.

It's close to two when we get back to the hotel and our respective rooms. I throw my packages on the bed, fill the tub with warm-to-hot water, and soak in bubbles for a long time. I can hear the television in Parnell's room through the wall. It's on much too loud. From the periodic hushes followed by polite applause, I can tell it's some part of the

PGA tour. Oddly disappointed, I run more hot water, creating competing noise and a real extravagance of bubbles. I could never love a man who watched television, especially golf, at such a volume in the middle of the day. Sinking into foam so high and thick that it stands in peaks, I sigh with a modicum of relief. It's good to have that point decided.

I'm standing in front of Mrs. Smith's three-decker in Jamaica Plain, having taken the Green Line from Haymarket. The high pitched roof sends a jagged shadow over the sidewalk. I shiver in a sharp wind, wrap another loop of scarf around my neck. When I dropped her off after our museum trip, I remember her opening the door to the first-floor apartment and being greeted by Jasper's happy barks. The same white-lace curtain hangs in that window, but plastic shades have been pulled tight behind the bowed front windows. I mount the few stairs leading up to a small porch, ring her bell, and hear a melodious chime inside. I wait. No one opens. I try the handle; it's locked.

I ring the bell for the second-floor apartment. A minute later, the stairway light flicks on, and the wooden stairs creak as someone lumbers down them. A woman, midforties, with a red kerchief tied around her head, pulls aside her curtain with a hooked index finger.

"Are you Jehovah's Witness?"

"No, ma'am."

"MASSPIRG? Greenpeace?"

"No, ma'am."

"Whaddya want?"

"I want to talk about Libby Smith."

The curtain falls, the bolt slides, and the door opens halfway. She's a large woman in cotton sweatpants and a T-shirt that bears a picture of Larry Bird above the caption "Legend."

"What about her?" she says. Her manner indicates that she's prepared to indulge me for a minute, no more.

"The night she died . . ."

"Yeah? Go on."

"Did you notice anything unusual?"

"I already told the cops."

"I was a friend. I'm just curious. As a friend."

The woman's eyes narrow. She knows there's something fishy, but that doesn't put her off. Instead, it seems to make me more interesting. But she doesn't invite me in, just stays on the small landing, keeping one arm behind the semiopen door, in case she has to shut it quickly.

"You work with her?"

"No. We . . . uh, we used to walk our dogs together at the pond. It used to be her and Jasper and me and Arnold, my Saint Bernard. Six o'clock every evening after work. We got to be really close. I guess it's just hard for me, not knowing what happened to her. The only information I have is from the newspaper obituary. And I'd love to know where Jasper is."

The woman's face has softened. "You'll be glad to know that Libby's son took him to live with his family in West Roxbury. Jasper's gone to a very good home. Libby would be so pleased.

"You know, it was Jasper who raised the alarm that night. He was barking . . . oh, was he barking! You'd think the world was about to end. It was three in the morning. I figured Libby would see to him, so I just put my earplugs in, and went back to sleep. But Jasper was still at it when I got up the next morning, so I knocked on Libby's door, and when she didn't answer, I went in with the key she gave me—we'd exchanged keys a couple of years ago in case one of us got locked out. Jasper was in a tizzy, scampering all around. His voice was hoarse from barking. Libby wasn't there, so I called the police; I didn't know what else to do. They stopped by and looked around the apartment, but didn't have much to say. A few hours later, my bell rings, and it's the cops again. Said there'd been a hit-and-run on the Jamaicaway early that morning. Wanted me to go with them to city morgue to see if I could identify the body. Sure enough, it was her. I couldn't believe it. It was so sad to see her that way, under a sheet, her face so white. That something like that would happen to her—who would have thought?"

"I wonder why she went out in the middle of the night."

"Dementia. That's what they said."

"When you went into her apartment, was anything out of place?"

"Looked the same as always."

"Did you hear anything before Jasper started barking? Or notice anything?"

"I was sound asleep until the dog woke me up."

"Any car outside?"

"Didn't check. Didn't think to. Why? You think someone picked her up?"

"I'm not sure. It just seems strange that she would walk off by herself at that time of night, leaving Jasper behind."

"Well, they say that's what happens when you got dementia."

"Well, thank you for your time, Mrs.—"

"Ramirez. And you?"

"Catherine. Catherine Johnson." It wouldn't do to have anyone know I'd been here.

"No trouble. It's a shame when something like this happens. Shakes everybody up." She starts to close the door, thinks better of it. "Sorry you lost your friend."

"Thanks. One more thing. Could I get into the apartment?"

"What for?"

"She had something of mine. . . ."

Mrs. Ramirez is already shaking her red-kerchiefed head. "No way. No one but family. If you want, you can leave me your number, and I'll give it to her son when he comes."

"That's OK. Thanks anyway."

I walk away dejected. The sun is bowing out with an orangey-pink fanfare at the sky's western edge, and the shadows of the tall houses are pooling together on the street. Maybe it's better to go to the police after all, spill everything I know. But my saner mind reminds me that I'd only be sucked into a complicated bureaucratic mess that would just tie up my time, leaving Johnny loose and Noah unprotected. No, I've got to think of something else.

At the end of Mrs. Smith's street, I turn onto South Huntington, a busy thoroughfare this time of day. The area has that worn-down, worn-out feeling: potholes a foot deep; telephone poles splintered at eye level from all the posters and church announcements that have been stapled to them over the years. Up ahead, the drab VA Hospital and the Home for Little Wanderers. A neighborhood with no illusions.

But that doesn't fully explain the odd sensation that begins to tingle along the back of my left shoulder as I walk along. It's the feeling you get when someone is watching you, or has quietly walked into a room behind you, and you turn and discover them, not quite sure how you knew they were there. I glance over my shoulder, but all I see is a fire hydrant, traffic moving sluggishly, and cars parked along the curb. I walk a little faster. Instead of fading, the prickling sensation gets stronger.

The Heath Street T stop is a couple of blocks ahead, on the other side of the street. I decide to cross early. I step off the curb, stand between two parked cars as I wait for the traffic to clear. I take this time to look to my left a good long way. Two blocks down, a blue Camry is traveling at about three miles per hour in the right-hand lane, causing other cars to slow and pull around it. The driver is gripping the wheel tightly, his hands at ten and two o'clock, and his eyes are scanning ahead of him and to his right. He appears to be hoping for a parking space to open up. As the car gets closer, I can see the driver better. *Shit.* It's Max. He must have followed me from Mrs. Smith's house.

I drop into a deep squat between the parked cars, hug my knees tightly to my chest, and hold my breath as the Camry slowly rolls by.

I wait through a good many beats of my rapidly beating heart before I stand up again. When I finally do, the Camry is several blocks away, still traveling slowly, but well past the concrete kiosk that marks the Heath Street stop.

I jog to the station and insert myself into the middle of a small crowd of people waiting on the curb. The trolley that stops a few minutes later looks completely full, but that doesn't stop all ten of us from clambering single-file up the steps, paying our fares, and streaming down the crowded center aisle of the attached cars, somehow finding places among the blank-faced inbound passengers.

I get to the last car, lean into a pole, and wrap my arm around it, stare out at the street as the trolley starts up with a jerk. I've got my eye peeled for the blue Camry, but it's nowhere in sight. We stop at Back of the Hill Station. Still no Camry. I may have given him the slip. At the intersection of South Huntington and Huntington Ave, the trolley stops again, letting more people off and on, then waiting for the light to change. As I look out the window, the blue Camry pulls up and stops right next to me, fourth or fifth in a line of cars also waiting at the light. Before I can lean away, Max glances up, apparently as sensitive to being watched as I had been, and our eyes lock as the trolley lurches forward. The Camry is quickly left behind, but it doesn't take a genius to know that Max will get through the light only a few moments after we do. Then he'll simply follow the trolley until he sees me get off. In the meantime, he'll call Johnny with my whereabouts, if he hasn't done that already.

The trolley shrieks mechanically in the curve, then rumbles along Huntington Ave at its usual slow pace. Pizza joints and coin-op laundries slide by the grimy window. My own face, distorted in the inside glare, is superimposed on the storefronts. I'm a sitting duck on this trolley. I've got to get out soon. A couple of stops go by—Mission Park, Fernwood. I squeeze through passengers and get next to one of the doors. As soon as they open at Brigham Circle, I'm off.

I sprint up to the first trolley car, cross in front of it, scoot across the outbound track, dodge oncoming cars in the lanes of outbound traffic, and run down Francis Street toward the heart of the medical area. I figure Max will have to make a U-turn to follow me, which will take several minutes at least. I'm looking for a side street to lose myself on, but the only ones are dead ends, and I don't want to become trapped. So I keep up a steady jog until I reach Brigham and Women's Hospital. I look over my shoulder to be sure I wasn't followed and see Max weaving through the people on the sidewalk. He must have simply abandoned his car on Huntington Ave and gotten across the tracks in time to see which way I went. It only takes a glance to see that he's a fit, fast runner and that he's got his eye on me.

Chapter 31

I dart through the hospital's drop-off area, clogged with double-parked cars and old people tottering on canes, and race to the main entrance of Brigham and Women's Hospital. I stumble my way through a revolving door into a bright, crowded atrium, randomly choose one of several corridors and sprint down it until I come to a bank of elevators with one door just closing. I stick my hand in; it opens, and I pile inside, turn around, and become just another blank, anonymous face going up.

I get off at the seventh floor, walk at a normal pace down a gleaming white corridor, find a waiting room bathed in soothing neutral tones, and collapse into a chair. I breathe, and breathe again. I know I've lost him now. I'm sure he saw me enter the hospital. But he wouldn't have seen which way I left the atrium, and he definitely wasn't with me on the elevator. He has no way of knowing that I'm sitting in a seventh-floor waiting room with a nice view of the Joslin Diabetes Center and a stack of *People* magazines to help me while away the time.

All I want to do is cry.

Which is exactly what the woman sitting across from me is doing.

Her sobs heave from deep within her chest; she tries to stifle them by pressing a wad of tissues to her mouth, which only distorts them to a strangled bark. The damp tissues being clearly inadequate to the job, she raises her right forearm, snags the cuff of her sweater with her left index finger, and sops up her tears with that. In the process, her glasses are dislodged. They fall. I pick them up and hand them to her.

"I'm very sorry," I say.

"Thank you," she gasps.

A short man comes in bearing two coffees in small paper cups. He hands one to her. She takes it and tries to steady her trembling lip on the rim.

"They didn't have Splenda, so I used Sweet'N Low," he says.

"Thank you." She gasps again, her eyes closed.

We're the only three people in the room. I want to give them space, but I also have to make a call, so I move to a seat in the corner, pull out my phone, and speed-dial Parnell. When I look up, the man is glaring at me. I end the call, feeling like a real shit.

I move into the hallway, looking for another place to sit, but there isn't one, so I hop into the next elevator that opens up, which turns out to be an express to the first floor. In the bright, busy, street-level corridor, I glance nervously in both directions, expecting Max to appear. A sign in front of me says Chapel with an arrow pointing down the hall. I scoot in that direction, pull open a strangely heavy door to a room of subdued lighting and blessed silence. Thank God there are no worshipers. On a handsome blue patterned rug, rows of chairs face a modest lectern and a table graced by a half-melted candle and a potted chrysanthemum. A few panels of nondenominational stained glass are backlit by electric bulbs.

I sink into a seat in the last row and mutter, "Fuck."

"You shouldn't say that in a church. Some of us are praying," a voice says.

I turn to see a teenage girl in goth regalia sitting in the shadowy corner of the room in a comfortable armchair probably intended for older, feebler folks. Her nasal septum is pierced by a fat silver ring, and her spiked black hair is streaked with metallic blue. She's got an iPad on her lap, fingerless black lace gloves poised above the screen.

"Really. Is there an app for praying?" I ask her.

She looks pensive. "Not that I know of. I could google it."

"Please don't."

She shows me pained, black-rimmed eyes and a tender, purple-painted mouth. "FYI: I play Angry Birds when I pray."

"Oh. Is that the trick? No wonder I never got the hang of praying."

Her eyes roll heavenward. "There's no trick to praying. You can do it however you want. I play Angry Birds because it helps me focus."

"Maybe if you weren't doing two things at once, you wouldn't need the help."

"You're very hostile. I can tell you're not comfortable with technology."

"Of course I am. Watch how fast I text."

I pull up my phone's keypad and type: *Where r u? Urgent. Call me pls.*

A few minutes of comatose meditation pass until my phone emits a cheerful tweet.

His message reads: *Where r u?*

But that's what I asked him. I reply: *U first.*

There's a long delay before I get his answer. *My apt.*

Why?!

Come over.

I stare at the screen angrily. He promised he wouldn't go there. He knows it's dangerous. So why is he asking me to join him there? Something's not right.

I call. It rings and rings. Something's definitely wrong.

I text: *Call me.* I place the phone on the seat next to me, as if it needed its own space in which to be a phone. I wait, look at it, wait, look at it. It doesn't make a sound. I can't believe he's not texting back.

I check the screen, go to Notifications. Everything's working. "Jesus Christ," I say.

"That's a little better, but not much," the girl says.

"I really don't need the commentary," I say drily without turning around.

"I don't need to hear your disrespect."

I sigh. "You're right. I'm sorry. I'm just a little tense."

"Why?"

I glance over my shoulder. "*Why?* Are you asking me *why?*"

"It's not such a strange question, is it?" She has silver sparkles along her cheekbones.

"I'm having a hard day."

"Around here, you're not having a hard day unless you're in the ICU."

"Yup. Good point. Right again. BTW, how old are you? Fifteen?"

"Fourteen."

"Well, you're very wise for someone barely out of childhood."

She regards me with alienated pity. "You really should do something about your hostility." Then she bends her head over the tablet on her lap.

It dawns on me that someone in her family is probably sick. "What's your name?" I ask.

"Sabrina."

"Mine's Pirio."

This gets a flicker of smile. "I like it."

"I like yours, too."

The phone rings. Thank God. I grab it. "Where are you?" I ask Parnell.

"Pirio—" His voice is small, tight.

"What's going on?"

There's fumbling, static, then his rushed cry: "Don't go there! Stay away!"

A loud thud, a sharp moan, more static and fumbling, and a husky voice slides into my ear. "Hey there, crazy girl. Your boyfriend wants to see you, bad."

"Johnny."

"Don't want to hurt him. But you know how I can get."

My stomach clenches. "If anything happens to him, I'll kill you, Johnny. I swear I will."

"Love your spirit, girl. I used to so enjoy fucking your brains out. Remember that?" He pauses; a muffled conversation takes place, and he gets back on the line. "I'm really dying to see you."

I break into a sweat.

"What? Not interested? You think you're too good for me, don't you? Too upper-crust. Or maybe you've just gotten old and lost your nerve. Maybe you need some motivation."

There's dead air for a few moments. Low voices. Then, not too far from the phone, a piercing male scream. Parnell.

"Johnny!" I yell into the phone.

"Yes, darlin'?"

"I'll be there."

"Better hurry. We're gonna keep hurting him till you get here."

"Leave him alone. I said I'd be there, didn't I?"

"That's my girl. Go out the main entrance and wait by the door. Max will pick you up. I want you to stay on this phone, having a nice conversation with me, right up until the moment you get in his car. 'Cause I don't want you calling anyone else. Fact, if any little detail I don't like happens between now and then, there'll be one less liberal journalist in this world. I know a lot of people who'd thank me for that."

"All right, take it easy. I'm on my way. What do you want to talk about?"

"Why don't you sing 'The Star-Spangled Banner'? I always liked that song."

"Funny. I thought you were more of an Allman Brothers guy."

"Start walking and talking, Pirio. Don't be embarrassed if people give you funny looks."

"You know I don't give a shit what people think."

"Let me hear it, then."

"O! say can you see . . ."

I look over at Sabrina. Her eyes are round and frightened. She's sitting close enough that she would have heard Parnell's scream, and she's certainly heard my half of the conversation.

"By the dawn's early light . . ."

I hold my fist about an inch below my chin, and give her an urgent glare.

She doesn't get it, is about to speak.

I firmly press my index finger to my lips.

"What so proudly we hailed . . ."

What? she mouths back, shaking her head slightly.

I try the fist in front of my mouth again.

She still doesn't get it.

I point to my phone, tug my ear dramatically, make the fist again, bring it up to my lips, and sing "At the twilight's last gleaming . . ." into my rolled thumb.

Sabrina's eyes light up. She gets it.

I wave her over.

"Whose broad stripes and bright stars . . ."

She leaves her pew and slides in next to me. Gets the microphone icon on her screen, presses the red light for *record*, and holds the tablet steady on her lap.

"I should be hearing people. It's too quiet," Johnny says.

"I'm in a quiet part of the hospital. The basement. I'm looking for the stairs."

"So keep singing."

"Do you remember what line comes next?"

365

"Start at the beginning."

I press speakerphone. "O! say can you see . . ."

"What's that? It sounds like speakerphone."

"It's not. I'm in a stairwell. It's echoey."

"Keep singing."

"By the dawn's early light . . . what so proudly set sail . . . Hold on; that's not the line. What did I say before? You remember, Johnny?"

"It doesn't matter. Say anything. Give me the fucking alphabet."

"No, I *want* to sing 'The Star-Spangled Banner.' It being your favorite song and all. And I like it, too."

"This is crap, Pirio. You want to hear him scream?"

"No! I'm going to sing 'The Star-Spangled Banner' like you told me to. But I don't see why we can't be honest with each other for one minute before I do. I mean, we *know* each other, Johnny. Why should we be playing this cheesy cat-and-mouse game when we both know exactly what's going on? I know for a fact that Hall and his boys were planning to murder me in Makkovik, which was your idea, apparently, and I also know that you killed Mrs. Smith, so what I can't help wondering right now is, what's to stop me from ending up like her the minute I walk out the door?"

"Don't be crazy. No one's going to run you over outside a hospital."

"You'll kill me later, I guess. Parnell, too. How many murders will that make?"

A pause. "Don't fuck with me, Pirio."

I let my voice go quiet. "What happened to you, Johnny? You didn't used to be a killer. Was it for money? A Lexus in the driveway? Orthodontist bills?"

"I said don't fuck with me."

"And when I'm gone . . . after you've tossed my body into the harbor . . . how many birdhouses are you going to have to make to forget about me?"

"You just start singing and get into that car. Unless you want to hear a sound you won't ever forget." His voice is tight and slow.

"At least I'd know he was alive."

"Oh, he is, barely. Here's proof."

I fairly leap out of the pew. "No, Johnny, don't—"

Parnell's protracted scream reverberates through the chapel. Sabrina looks at me in horror. The iPad almost slides out of her trembling hands.

"OK, Johnny. Take it easy! I'm on my way. Johnny! Johnny!" I yell into the phone until the scream subsides. I turn speakerphone off and go back to singing "The Star-Spangled Banner."

I sign for Sabrina to shut off her microphone, and mime *write* by scrolling through the air with an invisible pen.

She nods, puts the tablet down quietly, slides out of the pew, returns a moment later with a Hot Topic shopping bag, from which she pulls a school notebook with a pen stuffed into the wire spiral. I write my e-mail on a page of the notebook, then Milosa's for good measure, and watch as she sends the audio recording to both addresses. By the time she's done, I'm on *the land of the free and the home of the brave.*

"Where are you now? Why don't I hear anything?" Johnny says.

"Sick people don't make a lot of noise."

I slip out of the pew, with a grateful nod to Sabrina. The look on her face says that she wants to come with me, but she also seems unwilling to move.

I speed-walk along the noisy corridor until I reach the atrium, singing the whole time. No one reacts. Maybe they think I'm a psychiatric patient.

"Where are you now?" Johnny asks.

"The main entrance is right in front of me."

"Do you see Max?"

I crane my neck. "Not yet." I go through the revolving door.

"Do you see him now?"

The blue Camry's double-parked by the curb, with Max inside, scanning the entranceway. "Yeah, I see him."

"Get in the white SUV behind him."

"What?"

Before I can react, the back door of the SUV opens and a man gets out. Not a local fisherman in dirty jeans. A guy in a grubby suit, his white shirt open at the neck. Short arms, heavyset. He steps behind me in a way that herds me efficiently into the car. I get in and see another man sitting next to the far door. Before I can glimpse his face, his arm reaches up. Something covers my eyes, nose, and mouth. A sharp assault of chemicals. The first man is behind me now. I'm pushed into the seat. My muscles turn to gelatin, and everything stops.

A gull's cry pierces the air. Somewhere nearby heavy machinery clanks rhythmically. The air is cold and smells of mud—a salty, oily mud—mixed with the putrid gas of decaying fish. Added to that are several ambient odors: ammonia-washed metal, dry rust, and the persistent smell of human sweat. I don't need to see—which the blindfold prevents me from doing anyway—to know that I'm in the fish processing section of a large commercial ship.

On the *Galaxy*, even though it was huge, you could feel the tremor and strain of the working engine in the metal floors of the lower levels. The floor under my shoes now is tensionless, almost yielding in comparison. This ship isn't moving.

I'm upright in a straight-back chair, my hands cuffed behind me. My shoulders hurt; my head aches acutely. The rise and fall of my lungs is shallow and halting.

I think I'm alone, until a chair scrapes nearby. I feel the air displacement as someone approaches. The blindfold is yanked off. My eyes dully glimpse the edge of a suit jacket, a black leather belt. The man steps away, and I see, five feet in front of me, a pair of feet in dirty

Nike trainers, resting on a table. A face comes into focus gradually. At first it's just a cherubic white globe under a reddish glow. Then angles form, and it morphs into the flint-eyed, square-jawed, expressionless visage of John Oster. Feet on the table, upper body tilted back into the chair, hands folded across his chest.

Also on the table are an Apple notebook and a black-and-silver handgun about five inches long.

"Where's Parnell?" I say.

Johnny smiles slightly. "You like him better than me? Think he's smarter?"

"Don't pretend this is personal."

"I'll tell you, the guy pisses his pants after five minutes of torture. He's in there sobbing like a baby; tried to sell me his mother, but I refused the bitch."

We're in a cavernous room with two connecting steel tubs and a rubber conveyor belt that leads to a metal housing with plastic strips hanging over its maw. This setup is repeated two more times. Three processing stations. There are enormous metal hinges on the ceiling, holding up some kind of drop from the deck above, like a wide slide through which the fish must pour. Beyond the processing area, there's a big steel door rubberized all around, with a wheel about one foot in diameter to tighten the seal. A walk-in freezer.

When Johnny said *He's in there*, he tipped his head toward this door.

He offhandedly lobs a question at his minion. "How much oxygen in there?"

"Twenty minutes. Maybe thirty," the guy says. He's got a a scraggly black goatee, and a thick guttural accent that I think I recognize. Either he was one of the guys in the SUV, or there are any number of this suited variety wandering around.

"If you talk fast, you can get in there with him while he's still alive," Johnny says to me, tipping his head with sick gallantry.

369

"I have nothing to say."

Goatee Man is staring at me as if he expects me to become very interesting at any moment.

"You're right. You don't. We have his laptop, with his half-finished story and your film. By the way, I looked at your video. It wasn't any good. The images weren't clear at all. Bad time of day to shoot a film, I'd say." He slides his feet off the table. "Anyway, it will all be at the bottom of the harbor soon. And with you and Romeo disappeared, there'll be no one left who knows what went on up there."

"Not true. The Canadian authorities were notified. The story's going to break soon, if it hasn't already. Bob Jaeger, Dustin Hall, and Ocean Catch will be all over the news. My guess is, one of your sailors will crack, and everything will come to light. You might even find yourself answering questions down the line."

He smiles with sad condescension. "That's a nice story you're telling yourself. But you're forgetting something. Money. There isn't a government official alive or dead who can't be bribed, and Jaeger and his friends can spread a lot of cash around. A real lot. I figure they'll end up with a slap on the wrist for bad behavior, if that."

"But—"

"And down here in the States? Come on, think about it, Pirio. Who really cares about some dead fish in the arctic? If you had the film, then sure, maybe you'd have something. Everybody wants to see spear-throwers, bloody carcasses. If you put it on YouTube, it'd be a hit. But a couple of paragraphs buried in the back of a newspaper isn't going to make any difference. Especially if Lady Gaga's in town."

"It doesn't matter," I say, heart sinking. "The locals know."

He laughs outright. "The Inuit? You think they don't need money?"

I try to pull my wrists apart, predictably without luck. "So what are you waiting for? Why not get it over with?" In a corner of my mind, I try telling myself that if I'm gone, Johnny will have no reason to go after Noah. A silver lining that doesn't sit so well.

"You know what I don't like about you liberals?" he says, eyeing me with coy laziness.

"Do tell." I get the feeling he's been waiting for this moment—the moment when he can tell me how wrong about everything I am and have always been. The moment when he attempts to heal his own more-jilted-than-I-realized, class-conscious heart through elaborate self-justification presented in the form of a patronizing lecture.

"You overreact to the wrong things. A couple of guys out having fun on their yacht, and you start screaming like it's the end of the world. Save the whales, blah, blah. Lions and tigers and bears, oh my. But the whales aren't going anywhere. There are fucking thousands up there. Hiding out, honing their survival skills. Meanwhile, you don't see what's going on every day right before your eyes."

I look around obligingly. "Guess not."

He leans forward, lowers his head like a bull about to charge. "Where do you think you are?"

"In a big commercial fishing boat."

"How big?"

"I don't know."

"Big as a freighter?"

"Sure. If you say so."

"How many pounds of fish you think this holds?"

"I don't know, Johnny. You tell me."

"I don't know either. That's the point. Nobody knows, and nobody cares." He smirks. "There are forty-five thousand of these babies on the seas right now. One percent of the world's fishing fleet, employing two percent of the world's fishermen, landing fifty percent of the world's fish. The government made all these regulations for fishing in territorial waters—had to protect those precious groundfish, which were doing fine. So what did us fishermen do? We moved offshore, where there are no laws and plenty of fish. We got nets so big on this thing, you wouldn't believe it; steel cables dragging massive metal plates. We're making so much money, we can't count it fast enough. It's not even fishing anymore; it's more like mining."

"You sound kind of liberal yourself, Johnny. Crisis of conscience?"

"I'm just saying, you can't stop any of it. Not you, not your journalist. Nobody. Man was meant to hunt; man was meant to fish; man was meant to get rich if he possibly can. All you need is one tiny loophole in the government regs for the whole thing to unravel. Put an end to one practice, and somebody somewhere's gonna find a way to make an even bigger pile of money doing something else. *Where there's a will, there's a way*—truer words were never spoken." He leans back, folds his hands behind his head, well satisfied with mankind's eternal ingenuity.

"So what?" I say, figuring indifference is the only way I can piss him off. I strain my wrists against the cuffs. How much time does Parnell have left?

"You thought you were onto something, right? Thought you were going to break something big. You and your journalist who can't even hold a fucking pen in his hand. Well, what did you end up with, Pirio? Couple of minutes of video, some tusks in the sand—cripes, you were so far off base, it's pathetic. Now, on top of that, you're getting yourself killed."

"Fair enough. Let's get on with it."

He glances over his shoulder at Goatee Man. "How much more time we got?"

"Ten minutes?" The guy seems annoyed with the question.

Johnny turns to me. "You want to see him now, or when he's gasping his last breath, or when it's over?"

"First option, definitely. I hate waiting around."

Another guy walks in. This one's tall, with a confident snap in his step and a slightly better suit. He starts murmuring something to the first guy. My ears catch the familiar accent again. Russian.

I glance at Johnny in his dirty jeans and oil-smeared down vest. I think about his tired wife, his screaming brats, and his crappy house. His worn-down sneakers and completely baseless need to lecture me on the true ugliness of the unleashed profit motive.

Then I remember how Hall's minion, Dennis, automatically reacted when I cursed in Russian. *She could be with Petrenko.* As if Yevgeny Petrenko were the boss to fear. Something clicks. I smile at John Oster. "You're not in charge here. They are. You work for them, and they work for Petrenko. They throw you a few dollars now and then, just enough to keep you hooked. They promised you a big pay-off, but they're not going to deliver it, and in your heart you know you're a loser, no better than Troy was, just a bit higher up."

His face stiffens. The edge of his right eye is quivering. He softly hisses, "What do you know?" To the Russians, he yells, "She's ready to go."

The two Russians walk over.

"*Zdravstvuyte,*" I say.

They exchange a glance. One of them replies, "*Zdravstvuyte.*"

"Don't fall for it; she's American," Johnny says.

Snapping the cuffs, I say authoritatively, "Take these off and get Yevgeny Petrenko on the phone. You've got the wrong woman, and he's going to be very angry when he finds out. Hurry up. *Toropit'sya.*" My spotty college Russian might be enough to give me credibility.

Goatee Man snaps into action, takes a small key out of his jacket pocket, and moves behind me obediently.

"Don't listen to her! She made the film," Johnny yells.

I smile into the man's dull eyes, and say in Russian, "*He* made the film. He wants to bribe Petrenko."

The guy undoes the cuffs, tosses them on the table with a certain smugness. As far as he's concerned, Johnny's an American ass, while I'm practically a relative. All across the world, people are loyal to their tribe.

"What are you doing?" Johnny yells hysterically, leaping from his seat.

The dapper Russian has been watching all this silently. He puts his hand on the smaller guy's arm. *"Zhdat',"* he says, looking at me. "We have heard nothing of you. How do we know you're with Yevgeny?"

I assemble a calm expression, try not to blink. "He quotes Solzhenitsyn. He's got a fat blond woman whose elbow he likes to rub." Hardly proof, but my brain's a fear-soaked sponge, and that's what it gives me to say.

Goatee Man bobs his head like he just heard a good joke, but the tall one's not impressed.

"That doesn't mean anything! She saw Petrenko on the *Galaxy*!" Johnny reaches across the table and pulls the laptop toward him. "Here. Check this out." He clicks a few times and turns the screen to face the Russians and me.

It's my footage. The narwhals surge through the mouth of the inlet. They're dark, and so is the churning water. But you can still see them. And hear them. Their strange, unearthly noises come through the speakers. Then, quite clearly, you can hear my voice, Martin's, and Parnell's.

The tall guy gives me a backhanded slap across the face.

Johnny comes around the table and hauls me out of the chair. Clutching my upper arm, he drags me toward the freezer. There's no point in resisting. One part of my brain is telling me I'm about to die. The other part refuses to believe it.

We stand behind Goatee Man, who slowly turns the wheel on the door. He steps aside as it swings open. The inside is totally dark.

"There's supposed to be a light," Johnny mutters. He's momentarily confused, peering into blackness.

The freezer also appears to be empty.

He roughly pushes me forward. "He's in there somewhere. Go find him."

Almost before the words are out, a roar comes from the depths. Parnell lurches out, holding aloft what looks like a jousting spear. His left hand grips its front half; the other end is tucked under his armpit, pressed to the side of his body by his upper arm. He barrels forward, plunges the rod at Johnny's chest. It doesn't penetrate, breaks in half, but the force of the blow is enough to get Johnny off balance and loosen his grip on my arm. I twist out of his hold, and shove him in the direction that Parnell's strike has him moving. He lands heavily on the floor; I hear the fall rather than see it, as I am running across the room. I lunge across the table and grab the Colt. In quick succession, I cock the hammer with my thumb, slide the barrel back, and whirl to see that the smaller Russian is about to tackle me. I fire.

The bullet catches him in the shoulder. He stops, puts a hand over the wound, takes it away, sees blood, looks up at me with murderous hatred, and lunges at me again. This time I get his thigh, and he slumps to the ground, crying out in pain.

The sound of the gunshot reverberates, fades away.

"Put down the gun," Johnny says calmly. He's standing up now.

The tall Russian has Parnell in a one-armed headlock. His other hand is holding a handgun that is pointed directly at me.

Parnell's face is pasty white. The way he's slumped against the Russian makes it clear that he doesn't have much strength. He was probably well on his way to hypothermia when he made his charge.

"Come on, Pirio. Give me the gun," Johnny says. He is walking toward me slowly, his arm extended, palm up. In a few seconds, he'll be at my side.

Parnell's body may be weak, but his voice is clear and strong. "Don't give it to him," he says. His strange weapon is lying on the ground at his feet, broken in two. It's not a weapon, I realize. It's a narwhal tusk.

"Come on now, put it down," Johnny cajoles, continuing to approach me without apparent fear. Like he's talking to a little girl.

I raise the Colt, take careful aim, and shoot.

The bullet hits him in the throat. It leaves a hole that immediately fills with blood. Johnny falls to his knees, clamps his hands together over the hole. He starts gurgling, swaying on the short pillars of his upper legs. It looks like he's strangling himself.

The crack of a firearm fills the air. In a dim way, I know it's a bullet intended for me. But I'm watching Johnny die, in shock and horror, and it takes a few moments—during which everything that's happening seems slow, vivid, surreal, and fated (painfully, irrevocably fated)—to realize I'm not hit. Most likely, Parnell pushed him off balance somehow.

I hold the gun with two hands, and fire at the right side of the Russian's body, as far as possible from Parnell.

The bullet hits the Russian somewhere; Parnell is twisting free. He shouts "Behind you!" and I quickly step aside. The hand of the short man grabs thin air where it meant to grab my ankle. He had pulled himself along the floor on his elbows, leaving a trail of blood.

Johnny is rolling from side to side on his back, clutching his neck. Blood is spurting up forcefully between his fingers from the hole in his throat. I stare without comprehension, unable to think or move.

Parnell is next to me. He grabs my hand, and pulls me out of the processing area, up a flight of stairs, onto the deck, where a cold wind blows. The ship is ten times bigger than I thought it was. We run to the side. It's docked at a pier, but there's no gangplank—no way to get off. There's got to be a way, of course, but right now I don't feel like asking for directions. At the end of the pier, there's a ladder into the water. I recognize the low buildings of the Conley Terminal, the Boston skyline shrouded in a far-off western haze. I grab Parnell and pull him after me. We get to the flat, open back of the ship, where the nets are hauled and the catch is dumped. Parnell understands what we're doing. His eyes show no fear. We clasp hands and jump.

Chapter 32

The heavy tasseled curtains are drawn tight against the bright sunshine. There's a sour smell in the room. Unwashed sheets, meals brought on trays and left for hours uneaten. Milosa himself, unbathed. Only one lamp is on—a Tiffany on the night table, ornate and magical, with an amber shade. The walls are crowded with oil paintings—landscapes—in gilt frames. Mostly shallow, unpopulated hills rolling under heavy, variegated skies, they cast a suffocating, melancholic spell.

I go to throw open the curtains, but he waves me away. "No light," he says.

"Fresh air?"

"No, no. When did you get back?"

"Two days ago."

"You should have come right away."

Does this means he's failing rapidly? I can't bring myself to ask.

"How did it go?" he asks.

"It wasn't what I expected. It was worse."

He snorts. "It always is."

He's propped up in the king-size bed, against pillows that are arranged against a massive antique headboard. It's the bed he shared with my mother, in which Maureen slept briefly until his thrashing limbs, she said, drove her to a room down the hall. He hasn't moved to the middle, still keeps to his half, although no body has depressed the other side of the mattress for many years.

I'm standing near the foot of the bed. There's no place to sit.

"Come," he says, patting the mattress. "I'm not dangerous at the moment."

I've never sat on Milosa's side of the bed before. I perch.

"Tell me what happened. I could use a good story," he says. He neatly folds the sheet over the top of the blanket and smooths it out, making himself a more presentable audience.

"You might end up being proud of me." I can't believe I've said something so tender to Milosa Kasparov.

"I'll be the judge of that."

It's a relief to get it all out. And I do. Beginning, middle, and end. I leave out Martin, though, and Roger, and the small brown vial, which sits in my pocket as if it's only a small brown vial.

"Is that it?" he says when I'm finished.

"Isn't that enough?"

"You forgot the most important part!"

"What do you mean?"

"What about the boat?"

"What boat?"

"The one that sank the *Molly Jones*!" he roars.

"Oh, that. I'm pretty sure it was the Russian factory trawler *Kapitan Yolkov* owned by Yevgeny Petrenko. It's the biggest damn boat I've ever seen, short of a cruise ship. A dark gray color, just like I thought. Petrenko was using it to transport the narwhal tusks to European ports. When Ned Rizzo wanted out of the hunting operation, Dustin Hall tried to buy his silence with a lobster boat, but that wasn't good enough for Petrenko. He wanted Rizzo dead. So he crushed the *Molly*

Jones with the *Kapitan Yolkov*. And then Hall and John Oster had to cover it up."

"He must have put a location tracker on the lobster boat," Milosa says, with the smug authority of a veteran schemer.

"I guess. We'll never know the exact details."

A sly glint comes into his eyes. "So it *was* murder."

I manage a thin smile, prepare to choke on humble pie. "Yes, Milosa. It was murder. You were right."

"Ahhh." His lips come together gently as he savors his moment. But he's not one to rest for longer than that on his laurels. He shimmies his spine a bit higher on the bank of fluffy pillows. "And now, I assume, you are busy congratulating yourself."

"Why shouldn't I?" I say warily, realizing too late that this is exactly the question he wanted me to ask.

"Because you're not done!"

"Why not? What else is there?"

"What else is there?" His voice rises on ascending notes of mocking incredulity, and thuds back to flat earth with the next question. "Tell me, what do you know about the black market for narwhal tusks?"

"Not much, I guess. Parnell said there were hundreds of tusks tied together in small bundles in the ship's freezer. But I don't know if there were more tusks on board, or where they were headed, or how many other trips there had been."

"Let me tell you something that you should have figured out yourself by now: Petrenko couldn't have gotten that many tusks from Jaeger's group alone. He had to have had other sources as well."

"Oh, and I suppose you want me to find them," I say in a mockingly wooden tone.

"Someone ought to."

I cross my arms over my chest and bite back my impatience. The way he's sitting up in bed like that, with his hair sticking out, makes him look like a crazy old man. For the first time in my life, I wonder whether Milosa is, in fact, a little crazy. I try to sound reasonable. "The authorities will take it from here."

In fact, Parnell and I were at the police station from late Monday night until Tuesday morning, when Johnny's body and the tusks were carried off the *Kapitan Yolkov*. After a few hours of rest in my apartment, we went back to the station to give statements and descriptions, and to answer endless questions. It was all quite exhausting. I was glad to get it behind me, and to curl up on the couch in the evening with Parnell, eating Thai takeout. On the eleven o'clock news—local, not national—there was a story about Ocean Catch's alleged involvement in a Canadian whale-poaching ring. It was less than a minute long. Johnny might have been right when he said that no one would care.

"By the authorities, you mean the Coast Guard and police, I assume?" Milosa says drily.

"Uh-huh. Maybe some federal agency as well," I say, resisting his implications.

His watery eyes drift to the middle of the room and find something to fix on, perhaps one of his somber paintings, as if I have simply ceased to be of interest. "I see what's happened. You had a little adventure, a little victory, and now you're getting soft again. Giving up."

"I don't have to listen to this, you know."

"It takes so little to satisfy you Americans," he continues vaguely, gambling that I won't walk out. "You put a few facts together, and congratulate yourselves that you've uncovered the truth and told your story right up to the end. But truth doesn't have an end. It just keeps going, and if you don't have the guts to follow it, you start to die. Still, you comfortable people—you think you know it all." He nods with slow judiciousness, accepting my weakness, as his eyes return to my face. "I say it again, Pirio: Nothing's over. You're not done. You're simply tired and want to rest your feet."

My spine straightens, and I lean forward. For once, just once, I want him to give me credit for something good I did. "What's this about stories? What are you even talking about? I'm not telling a story. Almost drowning—was that a story? How about a sweet old woman murdered? Or a meth addict? Or all the whales? I've done plenty, in fact—more than my share. I just blew open a poaching ring and solved two murders. I don't *have* to do anything more. You want to know why? Because I live in a civilized country where there are judges and courts and a legal system and environmental protections in place. Sure, it's not perfect here, but in this country, this America, which you so revile though you've chosen to make it your home, some things actually work. Once in a while, the truth *does* come out. People can depend on each other. They can *trust*."

He sits up, leans toward me until our noses are only a foot apart. "Is it possible, what I hear? You lecture me about life? *You* lecture *me*? What you know could fill a thimble!"

Anger and reason vie for control of my mouth, and anger wins. I reduce the space between our noses to about six inches. "Really? Is that so? Just because you grew up in a fucking gulag or whatever it was, hacking off chicken heads and puking your vodka, doesn't give you the right to criticize my worldview!" At this point I hardly know what I'm saying. The words are just debris in a flood.

"Criticism," he sneers, leaning back into the pillows. "Is that what Pirio fears?"

"You're maddening!" I rise from the bed in a gust of fury. I actually stomp my foot. "No one can get along with you. You'd drive Mother Teresa insane. No wonder Isa was always storming out!"

His jaw tightens. "Another subject you know nothing about."

"Oh, don't push me on this one, Milosa. Because I know plenty, in fact." And I'm ready to fling it at him—Isa's affair. It would be so satisfying to see the pained expression on his face.

But a ray of sense holds me back. I see him sitting there, propped up like a feeble grandmother, wearing cotton pajamas with a food stain dribble down the front. He's alone in that empty bed, in his life. Dying. The blue of his eyes will never be brilliant again. His once-broad shoulders droop. Maureen's down the hall in her office, doing whatever she does when she's not in a theatrical whirlwind of put-upon impatience, scolding him like he's a child. *Mercy* is the word that comes to me.

I bite back my anger with difficulty, and to my surprise, tears form. "Can we stop? Can we please just stop?"

"Why?" His eyes taunt me. He wants a good fight. Maybe needs it in some way.

But I don't. I sit on the bed again, scoot closer. "Milosa, you're dying. Look, you're dying, OK? You're *dying*." I don't know why I need to keep repeating this. "Your choice to go fast, right? No meds, no dialysis. That's what you want. OK. I'm fine with that. But let's not waste the time that's left, saying all the shit we've said a hundred times before. Let's try something new. Let's be fucking nice."

His eyes widen. "*Nice*, you say. All right, then, if that's what you want. I give you *nice*." He folds his hands on top of his blanket primly. Lets his face go slack, and lights it with a beatific smile. He could pass for a Titian cherub were he not old, smelly, and bitter.

"Funny. Ha-ha. But I'm warning you: I'm not going to fight any-more. You'll have to find someone else."

"Who?" he pouts. "Maureen's no good at it. Not like Isa was. Or you."

I pick some lint off the sleeve of his pajamas. "Maybe you can hire someone. There must be people who will verbally abuse you for a fee. Now pay attention. I have something to give you. You'll know what it is right away, I think."

I produce the small brown vial. His eyes narrow as he takes it and unscrews the top. He knows it's perfume, of course, and brings it to his nose with a practiced blend of indifference and discrimination. The moment of recognition is visible on his face. You can almost see the

molecules streaming into his brainstem, finding their special recep-
tors, and, like tiny keys in tiny locks, opening long-closed doors. At
first he's startled. Then a mysterious expression appears, a glimpse of a
younger Milosa. Stronger, more supple, hopeful, warm. A young man
who played piano, who fell in love. This expression passes quickly.
Next he's agitated, clenching his jaw against the unexpected experience, quickly screwing on the top of the vial and handing it back to me.

"Where did you get it?" he asks tightly.

I halt in confusion. What should I say? "A man in Labrador had it.
A man who knew Isa."

A pause. His fingers curl tightly around the edge of the sheet. "Oh,
yes," he says in a casual tone. "That would be her lover. Her favorite
one."

"You knew about him?"

"How could I not know? Seeing her come back at the end of every
July, a changed woman. A peaceful, beautiful woman. I knew she'd
been well loved." He pauses. "Where is the man now?"

"He passed away a year ago."

"What a shame," he says with a hint of satisfaction. "You must
remember him yourself. I'm sure you met."

"I do remember him, actually." I'm about to say that even though
I was so young, I could see that he made Isa happy. But I close my
mouth firmly before the words are out because I don't want my father
to be hurt anymore.

"His name?" Milosa asks.

"Roger Naggek. A native."

Milosa nods thoughtfully. "A good name, I think."

"I was wondering whether . . . I might be—"

"His child?"

"Yes."

"Why would you think that?"

I swallow, hard. "I have black hair. I'm not as tall as you or Isa.

And . . . you never loved me like you should have. You sent me away when all I wanted was to be with you. And there's not a single picture of me in this house."

"You're mine, Pirio. You were conceived in this bedroom, on the bed you're sitting on now. I didn't love you like I should have because I . . ."—he squeezes his eyes closed and inhales sharply through his nose—"because I didn't love anyone like I should have. Not even your mother. I adored her, but I didn't give her what she needed. Only my obsession, my jealousy. I drove her away. Then you. And I failed at loving Maureen."

"You didn't drive me away, Milosa. I'm here. I'm sitting here right now." I reach out, touch the top of his hand with my fingertips. I've never touched him before.

A tear rolls slowly down his face. He doesn't wipe it.

"About the pictures," he says, moving quickly away from the emotion. "Isa wouldn't allow you to be photographed, wouldn't let a camera near you."

Except when she was in Labrador, where she felt safe, I think. Remembering the photo of me in Roger's box.

"She was completely irrational on the subject," Milosa continues, "as she was about many things. She said she wanted to protect you from what had happened to her." He gives a soft, derisive snort.

Suddenly we're circling the whirlpool again. The subject we can't talk about. I have to ask the question, this might be my last chance. "What *did* happen to her back in Russia, when you first met? I know there was something bad, something she never forgave you for." *You sold her, Milosa, and that's how you made the money to come to this country and established the contacts in New York that launched her in the fashion world.*

Milosa slowly closes his eyes. "There's nothing more you need to know."

I feel the question's urgency dissolve. He's right. Isa's gone, with

Milosa soon to follow. Their lives, their struggles and sufferings, are already fading into the nameless past, into a vast sea of countless millions of forgotten lives just as difficult, as tortured, as triumphant as theirs. What, really, does any of it matter anymore?

His hand reaches out and touches mine. His fingers are warm.

Now we've touched each other. Two simple, remarkable gestures. *What's love?* I wonder. *Is this it?*

Milosa sits up and straightens the sheet. He sips from the water glass and clears his throat. In a clear, brisk voice, he says: "So now you'll take your mother's fragrance, and build a successful company with it. And Isa will smile in heaven, if there is one, if they've waived the rules and let her in. And I'll track her down, kick out whatever scoundrel she's shacking up with, and if she's willing, she and I will try again."

He's actually beaming. I've never known him to be so fanciful. It's not the old bravado. Something bright and trusting has entered his spirit.

"You should come out to the patio. Sit in the sun. It's a lovely day. I'll have Jeffrey bring us tea."

"Maybe tomorrow." He shifts in the bed uncomfortably, and I notice trembling in his fingers. "Before you go, will you get a handkerchief out of my top drawer over there?"

I get one, bring it to him. It's starched, neatly folded, monogrammed in gold thread with the initials MK. It was always Milosa's pleasure to honk into fine linen with gusto whenever necessary. Isa would roll her eyes and pronounce it stable manners. At which he'd say, *Stable manners? I'll give you stable manners. My father used his fingers or his sleeve!*

Oh, dear, Isa would say. *Pirio, cover your ears. Your father's about to tell us how your grandfather plucked his own rotten teeth, and how freakishly often he farted in their tiny shack.*

Not just him, my sweet. And then, if he had it in him, Milosa would bend over slightly, raise a hip, and produce a gaseous gust. *For Mother Russia!* he'd cry.

Isa would sigh with bland, beleaguered patience. *Do you see what I put up with, darling? Who can blame me for calling this man an ass?*

Milosa opens his palm. "Now let me smell that wretched woman's scent again."

I lay the vial in his hand. He opens it and dabs some of the perfume on the cloth. He looks at the wet mark strangely, as if it might be living, dabs a bit more. He doesn't bring the moistened handkerchief to his nose, however. Just folds it neatly and puts it on the night table next to the Tiffany lamp.

"There. That's my ticket. For the journey," he says.

Tooling down Beacon Street as dusk approaches, I've got the windows and sunroof of the Saab wide open. I like things cold now, brisk, every window open, air streaming across my skin. Your body adapts if you let it, grows to fill the space it's given, does what's asked of it.

I stop at a light in Kenmore Square. Trapped in bumper-to-bumper rush-hour traffic, I sit considering the future of Inessa Mark, Inc. I'm going to make a big push with Isa's Scent—I think I'll even call it that. I'll put all the company's resources behind it. Gamble on my nose and my gut feeling; do what my heart is telling me. I want to start right away, with Maureen as product manager. Her experience will be invaluable. Not just for this product, but for all the other new ones we'll be rolling out as we struggle to raise Inessa Mark to the level of a luxury house.

The light changes. Only a dozen cars get through the five-way intersection before there's gridlock, which prompts an outcry of horns. I close the windows and sunroof, enjoying how the glass mutes the blare. I'm in no hurry. I'm home. This is my city, my Boston. The Citgo sign waves a big red triangle of hello.

I grab my cell, hit Thomasina's speed-dial number, and hold the phone to my ear. She and Noah got back from New Hampshire last night. Apparently, after a rocky start, they adjusted to life at the White Mountain resort, and eventually found themselves unwilling to leave the stunning views, the spa, and other amenities, or to miss a scheduled hayride through the hills. So they stayed a bit longer than they needed to. Noah was back in school today.

Parnell and I slept late this morning, lingered for a long time in bed, and had a legendary breakfast. He's planning to spend the day drafting an article about Caridad Jaeger before heading off to Falmouth to tell her that her allegations against her husband have finally been proved. I don't know what will happen to Caridad in the long run, but at least her true story will be told.

When I left the apartment at noon, the five fingers of Parnell's good hand were flying across his keyboard as if they were ten. I kissed the scruff of his unshaven cheek and the ropy tentacles of his uncombed hair. He barely noticed, so engrossed was he, and was easily forgiven, as we had spent the morning noticing every inch of each other, exploring like true adventurers, staking our selfish claims. I breathed his smell over and over, and let it fill me. It is not something to be described. It will never exist in this world again, and could never be bottled and sold. It is just himself, Parnell. A singular alchemy of cells, fluids, enzymes, antibodies, sweat. His body's signature in indelible ink on a new blank sheet of my heart that will always, forevermore, be his.

I feel his hand cupping my ass, the plump wetness of his lips—I'm almost drowning in sense memory when the ringing coming through my cell phone is cut off by Noah's voice.

"Hello?"

"Noah. Hi. It's Pirio."

"Oh, hi. How are you?"

"I'm fine, thank you. And you?"

"Pretty good."

"Did you enjoy your vacation?"

"Oh, yeah. It was cool. The place we stayed at had a game room and a heated pool. I had a mask and snorkel, and I rode bareback on a horse." A pause. "My mom said you were looking for the people who crashed into my dad's boat."

"I was."

"Did you find them?"

"No, I didn't. I'm sorry, Noah. I tried my best." I'll never tell him about the narwhals or the *Sea Wolf*'s special voyages. His father made a bad choice, tried to rectify it but only went halfway, and ended up making a bad deal that took him to the ocean floor. He had only half the courage he needed, which is what drove Thomasina crazy. But he came through as a dad. Noah's got his disk of narwhal tusk, which he thinks is whalebone. He's got happy memories of Red Sox and Bruins games and Ned pushing him on a swing. He felt a strong hand on his shoulder, at least some of the time. That's not nothing. It was real love. Sacred. Not to be disturbed.

"That's OK. They'll turn up," Noah says brightly. Reflexive optimism is his thin barrier against the crushing universe of non-sense.

"Do you and your mom want to have dinner?" I ask.

Noah holds the phone about six inches away from his mouth and bellows *MO-OM* down the hall.

"WHAT?" I hear Thomasina yell from another room.

"YOU WANT TO HAVE DINNER WITH PIRIO?"

"OF COURSE I DO," she bellows back.

There's some scrambling with the phone; then Noah's well-modulated voice comes over the line. "We can do that."

After dinner, when Noah's in his bedroom doing homework, I spread several printed sheets on Thomasina's kitchen table. Legal guardianship forms that I got from a lawyer this afternoon. He said the document was standard boilerplate, and went over it with me carefully, changing some of the wording to fit the situation. I gave him specific information with which to fill in the blanks, and he had his secretary type it all up and put the document in a legal-size envelope bearing the name of his firm. Now all I need is Thomasina's initials on every page and her undated signature at the end. Then, whenever I choose to add my signature and a date, Noah will become my ward.

Thomasina glances at the first page of the document. Her mouth twitches, but she doesn't say anything. She sits down heavily, pulls the pages nearer to her, and reads right through with close attention, shuffling each page behind the others when she gets to its end. When she's finished reading, she sits back, sighs, bites her lip. She doesn't look at me, just holds out a hand. "Do you have a pen?"

"I never want to file these papers, Thomasina."

"No, of course not. Where's the pen?"

I hand her one, and she grips it tightly, lowers her head, bears down hard on the shaft as she initials each page and signs on the blank line at the end. She stares at her signature for a few moments, then places the pen on the table gently.

"Thomasina, like I said, I never want—"

"No, no. Don't say anything. We'll file these papers if we ever have to, whenever you think it's right. You'll be the one to decide. I'll count on you to do that. Do you understand?" Without waiting for my answer, she stacks the pages neatly, slides them into the long envelope, and pushes it across the table to me.

"Thank you," she says with a firm voice, though her shoulders slump.

"But you—"

"I'm going to meetings. I'm trying again. That's all I can do." Her face is drawn; her lips are almost colorless. She pushes her hair off her face.

"How are you feeling?"

She looks at me frankly, with the full gray splendor of her troubled eyes. "Like shit. But dammit, I've got eighteen days."